Deceiving the Deceivers

Books by S. J. Hamrick
(W. T. Tyler)

The Man Who Lost the War

The Ants of God

Rogue's March

The Shadow Cabinet

The Lion and the Jackal

Last Train from Berlin

The Consul's Wife

Deceiving
the
Deceivers

Kim Philby
Donald Maclean
and Guy Burgess

S. J. HAMRICK

Yale University Press
New Haven and London

Designed by Mary Valencia
Set in Stone and Courier type by Binghamton Valley
Composition.
Printed in the United States of America.

Library of Congress Cataloging-in-Publication Data

Tyler, W. T.
Deceiving the deceivers : Kim Philby, Donald Maclean & Guy
Burgess / S.J. Hamrick.
  p. cm.
Includes bibliographical references and index.
ISBN 0-300-10416-2 (alk. paper)
1. Espionage, Soviet—Great Britain. 2. Philby, Kim, 1912-
3. Maclean, Donald, 1913- 4. Burgess, Guy, 1911-1963. 5.
Spies—Soviet Union—Biography. 6. Spies—Great Britain—
Biography. I. Title.

UB271.R92P477 2004
327.1247041'092'2—dc22

                                            2004053695

A catalogue record for this book is available from the
British Library.

The paper in this book meets the guidelines for permanence
and durability of the Committee on Production Guidelines for
Book Longevity of the Council on Library Resources.

10 9 8 7 6 5 4 3 2 1

To Nancy Ely-Raphel

Contents

details.—The search for Soviet codenames.—The Maclean cables.—Churchill, Roosevelt, and the Polish crisis.—Puzzling cryptologic failures.—Hiding Venona's Maclean texts.—Kept in the dark.—Whitehall misled.

NINE 159

Misplaced in time.—The CIA orphan.—U.S. military weakness.—London's Russia Committee.—Secret USAF-RAF cooperation.—U.S. war plans.—The Soviet specter.— Searching for a strategy.—Political and psychological warfare.—The Berlin crises.—The bomb as a deterrent to war.—The Foreign Office rebuffs the military.—The threat to Western Europe.—Philby's unlimited potentialities.

TEN 185

The CIA in transition.—Censure and scorn.—Admiral Hillenkoetter.—Philby and Angleton.—Delusional rubbish.— Albania and the Ukraine.—Displaced persons camps.—"A horrible mistake."—A pint-sized opportunity.—Philby's reports.

ELEVEN 204

Moscow and the bomb.—Deterrent to war.—Black operations.—A basis for deception.—The forgotten chiefs of staff.—Finding an agent.—General Sibert.—The British fly solo.—Only in memory.—Unresolved ambiguities.

TWELVE 228

Old myths revisited.—Why legends survive.—Field of vision.—Hijacking history.—Counterfeit cards.—No more to be learned.—The wartime generation.—The pygmy plan.

Preface

This is an improbable book that came about in an improbable way. It began in July 1995 when I was surprised to learn of the NSA's release of the Venona transcripts. As a Foreign Service officer I occasionally worked with NSA code-word material both overseas and in Washington and on a few rare occasions in 1977–1978 met with NSA cryptologists and linguists when interpretive problems arose. I knew how rigorously the NSA controlled its intercepts, limiting them to operational officers on a need-to-know basis for which there were no exceptions—not even for officers working under me. I was curious as to how much detail the NSA had given up.

I had returned to the State Department in February 1995 after an absence of a number of years and hadn't the opportunity to explore the Venona archive until late 1996. *Venona: Soviet Espionage and the American Response* proved to be an astonishing account of Arlington Hall's early codebreaking success, its tools, its methodology, and its personnel, which went far beyond my expectations. But I was puzzled by a few comments by the editors. Among them was the claim that "British liaison officer Kim Philby received actual translations and analyses [of Venona material] on a regular basis after he arrived for duty in Washington."[1]

My experience told me this was unlikely. I also knew of G-2's mistrust of civilian intelligence agencies both before and after the 1947 creation of the CIA, which was excluded from Venona until 1952. This exclusion made a civilian foreign-intelligence officer's access in 1949–1951 even more unlikely. Only out of necessity had the FBI been invited to share selective Venona transcripts in 1947–1948. What made the editors' claim equally questionable were their sources. To my surprise they didn't derive from NSA archives, but from a 1994 book on Philby written by a Russian journalist, Genrikh Borovik, and notes supplied to the editor by a recently deceased British journalist, John Costello. Either's knowledge of Venona prior to 1995 would have been based on hearsay. Why would two historians, one with the CIA, the other with the NSA, have been compelled to even raise the Philby issue much less rely on two unofficial sources? Although I didn't realize it until much later, they were misled by a long-established fiction regarding Philby and Venona that had been in circulation for years and that Borovik, Phillip Knightley, and John Costello had helped perpetuate.

In the early 1990s I had reviewed a number of books for the Sunday *Washington Post* and the *Chicago Tribune*. Among them was a book on Kim Philby. The author, Anthony Cave Brown, had made a similar claim, crediting Philby with unrestricted access to Venona.[2] Until I read and reviewed the Cave Brown book, I was only vaguely aware of the details of the Philby, Maclean, and Burgess affairs. I was posted to the American embassy in Beirut in the late autumn of 1962, when Philby was still roaming about, but I didn't arrive until five months after his January 1963 disappearance. I don't recall any great interest in his case among my embassy colleagues or the CIA officers at the CAS station (the CIA overseas acronym at the time). During the fifteen or so years that followed, I was posted abroad far from Washington, London, intelligence gossip, and the book reviews of the day. I had never read *My Silent War* and wasn't aware of the many books on Philby that appeared in the late 1960s and 1970s. In retrospect I suppose my ignorance gave me an advantage.

In late 1997 I began to explore the Venona documents at the National Archives in College Park, Maryland, and was struck by other inconsistencies in the series of Historical Monographs that accompanied the Venona releases. I was surprised by the absence of any factual detail on the British role in Venona apart from vague generalities. Not until I read Meredith Gardner's October 1951 report on the HOMER/GOMER chronology were my suspicions confirmed and I was convinced that something was very seriously wrong with traditional accounts of Venona's exposure of Donald Maclean and the 1949–1951 MI5 investigation. My search was transformed. It was then that I began to explore the innumerable official documents, memoirs, and books that are cited in the notes.

Protected by Britain's Official Secrets Act, the details of the MI5 investigation that led to the exposure of Donald Maclean as a Soviet agent were successfully suppressed for more than fifty years. Concealment began with the misleading 1955 official British White Paper which claimed Maclean wasn't identified until the spring of 1951. This widely accepted fiction was reinforced in the 1970s and 1980s by a deliberate leak in London of one detail from a brief June 1944 New York to Moscow Venona cable said to have identified Maclean. The leak could only have originated with MI5. In July 1995, however, the NSA broke down the walls and declassified the entire Venona archive. In 1996 it released all of Venona's decrypted Maclean cables containing Foreign Office telegrams he passed to his Soviet control officer in New York and Washington in 1944–1945. In an effort to deny any evidence that Maclean was identified any earlier than 1951, London successfully obscured the complete contents of those Venona cables first broken at Arlington Hall and subsequently decrypted more fully in London. Documents in the Venona archive not subject to British control confirm that Maclean would have been identified in August 1950 at the latest. In the 1980s a retired British diplomat in London innocently revealed that MI5 had exploited Maclean's exposure to its advantage in 1949–1951 in successfully deceiving both Kim Philby and Guy Burgess. He wasn't aware of the deception.

The precise date of MI5's identification of Maclean as a Soviet agent remains unclear but undoubtedly was made between mid-1948 and no later than August 1950. There are grounds for suspecting that he was identified on the basis of the 1945 Venona decrypts in the summer of 1948 while still in Washington. At the time Prime Minister Attlee's government was negotiating with Washington for the resumption of the exchange of nuclear weapons technology essential for Britain's creation of a nuclear deterrent. The identification would undoubtedly have been shared with Attlee, who would have ruled that the latter was far more important for Britain's national interests than taking immediate action against a Soviet agent at the British embassy who also had access to U.S. atomic secrets, as Maclean did. His 1948 identification, were it known in Washington, would have immediately shattered any possibility of Anglo-American nuclear cooperation. MI5 deferred any initiative until September 1949. Maclean was then in Cairo, Philby was preparing to depart for his Washington assignment, and the FBI had just notified MI5 that Klaus Fuchs, the British physicist, was a Soviet agent. Fuchs was arrested in Britain in February 1950, and Prime Minister Attlee's hopes of sharing U.S. nuclear technology were at an end.

The mid-1948 date is supported by a curious series of events which are inexplicable except as London's consistent effort to date the onset of MI5's Maclean investigation to no earlier than January 1949. They were initiated by a British cryptologist in December 1948 by a dubious claim identifying highly secret "telegrams from Churchill" found among the March 1945 Maclean cables. There is no identifiable Churchill cable among the Maclean cables released in 1996, but the claim enabled London to take full control of Venona's Maclean decrypts. That decision excluded the FBI from any further access to the Maclean decrypts beginning in January 1949, which meant that the FBI couldn't discover either currently or in retrospect what MI5 might have already known—that Donald Maclean, by then in far-off Cairo, was a Soviet agent. London has also withheld the identify and the activities of British cryptologists at Arlington Hall in 1946–1948 when the

Venona Maclean cables were first being broken. An NSA document together with Venona's Maclean cables establish beyond any doubt that British cryptologists, among the best in the world, were not fully sharing their success with Arlington Hall. London has also falsified the date on file at the Public Record Office by claiming that a parallel Venona operation was opened at Eastcote in London in December 1948 when, in fact, it commenced more than a year earlier. There are other anomalies in the Venona archive. The mid-1948 date, if accurate, would also help explain why London has been so resolute for so many decades in protecting a decision made by Prime Minister Attlee that otherwise might have been fifty years obsolete when the NSA declassified Venona. But there are other equally important reasons why London insists on maintaining the fiction of Maclean's 1951 identification, and they concern Kim Philby. But I am now getting too far ahead of myself.

Finally, I owe an enormous debt to those British journalists, writers, and historians whose work I have cited. Even if I disagreed with their conclusions, as I often did, without their efforts over the years this book wouldn't have been possible. I am also grateful to Jonathan Brent of Yale University Press and to Kim Hastings for her remarkable work in editing a very brambled thicket of prose.

S. J. Hamrick
Rappahannock County, Virginia

Acronyms

Abwehr	German general staff's intelligence and counterintelligence service.
AEC	Atomic Energy Commission. U.S.
AERE	Atomic Energy Research Establishment. British.
AFSA	Armed Forces Security Agency (Sigint). U.S. 1949–1952. Immediate forerunner of the NSA.
Amtorg	American-Soviet Trading Company. New York.
Arlington Hall	Informal name for army signals and cryptographic intelligence headquarters and working offices beginning in 1942. With the creation of the NSA in 1952, those offices were eventually moved from Virginia to Fort Meade, Maryland.
ASA	Army Security Agency (Sigint). U.S. From 1945.
AWRE	Atomic Weapons Research Establishment. British.
BJSM	British Joint Services Mission. British military mission in Washington in liaison with U.S. military. Established during World War II.
BRUSA	British-American communications agreement (Sigint). Signed May 17, 1943.
CIA	Central Intelligence Agency. U.S. Established 1947.
CIG	Central Intelligence Group. U.S. 1946–1947. Forerunner to the CIA.
Cominform	Communist Information Bureau. Created autumn 1947.
Comint	Communications intelligence. The interception and analysis of foreign communications transmitted by wire, radio, or other means, including encrypted communications.
Comintern	Communist International. 1919–1943.
CPC	Combined Policy Committee
DIA	Defense Intelligence Agency
EAC	European Advisory Commission. Established October 1943.
Enigma	Enciphering machine used by the German high command during World War II and reproduced by the British GC&CS to break German coded traffic.
FBI	Federal Bureau of Investigation
G-2	U.S. Army military intelligence
GC&CS	Government Code & Cipher School. British. Renamed GCHQ in 1944.
GCHQ	Government Communications Headquarters. British.
GRU	Soviet Military Intelligence

Humint	Intelligence gathered from human sources, usually foreign agents.
JCS	Joint Chiefs of Staff. U.S.
JIB	Joint Intelligence Bureau. Ministry of Defense.
JIC	Joint Intelligence Committee. British
JSPC	Joint Strategic Planning Committee
KGB	Soviet Security and Intelligence Agency. 1954–1991.
LCS	London Controlling Section. Established 1942. Responsible for devising and implementing deception operations.
LSIC	London Signals Intelligence Committee
MAD	Mutually Assured Destruction
MGB	Soviet Ministry for State Security. 1946–1953.
MI5	British Security Service.
MI6	British Intelligence Service. Also known as SIS.
MVD	Established 1953.
NATO	North Atlantic Treaty Organization. Established April 1949.
NIA	National Intelligence Authority
NKGB	Soviet Commissariat for State Security. 1943–1946.
NKVD	Soviet Commissariat for Internal Affairs. 1934–1941.
NSA	National Security Agency (Sigint). U.S. Established 1952.
NSC	National Security Council. U.S.
OGPU	Soviet Security and Intelligence Service. 1923–1934.
OO	Office of Operations. CIG.
OPC	Office of Policy Coordination. U.S. Created June 1948 as Office of Special Projects. Renamed July–August 1948.
OSO	Office of Special Operations. CIA.
OSP	Office of Special Projects. CIA.
OSS	Office of Strategic Services. Dissolved in 1945.
OUN	Organization of Ukrainian Nationalists
PM	Political-Military Bureau. State Department.
RAF	Royal Air Force. British.
RCMP	Royal Canadian Mounted Police
SAC	Strategic Air Command
SHAEF	Supreme Headquarters, Allied Expeditionary Force. World War II.
Sigint	Intelligence obtained from the interception of communications signals including both Comint and Elint.
SIS	Secret Intelligence Service
SOE	Special Operations Executive. British World War II special forces.
SSA	Signal Security Agency (Sigint). U.S. Army. 1942–1945. Renamed ASA.
SSU	Strategic Services Unit. War Department Intelligence group es-

tablished with the 1945 dissolution of the OSS. Integrated into the CIG and CIA to become the CIA's Office of Special Operations.

SVR   Russian Foreign Intelligence Service

Ultra   British and U.S. Sigint gathered during World War II. Often used to refer specifically to German high command encrypted communications broken by GC&CS at Bletchley Park using the Enigma machine.

USAF   U.S. Air Force

USCIB   U.S. Communications Intelligence Board

Deceiving the Deceivers

Chapter
ONE

Moscow bound: May 25, 1951.—Six conspirators.—

Unanswered questions.—The government

officially responds.—The 1955 White Paper.—

Philby reveals the secrets.—The hunt for HOMER.—

Journalists join the search.—Hearsay,

conjecture, and semiofficial leaks.—Washington

opens the Venona archive.—London's dilemma.

It was almost midnight as the pale Austin A-40 sedan careened out of the darkness into the thin gray twilight of the quay at Southampton. Abandoning the rented car, two men lept from the front seat, seized their luggage, and dashed for the 11:45 ferry bound for the French coast. The first was blond and slender, over six feet three, and a head taller than his stocky, dark-haired companion. As they jogged up the gangway, the ferry screws were already churning, adding their sea broth to the unmistakable smells of dockside and departure any place on earth: tar, brine, rotting wood, rusting iron, sea salt, oil, and diesel smoke, all promising the reprieve of new headlands, new countries to explore, and new adventures to be found no less than new lives discovered and old lives discarded. The two would never return to England. In their exile they would become among the most infamous Englishmen of their generation.

The date was May 25, 1951, the ferry was the SS *Falaise* bound for St. Malo, and the two men were the diplomats Donald Duart Maclean and Guy Francis de Moncy Burgess. Maclean, the taller, had celebrated his thirty-eighth birthday that day. He was acting head of the American Department at the Foreign Office in London. Burgess, two years older, had returned to England from the United States in early May after he had been sacked as second secretary at the British embassy in Washington. Sent home for irresponsible conduct, he now faced certain dismissal. If after fifty years both men now seem far younger in their fame than seems possible, Moscow, their destination, would transfix them in time, as ageless in memory as the scores of youthful photographs that would appear in newspapers, magazines, and books in the weeks, months, and years that followed. Only their legends would grow old. On May 25, 1951, they had been Moscow's faithful servants for seventeen years.

At the time of the SS *Falaise*'s sailing, the two were under surveillance by MI5, British counterintelligence, and Scotland Yard's Special Branch, but not beyond London.[1] Maclean had been followed by MI5 for much longer than Burgess. His surveillance had been officially ordered in mid-April by Foreign Secretary Herbert Morrison at the request of MI5 and senior Foreign Office officials who had learned that he was a suspected Soviet agent.[2] His recent MI5 and Special Branch watchers pursued him no farther than the gate at Charing Cross train station in London, where he punctually arrived and departed each day for the Sevenoaks station in Kent and on to Beaconshaw, his large Victorian house at Tatsfield, a village on the Kent-Surrey border. Over the weeks, his MI5 shadows had been as conspicuously predictable as his 5:19 train from London, or so it is claimed. Aware of their presence and the April suspension of his access to Foreign Office secret documents, he had been told he was under suspicion.

His informant was Burgess, who had known of MI5 suspicions before he left Washington for New York the last week in April. His mission was to spur Maclean's departure from England with the aid of his MGB[3] control officer at the Soviet embassy in London, Yuri Modin, and another of Moscow's English agents, Anthony Blunt. A former MI5 officer semiretired from Moscow's service since 1945, Blunt acted as an intermediary when not busy with his duties at the Courtauld Institute and as surveyor of the king's pictures. Blunt met Burgess at Southampton when he arrived on May 7 aboard the *Queen Mary* and drove him to London and his top-floor suite at the institute, where Burgess spent the night and enlisted Blunt's help. The next day Blunt met with Modin and passed on Burgess's warning. Alarmed that Maclean's interrogation would wipe out his entire Cambridge network but unsure of the next step, Modin scheduled another meeting two days later. During that second meeting, he insisted on talking with Burgess personally to confirm Maclean's predicament. He was also stalling for time. Without the authority to act alone, the KGB resident at the Soviet embassy had cabled Moscow Center for instructions. The reply soon authorized Maclean's defection to Moscow.[4]

At his meeting with Burgess, Modin brought along his superior, the imperious KGB resident Nikolai Borisovich Rodin (pseudonym Korovin). To Modin's disgust, he practiced his own eccentric tradecraft, sacrificing prudence to his own comfort and convenience; he had no hesitation phoning British agents under his control at their offices or arriving at an assignation in a Soviet embassy sedan. In June 1950 he had spent six and a half hours in a suburban London park chatting up a worried Burgess before he left for his Washington posting.[5]

At the meeting, the two Russians insisted that Burgess talk to Maclean immediately and convince him he had no alternative but to defect to the Soviet Union. Burgess obliged, visited Maclean at the Foreign Office, and subsequently met with him at the Reform Club. Maclean was indecisive. While he dithered, Burgess and Blunt continued their chats with the Russians. It was during a stroll with Modin in St. Regent's Park that Blunt suggested the pair escape by ship to the French coast. Modin thought it an interesting idea, visited a tour office, discussed boat schedules to France with the tour organizer, examined the brochures, and selected the SS *Falaise*. He recommended the *Falaise* escape route to Nikolai Rodin, who approved and soon met personally with Burgess to instruct him to book two berths on the *Falaise* for the May 25–27 weekend. Wary of Maclean's frail nerves and uncertain determination, Moscow had insisted that Burgess accompany Maclean. On Thursday, May 24, Burgess dropped by the travel agency and bought the two tickets. As must be evident by now, the four conspirators assumed their frequent meetings were unobserved, despite knowing full well that the fifth, Donald Maclean, had been under watch by MI5.

The arrangements were now complete. Early in the evening on May 25, Burgess arrived at the house in Tatsfield to fetch Maclean, interrupting his birthday dinner with his wife, Melinda, who was eight and a half months pregnant. Maclean introduced Burgess as Roger Styles and told her they were off for a weekend excursion. She was angry at not having known of his plans and the unexpected disruption of the birthday supper.[6] Twelve hours or so earlier, Foreign Secretary Morrison had signed the final order authorizing Maclean's arrest and interrogation between June 18 and June 25.[7] Despite many claims to the contrary, neither man was aware of the Foreign Office decision nor were their two Soviet accomplices. The timing was a matter of pure luck, so Burgess's voluble Soviet control Yuri Modin admitted in 1994.[8]

That May night, as the running lights of the SS *Falaise* vanished in the darkness of the estuary toward the English Channel, the Cambridge classmate who had recruited both men for Moscow's OGPU in late 1934 was still at his post at the British embassy in faraway Washington. Weeks earlier he had learned Maclean was under surveillance and had sent Burgess to warn Maclean in London and get him out. He was of course Harold A. R. Kim Philby, chief of station for MI6, British intelligence. A day earlier, on May 24, he had for a second time implored his KGB control officer, a semicompetent Soviet illegal named Valeri Makayev based in New York, to remove Maclean from England as soon as possible for fear he too would be in jeopardy.[9] He had also impatiently fired off a thinly disguised airmail alert to Burgess telling him, in effect, to get moving. Now he was anxiously awaiting the results.

After May 25, Philby's espionage career would be on its last legs, but his successes were behind him by then in any case. It hardly mattered. In time his renown would dwarf that of his outward-bound colleagues. He hadn't expected Burgess to accompany Maclean, explicitly cautioning him against it before Burgess left Washington. On the morning of June 7 he learned the worst: Burgess had disappeared as well. Burgess had shared Philby's house on Nebraska Avenue during his brief eight-month posting to the embassy and their close association and long friendship put him at risk. Although Philby assumed no one was the wiser, least of all MI5, for the past several years Burgess had been his sole cutout or message carrier to his Soviet control.[10] Burgess's absence had compelled him to meet Makayev and plead for Moscow's help. Predictably enough, Philby was now under suspicion. In June he was recalled to London, questioned inconclusively, and in late July asked to resign. Not until twelve years later, in January 1963, did he disappear from Beirut as mysteriously as Maclean and Burgess. Six months later he reappeared in Moscow and was given Soviet citizenship.

The tale has been told so many times the drama is thought to be wrung out by now, but there is far more to the story than is implied in its conclusion. If the many interpretations are to be believed, the last month of MI5's Maclean investigation was a debacle from beginning to end. The brief summary offered above suggests as much. The English and Russian conspirators' ability to roam around London with impunity, to meet, walk about, and talk undetected and unobserved seems curiously improbable, hardly descriptive of the work of experienced MI5 officers seriously attempting to disentangle and identify Moscow's clandestine espionage networks in the Foreign Office or elsewhere in England. The interpretative errors, including those blaming MI5 for gross incompetence, were based on the assumption by the Foreign Office and by the six conspirators, including Philby, that Maclean was the sole subject of the MI5 investigation. No one seemed to consider that he might be MI5's stalking horse.

MI5 had identified Donald Maclean as a Soviet agent long before May 25, 1951, perhaps as much as a year or two earlier but certainly no less than nine months or by mid-August 1950, as our narrative will show. As in many counterespionage initiatives, Maclean was MI5's instrument in an operation that searched far beyond a single Foreign Office diplomat. A simple fact began that MI5 operation and explains every decision that preceded it, whether made by MI5, by MI6, by the Foreign Office, by the KGB residence in London, by Philby and Burgess in Washington, or by KGB Center in Moscow. That fact, which has never been officially disclosed, is the date MI5 knew beyond any doubt that Donald Maclean was a KGB agent.

For more than fifty years Britain's Official Secrets Act has defied attempts by journalists, writers, and intelligence historians to unlock that secret or any other that would resolve the remaining mysteries associated with Kim Philby, Donald Maclean, and Guy Burgess. The search for answers began with Maclean and Burgess's May 25 flight from England and has continued episodically and inconclusively for more than five decades. As new information came to light over the years and old theories were discarded, interpretations have gradually evolved toward a reasonably credible reconstruction of their separate espionage careers. But the facts that explain their conclusive identification as Soviet agents are either missing, as with Philby and Burgess, or conjectural, in the case of Maclean. The date of his reported April 1951 identification by MI5 is based on evidence that is unverified, undocumented, and of questionable reliability. However persuasive those accounts appear—and many are persuasive enough to generate the belief that there is nothing more to be learned—they remain entirely speculative, even those that seem to be unofficially confirmed by comments by Foreign Office staff. The unanswered mysteries for all three are concealed in the precise date British intelligence knew beyond question that Donald Maclean was a Soviet agent.

The May 25 disappearance of Maclean and Burgess made banner headlines when London's *Daily Express* broke the story on June 7. Forewarned, the Foreign Office the same day announced that the two had been suspended on June 1 for being absent without leave. In Parliament, doubts were raised by the Conservative opposition in June and July but were turned aside by the Labor government, which insisted there was no reason to believe either had Communist associations. The brief fire smoldered and eventually died out but blazed up even more furiously in 1955, after press reports disclosed that a Soviet defector had insisted that the two missing diplomats were in Moscow and in fact were longtime Soviet agents.

Four years after Maclean and Burgess disappeared, the government was finally forced to abandon British intelligence policy of secrecy and silence and confront an issue it could no longer avoid. The Tories were now in power, not Labor, and fell back in defense of the establishment. In September 1955 the government issued its White Paper. The document sketched out a useful chronological outline but did little to resolve doubts or the larger mysteries.[11] It attempted to restore confidence in the integrity of the Foreign Office and British intelligence but the reassurance fell on deaf ears in Parliament in November when the issue was debated. The Labor opposition accused the government of a "cover up."[12] The government had inherited the mess and knew only as much as senior Foreign Office officials, who in turn knew only as much as British intelligence was willing to share. The White Paper, incomplete and intentionally vague, set forth only slightly less than Foreign Office seniors actually knew. The first draft was written by Sir Dick Goldsmith White, then Director General of MI5, assisted by a veteran MI5 officer, Graham Mitchell. Dick White knew far more than anyone else in London about the Donald Maclean case, including the date and the means by which he had been identified as a Soviet agent. The draft was subsequently reviewed by MI6 and Foreign Office officials, who knew far less.[13]

The White Paper disclosed that in January 1949 "British security officials" were notified that certain Foreign Office information "had been leaked to the Soviet authorities some years earlier." The 1949 warning offered "little more than a hint" as to the identity of the Soviet agent, an uncertainty that made it "impossible to attribute the leak to any particular individual." More than two years later, in mid-April 1951, the list of suspects was reduced to "two or three persons." By early May 1951 Maclean had become "the principal suspect." Because "legally admissible evidence" didn't support his prosecution, "security officials" began investigating his present "activities and contacts," meaning MI5 had put him under surveillance. At the time, he was seven months into his posting on the American desk at the Foreign Office. On May 25 Foreign Secretary Morrison "sanctioned" his interrogation between June 18 and June 25. That same night Maclean and Burgess fled England for the Continent. The White Paper explained that the watch on Maclean was confined to London and didn't include surveillance at his home at Tatsfield, which was "inadvisable" in the remote village because of the risk of compromise. Philby wasn't mentioned in the document.

For obvious reasons the government White Paper failed to reveal the source of the intelligence by which the unknown Soviet agent was discovered in January 1949 and Maclean identified as a suspect in the spring of 1951. It didn't characterize the substance or the sensitivity of the Foreign Office "information" passed to Moscow. While admitting Maclean was a principal suspect, the White Paper failed to declare his guilt. Those details were withheld because the intelligence operation that would have answered those questions was far too sensitive to be admissible. Not until July 1995 was that top-secret operation officially acknowledged and its archive declassified. The decision was made not by London, but by Washington, much to the amazement and displeasure of British intelligence.

Following the disappearance of Maclean and Burgess, Philby was summoned home and left for London on June 10. He was soon suspected by a few American officials of having alerted Maclean. Among them was CIA director Walter Bedell Smith, who wrote to MI6 chief Stewart Menzies in late June that Philby was no longer welcome in Washington. In London, Sir Dick White interrogated Philby to persuade him to confess, as did others. The attempts failed and in late July he was asked to resign. He remained in England until 1956, when he was allowed to move to Beirut as a correspondent for the *Observer* and the *Economist.* In 1962 MI5 unearthed more incriminating evidence, or so it claimed on the flimsiest hearsay. Flora Solomon, an English family friend of the Philbys, informed MI5 that she knew Philby to be a Soviet agent after he had asked her in 1938 to join him in working for the Communist International (Comintern). In January 1963 an MI6 officer and former Philby colleague, Nicholas Elliott, was dispatched to Beirut to confront him. After several long discussions, Philby typed out a partial confession admitting he had worked for the Comintern before World War II. He revealed nothing about his ties to the NKGB, the KGB, or the OGPU, the Soviet intelligence agency that recruited him in 1934. On the night of January 23, 1963, he vanished from Beirut, secretly smuggled aboard a Soviet freighter outbound for Odessa.[14]

Following Philby's disappearance, one puzzle that aroused some controversy in the November 1955 parliamentary debate on the White Paper appeared to be resolved. His apparent January defection from Beirut, although not immediately confirmed, supported the suspicion that he was "the Third Man" who had warned Maclean in April 1951 that he was suspected of being a Russian spy. Harold Macmillan, who years earlier as foreign secretary had defended Philby, confided in his diary in February 1963 that the mystery of who "tipped off" Maclean and Burgess was now solved.[15] So it was. On July 1 *Izvestia* revealed that Philby was in Moscow and had been given Soviet citizenship. In London the same day, Prime Minister Heath told Commons that before his disappearance from Beirut, Philby admitted he worked for the Soviet Union before 1946 and that "in 1951 he, in fact, had warned Maclean, through Burgess, that the security services were about to take action against him."[16] The three mysterious disappearances, finally connected, were now resolved, or so it seemed.

With the last of the three Soviet agents resident in the USSR, no further clarification was required. Philby's defection, like Maclean's and Burgess's, spoke for itself. British intelligence, responsible for the little that the government knew, had kept silent since the Burgess and Maclean disappearance was first publicized in June 1951, clarified somewhat in 1955, and Philby's guilt acknowledged in 1963. It remained silent. There was nothing more to add. But there *was* more to add, far more. In 1964 a distinguished English author, more known for her intellectual and literary gifts than for her knowledge of espionage's dirty trade, cast a scornful eye on the entire affair, particularly Prime Minister Heath's explanation to Commons that Philby had warned Maclean through Burgess. Dame Rebecca West found his explanation "incomprehensible": "It does not explain why a Soviet agent in England [Maclean], certainly in touch with local agents, could be warned that he was being watched by English security agents only by another Soviet agent in America [Philby] who sent a third [Burgess] all the way to England to tell him so. Soviet intelligence has better communications than that. This cannot be the story."[17]

Her conclusion was inescapable, so common sense told her, and she was right. This wasn't the whole story, far from it, but thirty years or more would pass before enough details could be collected from the KGB archives in Moscow, from other official sources in London, and from the Venona archive to piece together a different tale. In the meantime, few took notice of her doubts. A number of British writers and journalists were off on the chase after their own noisy fashion.

In 1967, four years after Philby's defection, his importance was finally established beyond any doubt. The most damaging details were disclosed by Phillip Knightley of the London *Sunday Times*. He had tracked down a former intelligence officer who let MI6's clandestine cat out of the bag.

Philby had been head of MI6's Section IX, responsible for collecting all intelligence identifying Soviet and Communist espionage agents. MI6's own principal Soviet spy catcher was a Soviet agent. The revelation was published in the *Sunday Times* on October 1, 1967. For the first time, readers on both sides of the Atlantic realized the enormity of Philby's espionage, or at least believed that they did. Knightley's exposure flushed more details from retired British diplomats willing to break their silence.

A year later, in 1968, to the astonishment of MI5 and MI6, Moscow allowed Philby's memoir *My Silent War* to be published in the West. Intended to exploit his growing prominence in the West to carry out what the KGB called an "active measure" campaign[18] to undermine MI6-CIA relations and injure the reputations of both, its author left no doubt about his work at MI6: he was indeed responsible "for the collection and interpretation of information concerning Soviet and communist espionage and subversion in all parts of the world outside British territory."[19] Enough additional information from unofficial sources had been accumulated by then to appear to authenticate Philby's triumph. MI5 and MI6 officials in London remained silent.

Among Philby's most important revelations was that a "Joint Anglo-American investigation" had uncovered a 1944–1945 leak at the British embassy in Washington. He claimed to have identified the source of the leak as Maclean soon after Sir Maurice Oldfield of MI6 first informed him of the unidentified Soviet agent during his briefing in late September 1949 prior to his departure for Washington. He disclosed that after his October arrival in Washington, "a sluggish trickle of information about the embassy leakage continued to reach us." Peter Dwyer, his MI6 predecessor, Geoffrey Patterson of MI5, and Robert Mackenzie, the embassy security officer, also saw the material. As Philby explained, by the time of Guy Burgess's arrival at the Washington embassy in August 1950, "We had received some dozen reports referring to the source, who appeared in the documents under the code name Homer." As the list of suspects was reduced to a final few, including Maclean, Philby conspired to send his Washington housemate and fellow spy Burgess to London to warn Maclean. Philby's comments made it clear that during his twenty months in Washington he was routinely informed of the progress of the search for HOMER.[20] Despite the clarity of his description—"reports" and "documents"—their origin wasn't obvious to many Philby chroniclers who had begun their reconstruction of the 1949–1951 Foreign Office and MI5/MI6 fiasco.

In Philby's 1968 account, he avoided mentioning the top-secret Anglo-

American codebreaking operation. In the 1990s, KGB files opened in Moscow to Western journalists show that in September 1949 he had attempted to pass details of the codebreaking project to his KGB control in London through Guy Burgess, who had bungled its disclosure to Modin for six months.[21] In 1968 a very few senior KGB officers already knew of the successful American codebreaking effort and had known for more than twenty years, even before Philby's report.[22] The reason for Philby's silence is obvious. The manuscript of *My Silent War* was vetted in Moscow before its release in the West. The decision to allow publication had created a rumpus in the Kremlin, where a few party troglodytes were opposed. They were overruled by the more progressive, who viewed Philby's memoir as an opportunity to trumpet the success of Soviet espionage to the humiliation of the British and American services and stir up mistrust between the two.[23] Disclosure of a major Russian cryptological failure blunted that point, even if no one in Moscow quite understood how it happened. The KGB hardly wanted it known that American and British cryptanalysts had successfully broken and read Soviet intelligence traffic. Philby's published comment was left deliberately vague.

Philby also claimed that the "investigation of the leads" that might identify HOMER was "in the hands of the FBI."[24] "Leads" is similarly ambiguous, but would have included any clues furnished to MI5 from Anglo-American penetrations of Soviet cable traffic and MI5's interrogation of British diplomats who had served with Maclean in Washington between 1944 and 1948. His claim that the FBI played a major role proves his 1949–1951 isolation from the heart of the MI5 investigation underway in London that concentrated on the Foreign Office's diplomatic ranks. The FBI was never substantively involved in that investigation. But in 1968 no one apart from a privileged few knew that or much of anything else. Yet Philby had lifted one corner of the curtain of secrecy, introduced the codename HOMER into circulation, described the search for HOMER, and erroneously assigned a major role to the FBI. His account added new elements to the case and was incorporated into many books published in the 1970s, 1980s, and 1990s. Facts on the Anglo-American codebreaking operation, the MI5 investigation of the embassy leaks, and the precise detail that betrayed Maclean remained shrouded in secrecy or were still too obscure for interpretation, as they had been for Philby.

In 1973 two British journalists, Patrick Seale and Maureen McConville, included Philby's revelations in their remarkable book, *Philby: The Long Road to Moscow*. In their comprehensive account of Philby's life and career, they offered clarification of a few details responsible for Maclean's 1951 exposure. They believed the Washington embassy leak had been uncovered in 1945 by British codebreakers in penetrating a New York to Moscow cable. When the cable was broken at Bletchley Park, MI6 was "astounded to learn" that the messages included the texts of Churchill to Truman cables. Only one of the messages gave British security a clue as to his identity: his twice weekly visits to New York. For six years British security worked on the case with the FBI, which was in "overall control." Before Philby left for Washington in 1949, MI6 had instructed him to work closely with the FBI in identifying the embassy spy, codenamed HOMER. Moscow told him to alert his Soviet control as soon as Maclean's identification seemed imminent so he "could make his getaway."

As more cables were recovered, so the two British journalists tell us, they disclosed that HOMER had delivered his secrets to the Soviet consulate general in New York during his twice weekly visits to his pregnant wife, Melinda Maclean. At the time, she was living apart from her husband, in New York, and would give birth to a son on September 22, 1944. This was the "giveaway," Seale and McConville declare, "on which a clever mind stumbled in London." They don't claim that Philby and Burgess knew of this recovery, but finesse that possibility, acknowledging only that both recognized that the net was closing on Maclean. Philby, whose account guided their own, used the same metaphor. Seale and McConville don't identify their sources.[25] Since only a selective few MI5 and even fewer Foreign Office officials were aware of these details, it isn't difficult to guess their provenance.

In *Wilderness of Mirrors*, published in 1980, the American journalist David Martin first identified by name the codebreaking operation cited by Seale and McConville. It was called Venona. Martin's book centered on the CIA, not the Anglo-American codebreakers, and broke new ground on CIA operations in several important ways. Pieced together from secondhand FBI and CIA sources who insisted on anonymity, some of his dates and details describing Venona were wrong. One source was undoubtedly FBI special agent Robert Lamphere, who had yet to write his own account of Venona and the search for HOMER and was embittered by his betrayal by MI5.[26] Lamphere was excluded from any crucial 1948–1951 Venona recoveries of the so-called HOMER cables and the results of the MI5 investigation in London. The CIA's James Angleton also cooperated with Martin for a time, but would have had little direct knowledge of Venona; the CIA wasn't privy to the 1949–1951 operation. Martin claimed Philby received "drop copies" of the HOMER cables decoded at Arlington Hall, a claim that ignores the absolute restrictions on the Venona material imposed by U.S. military intelligence. For many writers the claim seemed to clarify the source of Philby's receipt of "reports" and "documents" on the HOMER investigation as remarked in *My Silent War*. Crediting an unidentified CIA informant, Martin also alleged Philby was "specifically" assigned to work with the FBI in tracking down the British embassy spy. He repeated the Seale and McConville assertion, gathered from his own anonymous source, that Maclean was identified by a Venona decrypt disclosing that HOMER met with his Soviet contact in New York twice a week while visiting his pregnant wife (the "twice a week" refrain isn't found in the Venona traffic).

Martin also claimed Maclean was in charge of "the embassy code room" and "the Ambassador's private cipher in which Churchill's cables to Truman had been sent." Had Maclean been in charge of Ambassador Halifax's "private cipher" in 1944–1945, he would have been MI5's prime suspect at the onset of their investigation, alleged to have begun in January 1949. As we will learn, according to Foreign Office officials Maclean was not an early suspect and wouldn't be for another twenty-eight months as the MI5 investigation continued inconclusively (we leave aside for the moment what MI5 actually knew). Common sense tells us either that the "private cipher" claim was in error or, if not, that MI5 chose not to act on it immediately for reasons of its own. Leaving in place a foreign agent who has been identified without his knowledge is common intelligence practice. The purpose in such cases is to identify other Soviet espionage agents, operations, and their Soviet control. Martin mentioned neither possibility.[27]

Whoever Martin's informants, many in the CIA and particularly the FBI's Lamphere were still choleric at being stung, swindled, disgraced, or humiliated by Philby. Some blamed MI5 blundering, others MI6's arrogant complacency, but none was personally involved except Lamphere. His detail on the Venona cable identifying Maclean came to him from an MI5 officer in June 1951. Left out in the cold, Martin's informants also volunteered hearsay that in some instances effectively further discredited British intelligence. Mixed in the melee, however, was privileged information passed to the FBI or the CIA by MI5 officers.

Although several of Martin's facts, like those of Seale and McConville, were muddled or wrong in some detail, misleading or mischievous in others, they were near the mark in two instances: the so-called Churchill cables that launched the MI5 investigation, which the FBI's Robert Lamphere could have provided Martin, and the Venona cable citing HOMER's visit to his pregnant wife in New York. This Venona intelligence given to Seale,

McConville, and Martin accurately described the crucial Soviet New York to Moscow cable 915 of June 28, 1944, reporting GOMMER's travel to New York "where his wife is living with her mother while awaiting confinement."[28] To introduce a technical point, Maclean's Soviet codename was GOMER, not HOMER: the Cyrillic alphabet has no letter for the sound "H." In this single instance, a Soviet code clerk introduced the GOMMER variant. In any case, GOMMER was Donald Maclean.

Since Venona's Maclean intelligence was so tightly controlled, this single fragment, whether it traveled through FBI or CIA informants, could have originated only with MI5 or one of three senior Foreign Office diplomats privy to the general contents of the cable but not the text. Why would that intelligence have been leaked? The GOMMER cable was the source of the September 1955 White Paper assertion that Maclean didn't become the principal suspect until mid-April or early May 1951, no earlier. This leak supported that dubious claim, which had originated with MI5 and couldn't be challenged even by the Foreign Office as long as Venona's Maclean archive remained locked away in the top secret vaults of the National Security Agency (NSA) in Washington and Government Communications Headquarters (GCHQ) in London. This detail was more or less accepted as accurate, as it was in part, and added to the definitive Philby dossier cited by writers as late as 1999.

For many Philby sleuths and historians, the circle was now closed. By luck, design, or coincidence, at the time of the crucial April 1951 Venona decryption both Philby and Burgess were posted to the British embassy in Washington, sharing the same house at 4100 Nebraska Avenue. The source of Philby's knowledge of the Maclean investigation was now evident to many: his access to the Venona decrypts at Arlington Hall. With the recovery of a sentence from the decrypted June 1944 NKGB cable that disclosed his visit to his pregnant wife in New York, Maclean was conclusively identified as the British diplomat who had passed secret Foreign Office cables to his Soviet handler in Washington in 1944–1945. That New York and Venona cable alarmed Philby at the possibility of his own exposure, but instead of notifying his Soviet control officer in Washington, he dispatched Burgess to London to warn Maclean—that long journey Rebecca West found "incomprehensible." Informed by MI5 of the conclusive Venona recovery in April 1951, Foreign Secretary Herbert Morrison authorized his surveillance and MI5 began its five-week-long search for courtroom evidence. On May 25 Morrison signed the final interrogation order for mid-June. That same night Maclean fled Southampton with Burgess.

For the last couple of decades, this version of the Maclean, Burgess, and Philby affairs has been accepted and repeated with some variations by most writers retracing the events of 1950–1951. Other English conspiratorial fantasts are equally certain that neither Philby nor Venona but another MI5 officer and Soviet agent, Sir Roger Hollis, tipped off Maclean.[29] British intelligence has never clarified this chronological sequence. Forbidden to speak out by an archaic code of secrecy, it has created a hydra-headed dragon that many a British knight–errant scribbler have ridden out to slay but none successfully; its silence has also helped perpetuate a history that perversely continues to serve its interests. Like many other accounts, the accepted version is false in some detail and misleading in others.

The key to the remaining mysteries of all three Cambridge spies remains concealed in the precise date British intelligence knew beyond question that Donald Maclean was a Soviet agent. Until 1995, the impenetrable barrier of Britain's Official Secrets Act made it impossible to draw any closer to the truth than the assorted collections of spurious anecdotes, inaccurate hearsay, and fanciful conjecture that dominated the Maclean case for more than forty years.

On July 11, 1995, at CIA headquarters in Langley, Virginia, the directors of the National Security Agency, the Central Intelligence Agency, and the Federal Bureau of Investigation noisily intruded on London's forty-five years of privileged silence and flung open the doors of America's most highly sensitive repository of Cold War secrets. Together they announced that the Venona operation, which had long outlived its Cold War function, was officially open for examination. The Venona project, now declassified, was public property. The decision was a triumph of common sense over the intelligence oligarchs and the arrogant and often witless indulgences of executive privilege. That same day the NSA released the first of the many thousands of translations of Soviet telegrams buried for decades in its archives.

Venona was a codebreaking operation by a team of American and British cryptanalysts at the army's Signal Security Agency (SSA) headquarters at obscure Arlington Hall in northern Virginia. Closed down in 1980, Venona was the most highly sensitive secret in the American and British counterintelligence arsenal. The interception, decryption, and analysis of Soviet cable traffic had first revealed the enormity of Soviet espionage in the United States in the 1940s as well as networks in England, Australia, and elsewhere in the West. Only a select group of senior U.S. and British intelligence officers were aware of the details of Venona, its tools, its methodology, and its codebreaking triumphs.

The Venona effort at Arlington Hall was led by the remarkable linguist and cryptologist Meredith Gardner, who was among the principal transla-tors and analysts of what was first known as "the Gardner Material" and was later given other control names, including Cream, Dinar, Jade, Bride, and Drug. In 1961 it became Venona, a totally arbitrary codeword, like those assigned earlier, that designated a specific group of decryptions. By 1946, using classic or traditional cryptanalytic techniques, Gardner and others had reconstructed a KGB 1943–1946 codebook and Gardner broke the "spell table" for encoding English names and phrases from the Cyrillic alphabet. His success derived in part from a 1942 Soviet blunder in printing duplicate copies of the decryption "key" on thirty-five-thousand pages of one-time pads used to encipher KGB cables. The extensive use of two sets of one-time pads intended for only one use left them susceptible to cryptanalysis, but not completely and not without long and painstaking analysis.[30]

Gardner's reconstruction enabled him to read fragments of numerous Soviet telegrams on the Washington and New York to Moscow circuits. One led to his realization that Moscow agents had penetrated the Manhattan Project, the top-secret program that developed and detonated the first atomic bomb on the Jornado del Muerto desert flats at Alamogordo, New Mexico, at 5:29 A.M. on July 16, 1945 (on August 6 the atomic bomb was dropped on Hiroshima; the second dropped on Nagasaki on August 9). By September 1949 Gardner's work resulted in identifying the British nuclear physicist Klaus Fuchs, who had worked on the Manhattan Project at Los Alamos, as a Soviet agent.

In 1947 Gardner's Venona team first penetrated a series of six NKGB Washington to Moscow cables of March 29–31, 1945, that were to form the basis of the MI5 Maclean investigation. According to Gardner, the partial recoveries defied recognition until December 1948, when a British crypt-analyst recovered enough of the contents to recognize that "the contents were telegrams from Churchill, and in January 1949 the originals were iden-tified in London."[31] The September 1955 British White Paper cites the Jan-uary 1949 date that launched "highly secret but widespread and protracted inquiries by MI5 in its search for the source." The Churchill cables weren't mentioned.

The 1995 decision to release Venona was made at congressional urging, inspired in part by a similar decision in Moscow a few years earlier to selec-tively open secret documents from Soviet intelligence archives.[32] In September 1990 KGB chairman Vladimir Kryuchkov ordered the "wider use of KGB archive material" in a campaign designed to promote a more balanced and positive view of the Kremlin's predatory KGB ogre.[33] Western journalists and historians took full advantage of their opportunity. The files revealed more than had ever been acknowledged from official British sources about Philby, Burgess, and Maclean. The British writer Nigel West made excellent use of his access to the KGB's British branch files. With Oleg Tsarev he published his research in 1998 in *The Crown Jewels,* a remarkable account of KGB operations in Great Britain that included new episodes in the Philby and Burgess chronicle. From 1994 until 1996 Russia's new Foreign Intelligence Service (SVR) gave an American historian, Allen Weinstein, substantial access to many old KGB files. The result was *The Haunted Wood,* published in 1999, an extraordinary account of Soviet intelligence operations in the United States and the declining state of the KGB's Washington apparatus in the mid-to late 1940s.

During this same period other KGB documents also found their way to England but without official sanction. In 1992 Vasili Mitrokhin, a retired KGB archivist, smuggled out of Russia thousands of pages of notes transcribed from sensitive Soviet intelligence files he had secretly gathered from 1972 until 1984. Publication of *The Mitrokhin Archive* in 1999 revealed a far more substantial body of secret KGB documents than had ever been disclosed. Mitrokhin's six cases of KGB material contained some thirty thousand notes detailing Soviet intelligence operations from the 1920s through the 1980s. Edited and annotated by Christopher Andrew, a distinguished Cambridge University intelligence historian, the value of *The Mitrokhin Archive* is inestimable. Mitrokhin documented the many extraordinary successes of the KGB, its mindless blunders, and the bloody 1934–1939 Stalinist purges within the Soviet intelligence services that decimated the ranks of its most capable agents. A few Mitrokhin documents described crucial details that had long been a mystery in the Philby case.[34]

Over the two years following the July 1995 announcement of the declassification of Venona, more than twenty nine hundred Soviet cables amounting to five thousand pages of telegraphic text were made public in six separate releases. They described Soviet espionage operations in the United States, Mexico, Australia, and Great Britain, although documentary details regarding the latter were too sketchy to contribute much of significant value. An extremely useful if episodic introduction by NSA officials and historians, *Venona: Soviet Espionage and the American Response, 1939–1957,* explained the history and background of the Venona operation. Six complementary NSA Historical Monographs accompanied each new release between 1995 and 1997 and added comments on the new batch of cables. Much of the NSA introductory commentary is footnoted to refer the reader to external sources, including books published earlier on Philby, Maclean, and Burgess. The device allowed the NSA historians to cite various accounts in the public domain that expanded on the Maclean and Philby affairs and served as a substitute for the continued silence from official British sources who offered no help explaining the Maclean and Philby investigations. Some of that material is erroneous or outdated by the Venona disclosures and the details found in Moscow's KGB archives as published in the 1990s.

Had it been left to British intelligence, the 1944–1945 Venona cables would never have seen the light of day. Britain's Official Secrets Act had concealed the Maclean telegrams in impenetrable secrecy and now Washington threatened to break open the vault. Although Philby, Maclean, and Burgess were dead, as were all the 1950–1951 principals at the Foreign Office, MI5, and MI6, the full and unrestricted release of the Venona archive in all its precise detail would have raised those old spirits from the grave as accusingly as Banquo's ghost and stood hairs on end in London by repudiating the official and hearsay versions of the Maclean affair and possibly exposing the dagger that did him in. For decades MI5 and MI6 had looked on in silence as journalists, writers, and scholars had reconstructed the Maclean, Philby, and Burgess chronology on the basis of largely undocumented evidence amplified by their own fund of unsubstantiated gossip, rumor, and conjecture. A few had help from Philby as a result of personal interviews in Moscow or his self-serving memoir, *My Silent War*. MI5 had no reason to be too uncomfortable with the accepted versions, since the truth was even more embarrassing; MI5 had even contributed in various ways to their acceptance. The Foreign Office, dependent on details MI5 was willing to supply, was its unwitting accomplice.

Philby's reputation in particular had flourished. By 1995 his legend was well established. H. A. R. Kim Philby was the most celebrated and successful spy of his generation, a reputation both MI5 and MI6 knew to be fraudulent in numerous ways.[35] Yet both had become prisoners of the inadmissible secrets of the complete and accurate Maclean dossier and paradoxically of the Philby legend as well. As only MI5 and MI6 knew, the Maclean secrets were inextricably linked to the undisclosed secrets of Kim Philby and Guy Burgess. In 1995 British intelligence had no choice but to search for ways to elude Venona's full disclosure of the Maclean secrets, even at the price of sustaining espionage legends they knew to be fictitious. Unfortunately MI5 and MI6 were now hoisted by their own petard, victims of their own brilliantly conceived and daringly executed fifty-year-old deception based in part on the 1949–1951 MI5 investigation of Donald Maclean. Drawing on the example and the still-secret deception strategies of World War II, they had shared their initiative with no one, not two British governments, not the Foreign Office, not the FBI or the CIA in Washington. But this was peacetime, not wartime, and now the means had to be found to disable or at least neutralize the secrets of Venona's Maclean archive, the only documented database that might betray that operation.

Chapter
TWO

Old secrets at risk.—A legend in his time.—A
cold reception in Moscow.—Isolation and
mistrust.—Moscow merchandizes its hero.—A
broken-down pensioner.—Fetched from the
discard pile.—A fortunate marriage.—The
dutiful propagandist.—Sleepless nights and
secret fears.—Addicted to fame.—Pious liars
and public frauds.

The Philby secrets were those most dangerously at risk by the full disclosure of the 1944 1951 Venona archive. From October 1949 until June 1951 Philby had been MI6 chief of station in Washington. Clever, charming, modestly unassuming, and a bit rumpled at times, he had easily found his place as a welcome confidant and drinking companion among his many American friends at the CIA and the FBI, would enjoy their trust and share their secrets. As MI6 chief, he was responsible for liaison with the fledgling CIA still in transition and to a lesser extent the FBI. He had been a Soviet agent since the summer of 1934, when he was recruited in London for the OGPU. The dates of his recruitment are no longer in doubt and have been established by KGB files seen in Moscow by two Russians in particular, Vasili Mitrokhin and Genrikh Borovik.[1] The dates British intelligence knew beyond question that Philby was a Soviet agent are still missing and remain concealed by British intelligence. In an obscure way, that secret is the one jeopardized by Venona. If it could be shown that MI5 and MI6 knew far more about Philby in 1949 or even 1950 than either has ever divulged or official Washington has ever suspected, then something was very seriously wrong with our understanding of those Washington years and fifty years of Anglo-American intelligence history.

Those missing dates haven't troubled the popular legend that has flourished over the decades. Phillip Knightley calls Philby the most remarkable spy in the history of espionage. Anthony Cave Brown believes the Philby affair the spy case of the century. So does the KGB agent Yuri Modin, who rearranged a few facts in his own book to help persuade us. The more reliable Oleg Kalugin, the KGB officer responsible for Philby's rehabilitation in Moscow in 1972, was also faithful to the legend, although never professionally associated with Philby until he took up his reclamation. British and American journalists and their readers have been similarly faithful, even those of a generation far removed from the year of Philby's dismissal from MI6 or his defection to Moscow. After half a century his name still has enough buoyancy to bob to media notice with each new espionage exposé. On February 20, 2001, the American news network CNN reported from London that Philby's *My Silent War* had inspired Moscow's FBI spy Robert Hanssen, who had read the book as a fourteen-year-old in Chicago and decided to make Philby's treacherous career his own. CNN got a few facts wrong. Its reporter claimed Philby defected in 1962 and was made a KGB general. It hardly matters. Celebrity's name is all we know and all we remember.

Notoriety is indiscriminate. It claims the great and the small, the courageous, the cowardly, the infamous, and the obscure, the Lindberghs, the Lord Haw-Haws, even Sylvain Dornon, a Frenchman who in 1891 walked from Paris to Moscow on stilts. Philby got there by a less public route. No Czech sugar-beet harvesters or Polish pig farmers were drawn from their fields or sties to the lane to watch him clatter heroically past. But his treachery was extraordinary to many and still is. How else can we explain those investigative journalists who arrived twenty years later, notebooks in hand, to record his many exploits? In Great Britain his fame was assured by his humiliating penetration of MI6 from 1941 until 1951, a success that can't be denied even if the consequences are impossible to measure. England loathed him because he had betrayed English trust, traditions, and institutions and made fools of their lordly guardians, a humiliation welcomed by tattletale journalists who adopted Philby as one of their own. In America, had Philby never set foot in Washington or crossed a CIA threshold at the 2430 E Street compound or the clutter of CIA barracks down by the Reflecting Pool he would have been as little noted at the time and as dimly remembered now as John Cairncross, the fifth member of the Cambridge spy ring.

With the international publicity attracted by Phillip Knightley's London *Sunday Times* exposé followed by others and the release of *My Silent War*, Philby quickly became a celebrity. *Newsweek* devoted a few pages to his exploits on January 1, 1968, crediting him with speaking eight languages, including Hindi, Arabic, Turkish, and Russian.[2] The first three he didn't speak at all and Russian very poorly. Americans who took notice were aroused for different reasons. Many in official Washington were outraged at another betrayal by the English with whom we had shared our secrets: first Allan Nunn May and Klaus Fuchs, the British physicist, then Maclean and Burgess, now Philby. On Capitol Hill, where the McCarthyites and assorted foreign-policy primates once hung their hats and others still do these days, the furor was predictable. These Americans understood little about England—they didn't know that in 1941 the British were the first to recognize the potential of a nuclear weapon and begin work on an atomic bomb; they were unaware of the British contribution to radar, computer theory, and cryptology; they knew nothing about Ultra or Colossus, the first computer, or much else except that the whole affair was proof enough of the unreliability of our degenerate second-class ally, corrupted by fops, fools, and *Faerie Queens*. Others were merely bewildered that Philby had so easily flummoxed the CIA and the FBI, the overpublicized, overglamorized, and often inept guardians at the gate.

But for most, Philby merely personified Cold War mysteries few Americans knew anything about except that they were of great significance, undoubtedly concealing important truths still being hidden by Washington's conspiratorial bureaucrats, like those tiny alien bodies taken from a 1947 UFO wreck in the New Mexico desert near Roswell and still on ice at the Wright-Patton air force base in Dayton, Ohio. If in fact no one seemed to know precisely what Philby had done or what secrets he had passed, it didn't really matter. His name endures.

Curiously, during the decade following his defection, Philby's renown was more generously recognized in England and the United States than in the Soviet Union. He arrived in Moscow in January 1963, where he lived in exile for more than twenty-five years until his death in May 1988. For some years the Soviet Union failed to grant him the honors he expected. During his first months he was confined to a two-room KGB safe house where he was intensely questioned and debriefed.[3] Intense debriefing was normal KGB practice but not the severity of his isolation. During the 1940s and the wartime period of his KGB service, Moscow Center suspected him of being a disinformation agent under British control.[4] Although those early doubts had passed, in Moscow he remained under suspicion and was under constant surveillance. He was never elevated to KGB officer rank as he had anticipated and falsely claimed. For many years he was merely another retired KGB pensioner, another gray face in a gray Moscow crowd, silently stalked by other equally indistinguishable gray figures from his KGB security watch. After his debriefing he was given a four-room flat near Pushkin Square. His phone was tapped, his apartment bugged, his mail intercepted and read; the few visitors he was allowed were scrupulously screened. He wasn't permitted to enter the KGB's Lubyanka headquarters until fourteen years after his defection.[5]

It wasn't that Moscow soon forgets those who once served its cause. In 1961 Moscow's longtime American agents Lena and Morris Cohen were arrested in London. Unlike Philby, Maclean, or Burgess, the Cohen name is virtually unknown in the United States. Among her other successes, Lena Cohen had been a courier for the Los Alamos spy ring's theft of atomic secrets. In November 1969 she and her husband were released from prison in England and exchanged for an Englishman. In Moscow that same month they were given the Order of the Red Star and a lavishly furnished Moscow apartment, in contrast to Philby, who was then living in alcoholic isolation and misery. In 1993 Morris Cohen died in Moscow at the age of ninety and was posthumously awarded the title "Hero of the Russian Federation."[6] What equally decisive success did Philby bring Stalinist Russia during his American years? (His operational life ended before Stalin's death.) We aren't entirely sure. Evidently neither were the Russians during the first fourteen years of his exile in Moscow.

KGB files released in the 1990s indicate that Philby's espionage output during the war years didn't compare to that of his fellow Cambridge spies, Guy Burgess, Donald Maclean, Anthony Blunt, and John Cairncross. The secret-document yield passed to Moscow from 1941 until 1945 by Burgess and Maclean was fivefold greater than Philby's, Cairncross's more than sixfold greater.[7] After Philby's 1947 posting to Istanbul, no available KGB records either brought clandestinely or opened selectively in Moscow prove his espionage value to the KGB. A quantitative yardstick is hardly the measure of worth. It may be that Philby's more modest product was of infinitely greater value. If so, we don't know what it was. But we do know that for most of his twenty months in Washington he was out of contact with a Russian control officer.[8] Philby also claimed that Nicholas Elliott of MI6, who questioned him in Beirut in 1963, insisted that he was absolutely certain Philby had stopped working for the KGB in 1949. Elliott's assurance, supplied by MI6's Dick White, may have been designed to ease the way for Philby's full confession, implying that he might be forgiven. It failed.

Until the Maclean crisis erupted in April and May 1951, notes from KGB files tell us nothing of the substance of Philby's Washington contact with Makayev, his KGB illegal serving his novitiate, except his fear that he might be betrayed. Philby had known since September 1949 that Maclean was under suspicion and had done nothing for eighteen months. The OGPU agent who recruited him in 1934 had twice told Moscow Philby was indecisive. In Washington he had dithered too long, although his procrastination may have been helped by MI5's long search for Moscow's unknown agent HOMER from January 1949 until April 1951, unsuccessful for those twenty-seven months, or so we're told. In *My Silent War* Philby claimed that during his meetings with his Russian "friends" outside Washington, it was decided Maclean should stay in his post as long as possible. His claim is false, an invention intended to justify his delay.[9] Distraught when he realized that Maclean was under suspicion, he met with Makayev in April and again in May, desperate for Moscow's help in removing Maclean from England.

No other KGB files suggest the results of his Washington espionage or his 1949–1951 penetration of the CIA except for a questionable report on a single Ukraine airdrop. The KGB silence proves little except that the selective releases of the 1990s were confined to records intended to demonstrate Moscow's success, not its failure. Nigel West and Oleg Tsarev published some fifty pages of reports Philby sent to Moscow during the war. They reported that KGB classified files contained almost every one of the messages he passed to Moscow. Most now seem trivial, as they no doubt would after fifty years.[10] They included nothing for 1947–1951. Had the suspicions of senior KGB officers from 1963 to 1977 been based in part on the fragmentary KGB files opened in the late 1980s–1990s and those brought out by Mitrokhin in 1993, they might have concluded that Philby had given Moscow very little from 1947 until 1963. The Philby cupboard was bare. If that was the case, they might have questioned his purpose in defecting to the Soviet Union twelve years after he had left MI6, as some certainly did.

In isolation in Moscow those first years, Philby began writing his memoirs, *My Silent War*. Despite a few senior officers' suspicions, the KGB decided to extract a final benefit from the Philby legend that was attracting so much attention in the West. The KGB would fight fire with fire after the publication of the CIA-edited *Penkovsky Papers* describing a joint MI6-CIA espionage triumph in Moscow. Yuri Modin, our KGB guide, was assigned to lend a hand, or so he claimed in his own book. He had handled Burgess in London between 1949 and 1951 and, through Burgess, Philby, or so he alleged. The two had never met until Modin visited Philby in Moscow, so Modin asserted in his own memoir, telling us he reviewed Philby's drafts as KGB censor. If so, his intrusion isn't conspicuous and doesn't mar the narrative quality. Philby's book was composed at intervals over several years, completed in 1967, and published in England and America in 1968.

Philby was an able writer and *My Silent War* is well written. To pretend otherwise and condemn the book because of contempt for the man is understandable but silly. Philby was at his best in describing his former colleagues and explaining a few difficult British intelligence problems of the war years and their immediate aftermath. In those sections his descriptive and expository clarity, incisiveness, and self-deprecating wit are evident. If his better patches of prose are any indication, he found comfort in recapturing his past, not to flaunt his espionage triumphs, which were few indeed, but in recalling old friendships and old associates, often sympathetically, including those Americans he knew in Washington. The memories might have sustained him during those lonely early years of his Moscow exile.

There was a lingering malice in a few of Philby's recollections, however, and he couldn't refrain from an occasional barbed comment or innuendo he must have known to be false. He scorned FBI director J. Edgar Hoover for the usual and well-justified reasons. He denigrated those few British associates in whom he sensed a lurking ambiguity or doubt and belittled those he had reasons to resent. He mistrusted MI6's Sir Jack Easton, his immediate superior in 1949–1951, and dismissed Sir Dick Goldsmith White of MI5 and later MI6 as a former schoolteacher, a petty description he knew to be absurd. Both Easton and White had been active in British postwar deception operations. Allen Dulles, whom he met only briefly in Washington, despite Philby's claims of a longer association, was a convivial bumbler, but that judgment was based on Philby's Moscow newspaper readings and the Bay of Pigs disaster. On balance *My Silent War* is a reasonably accurate attempt to recover the past, the diverse personalities, problems, and character of Philby's difficult and troubling London years from 1940 until 1946. There are some errors of fact and a few falsifications.

It isn't difficult to understand why Moscow didn't publish *My Silent War* in the USSR until 1980 and then in a small bowdlerized printing with no publicity and no success. Soviet officialdom evidently snatched up the limited copies available. In memory, style, sophistication, and wit, it is an Englishman's book of minor recollections, not a routine exercise in Soviet propaganda, although it had its moments. After more than thirty years, the perfunctory tributes to Moscow have an unintended absurdity, but so do innumerable other books from the same period, whether written by American or English political analysts, many now unreadable. The various English personalities, internal problems, and issues Philby was recounting wouldn't have been of great interest to Russian readers. The exploits of Philby, the legendary KGB spy, and his benefit to Moscow are so minimal they might have raised questions as to the reasons for his renown.

In late 1967 two Russian journalists from *Izvestia* interviewed Philby and asked if he was "happy." "Yes, I am happy," he replied ponderously. "I would like to repeat the words of Felix Dzerzhinsky, the knight of the Revolution, the great humanist. If I had to begin my life again, I would begin it just as I did."[11] Those knowledgeable American readers who recognized his hero might have been stupefied by the tribute to the first Cheka leader and terrorist. Not Russian readers. The Philby interview was first published in *Izvestia* in December 1967 and intended for a Russian audience. A Russified Pole and fanatical Bolshevik, Dzerzhinsky, who died in 1926, was a popular hero of Stalinist culture.[12] *Izvestia* had given Philby a rare opportunity for public performance, one that would be seen by the inaccessible inner circle at the Kremlin. For an ambitious Moscovite, it wasn't unlike a onetime appearance on CBS's Ed Sullivan television show. In his homage to the revered Stalinist symbol, Philby, like a forgotten vaudeville hoofer being given his one big chance, was hoping to tapdance his way out of obscurity. It didn't work.

He didn't tell his *Izvestia* interviewers that he'd attempted suicide during those years or that his nightly descent into drunken incoherence was the least painful way to suicide, as he had once told his young wife, Rufina Philby. There were also his many sleepless nights, his fear of loneliness and abandonment, his slowly deteriorating health.[13] After the book was published in the West, Philby was dropped from official attention and cast aside. Despondent at being given no more work, he grew more isolated, his health deteriorated, and he drank even more heavily.

In his foreword to *My Silent War*, Philby had written that he recognized the many problems ahead faced by the Soviet Union. True to his commitment, he wasn't discouraged: "As I look over Moscow from my study window," he prophetically declared, "I can see the solid foundations of the future I glimpsed at Cambridge." If this was his view in 1968, it would soon fade from memory. In early 1972, a compassionate KGB officer on a recovery mission ascended in a creaking elevator toward the top floor of a decaying Moscow apartment house on Yuzhinsky Pereyulok. From the seventh floor he climbed up the stairs through the fetid twilight to the flat that held that study window and its heroic vision of the future. At the door he was met by a wreck of a man reeking of vodka who greeted him in savage denunciation of the Soviet "secret police, the Soviet government and the world at large." It was Oleg Kalugin's first meeting with the legendary Kim Philby.[14]

Inside the apartment, Kalugin attempted unsuccessfully to talk to an incoherent Philby and his young wife, Rufina. He left after twenty minutes, discouraged and upset at his KGB assignment to reclaim the "broken down drunk." The reclamation decision wasn't Kalugin's but had been made by Yuri Andropov, head of the KGB and later general secretary of the Soviet Communist Party. His plan was to visibly improve the lot of those many forgotten KGB agents, like Philby, who had defected to the USSR only to find themselves living as miserably, as impoverished, and as abandoned by the Communist state as the average Soviet citizen. Andropov's purpose was to so conspicuously improve the comforts of those old defectors as to make their lives in Moscow enviable enough to entice others to follow their example. His logic seems to have been that since Marxist-Leninist ideology had lost its attraction, material wealth, comfort, and well-being—those old capitalist bogeys—might serve in its place.

Harebrained it was, but then Andropov had never lived beyond the Iron Curtain. Isolated in the privileges of his rank, he may have thought Moscow's bright lights would have seductively beckoned to some underfed, underpaid foreign cabinet official doing donkeywork in pestholes like Bujumbura, Port au Prince, or Aden but hardly elsewhere. If the good life was to be the glittering lure to attract foreigners to KGB service, with its ultimate career reward a richly fulfilling retirement life, Moscow would hardly have been the city of choice. Miami, New York, Los Angeles, or Tucson would have been more seductive (for all the wrong reasons) and the CIA, not the KGB, would have been the foreign recruit's employment agency. The irony is that Andropov's promise of material rewards was responsible for the KGB's most significant success in recruiting American agents like the navy's John Walker in 1967 and the CIA's own Aldrich Ames in 1984. Both were walk-ins, both venal volunteers, both cash-and-carry operatives; both were misfits and both were paid substantial sums of money. The dollars the KGB gratefully doled out by the wagonload weren't intended to be spent in gay old Moscow.[15]

Oleg Kalugin, at the time the KGB deputy director of foreign counter-intelligence, was given the chore of rehabilitating the KGB discards and improving their circumstance. Philby was among the drunken wrecks on his pile. A decent and compassionate man, Kalugin was of a younger generation and had attended Columbia University. He was too young to have been personally involved with the Cambridge Five but knew of Philby's reputed exploits and renown, which were more widely celebrated among the younger cadre of KGB officers who knew little or nothing of Philby's operational successes. Kalugin was aware that a few in the KGB security apparatus and several KGB elders were suspicious of Philby, some because they considered Philby a double agent sent to penetrate the KGB. He wasn't among the doubters. He believed Philby was "one of the great spies for the USSR" who had been driven "half mad by the paranoia and idiocy of the KGB." His assessment of the cause of Philby's deterioration seems reasonable.

Half mad or not, the great spy was in deplorable condition when Kalugin began his rehabilitation. He was chronically depressed, drank heavily, often to incoherence—not a new habit by any means—and had been hospitalized for alcoholism. In 1969 he had again found what always seemed to bring him out of drunken depression: the consolation of female companionship. Rufina Ivanova was a lovely, intelligent, compassionate Russian woman thirty years his junior. They were married in December 1971. She was Philby's fourth wife and as devoted to him as he was to her, but her influence was limited and her relief only temporary for several years—obvious enough in the shattered drunk who greeted Kalugin at the door at their first meeting in 1972. During subsequent months Kalugin persuaded the KGB to reduce electronic surveillance, improve the couple's lot, paint the neglected flat, buy Rufina new furniture, limit Philby's drinking, and allow more visitors to reduce his imprisoned isolation. Kalugin also searched for ways to effectively use Philby's intelligence background and his extensive knowledge of British, American, and other Western intelligence agencies. As an indignant widow, Rufina Philby in her own account, published in 1999, would deny Kalugin's description of the Philby flat and the purchase of new furniture. She freely admitted her problems in coping with Philby's staggering drinking habits. After their marriage she was able to moderate his drinking, and bring it under control. But not his insomnia or his other fears, whatever they were and whatever their origin.[16]

In the abstract, Kalugin credits Philby's Moscow rehabilitation in part to Andropov's ambitious plan to raise the quality of life for KGB defectors and to show the munificent benefits of Moscow as a compassionate retirement house, all amenities available. Despite the suspicions of a number of KGB elders, Kalugin and others helped in the reconstruction. The credit belongs to Rufina Philby. Young and with a formidable will of her own, she gave him what no amount of official sanction could ever provide, an escape from his daily isolation, his nameless fears, and his pathetic loneliness. He recovered from his despondency, was used as a KGB lecturer, and was able to receive more visitors. But he remained "a run-of-the mill, semi-employed pensioner," wrote retired KGB colonel Mikhail Lyubimov in describing Philby at their first meeting in 1975. He derided Western press reports that Philby was among Andropov's advisers.[17] The semiretired pensioner appeared more content during his later years with his large library, his admiring visitors, his correspondence with his many followers abroad, his use of a dacha near Moscow, his international fame, and his occasional service to his adopted country. Near the end he was nominated for a notable Soviet award. The request was denied on higher authority and he received a more modest citation.

Whatever the reservations of the KGB skeptics—and they remained to the end, as did the microphones in his flat—Philby's usefulness to Moscow as a dutiful public servant and propagandist soon emerged. Any KGB doubts about his value—not the tiresome MI6 double-agent nonsense still remembered by a few—were set aside as irrelevant or immaterial as his role was defined and amplified. He became an occasional lecturer on English institutions to younger KGB cadres and his own grateful self-publicist. Those KGB officers who subsequently overpraised his invaluable past service to the KGB for the benefit of English journalists, even though they were as much in the dark as we are, were his eager collaborators. A cynic might conclude that legitimate doubts about his true espionage achievements for Moscow had been sacrificed to his renown in the West and its infatuation with his celebrity. They were. Peering into Lubyanka's dark windows for so many years, the face we saw in the reflecting glass wasn't Philby's but our own.

In light of what we now know or should know, by any sensible measure Philby's importance as a KGB agent has been preposterously exaggerated in the West. He has been credited with passing intelligence secrets he couldn't possibly have known or revealed even if he had known. His passivity in

Washington from 1949 until 1951 makes many of those claims absurd. Yet his name is constantly invoked, whether in explaining the Albanian fiasco of 1949, General MacArthur's defeats in Korea in the autumn of 1950, the theft of atomic secrets, or failures in the Ukraine. If a war that suits politicians is usually the wrong war, the same is true of covert operations that do little more than gratify the vanity of recklessly irresponsible intelligence officers. When failure came, Philby was always lurking about to explain their losses. When another inexplicable failure occurred, he was always there, that dim figure standing far off in the shadows who personified everything they didn't know, the proof of their honor, virtue, and innocence and the unfathomable duplicity on the other side. In truth he was merely the long shadow cast by the lamp of a common ignorance. It was far simpler to credit his treachery than to admit that their intelligence world had grown too infinitely complex, that the perplexity of institutions, people, secrets, lies, fabricated paper, real documents, and reconstructed events had outgrown their capacity to understand what they knew.

Philby's reputation was enlarged by officials in Washington who knew very little yet manufactured myriad espionage triumphs from multiple uncertainties, most particularly during his months in Washington. The memories of CIA officers who had absolutely nothing factual to contribute added their own conjectures, gossip, and hearsay that seemed to authenticate the legend. In England and America the inevitable result was to defer to a myth that lived and thrived quite independent of any documentary evidence. Mitrokhin's KGB archive smuggled out of Russia in 1992 and other KGB records help clarify the record and refute some of those myths. Philby's final years were evidence enough that he was continuing as Moscow's spokesman and his own self-promoter. The two roles were indistinguishable by then. Visitors came to indulge, flatter, and share the memories of an aging spy of limited importance still so honored in the West he could fancifully maintain a fraudulently overblown legend forty years obsolete.

Apart from his deception as a KGB agent, a cold undercurrent of betrayal runs through Philby's personal life in counterpoint to his espionage career. His disregard for those who had served his purpose is most evident in his failure to visit the dying Guy Burgess in a Moscow hospital after Philby's arrival in 1963, although the reasons are still unclear. Poor Burgess, Philby's often hapless, irresponsible, drunken, and faithful courier from 1947 through 1951, who remained an Englishman to the end. He died of liver failure in Moscow in August 1963. Philby had recruited him thirty years earlier and some believe he never forgave him for accompanying Maclean to Moscow, although the KGB, not Burgess, was responsible. Philby never saw Burgess again after 1951, evidently because the KGB denied his request for a hospital visit. He received Burgess's bequest of his large library and a tidy sum of money.

From time to time Philby borrowed other men's wives as mistresses—not terribly wicked if one doesn't make a habit of it. Philby did. He made it a vocation. He married one in Beirut, who faithfully followed him to Moscow; during her absence he fell out of the matrimonial bed and borrowed Donald Maclean's wife as his live-in mistress. We remember Donald Maclean. He was said to be impotent by then, which perhaps excuses his wife's infidelity but not Philby's. He had recruited Maclean in 1934, his first triumph over the English establishment he despised. In time his relationships with both wife and mistress grew stagnant and died. In Moscow he had the great fortune of meeting Rufina Ivanova and proposed soon after they met. She remained with him faithfully until his death in 1988.

During his final years Philby might have been an admirable rogue if he hadn't been such a pathetic liar. His endless efforts to justify himself put him well within our petty bourgeois moral reach and invite our contempt. A truly honest scoundrel wouldn't give a damn about our opinion, wouldn't have gathered together on his shelves the many books written about him to discover what new espionage triumphs had now been credited to him, wouldn't have studied new facts on old cases whose details he had totally botched in his memoir (the Fuchs case, for one), wouldn't comment further in his letters or revisit with his guests forgotten triumphs decades in the past. He might have been waiting in dread to learn what old secrets had finally and officially been released by GCHQ to the Public Record Office at Kew to expose the sham. None were, not in his lifetime. *My Silent War* in 1968 had been an interesting, well-written, and modest recollection, even if dishonest at times. Why say anything more? His July 1977 lecture to a group of three hundred or so KGB officers reveals his intent. It was a pitiful exercise in espionage banalities that deluded not only his listeners but the lecturer as well. His posting to Washington, he explained, was even more advantageous than his post as chief of MI6 counterintelligence in London, a claim that was as preposterous as his pretense. The latter had been the triumph of his career, not his twenty months in America, where he had lain low for more than a year and only met with a Soviet illegal those final months when desperation forced him to act to save his own skin.[18] But Washington had added the last gilded laurel to his fame and what did his young KGB audience know? Nothing except his heroic legend, and that when compared with America, Moscow's prime enemy, England was very small beer.

During that last decade Philby had been rejuvenated and reclaimed. The falling-down drunk was now a man of eminence. He received more foreign visitors, granted more interviews, and became more expansive. In 1988 in Moscow, when Phillip Knightley questioned the value of his 1963–1966 KGB debriefing twelve years after his contacts with the CIA—a reasonable point by the way—Philby was provoked: "Nonsense," he scoffed. "It's absolute nonsense to say that intelligence knowledge is ever out of date. Even today things still come in on which I have an opinion which is valuable, an instinct, a feeling for the situation."[19] Knightley had made an unforgivable error: he'd challenged the legend. Of course Philby had a feeling for his situation. It was his to exploit and exploit it he did. During those final years he attracted what the respectable scorn, a corrupt celebrity he gratefully indulged. He flattered his visitors' curiosity by mixing fact with fantasy in describing incidents forty years past that never happened.

Why did he continue his deceit in Moscow in the 1980s? His career was long over. He might have claimed the dignity of silence. *My Silent War* should have been enough. His reputation in the West—by then established far beyond reason, as senior KGB officers and he certainly knew—spoke for itself. But he didn't keep silent. Recognition and renown concealed his doubts and his pathetic uncertainty. "My ambition is fame," wrote his father, St. John Philby, an avaricious opportunist who might have become a Hindu if oil had first been found in the Pushtu rather than in King Saud's Arabia. Philby was his father's son even if he had no interest in excessive wealth except as it kept him in tobacco, whiskey, oysters occasionally, and a few necessities. Fame and Rufina Philby were the crutches that let him limp through those final years; celebrity was an addiction he couldn't resist.

He found it far more proof of his worth than the crippled, spavined, broken-down Communist nag he was obliged to mount and spur on, not to the bone yard or the glue factory where the old Marxist-Leninist cripple belonged, but to defend those final Cold War barricades then being torn down across Eastern Europe. He had no choice. His honor and that of his broken-down stable mount were at stake: to deny one was to deny the other, even if their union might suggest that the Don Quixote in the tattered saddle was a sadly demented fool. So he insisted on adding to his legend by generously providing more details. Because they were lies and because they were both trivial and gratuitous, they diminish any respect we might have for him, not a scoundrel at all, not an honorable rogue either, but merely another pathetic weakling craving popular recognition and acclaim. Toward the end of his life, the spy of renown became what had never been so obvious during his long career, a pious fraud.

What was lacking in Philby's case was a Swift, a Pope, an Orwell, or an H. L. Mencken who would have ripped away his pretense and our delusions. We got the English novelist Graham Greene instead. In 1968 Greene had paid tribute to Philby's *My Silent War* as "an honest autobiography, a dignified statement of Philby's beliefs and motives, not an instrument of communist propaganda."[20] His comments weren't totally off the mark if Philby's conspicuous but perfunctory tributes to Moscow are ignored. But Greene's review was dishonest. The literary essayist who could brilliantly penetrate the truths of Henry James's *Golden Bowl* and *Portrait of a Lady*, novels of treachery, deception, and spiritual evil (and why Greene called his lesser novels "entertainments"), had no insight into his own. His tribute was an exercise in pious phrase-making. He was grinding his own pitiably morbid ax, writing as a propagandist for his Jacobite cause. Philby was merely another neurotic excuse.

Twenty years later, the dying English novelist was a pilgrim visiting Philby's flat in Moscow. Why? For the same reason concealed in his review, the same reason Greene admired the obscure English Jesuit poet Robert Southwell far more than Shakespeare, a reverence that had nothing to do with creative genius. Southwell was hanged in 1595 for treason whereas Shakespeare went on writing plays. Southwell, a Jesuit brother, had secretly entered England to begin the spiritual conquest of Queen Elizabeth's Protestant dominion on behalf of Catholic Spain. He had formed a Popish cell in the Strand in London, was caught celebrating mass, was tortured to reveal his fellow priests, and was finally executed.[21] Of course Greene would have gone to Philby's flat. It was grist for his martyr's mill. As Orwell would write of Greene's devotion to similarly sanctified sinners in his novels, there was something rather *distingué* in being damned. Orwell would have treated the aging spy with the same withering contempt Graham Greene deserved.[22]

Philby's discussions with Yuri Modin in Moscow suggest he was never certain of MI6's intentions in Washington in June 1951, that is, in hinting that if he planned to escape, the time had come. Possibly he suspected London knew he was Moscow's agent long before his dismissal from MI6. If so, during his years in Moscow he may have been haunted by the uncertainty, a mystery he could never resolve but carried with him to his grave. Only

Rufina Philby, stronger than he was, gave him the affection and companionship he desperately needed to survive.

But even in our scorn for those conscious of history, fame, transience, and oblivion, the sight of Philby's swollen face in the photographs of those last years evokes pity and shame. Where was the stuttering, uncertain five-year-old boy brought to England by his father and abandoned to his relatives, who taught himself to silently resist the prejudices of the English public school system and ultimately rebel against the English class system responsible? The photographs and the reminiscent lies were all that remained, a bloated caricature of the legendary spy who had betrayed others and finally had been betrayed himself, and who no more belonged in Russia than he did anyplace on earth. Except England. In his own rebellious and aberrant way Philby remained an Englishman to the end.

Chapter
THREE

The Arlington Hall codebreakers.—The United
States and Britain collaborate.—The 1946 U.K.-
U.S. agreement.—Exchanging cryptologists.—The
British embassy leak.—The myth of London's
cooperation.—The HOMER codename.—London takes
charge.—Dubious cable texts.—Excluding the
FBI.—Attlee's nuclear deterrent.—Hoodwinking
J. Edgar Hoover.—Philby's MI6 cipher.—False
assumptions about Venona.—Fantasies, fabrica-
tions, and falsifications.—Who warned Philby?

The problems confronting London after Washington's decision to release
the Venona archive are difficult to identify without some understanding of
Anglo-American cooperation in attacking Soviet cable traffic. On February
1, 1943, U.S. military intelligence's Special Branch (cryptography) began to
study its repository of encrypted Soviet cables at the Signal Security Agency's
Arlington Hall headquarters on the instructions of Colonel Carter Clarke,
chief of Special Branch. The cables had been gathered during the war years
when U.S. censorship laws required that all international telegraphic traffic
entering or leaving the United States was subject to military inspection.
Three commercial carriers, Western Union, RCA Global, and ITT World
Communications, supplied U.S. military intelligence with copies of all foreign commercial traffic, including encrypted cables to and from Soviet diplomatic and trade missions in the United States. Known by various names,
including "the Russian Section," the modest SSA operation employed mil-

itary, naval, and civilian linguists and cryptanalysts. Colonel Clarke justified the project as an effort to detect any evidence that Nazi Germany and the USSR might conclude a separate peace agreement, a very dubious possibility in early 1943.[1] At the time, England's Government Code and Cipher School (GC&CS), Britain's codebreaking agency, had no such program. Operations targeting the USSR had been suspended on June 22, 1941, the day Germany smashed into Russia in Operation Barbarossa. Prime Minister Winston Churchill reportedly imposed the ban, although there is some doubt as to whether it was honored. Nevertheless GC&CS continued to collect Soviet communications intercepts.

On May 17, 1943, the United States and the United Kingdom signed the secret BRUSA agreement on communications intelligence. The pact established cooperation at the highest security level, including sharing the Ultra intelligence derived from Enigma decryptions of German military communiqués and commands. BRUSA formalized regulations and procedures, top-secret classifications, the Anglo-American exchange of personnel, and would govern U.S.-U.K. Sigint cooperation during the remaining years of the war.[2] By 1944 restrictions had eased on the Government Communications Headquarters (GCHQ), the renamed and reorganized codebreaking agency, and its analysts began attacking Soviet traffic. (GCHQ's functions weren't officially admitted in Parliament until 1984, more than forty years after its creation.) According to official KGB records available in Moscow in the 1980s, in August 1944 Kim Philby told his Soviet control in London that GCHQ at Bletchley Park was examining Soviet ciphers.[3] By 1945 the interception and analysis of Soviet cipher traffic had become GCHQ's principal activity and its highest priority. Documents in the British Public Record Office at Kew uncovered by an American historian, Bradley Smith, show that GCHQ had intercepted and successfully decrypted Soviet coded traffic in August 1945.[4]

The defeat of Germany and the Japanese surrender in August 1945 threatened the end of wartime censorship laws and military intelligence's access to international telegraphic traffic. On August 18, 1945, SSA officials began a secret campaign to enlist its wartime commercial telegraph collaborators in a peacetime intercept operation focused on "the enciphered telegrams of certain foreign targets." The appeal was successful and Western Union, RCA Global, and ITT World Communications agreed, although not without years of difficulty. Copies of international cables were supplied to military intelligence on microfilm or paper tapes and were sorted manually. In the 1960s the switch to magnetic tapes enabled cables to be broken out electronically. Beginning in August 1945 Operation Shamrock, as the top-secret intercept effort was called, obtained copies of millions of international telegrams sent to or from or transiting the United States.[5] In adapting to the new postwar environment, in September 1945 the SSA was reorganized as the Army Security Agency (ASA), whose headquarters remained at Arlington Hall, Virginia. Operating under the command of the director of military intelligence, the new agency's charter called for the creation of a worldwide network of field stations and a theater headquarters in the Far East and in Europe.

In the late summer of 1945 the United States and the United Kingdom began to collaborate on Soviet signals traffic. GCHQ was briefed on Arlington Hall's Soviet operations by cryptanalyst Cecil Phillips, a member of the team that broke one KGB cryptographic system in 1943–1944. On March 5, 1946, London and Washington were bound even more closely by a new top-secret U.K.-U.S. agreement to collaborate on all aspects of communications intelligence and share its results. Growing concern about the extent of Soviet espionage and the need for more extensive Sigint collection and collaboration effort were among the reasons for updating the 1943 BRUSA pact. The March 1946 agreement was in the form of a series of memoranda exchanged over several years as the original understanding was expanded and modified. Canada, Australia, and New Zealand would eventually be included.

Under the 1946 agreement, British cryptanalysts were assigned to Arlington Hall Station, maintaining an exchange begun with the original BRUSA pact. Under the latter, GCHQ had sent Colonel John H. Tiltman to Washington in May 1943 as a permanent liaison to the War Department and Arlington Hall's SSA. One of GCHQ's most experienced cryptanalysts, Tiltman had worked on Soviet communications since 1930, had broken and decrypted the Comintern's coded radio traffic between Moscow and its foreign radio stations, and at the time was head of GCHQ's General Cryptographic Section. He was reportedly instrumental in recognizing that the five-figure numbers on Russian one-time pads had been mechanically reproduced, an identification that led Arlington Hall cryptanalysts to ultimately reconstruct the pads. He would remain in Washington until 1954.[6] An encrypted telex link between Arlington Hall and GCHQ in London was installed; U.S. military intelligence controlled the U.S. end of the circuit and GCHQ the London terminal. A Senior United Kingdom Liaison Office in contact with Arlington Hall was opened in Washington in the Old Navy building on Constitution Avenue under the cover of the British Joint Services Mission established during World War II. The communications terminal and the Liaison Office were evidently opened in 1946. GCHQ military, civilian, and civil service cryptanalysts posted to Arlington Hall would have been under the authority of British services intelligence liaison officers assigned from GCHQ and the London Signals Intelligence Board.

Like its British counterpart GCHQ, Arlington Hall, now under the Army Security Agency, operated in absolute secrecy, as rigorously controlled as the wartime Ultra and Enigma secrets had once been at GC&CS's Bletchley Park. Known to only a few senior officials in U.S. military intelligence, GCHQ, MI5, and MI6, the Venona material was so tightly held and so narrowly distributed that senior officers at the Pentagon a few miles away were left in the dark, as was virtually all of official Washington. Until 1947, so was the FBI. The CIA didn't officially receive its first Venona translations until 1953, after Arlington Hall was absorbed by the National Security Agency in 1952. A few CIA officers were aware of Venona in 1948 but Arlington Hall's liaison with the agency was soon suspended because of the CIA's internal disarray.[7]

In late 1946, following Meredith Gardner's success in penetrating Soviet traffic, an unidentified British cryptographer from GCHQ was integrated into Gardner's team (GCHQ records released to Britain's Public Record Office in October 1996 don't give his name).[8] GCHQ's Philip Howse was assigned to Arlington Hall from February 1944 until early 1946. GCHQ's Russian linguist Geoffrey Sudbury was among the first sent to Arlington Hall to work with Meredith Gardner, probably in 1946 (he may be the unnamed officer in the GCHQ release).[9] Colonel John H. Tiltman, as noted earlier, had been working with Arlington Hall since May 1943 and was still there in 1947–1948. Evidently other GCHQ cryptanalysts were on assignment as well. The NSA documents tell us about the achievements of Meredith Gardner, Cecil Phillips, Lieutenant Richard Hallock, and other Americans working on Venona but not of their British counterparts. What was their role? We don't know, not from the NSA documents.

The NSA tells us that "from 1948 on there was complete and profitable U.S.-U.K. cooperation" on Venona. Although American and British cryptologists collaborated in their analytical work at Arlington Hall, GCHQ's cooperation in releasing the Venona archive in 1995–1997 isn't evident in the detail supplied in the NSA introduction or the six Historical Monographs that accompanied each release. The NSA documents fail to mention the assignments of Colonel Tiltman, Philip Howse, Geoffrey Sudbury, or any of the GCHQ officers who served at Arlington Hall. When they were occasionally identified in a memo by Meredith Gardner, their names were blanked out. We don't know whether the British had their own working section at Arlington Hall or were fully integrated into the Gardner Venona team, although the latter would not exclude the former. Nothing is said about the exchanges between the British at Arlington Hall and GCHQ in London to report new cryptologic breakthroughs, although we know from a 1997 NSA source that in May and June 1947 a GCHQ cryptographer and "the special UK liaison officer" in Washington were briefed in detail on Venona's progress in breaking into British Commonwealth traffic and began notifying their London superiors of the success.[10] The NSA introduction doesn't mention those or earlier exchanges and doesn't explain the British chain of command at Arlington Hall, at GCHQ, or at the controlling London Sigint authority. Although the NSA's Historical Monographs accompanying the releases describe Arlington Hall's cooperation with the FBI, they pass over in silence MI5's investigation of HOMER based on the Venona cables. These and other questions occur to anyone attempting to interpret Venona's Maclean cable recoveries and fully understand British participation. The NSA Venona monographs answer none of them.

In disclosing the extent of Soviet espionage in the United States, the 1995–1997 NSA Venona releases held back nothing in revealing the texts of the many Venona cables under its authority, including details on Arlington Hall's collaboration with the FBI in tracking down those American KGB agents identified by Venona. Only the names of those few Americans who were still alive were withheld to protect their privacy. The British, in contrast, embargoed any and all aspects of Venona that touched on British interests and identities. It is difficult to explain why the names of GCHQ officers detached to Arlington Hall would have been withheld almost fifty years later except as an effort to conceal the presence of several of Britain's best cryptologists who were working at Arlington Hall during 1947–1948, the most critical years of the HOMER recoveries. By omitting or ignoring intelligence details under its authority, London's cooperation in the 1995–1997 Venona releases was negligible, evasive, and in one major instance deliberately harmful.

The most damaging omission is the NSA failure to disclose the parallel GCHQ Venona operation established in London at Eastcote in Uxbridge in late 1947 or early 1948, if not earlier. In March 1947 Meredith Gardner first began breaking into Canberra-Moscow 1945–1947 cables that revealed Soviet penetration of the Australian Ministry for External Affairs. Some of the recovered cables were decrypted in near "real time," meaning soon after transmission. By September or October Gardner had been able to identify two documents prepared for the War Cabinet in London and passed to the KGB in Canberra. Gardner asked his GCHQ liaison to obtain London's copy of the originals, two top-secret British War Cabinet documents drafted by the Post Hostilities Planning Committee. Once these cribs were in hand, Gardner discovered that the complete texts of the two documents, "Security of India and the Indian Ocean" and "Security in the Eastern Mediterranean and the Eastern Atlantic," were contained in twenty KGB cables sent to Moscow from Canberra.[11] Washington's concern about lax Australian security betrayed by the Canberra breakthrough warranted a December 1947 visit to Washington by Sir Edward Travis, chief of the London Signals Intelligence Board. The U.K.-U.S. agreement was amended to more stringently restrict London's sharing Venona secrets with Commonwealth nations.[12]

Alarmed by the discovery of the NKGB Australian espionage network by an American cryptologist not under London's control, GCHQ established its own Venona cryptographic team at its Eastcote facility. GCHQ documents released to the Public Record Office falsely claim that the leak of British documents to the Soviet MGB residency in Canberra was discovered by Venona in December 1948 and led "soon after" to "the setting up of the UK's own cryptanalytic party" at GCHQ.[13] The December 1948 date is in error by at least a year, if not longer. As indicated above, Gardner first broke into the Canberra-Moscow traffic in March 1947 and six months later had recovered sections of a Soviet Canberra to Moscow cable alluding to the British War Cabinet documents. In February 1948, ten months before GCHQ claims the Canberra leak was uncovered and the Venona cell established, Sir Percy Sillitoe of MI5 arrived in Sydney to inform the Australians of the Soviet espionage network. He had in hand the codenames of External Affairs officers who had passed British documents to the NKGB in Canberra.[14] Sillitoe didn't mention Venona. Not until 1949 were the Australians told of the source.

Released by the Public Record Office in October 1996, the GCHQ review was intended to complement the 1995 NSA releases in Washington. It is impossible to know the reason for the error, but the date GCHQ launched its Venona operation in London is essential for knowing when the Eastcote cell began attacking Venona cables. In moving that date forward to December 1948, London was ignoring more than a year of activity. That omission is consistent with London's 1995–1996 determination to withhold any intelligence that might suggest Donald Maclean's espionage had been uncovered by GCHQ before December 1948 or that he had been identified as a Soviet agent prior to April 1951.

The 1996 NSA publication *Venona: Soviet Espionage and the American Response* omits any mention of a parallel GCHQ Venona project at Eastcote, as do the six Venona Historical Monographs. Nor do they mention Gardner's 1947 success with the British War Cabinet documents. One of the monographs reveals that in 1947–1948 the Venona project (then known by another name) became a combined American and British intelligence operation, but this acknowledgment ignores the 1943, 1944, and 1946 assignments of GCHQ officers to Arlington Hall. The work of the latter and the parallel Eastcote operation are crucial for a comprehensive understanding of Venona's role in exposing Maclean as a Soviet agent. Their exclusion from the NSA documents so violates the spirit of the NSA releases as to border on deception. The issue raises serious questions about the integrity of London's participation in Venona and the completeness and accuracy of the final Maclean cable texts released in February 1996.

The Venona archive published with the Third Release in February 1996 contains twelve Maclean telegrams.[15] Several include separately numbered sections transmitted individually by Soviet code clerks, but the 1996 release issued them as a single document with numbered sections. (The twelve Maclean cables are listed, described, and analyzed in appendix A.) Six of the twelve Maclean cables were sent from New York to Moscow in 1944 and six from Washington to Moscow March 29–31, 1945.[16] All were first recovered in 1947–1948 in broken fragments of varying lengths. Those initial recovery dates can be determined or inferred from Meredith Gardner's periodic listing of Russian cover names between September 1947 and August 1948 and his final comments in October 1951. The first HOMER cable recovery at Arlington Hall was made prior to September 26, 1947. Meredith Gardner referred to the cable (New York to Moscow 1263 of September 5, 1944, reporting a Churchill-Roosevelt meeting in Quebec on September 9) and its source in an internal ASA memo.[17] In his October 1951 summary he explained that there was nothing in that HOMER message "to suggest a connection with the Washington material of the following year." He was referring to the series of six Washington to Moscow cables of March 1945 that betrayed the British embassy leak.

None of the six March 29–31 Washington to Moscow cables refers to HOMER. Instead all cite "Material from 'H' or 'G.' " Only two of the twelve Maclean cables refer to HOMER (GOMER) as a source and both were sent from New York in 1944. Other 1944 New York to Moscow cables mention HOMER in the body of the text but none of the 1947–1948 initial recoveries of those telegrams was broken sufficiently or contained enough personal detail for Arlington Hall analysts to identify the source.

Intelligence analysts and historians studying Venona's twelve Maclean cables have assumed that their recovery and translations were entirely the work of an integrated Anglo-American team at Arlington Hall Station. They have also assumed that Arlington Hall's principal analyst, Meredith Gardner, and his Venona team knew the full content of those twelve cables. Both assumptions are false. All Gardner and his team knew about were those fragments first broken out at Arlington Hall before they were transferred to GCHQ's control in London for further decryption and analysis. Gardner mistakenly believed the "G" material was an arbitrary Soviet code designation, not a codename. He didn't know that the "G" ("H") cited in the March 29–31, 1945, series referred to GOMER (HOMER) until June 1951, when the FBI reported to the Armed Forces Security Agency (AFSA) that "G," HOMER, and GOMER were identical with Donald Duart Maclean. (The FBI source was MI5's Arthur Martin.) Gardner didn't have access to nor was he fully informed of the content or the results of any subsequent GCHQ Eastcote decryptions after January 1949, when GCHQ in London took control of the cables and MI5 the distribution.

In December 1948 more recoveries from the March 1945 cables first penetrated in 1947 led to the realization that Foreign Office secrets were being passed to Moscow. The original cables were identified in London in January 1949, or so Meredith Gardner was told. His October 11, 1951, report describes the March 29–31 series:

> From the earliest days of [blanked out] code-value recovery (1947) it was known that several Washington to Moscow messages of 29–31 March 1945 began with the stereotype: To the 8th Section. Materials G. The Eighth Section was known to receive political intelligence, and the scanty recoveries from the interior of the message confirmed that the contents concerned foreign policy and involved Sir Archibald Clark Kerr.
>
> In December 1948, further work by [blanked out] revealed that the contents were telegrams from Churchill, and in January 1949 the originals were identified in London.
>
> It was thought that "G" was probably an arbitrary code designation. When names are abbreviated to their initials in the traffic so far as it was then known the letter is followed by a period (inside the quotation marks, when there are quotation marks). Thus there was no reason to connect "G" with a person's name or cover name.[18]

Because the second name is blanked out, it isn't clear whether Gardner was referring to a British cryptanalyst at Arlington Hall or the GCHQ Venona cell at Eastcote. Either reference is possible. By December 1948, the GCHQ Venona cell had been at work for more than a year, an interval the 1996 GCHQ release to the Public Record Office attempted to obscure. December 1948 was also the month the GCHQ analyst told Gardner of the recoveries from the cables of March 1945. Those identical dates deny the possibility that Maclean's espionage could have been uncovered by GCHQ any earlier than December 1948.

The October 1996 release of GCHQ records to the British Public Record Office acknowledges the complementary GCHQ Venona operation at Eastcote. This was more than a year after the Washington announcement of Venona's declassification and received little attention in the United States. The GCHQ document explains that the American and British teams "worked very closely together, each undertaking different tasks" at the working level.[19] In the division of responsibility the Anglo-American team at Arlington Hall, whether integrated or working separately, and the British team in London would pursue those Venona transcripts in the Arlington Hall traffic relevant to their own national interests. The fragmented nature of the initial Venona recoveries at Arlington Hall made it difficult to immediately establish national authority. An American cryptanalyst working on a KGB New York to Moscow cable would assume the message relayed Soviet espionage collected from an American source until more recoveries from the body of the message clearly showed that British secrets were being compromised, as in the several March 29–31, 1945, Washington to Moscow cables. As noted above, their content wasn't known and the Foreign Office originals weren't identified until late 1948, or so Meredith Gardner was told.

Since the Canberra-Moscow cables were a British Commonwealth responsibility, GCHQ's Venona operation took over any further decryption of that traffic.[20] GCHQ control would have begun in the summer or autumn of 1947, not late 1948, as GCHQ claimed. In January 1949, once London had verified one of the March 29–31, 1945, Washington to Moscow cables as a Foreign Office or Churchill cable, the other five, all citing "Material from 'H' ['G']," would also have come under British authority and passed to GCHQ's Venona cell at Eastcote—if in fact they had not already been passed or read by GCHQ cryptologists at Arlington Hall.[21] There is reason to believe they were read and transferred much earlier in 1947–1948.

In May and June 1947 a GCHQ cryptographer and "the special UK liaison officer" in Washington began notifying their London superiors of Ar-

lington Hall's success.[22] After Meredith Gardner's disturbing Canberra recoveries in the autumn of 1947, an uneasy London would have kept a close
watch on Arlington Hall's Venona operation. The purpose in establishing
the London Venona cell in late 1947–early 1948 was to avoid any possible
repetition of the Canberra episode, when sensitive British War Department
secrets were first uncovered by the Americans. British analysts would take
control of any Venona recoveries at Arlington Hall that appeared even remotely relevant to British interests. In late 1946 Meredith Gardner had broken the Russian "spell table" for encrypting English letters, an invaluable
tool in helping identify cable content. In the 1947–1948 Venona penetrations, there was ample evidence of British names and content. Three of the
1944 HOMER cables mentioned Churchill. Other 1944 cables, citing HOMER
in the body of the text, referred to the Foreign Office, the British government, and the proper name of a British diplomat. Of the six March 1945
cables, two referred to the British ambassador in Moscow. Those references
would have drawn the attention of Colonel Tiltman and other British members of Gardner's team.

A comment by Gardner in October 1951 suggests that British analysts
at Arlington Hall had their own work section for deciphering Venona cables.
That separate section may have been the source of his information on the
Churchill cables. It also explains his comment that "the British surround
the handling of [blanked out] material with rigid safeguards," which suggests his personal observation.[23] Other British GCHQ officers were also mon-
itoring the Arlington Hall Venona operation. One of only seven top-secret
copies of Gardner's 1947 Special Report listing covernames in diplomatic
traffic taken from partially broken Soviet cables was sent to "LSIC thru Col
Marr-Johnson." LSIC was the acronym for the London Signals Intelligence
Committee. Colonel Marr-Johnson (whose name was overlooked by the
NSA's English name blotters), was a GCHQ officer working with the Royal
Air Force intelligence staff under the cover of the British Joint Services Mission with offices in the Old Navy building in Washington.[24] A March 1948
U.S. Air Force intelligence document on file at the National Archives shows
he represented RAF intelligence in collaborating with the U.S. Joint Operations staff at the Pentagon on Sigint in Europe directed at the Soviet Union,
a GCHQ function.[25] (Colonel Marr-Johnson's relevance to Philby's Washington assignment is described in chapter 11.)

It is difficult to believe that those experienced British GCHQ cryptologists in Washington wouldn't have begun attacking Venona cables judged
relevant to British interests as early as 1947–1948, and forwarding them to

London for further recoveries after the cell at Eastcote was established. It is likely, moreover, that the Eastcote operation was initiated for that express purpose. As mentioned above, years later Gardner would disclose that Geoffrey Sudbury, who had worked with him during the preceding years at Arlington Hall, led the GCHQ Eastcote Venona team. He was well aware of the 1944 HOMER cables and the March 1945 "G" series.

Not surprisingly, it was the Venona cell at Eastcote that identified the HOMER codename from the "G" and "H" designations in the March 1945 cables that had frustrated Arlington Hall. We don't know the date. The identification could have been made at any time in 1947–1948 after the GCHQ Venona team began further recoveries from the 1944 and 1945 cables first penetrated at Arlington Hall. An Eastcote analyst deduced that the opening to Washington to Moscow cable 1788 of March 29, 1945, "To the 8th Department. Material of 'G'," wasn't a code designation at all but the abbreviated codename for "an active and successful agent." "G" or "H" stood for GOMER (HOMER). In his comment on the cable, the GCHQ analyst noted: "Although there is no full stop after the G, it is certainly an abbreviation for GOMER [HOMER], the cover name for Donald Duart Maclean, who was 1st Secretary at the British Embassy, WASHINGTON, at this time. The brevity of the opening suggests that this was a routine type of signal and it is identical with that used on the LONDON to MOSCOW MGB link in respect to 'LEAF' (see London's 2905 of 23rd September 1941)."[26]

Although there were eight or nine Soviet cover names beginning with "G" in Meredith Gardner's listing of New York to Moscow cover names, the Eastcote Venona analyst unerringly concluded that "G" was HOMER, the name cited in Arlington Hall's group of six 1944 Venona New York to Moscow cables. His recognition gives us additional reason to believe that the New York to Moscow HOMER cables recovered in 1947–1948 were forwarded to the Venona Eastcote unit at that time. At the very least, those six cables were sent to GCHQ following London's January 1949 identification of the original Foreign Office March 1945 cables, the so-called Churchill cables, enabling the GCHQ analyst to draw his HOMER conclusion.

GCHQ's failure to inform Meredith Gardner that the "G" of "Materials 'G' " was the designation for HOMER is incomprehensible given the NSA claim of Anglo-American collaboration on Venona. The only possible explanation is that GCHQ was prohibited by MI5 from sharing its success with Arlington Hall. GCHQ cooperated only to the extent that it served MI5's interests. MI5 didn't want Gardner or his American team to recognize that London had been working successfully on those 1944 and 1945 cables since

1947–1948 and to discover that GCHQ knew far more about both HOMER and "G," the single source of the Washington embassy leak, than Arlington Hall realized. Telling Gardner all that GCHQ knew didn't serve MI5's purpose, most certainly not after the FBI's Robert Lamphere began working closely with Gardner in October 1948.

Sir Maurice Oldfield evidently used the HOMER codename in September 1949 when he briefed Philby in London on the 1944–1945 leaks from the British embassy and "the atomic energy establishment at Los Alamos."[27] Although Philby mentioned neither codename in describing his meeting with Oldfield in *My Silent War*, he used the HOMER codename in mentioning the reports he received in Washington. KGB files in Moscow disclose that he passed the CHARLES codename in his note to Burgess, evidence that Oldfield did cite Fuchs's codename and possibly HOMER.[28] Genrikh Borovik claims Oldfield did tell Philby the codename HOMER but Borovik isn't wholly reliable and sometimes borrowed from published sources.[29]

In the 1995–1997 Venona release of cables documenting Soviet espionage in the United States, the complete and final texts were published. After almost half a century, there was no reason to withhold whatever was found in the Venona archives. The Washington decision was intended to declassify Venona, and declassify it did—at least the American archive. In the case of the Maclean cables, however, GCHQ and MI5 control of the more complete or final traffic meant that the content of those telegrams released in 1996 was at London's discretion. The Maclean cable texts released with Venona could be from any number of those evolving stages, from an early 1947 1948 recovery by the Venona team at Arlington Hall, from GCHQ recoveries in London in 1948–1950, or from an even later GCHQ recovery in 1955– 1965. It is impossible to tell which version was published. We are asked to accept on faith that they were the full, unexpurgated texts known to MI5 during its 1949–1951 Maclean investigation.

There are grounds for dismissing that assumption. In early August 1950, a Mrs. Gray, an American analyst with the Gardner team at Arlington Hall, recovered fragments from a section of an August 1944 KGB New York to Moscow cable that shed new light on "G." Meredith Gardner commented:

> In August 1950 Mrs. Gray of AFSA recovered two stretches which read "work including the personal correspondence of Boar [? Churchill] with Captain [Roosevelt]" and "weeks ago G. was entrusted with deciphering a confidential telegram of Boar's [?] to Captain." These recov-

eries were communicated to the British 11 August 1950, who thereupon set up work-sheets for further recovery work. The suspicion that "G." was the source of material "G" occurred to people at AFSA immediately upon seeing Mrs. Gray's work and this suspicion was suggested to the British at the same time. Subsequent work on this message brought forth the suggestion that G. was married.[30]

The same August 2–3, 1944, cable released in 1996 omits the "subsequent work" fragment. Nor is there any suggestion that "G" was married. The "subsequent work" was completed after Mrs. Gray's recoveries were sent to the British on August 11. Gardner doesn't quote the later recovery, as he did the earlier fragments, presumably because in October 1951, when he wrote his final report, his only reference was the forwarded Arlington Hall text, which didn't include later recoveries. Had GCHQ analysts completed those recoveries, then their work should have duplicated Arlington Hall's. If the August 2–3 cable published in 1996 is the original Arlington Hall cable sent to London on August 11, not a later GCHQ recovery, the marital detail uncovered several days later hadn't yet been added. In either case, the NSA's publication of a partial cable text rather than a later, more complete GCHQ text raises serious doubts about the integrity of the Venona Maclean cables released by the NSA in 1995–1997.

The reasons for the failure to release the final and complete version of the August 2–3, 1944, cable text in 1996 as recovered at GCHQ, the controlling authority, aren't difficult to recognize. Virtually every published account of the Maclean and Philby affairs claims that an April 1951 recovery of a Soviet New York to Moscow cable at Arlington Hall Station finally and conclusively identified Donald Maclean as HOMER. He had passed Foreign Office secrets to his Soviet control while visiting his pregnant wife in New York in June 1944. This Venona secret was deliberately leaked in the 1970s and 1980s to support the September 1955 White Paper claim that Maclean wasn't identified until April 1951. The KGB New York to Moscow cable alleged to have identified him is one of six recovered at Arlington Hall Station in 1947–1948, and dated June 28, 1944 (no. 915). Only a fragment was recovered. Vladimir Pravin, the New York representative for TASS, a Soviet news agency heavily staffed with KGB officers, had met with GOMMER (HOMER). The relevant fragment reads: "SERGEJ's meeting with GOMMER took place on 25 June. GOMMER did not hand anything over. The next meeting will take place on 30 July in TYRE. It has been made possible for G. to summon SERGEJ in case of need. SIDON's original instruction has been altered. [34 groups unrecovered] travel to TYRE where his wife is living with her mother while awaiting confinement."

The GOMMER cable had been in the Arlington Hall inventory for several years. Until late March 1951 the body of the message was completely unknown to Meredith Gardner, who had no reason to believe GOMMER had any relevance to HOMER, "G," "H," the British embassy spy, or anyone else. On March 30, 1951, however, an English member (name blanked out) of his Venona team "transmitted to England the suggestion that G. was Homer [GOMER] and GOMMER."[31] And once again a British analyst or liaison officer, not an American analyst, was responsible for a decision that would result in a decisive Venona discovery. It had happened in December 1948 when a British analyst alerted Gardner to the "foreign policy" contents of a Materials "G" cable, the name of "Sir Archibald Clark-Kerr," and the January 1949 confirmation of the so-called Churchill telegrams. Now it had happened again. British analysts were no more prescient than Meredith Gardner but in those two instances their judgments were so accurate as to imply foreknowledge. Yes, the Churchill cables were identified in London in January 1949 and yes, GOMMER was HOMER. Both incidents suggest that in 1948 and again in 1951, unknown to Arlington Hall, the London Venona cell was working from a complete set of the twelve 1944 and 1945 Venona cables first broken at Arlington Hall 1947–1948 and acquired by the GCHQ Venona unit in 1947 and 1948.

Gardner wasn't certain why his British colleague had made his suggestion but guessed he may have come upon the GOMMER reference in compiling a routine index of KGB cover names, a frequent exercise at Arlington Hall that inventoried cover names, dates, and origins. The single identifying fragment was subsequently broken and translated at Eastcote in London, as the translation suggests: "awaiting confinement" is an English, not an American, locution.

The August 2–3 cable sent from New York to Moscow included detail quoted from an encrypted Churchill to Roosevelt cable on a military issue of major importance. It was passed by Maclean to his Soviet control in New York while visiting his pregnant wife, Melinda, whose actual confinement was much closer in August than in June (she gave birth on September 22, 1944). Had GCHQ released the most complete version of that cable in 1996, the reference to Maclean's marriage and his pregnant wife in New York would have demolished the claim that his marital status and his visits weren't discovered until April 1951 when the so-called identifying Maclean GOMMER cable was recovered by the GCHQ Venona cell at Eastcote.

Since the June 1944 GOMMER cable had proven impenetrable at Arlington Hall, it isn't easy to explain how it was so quickly broken at Eastcote. Nigel West claims it was decrypted in London on March 30, 1951, by GCHQ's Wilfred Bodsworth after "prolonged cryptographic attack." Since Gardner tells us that the GOMMER cable was passed to London on March 30, the GCHQ "attack" couldn't have been prolonged. GCHQ's Venona unit already had the GOMMER cable in its inventory and had broken it earlier. This should tell us that prescience didn't suggest to Gardner's British colleague that he single out that GOMMER cable; foreknowledge did. It had been broken much earlier by the Venona cell at Eastcote and was awaiting its moment. The GOMMER cable was MI5's instrument in finally closing out the Maclean investigation. With the moment at hand, a British analyst at Arlington Hall was told to forward his G/HOMER/GOMMER suggestion.

In commenting on GCHQ's decryption of the GOMMER cable and its disclosure that Maclean's visit to his pregnant wife in New York had identified him as HOMER, Nigel West asserts that "fortunately for Maclean, Philby was in a position in Washington D C to alert the Soviets to his immediate arrest and convey a warning to him."[32] He doesn't explain how Philby in Washington might have been aware of a GCHQ recovery at Eastcote.

West is wrong in this instance, as were many journalists, commentators, and historians in assuming that Arlington Hall cryptanalysts were responsible for the recoveries and translations of the Maclean cables. Meredith Gardner's report describing the transfer of the GOMMER cable to London, where the incriminating fragment was recovered by GCHQ's Venona unit at Eastcote, should banish that assumption. Philby's claim that the FBI played a major role in the Maclean investigation and the mistaken belief by so many that his liaison with Arlington Hall gave him access to the Venona secrets belong in the same rubbish bin.

The issue of FBI involvement is of minor importance, of interest principally in revealing much of the nonsense written about it. Philby's so-called access to Venona is far more significant. It leads to the question "Who told Philby that Maclean had been identified as a Soviet agent and prompted him to send Burgess to London?" The answer requires clarifying the FBI role and eliminating Venona.

The exclusion of the FBI from the Venona decrypts of the Maclean traffic began in January 1949, after GCHQ took control following London's confirmation of the March 29–31, 1945, Foreign Office telegrams. In early 1949 General Clarke, commander at Arlington Hall, also instructed his staff to withhold any Venona Special Reports from the Joint Counterintelligence Center established by the army and navy (and joined briefly by the CIA) to exploit signals intelligence opportunities. FBI special agent Robert Lamphere, who worked with Meredith Gardner on Arlington Hall's domestic codebreaking operations, no longer had access to the so-called HOMER cables. He took his exclusion personally and never forgot it. Embittered, he blamed MI5 and GCHQ.

It was Gardner who had introduced Lamphere to the Venona project. As Gardner broke into more KGB messages at Arlington Hall in 1946–1947, he became increasingly uneasy at the extent of KGB espionage operations in the United States and his inability to alert others to the Soviet penetration. The decrypted Venona codenames of Soviet agents were relatively meaningless to Arlington Hall's secluded analysts until clarified by the FBI's fund of names and suspects acquired from its own domestic counterintelligence operations. On August 30, 1947, Gardner drafted his Special Report "Covernames in Diplomatic Traffic," which included a number of names from his decrypted cables on U.S. KGB operations and sent it to his superiors.

His military chiefs took his point in questioning Venona's restrictive distribution. In 1947–1948 General Carter Clarke, then deputy director of military intelligence, began receiving from G-2's FBI liaison officer lists of the FBI's KGB and GRU cover names. At the time the FBI was investigating members of the U.S. Soviet espionage apparatus revealed by Elizabeth Bentley. A member of the U.S. Communist Party since 1935, she went underground in 1937 as a handler and courier for a Soviet espionage operation. In August 1945 she clandestinely contacted the FBI and subsequently produced a ninety-page statement identifying scores of individuals, some at the senior level of government in Washington, who were secretly supplying intelligence to the Russians.[33] The FBI forwarded a list of some two hundred names to Arlington Hall for analysis. In October 1948 Lamphere began liaison with Arlington Hall and Meredith Gardner.[34]

In his book published in 1986, Lamphere recalled that in late 1948 he knew of the existence of a fragment of a deciphered KGB message revealing a Soviet agent at the British embassy in 1944–1945. He doesn't explain whether he had seen the decrypt among the Venona messages sent to the FBI offices or during his visits to Arlington Hall.[35] He could only have been referring to one of the "scanty" recoveries from the Washington to Moscow "G" cables of March 29–31, 1945, described by Gardner and first penetrated in 1947 before GCHQ established authority. It is more probable that in late

December 1948 Lamphere learned from Gardner that "foreign policy" matters and Churchill cables had been uncovered. He could have assumed that there must have been a Soviet spy at the British embassy. Had he seen the cables, he would have known that they didn't cite HOMER. Lamphere's meddlesome presence at Arlington Hall beginning in October 1948 was another reason for GCHQ's failure to inform Meredith Gardner that "G" designated HOMER.

By the time Lamphere published his memoir, HOMER had become so synonymous with Maclean that he used the codename as a convenient analogue throughout his book. When he began formal liaison with Arlington Hall and Meredith Gardner in October 1948, there were but two HOMER-captioned cables; both were anomalous and neither offered enough detail to associate the name with an unknown spy at the British embassy. HOMER was also cited in several other 1944 cables and these may have been among the decrypted KGB cables with their Russian cover names sent to the FBI beginning in 1948, where they were analyzed, interpreted, and sometimes stored. But those 1944 textual fragments gave no clue as to their origin. Lamphere couldn't have known what Gardner didn't know: from 1949 until June 1951 Gardner had no idea who HOMER was. GCHQ and MI5 took control of those cables in January 1949 to the exclusion of Lamphere and the FBI after the so-called Churchill cables were identified in London the same month.

Lamphere also wrote that he gave Gardner copies of telegrams from Churchill to Truman, including some with the identifying numbers of the original cables.[36] He didn't disclose how he obtained these cables but his claim is incomprehensible. In diplomatic practice a cabled instruction to an embassy requesting that its substantive content be passed to the head of state or the foreign ministry is recast in the appropriate format, the text paraphrased, and so forwarded, usually by diplomatic note, or, if orally, by an aide-mémoire left with the host government official. Neither would ever include the original cable or its original language, the cable number, or any of the various operational markers found on a cable or an internal message center distribution copy. The original cabled instruction would be retained by the embassy and would never have found its way into the archives of the host country. Moreover, if Lamphere knew the cable numbers, he must have known the dates, August 1944 and March 1945: Roosevelt was still in the White House. There were no Churchill to Truman telegrams in the Venona inventory.

In late 1948, so Lamphere tells us, at the request of assistant FBI director

Mickey Ladd he told Dick Thistlewaite of MI5 and Peter Dwyer of MI6 from the British embassy of the decrypted fragment. Ladd had instructed him to deal with Dwyer on the deciphered messages, but told him "to be cautious about it," a warning that the intelligence was especially sensitive. Both Englishmen were astonished, insisting they knew nothing of the KGB decrypt or a suspected KGB agent at the British embassy. If Lamphere's dates are accurate—and he's careless about dates—their reaction isn't surprising since in late 1948 London hadn't yet verified the Foreign Office cables, or so Meredith Gardner informs us.

Dwyer and Thistlewaite agreed to work on a list of suspects. Thistlewaite of MI5 promised to collaborate with the FBI in the investigation and keep Lamphere informed (MI6 had no responsibility). As the months passed, Thistlewaite and his successor, Geoffrey Patterson, failed to keep their word. Despite Lamphere's repeated requests, Thistlewaite and Patterson insisted London had made no progress in identifying HOMER suspects.

In early October 1949 Lamphere was introduced to Philby by his MI6 predecessor, Peter Dwyer. They discussed HOMER but Lamphere gave no details. He claimed Philby didn't impress him, but his remark was made long after he had been duped and come to loathe Philby. Not surprisingly, post-facto reflections on Philby are often disparaging. Lamphere briefly referred to the Maclean investigation again when he wrote that in late 1950 or early 1951 he was informed HOMER had made weekly visits to New York to meet with a KGB agent. He doesn't identify his source but his reconstruction is erroneous. The Maclean visit to New York was never apparent to Meredith Gardner or Arlington Hall until April 1951, if then. Until June 1951 Gardner remained cautiously uncertain that GOMMER was HOMER.

From 1949 until June 1951, after Maclean and Burgess disappeared, Lamphere no longer had access to any so-called HOMER recoveries by the Anglo-American team at Arlington Hall, knew nothing of any suspects, and was unaware of the progress of the London MI5 investigation. Since early 1949, those initial Arlington Hall recoveries were under GCHQ control and were being more completely decrypted in London. Lamphere's other conclusions show his access to Arlington Hall Station was confined to Venona's domestic operation. He wasn't aware of the presence of GCHQ cryptographers when he began meeting with Gardner in October 1948, which strongly suggests the British had their own secluded work station. He mistakenly dated their appearance to 1949, and wrongly attributed their summons as an effort by annoyed GCHQ officials in London to bypass the FBI as a result of his informing MI5 and MI6 of the Venona fragments indicating a spy at the British embassy. Lamphere knew nothing of the details of the 1946 U.K.-U.S. Sigint agreement or the parallel GCHQ Venona operation in London.

But he was correct in his claim that London was upset by his knowledge of those Venona embassy spy fragments as he reported to Dwyer and Thistlewaite. London's anxiety had nothing to do with the assignment of British analysts to Arlington Hall and everything to do with the FBI's pursuit of a British diplomat who may have been guilty of atomic espionage in Washington. Under no circumstances would London have allowed the FBI to actively share in that investigation. In 1948–1949 there were far more serious issues at stake for Britain and more devastating implications in the search for HOMER than were apparent to the FBI. Among those issues was the Attlee government's determination to create an independent nuclear deterrent.

In the summer of 1945 British scientists were intent on duplicating for Great Britain the American atomic bomb several among them had helped create. In September 1945 they asked Prime Minister Attlee's approval for an Atomic Energy Research Establishment (AERE). The request was approved in October and British scientists began work on the first atomic pile at Risley in Lancashire. The AERE facility at Harwell would be opened on January 1, 1946, under Sir John Cockcroft. U.S. technical data was essential for building a plutonium bomb—the Nagasaki bomb—to which a leading British scientist was committed. Evidently it was also the bomb whose production methods, if not design, were relatively unknown to British scientists. Unlike the Manhattan Project facility at Los Alamos, the U.S. plutonium-producing works at Site W in Hanford, Washington, had been effectively isolated by the strictures of General Leslie Groves, the head of the Manhattan Project. Only one British physicist had visited Hanford.[37]

In November 1945 Attlee arrived in Washington seeking Truman's agreement for continued atomic energy collaboration. Churchill and Roosevelt had formed a wartime partnership for developing nuclear weapons with the August 1943 Quebec agreement and the September 18, 1944, Hyde Park aide-mémoire, both so secret that few in the Truman administration knew of their existence. On November 16, 1945, Truman and Attlee initialed a brief memorandum of intent expressing their desire for "full and effective cooperation in the field of atomic energy." A second memorandum recommended that the "development, design, construction and operation of [atomic] plants be regulated by *ad hoc* arrangements through the Combined Policy Committee (CPC)," established by the 1943 Quebec agreement as a coordinating body.[38]

Sir Roger Makins, the economic minister at the British embassy in Washington, became the joint secretary of the CPC soon after his January 1945 arrival. On February 15, 1946, the CPC considered a draft agreement prepared by Makins, General Groves, and the Canadian Lester Pearson to replace the wartime Quebec accord. The British had requested technical detail for the construction of a "large scale atomic plant" but Groves ruled out both the plant ("too vulnerable to Russian attack") and the allocation of ore required that would curtail U.S. nuclear production. Groves complained that the British were pressing for every secret the Manhattan Project possessed in the way of atomic development, design, and production, data that went beyond the Quebec agreement or any acceptable bilateral accord. As Attlee told Truman in April 11, 1946, however, "cooperation meant nothing less than the full exchange of information." Attlee repeated his plea on June 7 but got no reply. An atomic energy bill was under consideration as it had been since December 1945.[39]

In July 1946, after months of contentious debate, Congress passed the McMahon Act (the Atomic Energy Act). Signed by Truman on August 1, an Atomic Energy Commission (AEC) was established under civilian control. Among its many provisions, the McMahon bill prohibited formal agreements on nuclear cooperation, banning the exchange of nuclear weapons data or materials with any other nation. A contributing factor to the embargo was the growing hostility toward the USSR and increasing concern about Soviet espionage. Igor Gouzenko, the Soviet code clerk who defected in Ottawa in September 1945, had identified as a Soviet agent Allan Nunn May, the British physicist employed at the joint Canadian-British nuclear project in Canada. Gouzenko also claimed that hundreds of Soviet agents intent on stealing nuclear secrets were still uncovered in Canada and the United States. Thirteen Canadian scientists and technicians were arrested in Canada in early 1946. On March 4, 1946, Allan Nunn May was taken into custody in London and on May 1 was sentenced to ten years in prison for violation of the Official Secrets Act.[40] His arrest confirmed the doubts of many in the conservative Congress and the Truman administration that British security procedures offered adequate protection for U.S. atomic secrets.

With the restriction on the exchange of technical information, the work of the CPC was devoted principally to the Combined Development Trust, a CPC agent for acquiring essential uranium and other ores not under U.S. or

U.K. jurisdiction. At the British embassy the CPC remained as closely guarded a secret as ever. During a 1946 visit by George Carey-Foster, the head of Foreign Office security, Makins asked him to set up "a special Security zone for 'Tube Alloy' files [the British codeword for atomic energy] to which only Makins, Maclean and their respective secretaries would have access." After Makins returned to the Foreign Office in early 1947, Maclean succeeded him as joint secretary of the CPC.[41] Makins frequently returned to Washington to represent Britain at the most critical CPC meetings.

On December 31, 1946, the Atomic Energy Commission replaced the Manhattan Project as custodian of U.S. nuclear secrets. In January 1947, as noted earlier, Prime Minister Attlee decided to proceed with the construction of an atomic bomb. At the time neither Attlee nor Foreign Secretary Ernest Bevin was confident the United States intended to remain engaged in Europe or was prepared to consider Britain's defensive needs.[42] In August 1947 Harwell's first atomic pile was in operation and with the experience gained, British scientists had designed two atomic piles to produce plutonium for Harwell's military program, an atomic bomb.[43] In July Secretary of Defense James Forrestal had belatedly learned of the Quebec agreement and decided to help restore the British partnership. On January 7, 1948, at Blair House the CPC agreed to a modus vivendi providing for the exchange of information with Britain in nine specified areas not deemed "to pertain to military information." It didn't include atomic bomb design but it did provide favorable terms for the United States in the allocation of Belgian Congo ores vital to the U.S. program.[44]

In early July 1948 AEC technicians visiting England learned that the British were designing reactors to produce plutonium. Later the same month another AEC group traveled to England to discuss reactor materials and was authorized to exchange data on the "basic metallurgy of plutonium." The authorization was rescinded when AEC commissioner Lewis Strauss learned of it and alerted Republican senator Hickenlooper and others. Plutonium metallurgy was, as Hickenlooper warned, that "of an atomic bomb." Having been thwarted by the AEC in his effort to obtain technical information, Attlee directed that the request for weapons information be submitted directly to Forrestal.[45]

On September 1, 1948, Admiral Sir Henry Moore handed Forrestal a note from the British minister of defense proposing to "extend the areas of interchange" to include information on atomic weapons. The British request was referred to a meeting of ranking Defense, State Department, and AEC officers who recommended that their three agencies draft a proposal for consideration by the CPC. Lewis Strauss of the AEC vetoed the recommendation. When Secretary of State Acheson learned of the veto, he seized his opportunity and insisted that Anglo-American cooperation on atomic matters was a foreign-policy decision requiring review by the National Security Council. The Cold War was now underway, the North Atlantic Security Pact would soon be signed, and the U.S. commitment to Europe was no longer in doubt. A Special NSC Committee chaired by Acheson was appointed by the president on February 10, 1949. The final report recommended full cooperation with Britain and Canada on atomic energy matters and atomic weapons under a long-term agreement. It was approved by Truman on March 31, 1949.[46]

Months of long, slow, difficult but encouraging consultations with Congress followed. The 1948 modus vivendi would expire at the end of 1949 to the disadvantage of the United States, ending the favorable allocation of ores the AEC required. The British had moderated their requests and agreed that the "main effort in atomic energy matters would be made in the United States with British scientists cooperating fully in the joint program" and that "fabrication of atomic weapons would be concentrated on this side of the Atlantic for a certain number to be allotted to the United Kingdom." Acheson believed any differences with Britain might be resolved and that Congress too could be brought along. But then an unforeseen event occurred. On February 2, 1950, Moscow's spy at the Manhattan Project, Klaus Fuchs, was arrested in England. He was working at Britain's Atomic Energy Research Establishment at Harwell. The negotiations for resumption of the Anglo-American atomic weapons partnership were at an end. The British were left out in the cold.

The Attlee government's determination to acquire all the necessary technical data for the construction of a plutonium bomb raises a fundamental if unanswerable question. In mid-1948, had GCHQ sufficiently broken enough of the 1944–1945 Venona cables to lead MI5 to believe that the British embassy diplomat who had passed Foreign Office documents was the same diplomat then working with the CPC on atomic affairs, that intelligence undoubtedly would have been brought to the attention of Prime Minister Attlee. It is reasonable to assume that rather than fatally compromise the far more important negotiations with Washington on the exchange of nuclear weapons information vital to Britain's plans for a nuclear deterrent—and those prospects were promising—Maclean would have been quietly moved to another post after the end of his Washington assignment in September while London silently considered its problem and pondered an equally silent resolution.[47] This hypothetical construction exposes the difficulties London might have faced in 1948 and explains why Maclean could have been identified as early as the summer of 1948 without disclosure and without consequence as long as the much more important exchange of nuclear weapons technology with Washington hung in the balance.

The pattern of London's disclosures regarding the HOMER case is perplexing enough to suggest such an interpretation. London dated the HOMER investigation chronology from December 1948 when an unidentified GCHQ analyst told Meredith Gardner that further work on the March 1945 cables revealed that the contents were telegrams from Churchill, the originals of which were found in London in January 1949. Yet there are no clearly identified "Churchill cables" in the 1996 Venona releases. In 1996 the GCHQ release to the Public Record Office falsely dated the creation of the GCHQ Eastcote cell to December 1948, evidently to coincide with the notice given Gardner. But the Eastcote cell had been in operation for more than a year, if not longer, while the unnamed and unacknowledged GCHQ cryptologists had been working at Arlington Hall for several years. The 1955 White Paper maintained those dates and claimed that MI5 launched the HOMER investigation in January 1949. We have only London's word for this chronology, which obviously forecloses any possibility that Maclean was investigated any earlier than January 1949.

Had Maclean been identified by MI5 in 1948 and had Attlee ruled against any immediate action on his case, then MI5's burden in 1948–1951 would have been to establish a chronology that concealed that decision. This is purely a speculative deduction, but explains several baffling anomalies in the case not otherwise comprehensible. As it happened, Maclean left Washington on September 1, 1948. He was assigned to distant Cairo in late 1948 and was still there in early September 1949 when MI5 learned from the FBI that Fuchs had been identified on the basis of a Venona decrypt. MI5 began its surveillance of Fuchs at Harwell.[48] He was subsequently questioned and on February 2, 1950, he was arrested, shattering Britain's prospects of sharing U.S. nuclear weapons information. After Maclean's return to London in May 1950, he would become fair game for MI5.

Robert Lamphere was baffled for more than thirty years by his exclusion from the MI5 search for HOMER. He shouldn't have been. And neither should those British journalists like John Costello and Chapman Pincher who interviewed him, corresponded with him, and sympathized with him, concluding as he did that MI5 was guilty of malfeasance, ineptitude, and disorder. One of the most surprising aspects of the many reconstructed accounts of the Maclean affair is the inability of so many to understand why London would not have wanted the FBI involved in the hunt for an embassy spy who by the time they wrote their books years later was known to be Donald Maclean, who had shared U.S. atomic secrets while in Washington. Lamphere's field of vision was as limited as those others. But of course to even suggest Donald Maclean had been identified as a Soviet agent in 1948 was unthinkable. And yet it was far from unthinkable.

Not until June 1951, after Maclean and Burgess vanished, did Lamphere learn that Maclean had been identified as the KGB agent. His informant was Arthur Martin, the MI5 case officer in the Maclean investigation who helped handle liaison with GCHQ and had accompanied Sir Percy Sillitoe to Washington to explain the Maclean/Burgess debacle to J. Edgar Hoover. Martin also told Lamphere the Foreign Office had insisted the FBI not be informed of Maclean's identification, so Lamphere explained in his book. Martin's claim that the Foreign Office didn't inform the FBI of the progress of the Maclean investigation or of his final identification was denied thirty years later by Sir Patrick Reilly, the Foreign Office undersecretary at the time, one of only three Foreign Office senior officials kept apprised by MI5 of the case. From December 1949 until June 1953 he was also chairman of the Joint Intelligence Committee, composed of the various civilian and military intelligence chiefs and chaired by an official of the Foreign Office.

Reilly insisted that Sir Percy Sillitoe, director general of MI5, had kept FBI director J. Edgar Hoover informed of the developments in the HOMER case. The two had maintained cordial relations since 1933, when they had first met at a Chicago police convention. At the time Sillitoe was an obscure chief constable in Glasgow and Hoover the far more famous gangbusting FBI director.[49] According to Reilly, Sillitoe regularly sent Hoover cabled reports on the investigation. Because of their sensitivity, they were passed through the MI6 special security channel at the British embassy in Washington, meaning the text was coded and decrypted on one-time pads. The MI6 receiving officer and messenger was Kim Philby.[50] The three Foreign Office officials aware of MI5's progress were Sir William Strang, the permanent undersecretary; Patrick Reilly, who handled intelligence matters; and George Carey-Foster, the Foreign Office chief of security responsible for liaison with MI5. Reilly in particular knew of those sensitive MI5 messages and understood the need to keep the prickly FBI director informed.[51] Hoover, who had a passion for conspiracy, as many neurotic people do, was probably told that MI5's very sensitive progress reports weren't being shared with the CIA, his detested rivals. This privileged confidence would have helped neutralize him and his malicious meddling. Quite obviously he didn't realize he was being used by MI5 in London; perhaps "swindled" is a better word. FBI officers at the working level, including Robert Lamphere, didn't see those sensitive cabled reports.

Philby's description of the HOMER investigation reports in *My Silent War* clearly establishes the source of his knowledge of the latest developments in the Maclean case: the encrypted reports from Sir Percy Sillitoe to J. Edgar Hoover through his MI6 special cipher. No other interpretation so accurately fits his description. He remarks that the sluggish trickle of information continued to reach "us," meaning Dwyer, his MI6 predecessor, Patterson of MI5, and Robert Mackenzie, the embassy security officer. By August 1950, "We had received some dozen reports referring to the source of the embassy leak, cited in the documents under the code name Homer." From the nature of those reports, he concluded that the source was a Foreign Office diplomat of some stature and found it inexplicable that "the FBI was sending us reams about the embassy charladies and the inquiry into our menial personnel." He adds further that those MI5 reports eventually "informed us" that official papers were being withheld from Maclean and that "his movements would be put under surveillance." That detail was in the Sillitoe to Hoover report on or about April 17, 1951, and prompted Philby to send Burgess to London. A May 23 or 24 Sillitoe to Hoover message told him Maclean would soon be interrogated.[52]

Philby's references to the embassy menials describe the extent of FBI involvement in the Maclean case. His assertion that the FBI investigated the local or American staff at the British embassy—an FBI domestic operation—would have been a useful diversion. Copies of Foreign Office cables so sensitive they're decrypted on one-time pads aren't found in wastebaskets or trash bins by after-hours mop-up crews. Lamphere fails to mention these investigations in his own account, presumably because of his unwillingness to admit the FBI's wild goose chase.

It was Philby who in 1968 first introduced HOMER into circulation at a time when only a few MI5 and MI6 officials and the three Foreign Office seniors who were kept informed knew that codename. For more than thirty years many Philby commentators have assumed that his knowledge of the HOMER codename came from the Venona transcripts. They have also assumed that at Arlington Hall he read the decisive Venona decrypt in April

1951 that identified Maclean and prompted his decision to alert Maclean through Burgess. Both assumptions are false. In the decades following the publication of *My Silent War,* however, there appeared to be no alternative to that interpretation for those lacking knowledge of the 1950–1951 MI5 reports from London to Hoover through the MI6 cipher (disclosed by Reilly in 1986), the GCHQ Venona operation in London, and the actual texts of Venona's twelve Maclean cables, which remained concealed for half a century. That deduction seemed especially convincing for one Philby biographer who in 1994 in quoting from *My Silent War* went as far as to insert his own word [decrypts] in place of Philby's "documents," in describing the HOMER reports. It seemed to him a foregone conclusion that Venona was his source and he tidied up Philby's account to make it obvious.[53] His falsification is apparent in Philby's own description.

To briefly summarize, GCHQ analysts at Eastcote deduced that "H" ("G") was the abbreviation for HOMER (GOMER) on the basis of the 1944 New York to Moscow Maclean cables. They repeated the designation in each explanatory note accompanying the many phases of their recoveries from those twelve Maclean cables. MI5 adopted that codename in its periodic 1950–1951 reports to the Foreign Office and to FBI director Hoover in Washington. Philby's use of HOMER in 1968 led his many biographers and commentators into mistakenly assuming that the Venona decrypts at Arlington Hall must have been his source. Deception wasn't his intention, however, and he wouldn't be aware of his fictitious freedom of access to the Venona decrypts at Arlington Hall Station until years later in Moscow as he read their accounts of his stunning espionage triumph.

A final word for the skeptics. Even if Philby had had unlimited access to the Arlington Hall and the Venona cables—and he didn't—he would have learned nothing of value in those very few HOMER captioned cables. Most of the twelve Maclean cables had first been penetrated in 1947–1948; the first breakthrough came in December 1948–January 1949, with the identification of the Foreign Office cable in London, or so we're told, nine months before Philby's arrival in Washington. He had been told of the leak during his predeparture briefing in September 1949. At that time GCHQ and MI5 had control of the Maclean cables to the exclusion of the FBI and Arlington Hall. Gardner's Venona team didn't know the various "H" and "G" designations referred to HOMER or that Maclean was HOMER until June 1951. The June 1944 Venona cable that supposedly identified Maclean and warned Philby that he was in imminent danger in the spring of 1951 wasn't broken at Arlington Hall but by GCHQ at Eastcote.

Finally, U.S. military Sigint is restricted to those who hold an intelligence clearance higher and more sensitive than top secret, requiring a more extensive background investigation. Moreover, Sigint texts are further isolated from one another by distinctive codeword groups, TOP SECRET UMBRA, for example. Even with special intelligence clearance, access is confined to operational officers who are substantively involved; knowledge of one codeword designation doesn't bring access to others.[54] U.S. military intelligence policy so tightly restricted distribution of the Venona codeword material that other service intelligence agencies and the CIA were excluded. Special exception was made in the case of the FBI, but only to help identify specific Soviet codenames. Official liaison with the Arlington Hall military command was limited to military officers. GCHQ's official liaison was through its own military officer, Colonel John Tiltman, assigned to U.S. military intelligence. After January 1949 GCHQ and MI5, not Arlington Hall, controlled the Maclean cables. As already noted, Meredith Gardner reported that "the British surround the handling of [blanked out] material with rigid safeguards." Nigel West learned that the Bride material (as Venona was then called) was so tightly held in London that the head of GCHQ's Cryptanalytic Division wasn't aware of the progress being made.[55] Under no circumstances would Colonel Tiltman or other GCHQ personnel have shared "drop copy" decryptions of Venona material with those outside GCHQ ranks, as some CIA officials evidently alleged. MI6 was not active in the HOMER investigation. Philby, MI6 station chief, played no role. Similarly, he had no liaison responsibility with the AFSA or Arlington Hall Station. He undoubtedly paid a courtesy call to the facility, probably escorted by a GCHQ liaison officer, but assumptions about his regular access or his liaison duties are myths, as is his firsthand knowledge of the Venona traffic.[56]

In this instance as in others, Philby's many biographers and publicists by their conjectures and fanciful speculation have done his espionage work for him, crediting him with successes he never achieved and in fact never claimed. He collaborated in his fictitious triumphs by wisely remaining silent, as he did in Moscow decades later during his lengthy interviews, mutely passing over details that might have modified, corrupted, or demolished the legend. In 1988 Phillip Knightley, a resourceful London journalist whose early investigation had first unraveled many of the Philby mysteries, interviewed him in Moscow for more than twenty-five hours. In his 1989 book he claimed that "FBI cryptographers" had turned up Philby's Soviet codename STANLEY in 1948, and subsequently that as Philby "sat in his tiny FBI office and read the Venona material he saw the FBI steadily closing in on Maclean as the Soviet agent code-named Homer."[57] None of this is true. In 1994 Genrikh Borovik, a responsible Russian journalist who interviewed Philby over several years and was reliable in most respects, would tell us that those Venona telegrams were stored at the FBI and that some, to Philby's "horror," gave the dates of HOMER's meetings with his Soviet control in New York: "Homer will be in New York on such-and-such a date," the telegrams would read. "I will give him the instructions accordingly."[58] This was equally false. It was all fantasy, all a sham, and Philby, who might have admitted he never saw those critical Venona decrypts, knew it as well. But he kept his silence and so did British intelligence.

To rephrase our original question: if not Venona, then who told Philby that Maclean had been identified as a Soviet agent and prompted him to send Burgess to London to warn him? His source was Sir Percy Sillitoe, who undoubtedly was acting on behalf of Dick White, head of MI5's Division B. More than thirty years later, during a Moscow interview, Philby still recalled one of Sillitoe's memorable reports to Hoover. By then, after decades of thoughtful reflection and many a sleepless night, he may have deduced their purpose. But in 1950–1951, like the Foreign Office and J. Edgar Hoover, he too had been taken in and was oblivious to Dick White's true intent.

Chapter FOUR

British deception during World War II.—The
London Controlling Section.—Deceit and disin-
formation.—Dick Goldsmith White.—Deception in
peacetime.—Trevor-Roper's details.—The search
for Soviet codenames.—The Maclean cables.—
Churchill, Roosevelt, and the Polish crisis.—
Puzzling cryptologic failures.—Hiding
Venona's Maclean texts.—Kept in the dark.—
Whitehall misled.

In the aftermath of World War II and during the decades that followed, one of the undisclosed secrets of that war was the success of tactical and strategic deception. Military deception was as old as warfare itself, but it is doubtful whether any military command ever employed deception as a fundamental tool of strategic planning as completely and rigorously as did the British during World War II. They also showed a remarkable talent for cunning, imagination, and daring. During the first years of the war when Britain was faced with a superior enemy across the English Channel, deception was primarily a defensive tactic using disinformation to conceal Britain's weakness by falsely reporting its strength. In 1948 General Eisenhower aptly summed up London's predicament: "When Britain stood alone in 1940 and 1941, the British had little with which to oppose the Germans except deception. They resorted to every type of subterfuge." He concluded that "Out of this was born a habit that was later difficult to discard."[1]

In 1939 and 1940 British intelligence began what later became known as the double-cross system, named for the Roman XX or double cross; German agents in Britain and on the Continent were used to transmit bogus information to German intelligence. Aware of the identity of Abwehr agents in England for some years before the September 3, 1939, outbreak of war, MI5 and MI6 used that knowledge to their advantage. In some cases the agents were turned to become double agents under MI5 or MI6 control; in other instances they weren't aware they were being deceived. In January 1941 the British created the W Board, made up of the directors of the British services intelligence, to oversee deception operations and approve the intelligence to be passed (deception required that true coinage be mixed with the counterfeit to be credible). The W Board wasn't officially sanctioned, reported to no higher authority, and worked in absolute secrecy. A Twenty Committee was created to gather the intelligence to be passed to MI5's double agents in the United Kingdom and MI6's abroad in the double-cross system.[2]

In 1940 General Archibald Wavell, the British commander in the Middle East, established a Special Branch staff at his Cairo headquarters responsible for deception plans that were successfully deployed against the Italians in the Western Desert and East Africa in 1940–1941. In October 1941 the Chiefs of Staff Committee heard General Wavell's deception chief Lieutenant Colonel Dudley Clarke describe his Cairo operations and quickly decided to duplicate his organization in London. A controlling officer position, calling for a man of "considerable ingenuity and imagination, with an aptitude for improvisation, plenty of initiative and a good military background," was created to prepare deception plans. In May 1942 the chiefs of staff approved Lieutenant Colonel J. H. Bevan as controlling officer. His "Controlling Section," so named by the Joint Planning Staff, was responsible for strategic deception on a global scale but also was to include "any matter calculated to mystify or mislead the enemy wherever military advantage is to be gained."[3]

Within a short time Bevan's small staff of fewer than a dozen officers became the London Controlling Section (LCS), whose function was purely to "plan, coordinate, and supervise." Bevan had no executive authority, chaired no committees, but succeeded by establishing the closest working relationship with the military service staffs and their senior military commanders. In July 1942 the U.S. Joint Chiefs of Staff agreed to cooperate with the LCS and in August 1942 established its own unit at the Pentagon, the Joint Security Control. With the United States now in the war, the LCS moved more aggressively to the offensive and prepared a series of fictitious war plans to deceive the German high command by various "special means." The term described any channel of communication used to deceive and misinform, whether through an agent under MI5 control, false wireless signals employed by the Air Ministry in deceiving the Luftwaffe about Royal Air Force fighter dispersion and strength or bomber targeting over Germany, or a corpse found on a Spanish beach with a briefcase containing false documents chained to his wrist (Operation Mincemeat). The latter persuaded the German high command that the invasion of Greece was being planned. As a result the German defenders in Greece and the Balkans were reinforced by seventeen divisions. When Allied armies landed in Sicily, the intended target, only two German divisions were on the island to assist the Italians.[4] These operations adopted subterfuge, deceit, and disinformation in supplying false intelligence so credible—and "credible" is the key word—that the Germans were persuaded to draw disastrously wrong conclusions about military strategy, capability, and intent. Deception operations were carried out in the invasion of North Africa (codename Torch), Sicily (Husky), and the D-Day landings on the beaches of Normandy in June 1944 (Overlord), where the most elaborate deception plans had been prepared. Operation Fortitude, part of Overlord, misled the German high command with a fictitious plan for an Allied invasion in the Pas de Calais region.

From 1939 until 1945 Sir Dick Goldsmith White, who led the HOMER investigation as chief of MI5 counterintelligence, played an important role in the intelligence and military deceptions of World War II. Recruited by MI5 in 1935, he was a far more experienced intelligence officer than the former chief constable of the Kent County Police, Sir Percy Sillitoe, an outsider who was named director general of MI5 by Prime Minister Clement Attlee in 1945. Sillitoe was an unfortunate choice. He knew nothing of intelligence practices and, judging from his autobiography, had the dullest of minds—no imagination, no cunning, and no discernible sense of his own shortcomings.[5] By contrast, no one in the British intelligence services better understood the methods and technique of counterespionage and deception than Dick White or was more willing to dare its risks when the opportunity was offered. In Washington, only American military and air force officers who had been personally involved knew that those deception operations even existed. Their details would remain under lock and key for decades.

In contrast to many of his associates, White was no stranger to America. After his years at Christ Church, Oxford, where he had been an outstanding half-miler and miler—good enough to have been a member of the 1936 British Olympic team had he so chosen—in 1928 he won a Commonwealth

Fellowship to study American history and left England for the University of Michigan. Between terms he traveled in the east and south as time permitted. Dissatisfied at Ann Arbor, he moved on to the University of California at Berkeley, attended classes infrequently, read Proust, began work on a novel, and thought of becoming a writer. After two years in America he considered remaining as a teacher, but returned to England, cast about unsuccessfully for a job as a journalist, and in 1932 was taken on as an assistant schoolmaster, teaching history, French, and German. In 1935 his former Oxford tutor, John Masterman, recruited him for MI5.[6]

He worked on German affairs at MI5 and made a number of trips to prewar Germany. Returning to London by way of Paris in 1939, he was among those MI5 officers to whom a French Deuxième Bureau officer first suggested a deception scheme using turned or compromised German agents to send messages to their German command, a suggestion not new by any means. That same year White handled the first turned German agent, a Welsh-born Englishman codenamed SNOW, in the first MI5 double-cross operation.[7]

In 1943 White was appointed deputy counterintelligence adviser to General Walter Bedell Smith, General Eisenhower's chief of staff, working under General Sir Kenneth Strong, Eisenhower's intelligence chief. In January 1944 General Eisenhower became commander of Supreme Headquarters, Allied Expeditionary Force (SHAEF) and SHAEF executed strategic deception under General Smith. (In October 1950 Smith would become CIA director.) White was involved in deception operations planned before the Normandy landings. At the SHAEF War Room he had drafted the counterintelligence instructions that accompanied the Allied landing to thwart enemy intelligence operations and subversion.[8] Later he moved on with SHAEF to Paris. In June 1945 he was awarded the Legion of Merit at Eisenhower's recommendation and later the Croix de Guerre.[9]

In 1949 those LCS deception operations were still one of the undisclosed secrets of World War II. Their existence came to light only in the 1970s and then incompletely.[10] Even after sixty years some of those operations still haven't been disclosed. In total war, lesser military operations are sacrificed so that more important ones will succeed. In informing the enemy of genuine but more modest military offensives, lives are put at risk and sometimes lost for the success of a larger and more important offensive. Whatever the necessity of such sacrifices in war, in peacetime they would be difficult to explain. For an unknowing public, courage and valor win wars, not fraud and deceit, not at the sacrifice of their compatriots. Military deception offensives couldn't have been admitted by name without public recognition of those losses.

After the German surrender in May 1945, White was responsible for sending Hugh Trevor-Roper to Berlin to look into Hitler's final days. The successful result was Trevor-Roper's *Last Days of Hitler,* which White succeeded in getting approved for publication after MI6 had attempted to deny its release.[11] It was the most reliable account of that last week in the Berlin bunker. New evidence from KGB archives published in 1995 on the final disposition of Hitler's remains complemented Trevor-Roper's work but didn't replace it. After eighteen years at MI5, White in 1953 replaced Sillitoe as head. In 1956, he was named "C," head of MI6.

Dick White had been personally discredited by Philby in *My Silent War,* a work he knew to be false in a number of ways. After some hesitation, in 1968 he encouraged Hugh Trevor-Roper, now Regius Professor of History at Oxford, to write his own account of Philby, who had worked with Trevor-Roper at MI6 from 1941 until 1944.[12] Trevor-Roper had originally published two articles on Philby in *Encounter,* the British magazine partly funded by the CIA (not revealed until years later). In combining his two previous articles in book form, Trevor-Roper corrected his previous errors and added new details, but not those he truly wished to include.

His short 1968 book was a devastating critique of the pretenses of Philby's memoir and its purpose as an instrument of Soviet propaganda. He offered a number of intriguing comments on Philby's behavior as he'd observed him during those war years. As stinging as his dismissal of the Philby memoir was his contempt for the Secret Intelligence Service (MI6) and its cadre of "part-time stock-brokers and retired Indian policemen, the agreeable epicureans from the bars of White's and Boodle's, the jolly, conventional ex-naval officers and the robust adventurers from the bucket shops." He attributed Philby's success to SIS weaknesses and harshly criticized the SIS's disdain for its "old 'enemy,' M.I. 5." Dick White's appointment as head of MI6 had been a bitter defeat for the old guard (the "mandarinate," Trevor-Roper's often repeated derisive noun).

In his foreword, Trevor-Roper wrote cryptically that there were some secret details in the Philby story that "I would now like to add, for they do credit to my friends; but alas, my friends forbid it: so those last crowning touches must wait, perhaps for another eighteen years" (after the expiration of the thirty-year embargo imposed by the Official Secrets Act). He added his hope "that one of those friends will accept the dedication of this small volume, as a reminder of our special relationship." He was undoubtedly referring to Dick White, whom he mentioned further on in commending his appointment as the new "C," head of MI6 against the "solid opposition of the old [SIS] mandarinate." The new "C," he wrote, was the best choice for the position and, unlike his predecessor, was personally convinced of "Philby's guilt." White evidently shared with him the secret details he was forbidden to disclose. Trevor-Roper touches on them briefly and obscurely in alluding to the 1945 Volkov affair (discussed below, in chapter 7). He wrote that Philby's mishandling of the case "long rankled with those who had hoped, through it, to make a notable contribution to counter-espionage; and after 1951 their voice was heard. The memory of the mysterious Volkov affair then concentrated a suspicion which, otherwise, was diffuse: it formed the central and most persuasive change in the dossier which was now compiled, in M.I. 5, for the interrogation of Philby."[13]

We're on very murky ground here and so was Trevor-Roper, who was delicately circling the thicket of privileged if not extremely sensitive intelligence. His comment was so discreetly and abstractly phrased as to defy interpretation except by MI5 and MI6 officers familiar with the issue that divided SIS and MI5, evidently on the Philby case. He implies that MI5 (most evidently, Dick White) recognized the Volkov affair as an opportunity that could be exploited but was denied by MI6 seniors who could find no reason to suspect Philby. After 1951 those MI5 suspicions were finally given a voice.

Trevor-Roper's analysis might have dashed cold water on Philby's emerging fame had it been read by a wider audience. But it was written by an intellectual, a historian-scholar with a classicist's memory for Latin odes and Greek myth as well as a literary stylist who disdained the commonplace, whether newspaper journalism or the popular imagination (he also skewered John le Carré and Graham Greene with a few nimble thrusts of his épée but not at such length as his broadsword once disemboweled Arnold Toynbee). His audience was probably not much larger than the combined circulation of *Encounter*, the *Spectator*, the *New Statesman*, and the *Times Literary Supplement*, where his historical essays appeared. His book was never published in the United States. Regrettably, it did very little to diminish Philby's growing notoriety and renown.

The lessons White learned during his war years working with the Double Cross Committee, the W Board, the London Controlling Section, and in the various SHAEF deception operations never left him. Absolute secrecy was indispensable. Without it, any deception operation was at risk and would be compromised in one way or another. The fewer who knew, the better the chances of success. Utter and inviolable secrecy also brought complete freedom of action: no bureaucratic dithering, no fussy Whitehall meddling, no interminable executive committee squabbles, no interdepartment wars, no oversight, and no disclosure. One series of incidents in particular describes his insistence on absolute secrecy even decades after its purpose had been served.

In the 1950s, J. C. Masterman, the old Oxford don who had recruited White for MI5 and worked with the double-cross system, asked permission to publish his account originally written in 1945 as a documentary record. White, by then head of MI6, was vigorously opposed and publication was denied. Masterman continued to doggedly press his case and in 1972, despite White's protests, he was finally granted permission. This was more than twenty-seven years after those operations had concluded. White was outraged.[14] Masterman failed to mention White's name in his groundbreaking account, *The Double Cross System*, probably at White's insistence. Although World War II had ended, the Cold War was then underway and deception still had its purpose; the group that designed and carried out British peacetime deception was as closely guarded as the wartime operations.

In 1945 Britain's wartime deception habit, which Eisenhower had described as "difficult to discard," wasn't shed at all but survived. Britain's deception operations continued under the London Controlling Section, which was "reconstituted in January 1947 with its primary target the Soviet Union and its satellites." Evidently it operated as a subcommittee under Major General Sir Leslie Hollis, secretary of the Chiefs of Staff Committee.[15] During the war Hollis was deputy to Lord General Hastings Ismay, Prime Minister Churchill's chief of staff and military secretary. Churchill took an active interest in deception operations, and Hollis as Ismay's deputy had worked closely with both Churchill and the LCS. But with Britain at peace once again, strategic deception was of a different order and the strategies of 1940–1944 a bit anachronistic. Armies were being demobilized, not readied for new offensives across entire continents. Any plans underway were contingencies for the future. In 1947 the British Joint Planning Staff strategy paper recognized that "the only effective deterrent to a potential aggressor is tangible evidence of our intention and ability to withstand attack and to retaliate immediately."[16] Tangible evidence had been on the mind of Dennis Wheatley two years earlier. An RAF wing commander assigned to the London Controlling Section, Wheatley, as Professor Michael Howard tells us, had been feeding "stimulating and unorthodox ideas into the Joint Planning Staff since 1940."[17] He believed that in peacetime the value of traditional military deception was no longer appropriate and that the key to "persuading our potential enemies that Britain was to be feared" lay with "scientific deception." In saying his farewells at LCS in 1945, Wheatley had hoped to see the chief of air staff, Sir Charles Portal, but was unable to do so. He had intended to submit to Portal his ideas about "deception for the future," but instead sent his ideas to the assistant chief. In his letter he proposed the creation of a fictitious air base from which would be deployed "a new scientific weapon of great power—perhaps one which would enable us to bombard Moscow with atom bombs."[18] A similar notion or at least a variation was considered by General Hollis's LCS two years later.

In 1947 the LCS considered a deception operation under the name Atomic Scientific Research and Production intended to mislead Moscow on Great Britain's nuclear weapons capability. What it lacked was a credible candidate—an identified Soviet agent—for delivering its message to Moscow. The defection of Igor Gouzenko in Ottawa in September 1945 revealed that the Soviets had penetrated the top-secret joint Canadian-British nuclear research center in Canada; Allan Nunn May had passed atomic secrets and traces of uranium-235 to the Soviet embassy in Ottawa. Fearing failure and that Soviet agents had sufficiently penetrated British nuclear and weapons development to enable Moscow to identify the deception, the LCS shelved the plan until more was known about Soviet penetration.[19]

One source in the search for opportunities for intelligence deception was GCHQ, with its broken Soviet cables. The conjunction was a natural alliance. Successful GCHQ penetrations of the London-Moscow circuit would have been grist for the London Controlling Section's mill. A Russian codename on a Moscow to London cable broken by GCHQ cryptanalysts and identified by MI5 or MI6 would offer the possibility of exploiting that secret to advantage. If the Russian agent's codename had been broken out of a GCHQ recovery, more recoveries might have revealed fragments of the secrets passed, enabling MI5 to establish who would have had access to those secrets. If MI5 successfully identified the agent, then the deception experts would set to work to determine how he or she might be used. As chief of MI5 counterintelligence, Dick White would have collaborated with General Hollis's London Controlling Section. An MI6 officer in contact with GCHQ and the LCS was Jack Easton, responsible for liaison with the CIA, which often took him to Washington. A former Royal Air Force commodore, he was the RAF assistant director for intelligence during World War II. In 1948 he chaired MI6's Defectors Committee.[20]

Dick White was responsible for the 1949–1951 HOMER investigation as well as MI5's surveillance of Maclean during those final weeks in May 1951. It hardly seemed a fair match. One former MI5 officer, not without his own peculiar prejudices nor wholly reliable, called White a "brilliant, intuitive intelligence officer" (White had hired him for MI5) and "almost certainly the greatest [counterintelligence officer] of the 20th Century."[21] However accurate that description, White's talents were among the best England had to offer. His adversaries were the feckless Soviet resident in London, Nikolai Rodin, comfortably chauffeured about in his embassy sedan, and the one-time translator and code clerk Yuri Modin, a newcomer to his trade. Pressed into service in London in 1948, he had to learn on the trot. His mentor in dodging surveillance in the street was the eminent London art critic and Poussin expert Anthony Blunt, who had been taught by MI5. No Soviet illegals were involved, only the two Russians, the three Englishmen, and an army of MI5 and Special Branch ferrets. No wonder so many tongues wagged so cruelly when the two hares eluded the hounds and bounded clear of meadow, forest, and sea all the way to Moscow.

During the 1949–1951 MI5 investigation, Foreign Office officials had found it unthinkable that a Communist could be found among its senior diplomats, least of all a Communist spy. The unknown agent HOMER was an anomaly, an aberrant exception who clearly wasn't to be found on or near the Foreign Office bridge but came from the nether ranks among those who fed on bitterness and hard tack down in the bilge. In early 1951, when MI5 told the three Foreign Office officials kept informed of its investigation that HOMER was a diplomat of some importance, they were skeptical. In April 1951, when they learned Maclean had been identified, they were speechless.[22]

As the MI5 surveillance of Maclean wearily dragged on from mid-April until late May 1951, they grew increasingly annoyed and impatient at the delay. They wanted him fetched in, interrogated, and the whole matter brought to a dignified end. His treason would be kept from disclosure, the Foreign Office's reputation would remain intact, his resignation would be arranged, and the whole dreadful affair would be mercifully ended. But Foreign Office policy is not necessarily MI5 policy. In 1949 the interests of Dick White and MI5 and those of the Foreign Office weren't identical.

In July 1951, during the parliamentary challenges raised by Maclean's disappearance, in answering Tory charges of negligence in rooting out known Communists or Communist sympathizers, Foreign Secretary Morrison pointed out that in 1950 forty-three civil servants had been suspended as security risks. Fifteen were dismissed or resigned and the remaining were reinstated or transferred to less sensitive positions. He was citing the most recent rewards of Prime Minister Attlee's revised security policy of denying employment to Communist Party members or those with Communist associations. Attlee's 1948 reversal of his earlier 1945 policy untied MI5's hands and allowed the use of counterintelligence methods previously denied: the infiltration of subversive organizations, wire and telephone taps, and mail cover that were even extended to extreme left-wing Laborites sitting in Parliament. The change was the result of the Attlee government's growing recognition of Stalin's Soviet Union as its unrelenting adversary, whether openly and defiantly, as in the Berlin crisis of 1948, or secretly and clandestinely. The Cold War was now underway.[23] Communist Party membership or Communist affiliations might seem merely a benign presence among British civil servants but the risk lay with their possible links to Soviet espionage.

In England the American furor about Communist infiltration was seen as a heinous witch hunt, typical of a barely civilized nation that could be whipped to frenzy by a demagogue like Senator McCarthy. Where was civility, where was decency, where were civil liberties, where was that quiet cup of tea a chap could enjoy in the Communist Party reading room as he browsed through the *Daily Worker?* But the truth to some of those American espionage trials so widely publicized and deplored would lie concealed for decades in the Venona recoveries. Like the FBI and its inadmissible courtroom secrets, MI5 knew far more about Soviet subversion in England than was apparent elsewhere. The American virus hadn't yet reached London, or so many believed. Except for the arrests of the two British physicists, Allan Nunn May and Klaus Fuchs, both high-minded amateurs, both of whom had confessed, no comparable KGB espionage operations had yet been publicly identified in Great Britain, which had escaped attack, or so it might have been believed.

Since 1945 the interception and analysis of Soviet intelligence traffic had been GCHQ's highest priority. During September 1945, innumerable Moscow to London cables had been intercepted and subsequently penetrated by British cryptanalysts. That month alone GCHQ recoveries revealed that at the very least twenty Soviet agents were known to be operating in

Great Britain.[24] If twenty Soviet cover names could be identified in thirty days, there were obviously many more. In 1947–1948 Arlington Hall crypt-analysts had successfully exploited a 1943–1946 KGB codebook in exposing Soviet networks in the United States and Australia. By 1948 London's GCHQ analysts would have achieved comparable results with the identical KGB codebook and the same cryptanalytic tools in attacking those many 1945 Moscow to London cables. By 1947 and 1948 Dick White and MI5 were deeply troubled by the extent of Soviet espionage in England and the many unidentified English agents suggested by the September 1945 and other in-tercepts. The challenge was to match the many codenames with those on MI5's watch list or other suspected Britons. In 1949–1951 White's MI5 re-sponsibilities probed considerably beyond the hunt for one unidentified spy resident in the Foreign Office ranks.

GCHQ was a rigorously compartmentalized organization, even more so than Arlington Hall Station. One of the many divisions in the Directorate of Operations concentrated on intercepting Soviet signals; cryptanalysis was the responsibility of another division. The various cryptanalytic teams within the division were also secluded from one another. In the case of the Maclean cables, the head of the cryptanalysis division didn't know of the progress being made by the Eastcote Venona team. They were so tightly held that their content wasn't known to other GCHQ codebreaking units. MI5's liaison with GCHQ was under Dick White, who would also have worked with the GCHQ Counter-Clandestine Committee that included senior members from MI6 and MI5 who were informed of any new or revealing cryptanalytic successes.[25] Evidently MI5's Arthur Martin, the HOMER case of-ficer, also shared the GCHQ decrypts. Dick White would have prohibited any disclosures of those GCHQ recoveries from Venona's Maclean cables. Under normal circumstances there would have been no reason to inform Arlington Hall cryptanalysts about the progress of penetrations that in-volved British security interests. MI5's liaison, when necessary, would have been with the FBI. In the Maclean investigation, however, not only were FBI agents excluded from the case but so were both MI5 and MI6 officers attached to the British embassy in Washington. Their knowledge, like Philby's, came from the Sillitoe to Hoover cable reports.

Maclean served in Washington for more than four years, from May 1944 until early September 1948. In view of his length of service and the often publicized importance of his responsibilities at the embassy—and they were very important for Moscow, particularly work on the Combined Policy

Committee and his access to documents relating to the Manhattan Project—analysts would assume that there were innumerable Soviet cables in the Venona archive revealing the intelligence he passed to his Soviet control.[26] As those many Venona cables were decrypted, analyzed, and refined at Arlington Hall from 1949 until 1951, incriminating details that would identify HOMER would emerge slowly and inexorably from the accumulating fragments. This was the tightening noose or "closing net" analogy described by Philby and others. This was also implicit in the view of senior Foreign Office officials who recalled that the hundreds of original candidates were gradually reduced to several dozen, then five or six, and finally Donald Maclean. This was the view, too, encouraged by MI5, which had complete control of the Venona telegrams to the exclusion of the Foreign Office. Although the tightening noose paradigm was misleading, a slowly developing identification process served MI5's purpose.

As we now know, there were only twelve Maclean telegrams in the Venona archive and all were from 1944 and 1945. Almost all were first recovered, albeit in meaningless fragments, in 1947–1948, long before Philby arrived in Washington. The six Washington to Moscow cables were transmitted during a three-day period, March 29–31, 1945. They all cite "Materials of 'G' or 'H.' " One led to a British analyst's realization that Foreign Office secrets were being passed to Moscow, or so Meredith Gardner was told. Five of the six were from the Foreign Office to the British embassy in Washington and one was from Lord Halifax, the British ambassador in Washington, to the Foreign Office. The six cables aren't numbered in their original sequence and their few technical details are maddeningly obscure, all of which hobble easy analysis. The original Halifax cable (1815), dated March 7, 1945, was the first in the series. Three of the five remaining original Foreign Office cables were dated the following day, March 8 (1788, 1791, and 1808–1809), and two March 16 (1793 and 1826).

Fifty years later it is impossible to recognize from the Venona texts released in February 1996 the sensitivity, significance, and urgency of the six March 1945 cables. They dealt with Stalin's betrayal of the agreements signed at Yalta in February 1945 and Churchill's urgent appeals to Roosevelt to join him in taking a much harder line with Stalin. At the Crimea conference Stalin had agreed to the Declaration on Poland calling for a reorganization of the Polish provisional government on a broadly representative basis to include democratic leaders from within Poland and from abroad.[27] After the conference Churchill had assured the House of Commons that in the spirit of Yalta the transition to a new Polish government of national unity would bring Poland under majority rule.[28] Stalin was making a mockery of that assurance by his recognition of the Warsaw group, the Lublin Poles, the instrument of Soviet power. By late February 1945 the Red Army had liberated virtually all of Poland and had advanced to the Oder River in the West. Moscow considered Poland a battle zone and had denied entry to British and American observers. Washington had little idea what was going on under the Russian occupation; London was better informed through the Polish government in exile in London. Since January 1945 the Soviet army and the NKGB had begun the systematic arrest, deportation to the USSR, and execution of those Polish leaders or factions that challenged Communist rule. Churchill feared that the political purges underway would make it impossible to establish a freely elected government in Warsaw as promised in the Crimea agreement. Stalin had also ignored the Declaration on Liberated Europe, which obliged Moscow to refrain from any unilateral action to impose its will on the former Axis satellite nations of Eastern Europe. By March 1945 he had installed a minority Communist regime in Romania by military force.

All six of the March 29–31 Maclean cables dealt with the Polish crisis. Although the fragmentary nature of the Venona texts makes it difficult to clearly identify their context, it is evident when studied with Churchill's many telegrams of the same period published in the 1980s. To implement the Declaration on Poland, the Yalta conference created a commission made up of Soviet foreign minister Viacheslav Molotov, the British ambassador in Moscow, Sir Archibald Clark-Kerr, and American ambassador Averill Harriman. The three began talks in Moscow on February 23. On February 28 Churchill sent Clark-Kerr a cable asking him to obtain Molotov's immediate agreement to permit "two or three trustworthy" observers to enter Poland to report on the situation. A day earlier, on February 27, Molotov had agreed that the Allies might send in observers, but several days later told Clark-Kerr that the request must be addressed for the approval of the Warsaw group, the provisional Polish government, thus ignoring the Yalta agreement.[29]

On March 6 Harriman reported to Washington that every argument he and Clark-Kerr advanced to Molotov was brushed aside. "I told him [Molotov] that I knew that the President would be shocked to learn of Molotov's obstruction to the work of the commission in objecting to our calling representative Polish leaders to Moscow."[30] Molotov's tactics had also provoked London. That same week Foreign Secretary Anthony Eden forwarded to Lord Halifax in Washington a proposed U.K.-U.S. draft note to be sent to

Molotov for review by the State Department (London 2078). Eden's cable isn't in the Venona traffic. Lord Halifax's March 7 cable to London (Venona, Washington to Moscow 1815, March 30) is in response to Eden's instruction and is the first in the Venona series of six March 29–31 cables. The Russian translation of the Halifax original begins blankly and abruptly.

From: Washington
To: Moscow
No: 1815   30 March 1945
    [seventy-five groups unrecoverable]
questions, although there are some major differences of tactics. This morning a member of my department discussed this question at some length in the State Department. Set forth below
    [forty-six groups unrecoverable]
on this question and considers it essential to get a clear definition on the basis on which the Commission is to work.

The above are fragments of paragraph 2 of the Halifax cable, which goes on to discuss the basis of the commission's work and cites the relevant paragraph of the Crimea communiqué. On the question of the commission's invitation to the Poles, paragraph 3 declares that the commission "must itself agree on lists of Poles who are to be invited for consultation. One cannot allow any outside organization to influence the composition of this list."

Paragraphs 4 and 5 are even less helpful:

It is necessary to achieve a moratorium on political persecution in Poland. All Poles should now act in such a way as to create an atmosphere of freedom and independence, since only under such circumstance can [two groups unrecovered] a representative government or conduct free elections. In this connection the State Department feels that the text of the draft note to MOLOTOV, set out in your telegram no. 2078, is too sharp and shows too great a distrust of Soviet intentions in Poland; they entirely agree with those objectives which you set, but feel that we will gain nothing if we are too harsh at this stage; they are considering now the possibility of issuing instructions to HARRIMAN—to make a demarche on similar lines, but somewhat softened down in tone; at the present time, in their opinion, it is inadvisable to face MOLOTOV with a combined note on this subject.

5. Observers

The State Department learned with gratification that you for the moment do not intend to go ahead with your idea of sending Sir A. Clark KERR to press for full facilities for sending to Poland a somewhat lower level technical commission. The aim of this commission will be to gather first hand information about conditions pertaining there in so far as they affect the question of appointing a government and the later elections.

The State Department's response to London's appeal was utterly useless for the Foreign Office. What was required wasn't a reiteration of the obvious but the political muscle needed to remove Molotov's obstruction of Clark-Kerr and Harriman's work in Moscow. Only Roosevelt's direct intervention could supply that. In fairness to State, however, the Foreign Office's appeals wouldn't have been helped by Ambassador Harriman's earlier March 4 cable to Washington (not in the Venona archive) advising that Clark-Kerr was "handicapped by being directed at every turn by the Foreign Office" and that "Downing Street is viewing the work of the Commission more from the standpoint of the debate in the House of Commons than from the urgent need of making progress in implementing the Crimea Agreement."[31] He meant that for Churchill Poland was also a critical domestic political issue with British Conservatives who were deeply suspicions of Soviet intentions in Europe.

Apart from the cable's general worthlessness, several curious features set it apart from other Venona telegrams. In every other instance, those March Maclean cables are prefaced by the transmitting officer's identification of the material and source: "Materials of 'G.' I am transmitting a telegram of the NOOK [Foreign Office] to the POOL [British embassy]." Because that routine preface was omitted, the GCHQ analyst was obliged to hedge: "This is probably material from 'H'/HOMER, i.e., a telegram stolen by Maclean." A further note explained that "The 75-group gap presumably contains the introductory remarks by the WASHINGTON MGB officer and the beginning of the text of the stolen telegram." The less familiar word groups in his comment might have been unrecoverable, but it is far less plausible that the GCHQ cryptologists would have claimed that the same repeatedly used and repeatedly recognized word groups that preface the other Venona "G" and "H" cables would be "unrecoverable." Just as incomprehensible is the GCHQ failure to recover the opening sentences of paragraph 2, which should have been broken, as were parts of the remainder of the cable, had GCHQ used Halifax's original telegram as a crib.

The GCHQ assumption about "introductory remarks" by the MGB officer raises further suspicions. In forwarding Maclean's filched copies of British telegrams to Moscow, the transmitting officer usually reproduced the full text without personal comment. In only two of the twelve Maclean cables did the transmitting officer inject explanatory remarks. In a New York to Moscow cable of August 2–3, 1944, he mentioned "G" 's marital status. As we know, that remark wasn't included in the February 1996 Venona release of the same cable. In the same cable he also described two of "G" 's embassy responsibilities but these couldn't be entirely suppressed because the Arlington Hall recovery was quoted word for word by Meredith Gardner in October 1951.

The only other cable to include an explanatory remark was the GOMMER cable of June 28, 1944, mentioning his upcoming visit to his pregnant wife living in New York. London had no hesitation in publishing that comment in February 1996 since it claimed it had finally and belatedly identified Maclean as HOMER. What is apparent is that those Venona cables released in February 1996 exclude any of the transmitting officer's explanatory remarks that might have identified Maclean any earlier than the April 1951 recovery of the GOMMER cable. The original Halifax cable was dated March 7 and was the first in the six-cable March series. It is reasonable to assume that the transmitting officer commented on his embassy source, "G," as he did in the August 2–3, 1944, cable, as well as London's addressee, Foreign Secretary Anthony Eden.

The next three March 29–31 Venona cables forwarded to Moscow British Foreign Office telegrams sent to Washington on March 8. The first was a repetition to Lord Halifax of Clark-Kerr's cable to the Foreign Office (1788, dated March 29). The first sixty-six word groups were "unrecoverable" but part of the cable contained Clark-Kerr's draft note to the Soviet Foreign Ministry to be presented either jointly with the United States or separately. Once again, the issue was Moscow's approval for inviting Poles who were not part of the Warsaw group to the Moscow meetings. Two hundred and seventeen other word groups were "unrecoverable" in the Venona text. The second March 8 cable sent Halifax a copy of Clark-Kerr's cable (1791, March 29) listing Harriman's recommendations to the State Department in pressing Molotov to invite nonmembers of the Warsaw group to join in the Moscow consultations on a future Polish government.

By March 8 Churchill's patience was exhausted. He sent a personal and top-secret cable to Roosevelt (905) of some seventeen hundred words reviewing the situation in Romania, Greece, the Black Sea Balkan countries, and most especially Poland:

> I have based myself in Parliament on the assumption that the words of the Yalta Declaration will be carried out in the letter and the spirit. Once it is seen that we have been deceived and that the well known communist technique is being applied behind closed doors in Poland, either directly by the Russians or through their Lublin puppets, a very grave situation in British public opinion will be reached. . . . I feel that this is the test case between us and the Russians of the meaning which is to be attached to such terms as Democracy, Sovereignty, Independence, Representative Government and free and unfettered elections.[32]

Churchill feared that the systematic murder, imprisonment, and exile of the enemies of the Warsaw group meant that Moscow was moving inexorably toward a puppet regime under Soviet control that would eliminate any possibility of free and open elections. He believed the time had come to end Molotov's repeated denials of the Yalta agreement and send Stalin a personal message urging an early settlement to the Polish question on the basis of the Yalta decisions ("based on the ideas in Eden's telegram to Halifax number 2078"). He hoped Roosevelt would join him and send Stalin a similar message. He promised to delay his cable until he heard from Roosevelt, included his telegram to Stalin, and asked that British and American observers be permitted to visit Poland and report on conditions there. "I should be grateful to know your views," he asked Roosevelt in closing. "Pray let this telegram be between you and me."

This brings us to the third March 8 Venona cable to the British embassy, the only March cable that might qualify even remotely as a Churchill cable, as Gardner was told. It was from the Foreign Office (London's 2213) and was copied in Venona's Washington to Moscow 1808–1809, March 30. The cable is in the first person—both "we" and "I" are found in the text. It was repeated to Moscow, CASERTA, and SAVING in Paris and opens with the drafter's preface "Supplementary to my telegram no. 1018 to Moscow." Paragraph 1 begins by noting: "The rapid deterioration of the situation in ROUMANIA" and breaks off with 150 groups unrecoverable. It mentions the Polish commission as it does the "Declaration," but the two following groups were "unrecovered." The reference was either to the Declaration on Liberated Europe agreed to at Yalta, which Moscow violated in its actions in Romania, or to the Declaration on Poland. The Russian text was sent to Moscow in two parts and is so designated in the Venona cable, which meant that it was very long, as was the Foreign Office original of March 8. Finally, 374 word groups in the cable were "unrecoverable," meaning that very little of the body of the text was recovered.

Despite these obstacles, a few clarifying deductions are possible. Since the cable originated in the Foreign Office in the first person, it was either from Foreign Secretary Eden or sent on behalf of Prime Minister Churchill.[33] It was sent on the same day as Churchill's long personal and top-secret telegram to Roosevelt (905), which also begins with Churchill's comment on Romania. But it isn't a Churchill to Roosevelt cable. (His personal telegrams to Roosevelt were sent "via U.S. Army" communications.) A sensitive, personal, top-secret Churchill to Roosevelt telegram would never have been copied to Moscow, CASERTA, and SAVING in Paris, acronyms for Allied European military headquarters. The original March 8 Foreign Office cable is similar to the opening of the March 8 Churchill to Roosevelt cable that also reviews the situation in Romania before beginning his personal appeals to Roosevelt. It is possible that those opening paragraphs were from a Foreign Office circular telegram sent on the prime minister's instructions as his own personal tour d'horizon reviewing alarming developments in the Balkans and Eastern Europe for the addressees, including the British embassy in Washington. In that sense it may be a Churchill cable, but this is merely a supposition. There is nothing in the text released by Venona in 1996 that would conclusively identify it as a Churchill cable.

On March 10 Churchill sent two more telegrams to Roosevelt on the Polish crisis. The first (907) was provoked by a half-witted State Department instruction to Ambassador Harriman passed to London by Lord Halifax requesting that the rival Polish factions "adopt a political truce." Churchill must have been shocked beyond belief as he read the instruction but he suppressed his rage in a sensible repudiation of the entire notion. A truce, he warned Roosevelt with more common sense than Washington could muster, would substantially benefit the Soviets in their ruthless suppression of the non-Communist opposition. To sanction a long period of delay or a truce would guarantee the "liquidation of elements unfavorable to them or their puppets." He begged Roosevelt to give full consideration to his long March 8 cable in support of a direct approach to Stalin and suspend the Harriman instructions until Churchill received his reply and could respond. Churchill's second March 10 cable (909) reinforced the first in a long summary of Soviet and NKGB executions, arrests, deportations, and suppression throughout Poland from January through February 1945 as given to him by the Polish prime minister in exile in London.[34]

On March 11 Roosevelt replied to Churchill in two cables, both drafted by the State Department with help from Admiral Leahy, the White House chief of staff (the drafters probably included Alger Hiss, the Yalta legal expert, then head of the Office of Special Political Affairs, who had a hand in drafting the Declaration on Liberated Europe).[35] Churchill's plea for Roosevelt's personal response had been ignored. One cable insisted on maintaining the call for a general political truce but agreed to low-level observers; the second suggested they not approach Stalin "personally" but let their ambassadors in Moscow continue their attempts at resolving the Polish impasse with Molotov.[36] The reply was as illogical as the call for a truce. Why would Molotov yield when his tactics were working? On March 13 Churchill, at wit's end, answered with a telegram to Roosevelt warning that they were "in the presence of a great failure and an utter breakdown of what was settled at Yalta." He also insisted "that combined dogged pressure and persistence on which we have been working and my proposed draft message to Stalin would very likely succeed."[37] Powerless alone, he could succeed only if supported by Roosevelt. Churchill's fears, however, like his foresight and foreboding, weren't Roosevelt's.

Still trusting that the United States and the USSR could be partners in peace as they were in war, Roosevelt's State Department drafting team and Admiral Leahy responded on March 16. They denied that they were faced "with a breakdown of the Yalta agreement until we have made the effort to overcome the obstacles incurred in the negotiations in Moscow." They commented on several negotiating points made by Churchill in his March 8 message, suggested others, and asked for an urgent reply so that their two ambassadors could proceed with their instructions.[38] Churchill sent a rejoinder to Roosevelt the same day. Opening with a note of gratitude that their disagreement concerned tactics rather than fundamentals, he left it to Lord Halifax "to explain to you in detail" his views on various essential points, which meant that he was conceding the game to the moralizing didacticians at Foggy Bottom. But he expressed grave doubts for the future and included a cautionary comment on the collapsing state of affairs in Poland, now shrouded in even greater secrecy, that would be rephrased in more starkly forbidding terms a year later: "An impenetrable veil has been drawn upon the scene."[39]

The final two March 29–31, 1945, Maclean cables were sent to Washington from the Foreign Office on March 16. Both followed from the Churchill exchanges with Roosevelt (Venona, Washington to Moscow 1793, March 29, and Washington to Moscow 1826, March 31). The former (Foreign Office 2535) references Roosevelt's cable to Churchill (719) and Churchill's answer (912). As promised in Churchill's telegram to Roosevelt, Foreign Secretary Eden instructed Halifax to see Secretary of State Stettinius as soon as possible, "and after that, if you can, the President and show them [2 groups unrecovered but obviously Clark-Kerr's draft note] to Molotov." Halifax was told to use every argument at his disposal to "induce them to make a concerted effort with us on the basis of this draft." Eden's cable also noted that "From the Prime Minister's message you will see that the point on which we can't give way is the question of a truce." Eden followed immediately on March 16 with a supplementary cable passing on more advice to Halifax for his conversations with Stettinius and the president (231 groups were unrecoverable). So ends the series of six Venona March 29–31, 1945, cables, but not the Churchill-Roosevelt telegraphic correspondence.

Convinced by the tenor of Roosevelt's replies that they had been drafted by others and having exhausted his appeals, Churchill followed on March 18 with a personal message expressing his hope "that the rather numerous telegrams I have sent you on our many difficult and intertwined affairs aren't becoming a burden to you. Our friendship is the rock on which I build for the future of the world, so long as I am one of the builders."[40] Roosevelt sent a message of appreciation on March 20, to which Churchill replied on March 21. Roosevelt soon learned that Molotov wouldn't be attending the founding conference of the United Nations at San Francisco, the rock on which Roosevelt had built his own hopes for the future. Fearing Molotov's absence would be interpreted as a Soviet rejection of the U.N., he cabled Stalin on March 24 asking that Molotov attend. Stalin's dismissive reply bothered Roosevelt and on March 29 he decided the time had come to take up "directly with Stalin the broader aspects of the Soviet attitude with particular reference to Poland."[41] He sent the text to Churchill, who approved, although it didn't fully express his views, and the cable was sent on April 1.[42]

Roosevelt had already left Washington on March 29 for a few weeks of rest and recuperation at Warm Springs, Georgia, before his contemplated June trip to England and the Continent. At one o'clock in the afternoon of April 12, he suffered a massive stroke and died of a cerebral hemorrhage three hours later. On April 22 Moscow signed a treaty of mutual assistance with the minority Warsaw regime. Churchill had lost his battle. In early May he returned to the offensive and urged President Truman to maintain the American armies in position in Yugoslavia, Austria, and Czechoslovakia to counter the presence of the Red Army and thwart Moscow's ambitions in imposing Communist rule in Eastern European countries occupied by Soviet troops. Truman and his advisers turned aside his appeal and Allied troops withdrew to their occupation zones.[43] Churchill's fears eventually came to pass. On March 5, 1946, having retired to civilian life after his defeat in the July 1945 elections, he broadcast the consequences to the world from Fulton, Missouri: "From Stettin in the Baltic to Trieste in the Adriatic, an Iron Curtain has descended across the continent."

As noted earlier, there are no clearly recognizable Churchill cables in the March 29–31 Venona series. Washington to Moscow 1808–1809 of March 30, 1945, might conceivably be a Churchill cable sent through the Foreign Office, but this is only an inference. While Churchill's shadow is everywhere visible, his voice is nowhere present despite the ten telegrams he sent to Roosevelt between March 8 and March 18, 1945, the period covered by Venona's Maclean cables. The six Venona cables directly involved Churchill only in the sense that they were provoked by his alarm at Stalin's repudiation of the Yalta agreement and his determination to resist Molotov's and Stalin's designs for Poland before it was too late. The absence of an identifiable Churchill cable doesn't necessarily contradict the information given to Meredith Gardner by a British GCHQ colleague in December 1948 and reaffirmed in January 1949 when those Churchill "cables" were identified in London. But it does raise questions about the evidence on which that conclusion was based. Our reconstruction of the March 1945 cables as outlined above was made possible only by reviewing Prime Minister Churchill's March 1945 telegrams to President Roosevelt and the accompanying commentary by American and British historians published decades later. If the only Venona cable in the March 1945 series that might qualify as a Churchill cable is the Foreign Office cable of March 8 (London's 2213), such a conclusion isn't possible in reading the incomplete fractured text of the 1996 Venona release. What then was the basis for the GCHQ officer's alert to Meredith Gardner in December 1948?

Once again the very little we know about GCHQ's effort on the Venona cables returns us to inference and deduction. As already observed, GCHQ officers whether in London or at Arlington Hall showed a surprising ability to anticipate conclusions later verified in London. This was true in transferring the GOMMER cable to GCHQ in March 1951 and it was true in sending the March 1945 "G" or "Churchill" cables to GCHQ in London in December

1948. The purpose of the London Venona operation established in 1947–1948 was to avoid any possible repetition of the Canberra episode when sensitive British War Department secrets were first uncovered by Arlington Hall. In 1948–1949, had Arlington Hall first discovered that sensitive Foreign Office secrets were being passed to Moscow from Washington or New York by a British embassy diplomat and that intelligence escaped London's control—leaked to the public and Congress by the FBI, for example—the consequences could have been far more catastrophic for Britain's policy goals in Washington than the Canberra revelations; most notably the sharing of U.S. atomic weapons technology.

In October 1948 the FBI's Robert Lamphere had begun cooperating with Meredith Gardner on Venona, working from a list of hundreds of Soviet codenames. Buried among them were HOMER (GOMER) and "G" ("H") cables. GCHQ's liaison officer at Arlington Hall and other British analysts were aware of Lamphere's intrusion. By December 1948 it must have become apparent to London that sooner or later Meredith Gardner's Venona team at Arlington Hall would recover enough additional fragments from the 1944 HOMER cables or the March 29–31 "G" cables to recognize, as London had already concluded, that British Foreign Office telegrams had been compromised in Washington.

The December 1948 notice to Meredith Gardner that the "contents were telegrams from Churchill" and the official confirmation in January 1949 brought them under exclusive British jurisdiction, as would be any future Arlington Hall decryptions relevant to the "G" or Maclean case. The FBI and Robert Lamphere were effectively shut out. Ending the FBI's access to the HOMER decrypts explains GCHQ's logic in identifying the so-called Churchill cables for Arlington Hall

The six March 29–31 cables disclosing British and American attempts to resolve the Polish crisis would have had an immediate and explosive effect had they been seen at the Foreign Office in 1949. The magnitude of betrayal was evident in their text: HOMER had compromised Churchill's efforts to resolve the Polish crisis, the issue that had fully engaged the prime minister's energies and aroused his fury from late February through April 1945. His failure in Poland had also helped weaken him domestically with his Conservative base. Four years later, in early 1949, at the onset of the MI5 investigation, senior British Foreign Office and cabinet officials would have had no difficulty recalling Yalta, the futile March 1945 negotiations with Molotov, Churchill's struggle with Stalin to restructure the Polish provisional government as he had promised Commons, and the sensitivity of his policy differences with Roosevelt.

Had Dick White's sole purpose been to identify the diplomat responsible for passing those Foreign Office cables to the Russians in 1944 and 1945, full disclosure of the Venona cables to the Foreign Office in early 1949 would have drastically affected the MI5 investigation. The sensitivity of Foreign Office cables so closely held they required decryption by Ambassador Halifax's personal cipher would have reduced the suspects to a small number of diplomats at the British embassy in March 1945. Only the decrypting officer and a very few embassy diplomats would have had access. But quickly ending the investigation wasn't Dick White's aim.

For those reasons senior Foreign Office officials never saw the actual GCHQ texts of Venona's twelve Maclean telegrams. Their content made it impossible for Dick White to share the recoveries and transcripts without compromising his purpose. In his 1960 memoir, Herbert Morrison gave scant attention to the Maclean affair but repeated the official 1955 White Paper claim about the British embassy leak and the vagueness of the evidence in identifying the source. He didn't mention codebreaking but he did comment that after the discovery of the leak there followed a "highly secret investigation at a level which would be over the head of the Foreign Secretary and known only to the Prime Minister."[44] He meant at the level of GCHQ, the supersecret British codebreaking agency whose work was far too sensitive to be known except to the rare few. As a member of Churchill's War Cabinet from 1942 to 1945—he was home secretary—Morrison would have had little difficulty recognizing the sensitivity of the March 1945 cables had he been shown the texts. But he didn't see them.

Neither did Anthony Eden. In September 1955, when Dick White was drafting the White Paper, the Conservatives had returned to power and Eden was prime minister. Had he been shown Venona's Maclean archive even in fragmentary form, he would have recognized his three cables to Lord Halifax in Washington on the Polish negotiations in Moscow. Trusting British intelligence, he didn't see the GCHQ recoveries. For the same reason, neither did Foreign Minister Macmillan, a member of Churchill's caretaker government in May–July 1945. In defending the White Paper in the House of Commons in November 1955, Macmillan spoke of searching a "field of 6,000" suspects in identifying the leak of Foreign Office "information" to the Russians. Evidently he had been very seriously misled. But then so were they all.

Chapter
FIVE

London's Venona choices.—Informing the Foreign

Office.—Sir Roger Makins.—Mrs. Gray's August

2-3, 1944, "G" cable.—Maclean in Cairo.—

Burgess and Blunt blunder.—Yuri Modin and

Nikolai Rodin.—Philby's strange silence.—

Three at Cambridge.

Soviet cables under attack by American and British analysts during the Venona operation gave up their secrets very slowly. Sometimes they yielded a few fragments in a few months, sometimes never at all. A partially comprehensible text might take a year or even longer to recover. In the long process of recovery, an encrypted Russian cable would pass through a number of evolutionary stages before it might yield enough weight, substance, and heft for counterintelligence officers to begin trolling for the source. More often the recovery work was abandoned without conclusive results. The mind-numbing work was helped immeasurably if the cryptologist had recovered enough fragments to identify the original document or cable the Russian agent had copied verbatim.

In attacking the six Washington to Moscow cables on the Polish crisis, GCHQ Venona codebreakers in London had the complete texts of the original March 7–16 Foreign Office and embassy telegrams. In 1947, as we know, Meredith Gardner was able to recover the complete texts of two British War Cabinet documents passed from Canberra to Moscow using the originals London gave him. The original March 1945 cable texts should have been invaluable as cribs in breaking out the enciphered word groups from the Russian cables. But that wasn't the case. The texts were only partially broken. Large sections that should have been intelligible were marked "unrecoverable." Left for us fifty years later is the detritus, the broken fragments, as difficult to identify and reconstruct as shattered beach litter after a storm at sea: a schooner, a dory, or a lifeboat? We can't tell. The GCHQ translations take no account of London's possession of the six original British cables copied by the Soviet embassy in Washington.

The reason is apparent enough. The Third Venona Release of the Maclean cables in February 1996 combines the Arlington Hall collection of recoveries with those amended by GCHQ. They aren't the final GCHQ recoveries and translations. Would the complete translation of the Foreign Office cable transmitted on March 8, 1945, have revealed that it was a Churchill tour d'horizon? We don't know. Would the Russian transmitting officer's unrecovered preface and introductory remarks in the cable from Lord Halifax to the Foreign Office have boasted of "G" 's being entrusted with negotiating with the State Department on the Polish crisis? His Soviet colleague made similar boasts in a cable from New York to Moscow on August 2–3, 1944. All we can assume is that complete GCHQ translations of the March 1945 cables were withheld because they could have revealed Maclean's identity as a Soviet agent prior to April 1951.

British intelligence never intended, guessed, or even imagined that the Venona Maclean cables would ever see the light of day. The most sensitive British intelligence is never disclosed to the public and the GCHQ cache of broken Soviet telegrams was considered especially invulnerable. The publication of the Venona traffic in particular would have scandalously exposed the distortions of the Maclean case outlined in the September 1955 White Paper, accused its authors, and perhaps brought on a parliamentary inquiry. The NSA's 1995 decision to declassify Venona shocked London and confronted British intelligence with an impossible problem.

The initial 1947–1948 recoveries of the Maclean cables in the Venona archive at Arlington Hall were under U.S. military authority at the time; Washington would have pressed on with their declassification whether or not London agreed to cooperate. Confronted with the 1995 NSA decision, London had a choice to make. It could collaborate with the NSA and issue the complete Maclean archive as broken by GCHQ cryptologists or it could avoid full disclosure by limiting the February 1996 releases to those cable sections broken by Arlington Hall in 1947–1948 without the benefit of the original British cables.

London chose the latter option. The fragmentary texts of the six March 1945 cables separated by hundreds of "unrecovered" word groups are convincing evidence of that decision. Since the so-called Churchill telegrams identified in London in January 1949 aren't recognizable in the 1996 NSA releases, then obviously those weren't the cables or cable that enabled GCHQ to identify their Churchill content in December 1948. That Churchill cable, if it existed, had been identified earlier by GCHQ analysts at Arlington Hall and broken by the GCHQ Venona cell using the original Foreign Office text. Few of those Maclean cables go beyond the Arlington Hall recoveries or at least what we know of those recoveries as quoted by Meredith Gardner. In two minor instances GCHQ cryptologists added "attachments" identifying word groups previously "unrecovered" in the "NSA version" (Washington to Moscow 1791 and 1793 of March 29) but neither adds significance to the cable. That choice may explain why the NSA didn't mention the GCHQ Venona cell at Eastcote, perhaps at London's insistence in its talks or negotiations with the NSA. The six March 1945 cables are also the only Venona Maclean telegrams released to the Public Record Office and attributed to Washington.[1] The HOMER cables of 1944 are ignored.

As stated earlier, from early 1949 until spring 1951 Dick White kept three senior Foreign Office officials informed of the progress of the HOMER investigation: Sir William Strang, the permanent undersecretary, Sir Patrick Reilly, the acting undersecretary, and George Carey-Foster, the security chief and MI5's official liaison. In 1986 Reilly explained that by autumn 1950 there were thirty-five possible HOMER suspects and that the MI5 investigation of each had been long and tedious. For Reilly it wasn't surprising that "for a long time MI5 had nothing to report." At a fairly late stage, however, "a message became available showing that Homer was being consulted by the Russians." The "new message" showed that the spy was "someone of some importance" and a relatively short list of about nine was produced.[2] There was still nothing pointing to Maclean. There are no Venona HOMER cables among the 1996 releases that even hint Maclean was ever consulted by the Russians. Normally any Soviet cable that requested consultations would have been incoming from Moscow. All twelve Venona cables are outgoing Washington or New York to Moscow. Reilly's comments confirm that he didn't see the actual GCHQ texts but depended on information White was willing to share. Strang was similarly in the dark, with good reason.

From 1943 until 1945 Strang was the British representative on the European Advisory Commission (EAC). Established at the October 1943 Moscow conference of foreign ministers, one of its tasks was to prepare plans for the surrender, occupation, and control of Germany. Strang was based in London from 1943 to 1945; the EAC meetings were held at Lancaster House.[3] In July 1944 Maclean was the embassy's representative in Washington preparations for meetings of the EAC considering plans for postwar Germany. In a New York to Moscow cable of September 7, 1944 (1271–1274), the Russian transmitting officer quoted from HOMER's report of September 2: "Citing the Strang documents which you know of, H. [G.] emphasizes that the plans of the British, in large measure, are based on the opinion of the British Foreign Office. A sub-committee on post hostilities planning of the British Chiefs of Staff issued a paper on 19th August."

"H" had passed Strang's documents earlier to his KGB control. The cable continues with several paragraphs on the occupation of Germany and the major differences on German policy within the Roosevelt administration. Strang would have been familiar with the content. He would have known that Maclean represented the embassy in the Washington preparations for the EAC meetings at Lancaster House. The August 2–3, 1944, New York to Moscow cable refers to the EAC meeting in London and boasts that "Almost all of the work is done by H. [G.] who is present at all the sessions." For those reasons Strang would never have seen either cable. He, Reilly, and Carey-Foster mistakenly assumed that Dick White passed on any new details on HOMER's identity as they were recovered from the Soviet cables by GCHQ cryptanalysts. The three Foreign Office seniors weren't shown those cables, with the possible exception of the so-called decisive GOMMER decrypt that identified Maclean in April 1951 as a result of his visits to his pregnant wife in New York. Not surprisingly, this is the only Maclean cable that had no substantive content. But even the full disclosure of that cable is questionable.

The secrecy surrounding GCHQ and the sensitivity of the GCHQ Venona cables gave Dick White an impenetrable cover as well as complete freedom of action. He could choose the time and place to use those decrypts as he wished in managing the pace of the investigation, protected against exposure by their absolute secrecy. Since the Venona decrypts had first identified the Soviet agent at the British embassy, the three Foreign Office officials had been led to believe that new GCHQ recoveries would inevitably identify Moscow's agent. Yet they didn't learn that HOMER was "someone of importance" until early 1951. This was obvious to White in January 1949, if not months earlier, and would have been so to Reilly, Strang, and Carey-Foster had they been shown the March 29–31, 1945, Venona cables even in fragmentary form.

Although only one of the March Foreign Office cables passed to the Russians was identified as in cipher, it is likely that all six were, especially the three from Foreign Secretary Eden. Foreign Office telegrams so closely held as to require decryption by Ambassador Halifax's cipher would have contradicted MI5 claims that there were a hundred or so initial HOMER suspects, gradually reduced to three dozen by mid-1950, to nine by early 1951, and ultimately to Maclean. This is the tightening noose paradigm mentioned by Philby. Lord Halifax and his embassy counselors would have recalled who had charge of the ambassador's cipher, who was responsible for deciphering the Foreign Office cables, or who had privileged access to the cables during those hectic March days when the embassy was seized with the Polish crisis, was coping with the decryption of a blizzard of Foreign Office telegrams, and was in constant consultations with the State Department in negotiating with Molotov in Moscow. They might even have remembered which embassy officer discussed the Polish problem at such length at the State Department on March 7, 1945.[4]

Among those embassy diplomats was second secretary Donald Maclean, who had been welcomed on his posting by a warm letter from Lord Halifax, a friend of his late father, and was given several important responsibilities exceeding his rank soon after his May 1944 arrival. In 1944, as noted above, he took part in Washington preparations for EAC meetings concerning postwar Germany. He was also active in Anglo-American preparations for the Churchill-Roosevelt meeting at the second Quebec conference in early September 1944. On April 17, 1945, he was promoted to first secretary.

As we know, among Ambassador Halifax's embassy ministers was Economic Minister Sir Roger Makins (later Lord Sherfield). In March 1945 he represented Halifax on the Anglo-American–Canadian Combined Policy Committee secretariat created by the Quebec agreement of August 1943. He had worked on the Truman-Attlee accords on nuclear cooperation until that effort was suspended following Fuchs's arrest in February 1950. In January 1949, when MI5 began its investigation, Dick White would have had to look no farther than Whitehall to ask his confidant Roger Makins if he recalled those hectic days and nights at the embassy during the week of March 8–13. In January 1949 Makins was undersecretary at the Foreign Office, second in rank to Sir William Strang. White maintained excellent relations with Makins and called on him from time to time to discuss sensitive MI5 intelligence reports he thought Makins might find of interest. Makins stood apart from many of his Foreign Office colleagues in recognizing, like Churchill, Moscow's ambitions in Eastern Europe earlier than others at the Foreign Office were finally forced to admit.[5] A friend of Secretary of State Dean Acheson, in 1953 he was appointed ambassador to Washington by the Churchill government.

Makins might have remembered those busy March days in 1945, recalled who had encrypted the Halifax cable to Foreign Secretary Anthony Eden or decrypted the telegrams from Eden, the Foreign Office, or even a Churchill cable to the Washington embassy. He might also have known who was charged with consultations at the State Department in coordinating instructions to their two ambassadors in Moscow. If Roger Makins was told of the substance of those March 29–31 British cables or of the 1944 HOMER cables or at least was told enough by Dick White to explain his innumerable questions, he was the only Foreign Office senior privy to that intelligence. White released details on HOMER to the three other Foreign Office officials and to J. Edgar Hoover only as they served his more particular purpose, one that Roger Makins too might have shared.

As already noted, in early August 1950 a New York to Moscow August 2–3, 1944, cable was partially broken by Mrs. Gray, a cryptologist on Meredith Gardner's Venona team at Arlington Hall. Her fragments contained the NKGB transmitting officer's boast that the work of its source "G" included Churchill's personal telegraphic correspondence and that "weeks ago" he was entrusted with deciphering a confidential Churchill to Roosevelt telegram. Makins didn't arrive in Washington until January 1945 but he would have known Maclean's duties in March of that year and whether he was responsible for decrypting the most sensitive embassy cables. Dick White's realization that Maclean was "G" or HOMER might date from his discussions with Roger Makins in London in early 1949. More probably Maclean had been identified by late December 1948, when London decided the time had come to take full control of those Venona cables. His identification would have followed from the GCHQ Venona cell's successful recoveries of the 1944 New York to Moscow HOMER cables and the series of March 29–31, 1945, cables based on the original texts.

In January 1949, when the original March 1945 "Churchill telegrams" were supposedly identified in London, Maclean was stationed in Cairo, the youngest head of chancery in the British diplomatic service. It isn't known whether he was questioned in Cairo that spring, either by the Cairo embassy's security officer, a Major S. Sansom, or by an officer sent by MI5 from London. What is known is that by spring and summer 1949, several months after MI5 began its investigation, Maclean's behavior in Cairo had begun its chaotic deterioration. Several incidents in Washington prior to his September 1948 departure might have triggered Maclean's instability and uncertainty.

On June 26, 1948, his Washington handler, Boris Krotov, found himself under FBI surveillance while approaching a meeting with Maclean and broke off contact. The KGB station at the embassy subsequently told Maclean to deliver his materials through dead drops, a routine Maclean disliked, probably because being separated from his intelligence material would put him at risk were he under surveillance. An accommodation was eventually worked out using both dead drops and personal meetings.[6] On August 3, Whittaker Chambers, who had served in the KGB underground in the 1930s, was summoned by the House Un-American Activities Committee. In public session he named several members of the Communist Party underground, including Alger Hiss. Maclean had met with Hiss from time to time on official business at the State Department in 1945–1946, although they were unaware of each other's espionage. The charges against Hiss dated from years earlier, although neglected and clumsily mishandled for several years by the FBI. In November 1945 the FBI asked Attorney General Tom Clark to permit technical surveillance in Hiss's office at State; it was approved in December.[7] Hiss resigned in late 1947. The Hiss case made headlines the remaining months of 1948 and on through 1949. At the conclusion of his second trial, on January 21, 1950, the jury returned a verdict of guilty on all counts. He was sentenced to five years in prison for perjury. (We don't know if Maclean met with Hiss in March 1945 in resolving differences on the Polish crisis.)

Maclean was miserable in his new post in Cairo. He was drinking heavily and his behavior had grown increasingly bizarre. On some evenings he would drunkenly disappear, not to be found until the next morning, muddled and disheveled. During a boating party on the Nile he had gotten savagely drunk and throttled his wife by the throat. On the quay he had seized the night guard's rifle and in the struggle with the embassy first secretary, who had attempted to retrieve the weapon, Maclean had broken his colleague's leg.[8] His personal crisis, whatever its source, would worsen as the year wore on. In December 1949 he sent a note to the Soviet KGB residency in Cairo asking that he be allowed to leave KGB service. His note was for-warded unread to Moscow, where it was ignored for some time. In April 1950 he again appealed to Moscow through the Soviet residency in Cairo to allow him to end the unendurable stress of his double life as a Soviet agent.[9] In May, following his last cry for relief, the turmoil he had too long suppressed exploded in drunken rage when he broke into the Cairo flat of two American women—one was secretary to the American ambassador—and demolished some of its contents, proving in fury what he had fore-warned in his pleas for remission. He ended up in anonymous delirium in an Alexandria jail among drunken sailors, too incoherent to identify himself for two days. His wife met with the permissive British ambassador in Cairo to urge his recall. On May 11, 1950, the Foreign Office obliged. Escorted to the airport, Maclean flew back to London, where he was given extended leave for psychiatric counseling. The psychiatrist diagnosed "overwork, marital problems and repressed homosexuality." Maclean was given six months convalescent leave ending on or about the first week of November 1950.[10]

In accounts of his disintegration and breakdown, commentators have speculated that in Cairo Maclean was warned by the KGB of the MI5 inves-tigation after Philby had reported the embassy leak to Moscow in September 1949, as he claimed in *My Silent War.* As we know, before Philby left London for Washington, he was briefed by MI6's Sir Maurice Oldfield, who described the Anglo-American codebreaking operation that had uncovered the leak and an unidentified Los Alamos KGB spy, codenamed CHARLES (Klaus Fuchs). In his memoir Philby recalled that after his briefing he visited the MI6 li-brary to explore the British diplomatic lists, found Maclean's name on the British embassy roster for Washington 1944–1945, realized the spy's iden-tity, and passed the intelligence to his "Russian friend." Forty years later, Philby repeated his original account but added a few flourishes. In Moscow he insisted he immediately passed on the intelligence to his Soviet control, a KGB officer at the London residence whom he knew as Max and had first met in 1946; they had worked together for a year and a half in Turkey in what Philby called an agreeable relationship. Max was alarmed at Philby's revelations about the Anglo-American codebreakers, Fuchs, and Maclean, or so Philby claimed, and immediately reported them to Moscow.[11]

This is Philby's version of his quick, decisive, and full disclosure of his London briefing by Oldfield. It is totally false, contradicted on every count by KGB files opened in the 1990s, and so precise there's no doubt his details are as specious as many of his Moscow reminiscences. According to the KGB archive examined by Nigel West, Philby was briefed by Oldfield after, not before, his final September 21 meeting with his controller, Mikhail Shishkin, whom Philby called Max. The meeting took place too late to pass on the Oldfield details. Instead, before departing by ship on September 28, Philby relayed the intelligence to Guy Burgess, who included it in a note delivered to Anthony Blunt, along with Foreign Office documents Blunt was to photograph for delivery to his new KGB handler, Yuri Modin. On October 11, Blunt delivered the film but had so botched the camera work the over-exposed films were worthless.

Owing to these blunders, Burgess didn't report the Oldfield detail about the U.S.-U.K. codebreakers until he met with Yuri Modin on February 10, 1950, five months after Philby's briefing. Moscow Center was upset when it eventually learned the details. Philby's CHARLES warning had come too late. Klaus Fuchs had been twice questioned by MI5 in December and twice again in January. On January 24 he confessed, on February 2 was officially charged, and on February 10 was sentenced to fourteen years in prison. In straightening out the muddle during these exchanges from February until June 1950 among Burgess, Modin, and Nikolai Rodin, the KGB chief of station, Maclean was never mentioned. Not a single KGB file opened years later shows that Philby warned Moscow of the Maclean investigation until April 1951. Burgess, who was Philby's courier, never raised the Maclean inquiry with his new case officer, Yuri Modin, or with Nikolai Rodin, who had intervened on occasion to take more direct control. The possible exposure of Maclean, who would return to London from Cairo in early May, was ignored.[12]

Although in later years Maclean's name would be consistently linked with Philby, the two were never intimates either at Cambridge or during their espionage careers. Their paths diverged after 1934 and seldom crossed; they hadn't met in years. Their families and Cambridge backgrounds are as different as their intellects, characters, emotional makeup, and physical appearance. Philby entered Trinity College, Cambridge, in October 1929 as a seventeen-year-old scholarship student intending to read history. Guy Burgess followed in 1930 from Eton and Donald Maclean in 1931 from Gresham's School, a progressive public school where he had declared himself a Communist. At Cambridge Maclean was the most politically active. Articulate and widely read, he knew his own mind long before Philby, and joined a Communist cell organized at Cambridge in the summer of 1931. The son of a minor liberal cabinet minister, he read modern languages, took first class honors, and considered teaching in Russia. He should have been encouraged to pack his bags.[13]

Of the three, Maclean was the most poorly served by his recruitment by Philby to the OGPU in 1934. His self-destructive collapses had been evident for years. In Paris in 1938 he had drunkenly admitted to being a KGB agent, a pattern he would later repeat after his return to London in May 1950. He was badly equipped temperamentally for espionage, a role he held in contempt even if essential for the onward march of international socialism. In Moscow years later he compared espionage to being a lavatory attendant: "It stinks, but someone has to do it."[14] Far more dedicated ideologically than Philby or Burgess as his final years in Moscow proved, he was a study in contrasts, now gracious and charming, now coldly aloof. Like Burgess, he was a chaotic drunk. He seemed to move between personae, struggling to control a dangerously multiple nature. Whatever his inner turmoil, his drinking sometimes crumbled his defenses and brought on confession, violence, and hysteria.

Philby was remembered for quietly guarding his thoughts and his silence, was more ordinary and far less conspicuous at Cambridge than Maclean. He was known as a solitary, modestly indistinguishable from the crowd, satisfied politically by his membership in the University Socialist Society. In 1931, two years after entering Cambridge, he changed from history to economics and in his final year discovered Marx and Communism. He never joined the Communist Party. The shorter, flamboyant Guy Burgess, by all accounts the most gifted of the three and evidently the quickest mind, joined the Communist Party cell at Cambridge but not from studious conviction. Concealment didn't matter to Burgess. Invulnerable to shame or humiliation, he never disguised his ego, his impressive knowledge, his fierce opinions, whatever the subject, or his promiscuous homosexuality. Unlike Maclean, he had no inner walls. His drinking resulted in insults, rowdiness, and barroom brawls. Called brilliant by some, he was also a tiresome exhibitionist, vulgar, impenitent, and impregnable even as others grew tired of his escapades. He never changed except by exhausting his peculiar genius. Noel Annan, his contemporary, wrote that Burgess remained an undergraduate all his days, "reading the same books, listening to the same music and repeating the same themes."[15] Another contemporary, Cyril Connolly, believed that the intensity of English boys' experiences at the great public schools permanently arrested their development. Burgess's life suggests as much. He never realized his promise. But these are mere thumbnail sketches.

By 1949 and 1950 the years of deception had worn down the defenses of all three in different ways. Maclean began to go to pieces in Cairo, although whether his questioning by MI5 in 1949 accelerated his disintegration is open to question. Burgess's behavior was more erratic than ever. In 1949–1950 he was the subject of an official inquiry at the Foreign Office. During an autumn 1949 holiday in Tangier and Gibraltar, he was often drunk, failed to pay his hotel bills, had an altercation with a British intelligence officer, and had publicly identified two British intelligence officers. MI6 had complained to the Foreign Office. The charges were similar to those made during the war when Gladwyn Jebb had dismissed him as "dissolute, indiscreet, and unfitted for any kind of confidential work." In Parliament in 1955 the Cambridge undergraduate who had been called the "most brilliant of his day" was described as a "dirty, drunken, sexual inebriate."[16] After 1947 Philby retreated into relative passivity, daring less and less.

Philby's failure to warn Burgess or to alert Yuri Modin through Burgess is curious but not inexplicable. Had Philby told Burgess in September 1949 after the Oldfield briefing of Maclean's possible exposure, Burgess would also have realized Maclean's interrogation would have made them all vulnerable. Maclean's behavior was so unpredictable Philby might have feared that had Maclean known he was under suspicion, he might have gone to MI5 or others and made a clean breast of it. In *My Silent War* Philby described his intended strategy: the Maclean investigation would "require minute watching" on his arrival in Washington and would no doubt require "drastic action" before his next posting, otherwise he "might well lose all control of the case." As self-serving as this rationale appears, it wasn't without its logic. Had he immediately passed on the Maclean warning, quite apart from alarming both Burgess and Maclean (Burgess was frightened enough by the Anglo-American codebreakers), Philby would have forfeited to Moscow the decision about managing the Maclean problem. In Washington, he might handle matters to his advantage. He would wait and see. Indecision isn't mentioned in the many accounts of Philby's career, yet on two occasions the OGPU agent who recruited him in London in 1934 described him in his reports to Moscow as "indecisive" or "somewhat indecisive."[17] His silence in the case of Maclean might well have been simply another instance of indecision. A simpler explanation and one Philby would never have been willing to admit is that he didn't realize Maclean was HOMER until he saw his name on the April 1951 list. But this is speculation.

As explained earlier, Rebecca West found incomprehensible Prime Minister Heath's explanation that in 1951 Philby in Washington had warned

Maclean in London by sending Burgess, also in Washington, to warn him that he was in danger. "Soviet intelligence," she insisted, "has better communications than that. This cannot be the story." Moscow did have better communications than that. Philby had been out of contact with a KGB control officer for most of his twenty months in Washington. Genrikh Borovik, the sympathetic Russian writer who interviewed Philby extensively between 1985 and 1988 and had limited access to KGB files, insists that for more than two years (1949–1951) Maclean had no contact "with the people who could have warned him of the coming danger." He also claims Philby hadn't seen Maclean since 1940 and in the winter of 1951 believed Maclean had broken off contact with the KGB "two years earlier."[18] Moscow Center didn't learn that Maclean was at risk until May 1951.

KGB files in Moscow indicated that Philby never mentioned the Maclean investigation to the KGB until April 1951, eighteen months after his arrival in the United States. Even then, Yuri Modin and Nikolai Rodin weren't aware of Maclean's distress until Burgess informed them in early May 1951. Not until then did Maclean's possible exposure as a Soviet agent finally force Philby to confront a threat he could no longer ignore. In desperation he met with a Soviet illegal, Valeri Makayev. His secret source, as we already know, wasn't Venona at Arlington Hall Station, as many Philby sleuths insist, but MI5's Dick White through Sir Percy Sillitoe, who warned in mid-April 1951 and again on May 23 or 24, 1951, that the seemingly interminable search for the 1944–1945 Soviet agent at the British embassy in Washington had reached its final stages.[19]

Chapter SIX

Secluded in Washington.—Burgess as courier.—
The Soviet illegal.—Mrs. Gray's "G" recovery.—
"G" and the Churchill traffic.—Makins returns
Maclean to the Foreign Office.—Under unofficial
surveillance.—Moving toward closure.—The GOMMER
cable.—Under official surveillance.—Philby
informed.—Burgess returns to London.—The
Maclean interrogation order.

In August 1950, almost a year after Philby's arrival in Washington and seventeen months after London had learned of the Russian agent at the British embassy, the MI5 investigation remained inconclusive, or so it is commonly believed. The identification of the embassy spy was extraordinarily slow in coming. GCHQ and the Eastcote Venona operation had taken control of Arlington Hall intercepts identified as relevant to the case, and Dick White restricted disclosure. According to the Foreign Office's Sir Patrick Reilly in a letter written in 1986, at the time some thirty-five names were included on MI5's list of suspects. Donald Maclean was among them.[1] In London, he was still on convalescent leave, still consulting a psychiatrist, and still adrift in alcoholism, marked by the occasional drunken altercation and by *delirium tremens* clearly visible to his friends. In one drunken encounter, Maclean blurted, "I'm the English Hiss."[2] The remark has been interpreted as an admission of guilt. Hiss had been accused of espionage but was tried and convicted for perjury. It is possible Maclean meant that he'd been questioned by MI5, which implied an accusation.

In Washington, Guy Burgess had joined Philby at the British embassy and was living in the basement of the Philby residence on Nebraska Avenue, much to Mrs. Philby's annoyance. Told of his posting to Washington in May 1950, he arrived in August. His assignment hadn't been well received elsewhere either, most particularly by the embassy security officer, Robert Mackenzie. But he had been assured that if Burgess didn't behave, he would be sacked. As for Philby, after ten months in Washington the most celebrated spy of his time was in seclusion. He had been out of contact with the KGB since his October arrival and would remain cloistered for many months to come. During his wartime espionage from 1940 until 1945 and the two following years he maintained regular contact with his Soviet case officer in London, although there were periods when those meetings were suspended. That era had passed. Once in Washington, Philby refused any contact with the KGB residency at the Soviet embassy. The Mitrokhin archives and Philby's Moscow recollections during the 1980s confirm his isolation, which is corroborated by Yuri Modin in his 1994 memoir. Modin insists Philby had no contact with any KGB agent in Washington, either legal or illegal. He gave two reasons: Moscow Center believed contact was "too hazardous" and hoped Philby might yet become head of the British secret service, MI6.[3]

Modin, our KGB raconteur, is a congenial companion in escorting his reader through the mazes of 1949–1951, as eager as any museum guide in letting no question go unanswered before he shows his visitors the door. Reliable in explaining episodes in which he participated, without firsthand knowledge he's as lost as everyone else, but never concedes defeat. It's then that his inventions begin, a pastiche of fact, fancy, and authorial improvisation, many farcically wrong. (See appendix B.) In Washington Philby resumed the same defensive tactics begun in Istanbul in early 1947 following his dismissal in December 1946 as head of MI6's IX Counter-Soviet Section in London. Until Burgess joined him in Washington in August 1950, he used a slow and cumbersome mail route to Burgess in London, who passed his messages to Modin, his KGB control. Modin insists that even those messages were rare, "for the very act of sending a letter or a telegram was liable to put the network at risk."[4]

In Moscow in the 1980s Philby told Genrikh Borovik that he had no Soviet contact during his first nine or ten months in Washington.[5] If the KGB files brought out secretly by Vasili Mitrokhin are reliable, once in Washington Philby was out of direct contact with any KGB officer for much longer. He didn't meet with a Soviet illegal until April and May 1951, almost eighteen months after his arrival. (Modin wasn't aware of those meetings.)

Philby's admission of inactivity is unusual given his habit of concealing or fancifully embroidering the facts. His Moscow recollections, like those of *My Silent War,* always serve a purpose and this one is difficult but not impossible to explain. During his Moscow reminiscences before his death in 1988, except for his claim of a nine- to ten-month hiatus, he never acknowledged any deviation from his 1940–1951 clandestine routine. The tales he repeated decades later in annotating his remarkable career are occasionally as false in detail as his account of reporting the Maclean investigation to Moscow. He told Borovik that he had a Soviet case officer in Istanbul 1948–1949, a controller he met very briefly—"a minute or two" at a time during his tour. According to Yuri Modin, who handled Burgess at the time, he had no regular Soviet controller or case officer in Istanbul. He used a courier or mail route to Burgess in London.[6]

Philby's dependence on Guy Burgess as his intermediary or cutout from 1947 until 1951 was never admitted in his Moscow reminiscences. Instead, he always had his Soviet case officer on call or close at hand, the two a quick, confident, and smoothly functioning espionage team who easily eluded detection. KGB files tell a different story, as does Modin. Philby was wholly dependent on Burgess. For the skeptics, this reliance might explain Burgess's incomprehensible posting to the British embassy in Washington in May 1950, three months before his arrival, a Foreign Office decision that made no sense to anyone at the time or years later.[7] Evidently there were few messages.

In August 1950 Philby kept himself abreast of the progress of MI5's MacLean investigation by reading the reports sent through his MI6 cipher by Percy Sillitoe to J. Edgar Hoover. If his memory is reliable, by the time of Burgess's arrival in Washington he had seen dozens of reports citing the HOMER codename. There was nothing alarming in those reports. The list of suspects had been reduced to three dozen or so, a comfortable margin, not yet the moment to seize the initiative. His KGB illegal, Valeri Makayev, who had arrived in New York in March, was establishing his bona fides in New York and diverting himself with an affair with the Polish-born operator of a dance studio.[8] The Korean War had erupted unexpectedly in June, dramatically changing the Washington atmosphere. In the oppressive heat of a Washington August, at Arlington Hall Station Meredith Gardner's team of Anglo-American Venona cryptanalysts were tirelessly working their way through the inventory of KGB intercepts.

During those first eleven days of August, Mrs. Gray, an American analyst with the Gardner team, made the recovery already described. She decrypted two fragments of an August 2–3, 1944, KGB New York to Moscow cable citing its British embassy source, who was very specifically and very foolishly identified by his KGB control officer in New York. Gardner described Gray's recovery in October 1951. He was commenting on the link between material "G" and New York to Moscow messages and a six-part message of August 2 and 3, 1944:

"In August 1950, Mrs. Gray of AFSA recovered two stretches which read 'work including the personal telegraphic correspondence of Boar [? Churchill] with Captain [Roosevelt]' and 'weeks ago G. was entrusted with deciphering a confidential telegram of Boar's [?] to Captain.' "9

Mrs. Gray's recovery was the only breakthrough in the Venona Maclean traffic not initiated by a British analyst, which means it wasn't contrived by GCHQ or MI5 in London. Since her few fragments were described word for word by Meredith Gardner in his October 11, 1951, report, they couldn't be denied in a 1996 GCHQ-released cable by claiming those word groups were "unrecoverable." Gardner's report, issued in the final, September 27, 1997, NSA release, nineteen months after Venona's Maclean cables, confronted London with a serious problem. NSA editor Robert Benson recognized the difficulty and warned that Gardner's report "must not be taken as a full representation of the counterintelligence investigation chronology."10 He meant that Gardner's report shouldn't be interpreted as contradicting the accepted version of Maclean's identification as HOMER in April 1951. His caveat is no more credible than his bizarre attempt to affirm the integrity of "the counterintelligence investigation chronology" he knew nothing about. The NSA and Benson had no more idea of the MI5 investigation chronology than William Strang, Patrick Reilly, George Carey-Foster, or Kim Philby. MI5 had abandoned the NSA and everyone else to a dark alley chasing stray cats while withholding all details about their investigation and the Venona chronology except those that served its purpose. Benson and Warner were forced to rely on secondary sources, all of them questionable and some unreliable.11

Mrs. Gray's fragment was passed to the British on August 11, 1950, quoting "G" 's Russian control officer, who credited him with responsibility for the "personal telegraphic correspondence" between Churchill and Roosevelt. Weeks earlier he "was entrusted with deciphering a confidential telegram of Boar's." If ever a Venona cable was to enable MI5 to identify "G," as the three Foreign Office officials expected, no more was needed. The embassy officer responsible for the Roosevelt-Churchill telegraphic correspondence who had recently decrypted a Churchill cable would have been known to the ambassador, Lord Halifax, and his ministers. The original Churchill cable was one of particular sensitivity: an attempt to persuade Roosevelt to agree to changing Allied invasion plans from the south of France (ANVIL) in favor of a massive offensive through northeastern Italy, Venice, and Trieste, and on to the north, through the Ljubljana Gap, to Austria. Roosevelt and "his Generals" were opposed. The cable wasn't included in the August 2–3 text but was briefly cited.

Mrs. Gray's fragment should have ended Dick White's MI5 investigation if his search hadn't identified Maclean many months earlier, as is more likely. It is also likely that the GCHQ Venona cell in London had received the August 2–3 cable earlier in 1948 and had already recovered Mrs. Gray's fragment.

Meredith Gardner's report also gives us our only opportunity to compare an original Arlington Hall Venona recovery from 1950 with the published version issued in February 1996. As explained earlier, London avoided full disclosure of the March 1945 Venona cables by limiting the February 1996 releases to those Arlington Hall recoveries made without the benefit of the original British cables copied by Maclean and available to GCHQ. The August 2–3, 1944, cable released in 1996 shows that forty-six years later GCHQ cryptologists had made no additional or clarifying recoveries from that portion broken out by Mrs. Gray. This release isn't the complete and final GCHQ recovery.

The August 2–3 telegram was in six parts, each separately numbered and sent from New York to Moscow over a two-day period. One section of that cable had been partially recovered in 1946–1947 and was listed in one of Meredith Gardner's covername indexes. The 1996 Venona version doesn't separate the individual sections and also excludes the Russian transmitting officer's preface. The cable is titled "H.'s Work for a Committee" but that heading was undoubtedly added much later by the Arlington Hall analysts. Some 750 word groups were "unrecoverable," including the 149-word preface or introduction that would have included the opening comments by the Soviet transmitting officer. Mrs. Gray had evidently been working her way through a section of the text in early August. Since the first word groups were "unrecoverable," the cable begins with a reference to an upcoming meeting of the European Advisory Commission (EAC) in SIDON (London). The fragment continues: "is/are taking part in the work of the Committee. Almost all the work is done by H. [G.] who is present at all the sessions. In connexion with this work H. [G.] obtains secret documents [six groups unrecovered]." This section should also have identified Maclean, who represented the British embassy in Washington consultations for the EAC meeting in London. Since it isn't included in Mrs. Gray's word groups, we'll leave it aside. Farther along, near the end of the text's intelligible word groups, she recovered her identifying fragment: "H. [G] was entrusted with deciphering" a Churchill cable.

Had Dick White so decided, Maclean could have been brought in for interrogation. The timing would have been propitious. He had returned in early May after a disastrous ending to his Cairo posting when his drunken rage had demolished his hopes for advancement, but had shown no improvement as his inexplicably drunken behavior had continued. With Klaus Fuchs behind bars and Britain's negotiations with Washington on the exchange of nuclear technology shattered to pieces, there were no overriding policy considerations that would have ruled against the interrogation and possible arrest of Moscow's English agent.

By the late summer all that the three senior Foreign Office officials knew about the MI5 investigation was the list of thirty-five suspects who in March 1945 might have leaked Foreign Office secrets. Maclean was one among many. The Foreign Office wanted to root out the traitor within its ranks as quickly and quietly as possible. Had White revealed that Maclean had finally been identified and cited Mrs. Gray's brief August 1950 recoveries by way of putting an end to the tiresome Maclean affair, Foreign Office officials would have insisted that he be confronted, questioned in secret, and persuaded to confess. Foreign Secretary Ernest Bevin in particular would have insisted that Maclean be interrogated. "Deal with the suspect and deal with him promptly," he might have demanded.

Had Maclean been questioned in Cairo in the spring of 1949, a second, more intensive interrogation in the summer and autumn of 1950 by MI5's most experienced interrogators might have found him fragile and vulnerable. He might have broken down and confessed, finally ridding himself of the intolerable burden of his despised double life as a Soviet agent. Certainly an accommodation might have been reached had he told White and MI5 all they wanted to know.

But Foreign Office interests and Dick White's interests weren't identical. MI5 had wanted to identify him as well but for different reasons. Donald Maclean, as an identified Soviet agent, was White's means to a much more audacious and inclusive end. And here we reach the end of one episode and the beginning of another.

MI5's surveillance of Donald Maclean didn't begin in April 1951, as the Foreign Office mistakenly believed. It began on November 6, 1950, the date he was brought back to the Foreign Office at the end of his six-month convalescent leave. (Medically unfit, Maclean couldn't have been recalled any earlier.) MI5 began his surveillance without the knowledge or the approval of Ernest Bevin or other senior Foreign Office officials. Who was responsible for Maclean's return? Dick White's trusted colleague and confidant, Deputy Undersecretary Roger Makins, the senior member of the Foreign Office Promotions Board who made Maclean temporary head of his American section. The date of the assignment isn't clear, although it was evidently made by the 1950 summer Promotions Board.[12] In November 1985 Makins disclosed that he had known for several months of the suspicions of Maclean, which suggests that he might have identified Maclean for Dick White. He also revealed that as it was known that he liked Maclean, he "was asked to employ him in Whitehall in order to keep an eye on what he did." MI5 assured him Maclean would be trailed only in London.[13] If Makins was approached before the summer assignment, Maclean's return had probably been planned as soon as he was physically able and before Mrs. Gray's August decrypt. But this is speculation.

Makins might have had a personal reason for accommodating White. More familiar than anyone in London and the Foreign Office with the details of U.S.-U.K. atomic collaboration, he would have known the consequences of Maclean's espionage. As we know, Maclean had worked under him on the top-secret Combined Policy Committee (CPC) dealing with nuclear issues. When Makins departed in early 1947, Maclean was appointed to replace him as CPC joint secretary. Despite the dignity of his later title, Lord Sherfield (i.e., Makins) wasn't averse to bending or breaking the law when British security was at stake. In early 1947, before he returned to London as director of the Office of Atomic Energy, he called on Secretary Dean Acheson, ill at home at the time, and attempted to persuade him to ignore the August 1946 McMahon Act. Britain needed certain engineering details that would allow Britain to construct its atomic energy plant. Acheson refused.[14]

In explaining why he had been approached, Makins said that he knew and liked Maclean. He recalled that in Washington, Maclean was an extremely good officer but after Cairo was a "liability." Yet knowing this, he had arranged for his assignment. He also remembered that the position was the least sensitive he could find without arousing Maclean's suspicions. It was relatively unimportant, he claimed, since Makins dealt personally with all the most secret issues, including nuclear matters. We leave aside any MI5 intent to carry out a disinformation rather than a counterespionage operation.

Maclean reported for duty at the end of his six months' leave on November 6, 1950 (he got smashingly drunk the night before).[15] Dick White and MI5 now had the opportunity every counterespionage officer searches for but infrequently finds. A known Soviet agent was given access to official documents to identify other Soviet agents and Soviet networks in England, whether in the Foreign Office or elsewhere, as well as their Soviet control, legal or illegal. This was routine counterintelligence practice. Since Ernest Bevin, the foreign secretary, hadn't signed an order approved by the home secretary officially authorizing MI5's surveillance of Maclean, technically at least it was an illegal operation (Bevin disdained clandestine operations). Not until six months later, on April 17, 1951, would his successor, the more compliant Herbert Morrison, sign the formal surveillance documents based on the so-called identifying Venona recovery, the March 30 decryption of the GOMMER cable.

In 1986 Patrick Reilly recalled that a short list of nine or so was produced in early 1951. Maclean still wasn't the primary suspect. Philby visited London in January 1951 and met with George Carey-Foster, the Foreign Office's chief of security. Carey-Foster invited Dick White to join them and discuss the MI5 investigation. During the meeting, so Carey-Foster recalled years later, White told the Foreign Office gathering, including Philby: "You should look for someone who is unstable, living on his nerves. That will be our man."[16] Philby's visit to London that week and his presence that day at the Foreign Office gave White the opportunity to drop his fly over Philby. It should have been tempting. Donald Maclean had been living on his nerves for almost two years, but so had Philby, who evidently failed to take that message elsewhere as he had so quickly after Maurice Oldfield's briefing more than a year earlier. Burgess, his faithful courier, was in Washington. Yuri Modin was lurking about London somewhere, no doubt on the dodge, but he heard nothing.

White resumed the reports MI5 chief Sillitoe periodically sent J. Edgar Hoover on the HOMER investigation passed through the MI6 special cipher. Perhaps Philby had reasoned that if MI6 was close to identification, he'd soon hear more. The Sillitoe to Hoover reports were an essential part of the Maclean counterespionage deception and evidently similar to the summaries seen by the three officials at the Foreign Office. They had been misled by necessity; Philby was being deceived by design.

For five months after Maclean's November 1950 return to the Foreign Office until April 17, 1951, his MI5 watchers watched and waited. Yuri Modin maintains that the KGB in London decided to suspend contact with Maclean after his November return to the Foreign Office.[17] On Maclean's own initiative, however—or so Modin claims—he supplied intelligence through Burgess. Since Maclean resumed his Foreign Office career in November 1950 and Burgess was in Washington from August 1950 until his return to London in early May 1951, after Maclean had been denied access to secret documents, Modin is in error. There's no doubt Modin established contact with Burgess after his return to London in early May 1951, as described in chapter 1. To Modin's credit, however, he was as much at a loss to explain Maclean's November return to the Foreign Office as Burgess's May 1950 assignment to Washington. What Burgess needed instead, Modin thought, was serious medical treatment. He also said the same thing about Maclean.

While Maclean was recovering at the Foreign Office and behaving in a respectable manner suitable to his rehabilitation, Burgess, then in Washington, was again behaving as disagreeably as he had so often during his civil service and Foreign Office career. During his duty hours he was often in an alcoholic stupor. His drunken mishaps off-duty were also becoming increasingly obnoxious as was his recklessness. In January, during a party at the Philby house, he had infuriated Philby's American guests and humiliated his host. On February 28 he had flagrantly and repeatedly broken Virginia speeding laws three times and was arrested. He pleaded diplomatic immunity and was released. In mid-March 1951 an enraged Virginia governor wrote to the State Department in bitter protest. Ambassador Oliver Franks was on consultations in London at the time.[18]

The fatally ill foreign secretary, Ernest Bevin, had resigned on March 9 and was replaced by Herbert Morrison on March 12 (Bevin died on April 14). Apart from the changing of the Foreign Office guard, one subject on Ambassador Franks's London agenda was Great Britain's deteriorating relations with the United States as a result of differences on the Korean War as well as divergences on Chinese and Taiwan policy. The State Department complaint wasn't sent to the British embassy until Franks returned. On April 7 State was told that the ambassador was discussing the action to be taken with the Foreign Office. In the meantime, Maclean was under surveillance, and Sillitoe was telling Philby of the progress of the MI5 investigation through the British embassy's MI6 special cipher.

The MI5 counterespionage deception was reasonable enough in design. Maclean was fetched back to the Foreign Office to be watched, Burgess was posted to Washington in May 1950, and Philby was to be falsely informed. But in Washington Burgess's antics were becoming more unpredictable and his behavior more insufferable. In mid-April 1951 the operation moved in another direction. Several factors might account for Dick White's change in tack: Communist China's intervention in the Korean War in November 1950, Foreign Secretary Bevin's fatal illness and his replacement by the more malleable Herbert Morrison, Burgess's ungovernable behavior in Washington. Furthermore, if Maclean's surveillance had yielded no results, the time had come to force the issue.

In the summer of 1950 when Roger Makins had arranged Maclean's assignment to the American desk, British-American military cooperation in Korea under the United Nations was relatively untroubled. MacArthur's October drive north across the 38th Parallel totally transformed the Korean War. Five days before Maclean took up his post on November 6, scattered Chinese army units attacked South Korean and American forces but not in great numbers; the forays seemed insignificant to MacArthur's command and to Washington, although not to the Armed Forces' Security Agency intercept stations in the Far East.[19] On November 24 MacArthur began a massive envelopment maneuver against North Korean forces. Three nights later, on November 27, the Korean front exploded as twelve Chinese divisions of 120,000 men hidden in the mountains of northeastern Korea launched their attack. Sixty thousand Chinese would trap the U.S. lst Marine Division in a disastrous defeat. Chinese intervention had created a completely new war, one the Joint Chiefs weren't ready to fight; instead they were prepared to withdraw U.S. forces. The senior policymakers' resolve in pressing on in Korea began to weaken but would finally return in the recognition that the United States had no choice other than to stay the course. But MacArthur had to go.[20]

Chinese intervention also crumbled Anglo-American solidarity on the Korean War as Prime Minister Attlee began to express serious doubts about the course of the war. His fears were made worse by General MacArthur's bluster about dropping the atomic bomb. An erroneous report that MacArthur might be given discretion to use the weapon inflamed a foreign-policy debate in the House of Commons. Attlee flew to Washington to sound his alarm and obtain reassurances from Truman.[21]

The five days of British-American talks in Washington and the Truman-Attlee summit were complex and difficult as was the agenda (Sir Roger Makins attended). Attlee favored American withdrawal from Korea, an end to the war against China, recognition of China's rights in Taiwan, and resumption of a more vigorous U.S. role in the defense of Europe, all sensible positions that grow even more sensible as the decades pass. Truman made no commitment but, after a private one-on-one talk with Attlee, agreed that neither would use the atomic bomb without "prior consultations with the other." When Secretary of State Acheson read those words, he immediately backed Truman away from any language that compromised his presidential freedom of action. The final communiqué made public and drafted in part by British ambassador Oliver Franks stated that "it was his [Truman's] hope that world conditions would never call for the use of the atomic bomb." He assured Attlee that it was his desire to "at all times keep him informed of developments which might bring about a change in the situation."[22]

Although not a crisis in British-American relations, substantial foreign-policy differences were clearly introduced by China's explosive entry into the Korean War. The Labor government had recognized Communist China on January 6, 1950, before the North Korean invasion of the south, and had withdrawn recognition from the Chiang regime a day earlier. The new Korean war also brought with it other questions about Asian policy, including the legitimacy of South Korea's oppressive rule, the seating of Communist China at the U.N., and the Taiwan issue. In 1949 the British chiefs of staff defined long-term military strategy in terms of "three pillars"—defense of the United Kingdom, defense of sea communications, and defense of the Middle East.[23] Korea didn't figure in their strategic reckoning, not with Peking now in the war; least of all was London interested in being held hostage of the American Caesar in Tokyo, General MacArthur. Maclean had been recalled during a quiet interlude in British-American relations. Now he had his ear at the door during a more turbulent period. His November assignment was more troubling as the character of Anglo-American relations changed. Although MacArthur was finally removed from command in April 1951, Maclean's presence on the American desk may have complicated White's purpose.

Probably the most compelling reason for Dick White's decision to move toward closure was Ernest Bevin's March departure from the Foreign Office.

His absence gave White greater flexibility in moving the counterespionage deception toward its conclusion. Herbert Morrison, Bevin's replacement, would be more sympathetic to MI5 and wouldn't force the pace of the investigation, as the stormy Bevin might have done. With Burgess's conduct in Washington attracting embarrassing notice, the time was opportune to quicken the pace. A March 30 message from Arlington Hall Station to GCHQ in London gave White his opportunity: the GCHQ penetration of the GOM-MER cable citing Maclean's New York visits to his pregnant wife. Whether collusion was responsible for the transfer of that cable from Arlington Hall to London, where it had been broken some time earlier, is unanswerable but not unlikely. In any case, Maclean's visits to his wife (Meredith Gardner's "marital detail") had been known to London since early August 1950 at the latest.

With the GOMMER cable in hand, Dick White could inform the Foreign Office seniors that a newly recovered Venona cable had finally and conclusively identified Maclean as HOMER. He could do so without compromising MI5's identification of Maclean as a Soviet agent prior to his November 1950 recall to the Foreign Office. Until British declassification policy is overhauled, we will never know when nor how Maclean's guilt had been established. It might have been as early as mid-1948 or as late as the first months of 1949. What is certain is that the June 1944 GOMMER cable didn't first or conclusively identify Maclean. Dick White could give the Foreign Office that Venona intelligence because it served his purpose, not because it was MI5's vital clue that finally and belatedly established Maclean as the source of the embassy leaks.

Official documents released in London in 1963 supply a few details on the consequences of the GOMMER cable but without identifying it as the source. On April 16, 1951, Sir William Strang, the Foreign Office permanent undersecretary, met with unnamed "Security Service" officials, including Sillitoe and White, to review the Maclean case. The Foreign Office account noted that Maclean had come under suspicion but that he wasn't the only or sole suspect.[24] That record doesn't clarify whether White disclosed that a new Venona decrypt had positively identified Maclean or postponed the disclosure until later to forestall any Foreign Office request that Maclean be immediately interrogated, an insistence that would have ended the MI5 deception. It is possible he cited the incriminating GOMMER cable but pleaded for additional time to put Maclean under surveillance to take advantage of what Foreign Office officials would believe was MI5's apparently new and unique opportunity to learn where the espionage trail might lead.

In agreeing to White's request, Strang would have excused the Foreign Office's indulgence of MI5 in not immediately confronting Maclean by claiming he was only one of several suspects. The official record doesn't clarify the matter.

At a meeting the following day, Maclean was singled out. On April 17, Strang met with Morrison and proposed that MI5 investigate Maclean's past history and his "present activities," meaning officially put him under MI5 surveillance. Morrison agreed and signed the order formally authorizing Maclean's watch and limiting his access to sensitive intelligence.[25] Sillitoe immediately informed Hoover in Washington through Philby's MI6 cipher that Maclean now was under surveillance. Sillitoe's April 17 message is confirmed by Philby's comment in *My Silent War* that he had been told by MI5 that certain Foreign Office papers would be withheld from Maclean and his movements put under surveillance.[26] In Moscow in the 1980s he told Genrikh Borovik that he was the first to learn Maclean was under surveillance and had handed the information personally to the FBI, presumably to deputy director Mickey Ladd.[27]

Dick White's intent was to prompt Philby to action, as he soon did. Philby arranged to send Burgess to London to warn Maclean. On April 16 or 17, Ambassador Franks made the complementary decision: he summoned Burgess and dismissed him. He would be sent home. The April 17 Sillitoe report to Hoover also provoked Philby to send a memo to MI6 in London suggesting further exploration of a 1940 allegation by a Soviet defector, Walter Krivitsky, that a well-born Englishman in the Foreign Ministry was a Soviet agent. By singling out Maclean, now a suspect, Philby hoped to escape suspicion himself, reasoning that after Maclean fled he could claim he had helped identify HOMER.[28] His Krivitsky memo made no sense unless Maclean escaped from England before he was interrogated. Maclean's escape was precisely what Philby was planning. In one of only two of Philby's documented face-to-face meetings with his KGB illegal, Makayev found him distraught: STANLEY, he reported, "demanded HOMER's immediate exfiltration to the USSR, so that he himself would not be compromised."[29]

In 1986 Sir Patrick Reilly recalled that the Foreign Office, with typical eagerness to cleanse its stable, was impatient to bring Maclean in for questioning but that Dick White continued to insist on the delay. White needed additional time, not to investigate Maclean, but to await Burgess's arrival in England. Reilly and the Foreign Office knew nothing of the purpose of Maclean's recall to the Foreign Office and had no reason to believe MI5's inquiry extended beyond Maclean. Reilly was told the intent of Sillitoe's messages through the MI6 cipher was to keep Hoover abreast of the latest developments in the Maclean case and avoid any difficulties with the easily offended director, who had been outraged at a British magistrate's decision forbidding the FBI's interrogation of Klaus Fuchs until after his February 1950 sentencing. Hoover's fury was widely known, as Dick White recognized very well: in early 1950 Hoover had threatened to break off cooperation with MI5. The intent was plausible and Reilly didn't question it.

At some time before Burgess's departure, Valentine Vivian of MI6, who wasn't privy to Dick White's purpose, answered Philby's memo and told him the Krivitsky suggestion had been on their minds. How seriously? Enough that a short list of "perhaps six names" or suspects was soon sent from London to Philby to prove MI5 and MI6 sincerity. The names included Paul Gore-Booth, Michael Wright, Donald Maclean, and Roger Makins.[30] Robert Mackenzie, the British embassy security officer, confirmed that Makins's name was on the list.[31] (Makins wasn't posted to Washington until early 1945, after the New York to Moscow cables of August 1944.)

As we've seen, Roger Makins was Dick White's accessory. He had arranged for Maclean to resume his career at the Foreign Office in November 1950 so he could be watched, and perhaps arranged Burgess's May 1950 assignment to Washington as well. Now Makins's name was given to Philby as among the final HOMER suspects identified by MI5 and passed on to him by MI6. Since the first list of suspects had been drawn up, Philby had been deliberately misled on the progress of the investigation. Far from being the abandoned victim of the flight of Maclean and Burgess when it was thought he first came under suspicion, he was as much the object of the MI5 deception as Maclean. He was being flummoxed, as was his surrogate messenger Guy Burgess.

Burgess didn't leave Washington quickly, as Philby no doubt hoped and MI5 might have expected. He dallied about New York and Washington for a time, said his farewells, had a final dinner with Philby in New York, and sailed for London on May 1. He arrived on May 7 and was met by Anthony Blunt, who alerted Yuri Modin, as described earlier. MI5 continued to watch and wait through those last weeks. The watch didn't extend to Maclean's house at Tatsfield, as we know, but by May, Dick White's MI5 A Branch electronic eavesdroppers would have had seven months to install an S.F. or Special Facility operation, planting a phone tap or a microphone at the Maclean residence, and establish other surveillance posts nearby in the village, a common practice.

Toward the end of May, as Reilly recalled—undoubtedly during the May

21–25 work week at the Foreign Office—Dick White finally declared MI5 ready to interrogate Maclean. Reilly remembered too that "some hitch with the FBI caused a last minute delay." Again the Foreign Office was impatient but Sillitoe wanted to be "in step with the FBI," whatever that meant. Reilly didn't explain because he didn't know. During that week Foreign officials, including Strang and Reilly, drafted the necessary documents for submission to the foreign secretary ordering Maclean's arrest and interrogation, including the proposed dates. On May 23 or 24 Sillitoe informed Hoover. Reilly recalled that the "full details of the plan were telegraphed to Washington (via Philby)" through the MI6 channel in Washington.[32]

Philby read the Sillitoe message and wrongly concluded MI5 had been mobilized by his own suggestion weeks earlier to explore the Krivitsky claim. He was stunned by the speed with which his lead was pursued and Maclean identified. Now Maclean was to be arrested and interrogated. In despair, Philby met on May 24 with his Soviet illegal, Makayev, who found him "alarmed and concerned for his own security." He insisted that he would be at risk if Burgess fled to Moscow with Maclean.[33] This is the second of the two documented meetings Philby had with Makayev, who wouldn't have been of immediate help. His channel to Moscow was by way of a mail or courier route; the mail route was to a mail drop in London, the courier route through Finland using a Finnish sailor. (Had GCHQ believed Philby's distress would have resulted in a flurry of Washington to London traffic from the Soviet embassy in Washington, they would have been disappointed.)

Impatient for word, Philby had also sent off a cleverly disguised airmail letter to Burgess warning him that "if he did not act at once it would be too late." He was referring to the disposition of Burgess's abandoned Lincoln Continental, which might soon be impounded, but his words "It is getting hot here" meant Maclean had to be gotten out of England. So he was.[34]

On May 25 Strang submitted a summary of the Maclean case to Morrison proposing that Maclean be interviewed by MI5 between June 18 and June 25. Morrison agreed. (The official Foreign Office version differs from the recollection of Patrick Reilly, who mistakenly believed Maclean was to be interrogated the week of May 28.) And so on Friday, May 25, 1951, more than a month after the foreign secretary's April 17 surveillance order and Burgess's dismissal, seven months after Maclean was welcomed back to the Foreign Office as the suspected spy, and twenty-eight interminable months after MI5 launched its investigation, Morrison formally authorized his arrest and interrogation. MI5 would soon have in hand the results of its inquiry, or so the Foreign Office imagined; Maclean would quickly break down; and MI5 would obtain a full and complete admission of guilt, as had happened so easily and quickly with Allan Nunn May and Klaus Fuchs. At long last, after more than two troubling years, the Foreign Office ranks would be swept clean. The prospects must have seemed promising, to the relief of the Foreign Office's William Strang, Patrick Reilly, and Carey-Foster that Friday evening as they left Whitehall. That night Maclean and Burgess sailed off to St. Malo on the SS *Falaise*. On Monday morning, and during the weeks, months, and years that followed, things only got worse.

For years to come, journalists, writers, intelligence analysts, and historians would search for final answers. How did it happen? What went wrong? Who was responsible? As the years passed, the search would widen as the answers multiplied and flourished, fed by hearsay, error, rumor, innuendo, and ignorance. Suspicion settled on others, British Soviet agents in high places who were undoubtedly involved and most likely had warned Maclean and Burgess. Were they within Whitehall, MI5's Leconfield House, or MI6 at 54 Broadway or 21 Queen Anne's Gate? Confidence in the British intelligence services would be steadily and disastrously eroded, ugly consequences that were far from Dick White's objectives. There could be no final answers. If the relatively routine counterespionage operation had secretly succeeded, public scorn, suspicion, and contempt overwhelmingly compromised its success.

Chapter SEVEN

Making sense of it.—What everyone believed.—No
more than two.—Miscalculation.—Yuri Modin's
account.—A few red herrings.—Was Cairncross
flummoxed?—Modin's network wiped out.—Philby
ponders the past.—The enigmatic Jack Easton.—
General Leslie Hollis visits the Joint Chiefs.—
Sillitoe calls on Hoover.—MI5's Philby file.—
The Volkov affair.—Litzi Philby.—Philby is
offered Washington.—Makayev in New York.

The Maclean case baffled the Foreign Office and the three officials who had unwittingly helped Dick White carry out the MI5 counterespionage deception. Over time, a few added scraps from their own memories of those final months in 1950–1951, as did Patrick Reilly. So did Sir Roger Makins but his November 1985 explanations of Maclean's November 1950 recall were ignored. Not widely known, they were given to a British historian, Anthony Glees, unfairly dismissed by one Maclean chronicler, Robert Cecil, as an "ill-informed academic writer." Cecil had read Glees's account and was near completion of his own very useful book; Makins's comment compromised several of his conclusions.

Sir Patrick Reilly didn't mention the April 1951 decrypt to Professor Glees, but he may have been a confidential source for others. Venona, then known as Bride, had finally supplied the identifying detail the three Foreign Office officials had been expecting for many, many months but they had to trust the interpretations of their source, Dick White, whose secrets came to them secondhand. Yet the secret got out. Robert Cecil was able to write that by mid-April the final piece of cryptanalytical evidence had come in and it was clear that Maclean was HOMER. White had never uttered a word of clarification in public or in private and Cecil's source was "private information."[1] Venona's twelve Maclean cables in their full and final versions would have told a different story but they remained closed. After their 1996 publication in incomplete or fragmented versions, they attracted little notice. It didn't help that they were scattered at random among some three thousand Venona texts. The same faulty interpretations that had prevailed over the decades were sustained.

Also curious was the freedom of the Russian and English conspirators dodging about London or motoring away from the Soviet embassy at 13 Kensington Palace Garden those several weeks in May. Where were the MI5 and Special Branch watchers during the conversational strolls in St. George's Park in Wandsworth, a Russian favorite, and elsewhere? And then there was Blunt, meeting with Burgess, and Burgess himself, vanished inexplicably with Maclean, condemning Philby, if only by his association, to his final exile. Who could make sense of it?

The Foreign Office couldn't. In April and May, Strang, Reilly, and Carey-Foster assumed MI5's pursuit was confined to Donald Maclean and no one else. None had any reason to suppose the purpose in obtaining Foreign Secretary Morrison's April surveillance order and the ensuing delay until May 25, 1951, was intended to do anything other than gather enough additional evidence for Maclean's successful interrogation. This was what the Foreign Office believed, what Kim Philby, Guy Burgess, Anthony Blunt, Yuri Modin, the KGB residency, and its chief, Rodin, believed. Reilly's comments in 1985–1986 show he had no reason to suspect anyone other than Maclean. Not until the flight of Burgess and Maclean did he realize Burgess and Philby were also involved.[2] The Foreign Office knew nothing of Dick White's interest in anyone other than Maclean. The KGB's footsore but tirelessly resourceful Yuri Modin, who has told us much of what we know about those weeks, knew only his own success in planning and executing Maclean's escape.

The expectation that the MI5 interrogation would soon take place had provoked all to action. In Washington, Philby sent Burgess to London; Burgess enlisted the help of Blunt, who told Modin, who dutifully informed Rodin, who then had to ask for instructions from Moscow Center. As Rebecca West pointed out in 1964, long before rumor, hearsay, and conjecture had trampled over the huntmen's casting ground, it was a very odd way of doing business, so odd in fact she found it "incomprehensible."[3] Philby had merely to tell his Russian control in Washington that Maclean was under suspicion and was to be interrogated, and the Soviet communications network would have quickly carried the message to London. But it didn't happen that way. Philby had twice appealed to his Soviet illegal for help. His second appeal came after Burgess was already in London. If Modin is to be believed, the Soviet residence in London knew nothing of the threat to Maclean until Modin received Blunt's call for help, which he had to confirm in a personal meeting with Burgess (Modin knew nothing of the Soviet illegal in New York).

As Dick White no doubt had foreseen, all five had conspired in anticipation of an interrogation that never took place; each had his own reasons for making sure it didn't. Philby feared he would be at risk; Burgess did too, but unlike Philby he was moved by his devotion to Maclean. Modin feared the interrogation "would wipe out our entire network," as Blunt told him in passing on Burgess's message.[4] Nikolai Rodin's concern was probably similar. For senior Foreign Office diplomats, however, unaware of all that Dick White knew and planned or that the conspirators knew and feared, Maclean was the beginning and the end. Impatient at White's delay from mid-April through May, they were determined to bring him to account, an impatience that was as much personal as professional. He was the betrayer, the anomaly, a single aberrant diplomat who had disgraced the Foreign Office and Her Majesty's Government. For Dick White, Maclean wasn't the end but the means to a larger and more inclusive end that embraced anyone and everyone to whom Yuri Modin, Nikolai Rodin, Maclean, and Burgess would lead him in London. But most particularly for those MI6's doubters in Trevor-Roper's mandarinate, he would expose Kim Philby as a Soviet agent.

From Burgess's return to London the first week in May until May 25, the most surprising aspect of Soviet control of London's Cambridge Five as described by Yuri Modin was the fact that only two Russians were involved. Had MI5 been discreetly on the heels of the conspirators in London after Burgess's return, they may have been astonished as well. At the time, there were more than a hundred Russians on the Soviet embassy staff and an additional hundred or so attached to the Soviet trade delegation. Unknown to anyone except the Soviet embassy and MI5, however, only two KGB officers handled Burgess and Blunt, Yuri Modin and Nikolai Rodin. Modin also controlled two other London agents, the semiretired Anthony Blunt, who was not as retired as everyone thought, and the active John Cairncross. The KGB pair had worked together since September 1949, when Philby passed the results of his briefing by Maurice Oldfield to Burgess for onward delivery to Modin, and they now worked in planning the escape of Maclean and

Burgess. No Soviet illegals were brought into service, as with Philby in Washington; nor were other Soviet agents dispatched in and out of London to lend support, which remained in the hands of the same pair at the Soviet embassy.

It is possible Moscow Center gave only minimal significance and support to Maclean and Burgess, the "two burnt-out agents on our hands," as Yuri Modin cynically commented. Given the simplicity of KGB control and the presence of only two moving Russian targets, MI5's aim was also simplified and at least one purpose achieved, although a month or so would have been necessary for conclusive verification that Soviet control consisted of a solitary pair whose London network didn't reach beyond Burgess, Blunt, and Maclean (we'll come to Cairncross later). This would have been important for MI5. If its purpose had been achieved, Maclean's delayed interrogation may no longer have mattered—or perhaps was never intended to take place, but that is most unlikely.

At Arlington Hall Station reconstruction of a KGB codebook had enabled Meredith Gardner's team to read hundreds of Soviet messages sent from November 1943 until early 1946. They also included hundreds of Soviet cover names, so many that in 1948 the FBI was called in to help the ASA's cryptologists by matching detail contained in the broken Venona messages with information in the FBI's own extensive files.[5] In England GCHQ's attack on Soviet traffic paralleled Arlington Hall's Venona project as did its success in recovering Soviet texts and codenames from the London to Moscow circuit. MI5 played the same role as the FBI in Washington in matching GCHQ Soviet cover names and detail in the broken texts with information in MI5 files and watch lists in the search for candidates or suspects. By 1948 and 1949, if not earlier, those GCHQ recoveries had begun to yield scores of KGB codenames, including HICKS (Burgess), JOHNSON (Blunt), MOLIERE (Cairncross), and STANLEY (Philby).[6]

Besides believing Donald Maclean was the sole object of the MI5 investigation, Philby, Burgess, Blunt, Yuri Modin, and Nikolai Rodin were convinced Maclean's confession was essential for MI5. And for the three Foreign Office seniors who knew the Venona material would never be used in court and who had little idea of the many Foreign Office secrets Maclean had passed to Moscow, the purpose of the prolonged delay from mid-April until late May was to gather courtroom evidence. An arrest and interrogation that resulted in a full confession would confirm his guilt and produce even more useful intelligence. Dick White, however, knew all he needed to know about

Maclean's espionage as well as the complicity of his two Cambridge colleagues, Philby and Burgess, who were included in the deception. Maclean's guilt had been established beyond question by the 1948–1950 Venona decrypts the Foreign Office had never read: he had betrayed top-secret information to Moscow in 1944–1945, including details on the Yalta negotiations and a few details from at least one Churchill to Roosevelt cable of July 1944 discussing Anglo-American war plans for the Mediterranean.

Had White been convinced Maclean's interrogation and confession were essential to corroborate what he already knew or turn up other important details, physical surveillance of Maclean and Burgess at Tatsfield or elsewhere in England wouldn't have been forfeited. Had more watchers been needed by MI5, they could easily have been pressed into service. In January 1961, during a much larger and more complex operation, MI5 had no hesitation in asking Special Branch (Scotland Yard) for help in supplying the additional men required to successfully bring in three very experienced and elusive Soviet illegals and their English agent.

The Soviet illegals were the slippery Gordon Lonsdale, and the equally slippery American couple Peter and Helen Kroger; Harry Houghton was the luckless British agent. None was in contact with the Soviet embassy in London. Having covertly identified all three, MI5 had no intention of bringing them in but planned to maintain surveillance to identify any other British agents under their control. To MI5's chagrin, the advantage was lost after a Polish CIA agent whose information had led to Houghton sent word he would soon defect. With his defection known, the three Soviet illegals would quickly vanish, as they had in years past. So too would any other English KGB agents under their control as yet unidentified. MI5 was forced to act and act it did; all three very cunning Soviet illegals were successfully bagged.[7]

MI5's failure to extend its physical surveillance to Tatsfield in May 1951 because of a shortage of foot soldiers might have been a convenient fiction. By May 25 Maclean and Burgess had served their purpose to a limited extent. There were no Gordon Lonsdales, no Peter and Helen Krogers, just Modin and the chief he held in silent contempt, Nikolai Rodin. Their careers were over, as Modin's "burnt-out agents" description suggests. Flight would confirm Maclean's guilt as it did Burgess's, even if it remained ambiguous for everyone else for more than three years. It could be argued that whether or not they took to their heels wasn't of great consequence or, as others have suggested, that they were simply permitted to escape. The White Paper claim that surveillance at the small village of Tatsfield would have been too conspicuous is true enough. MI5 was similarly cautious in its September–December 1949 surveillance of Klaus Fuchs at Harwell; and both were the responsibility of the same MI5 officer, James Robertson.

Nevertheless, it is impossible to believe that Dick White didn't intend to interrogate Maclean during the week of June 18–25 with the grilling of both Burgess and Philby to follow. The dates suggest Maclean's questioning was to take place during Melinda Maclean's hospitalization when she gave birth to another child. Even if the Venona cables and his 1944–1945 duties at the Washington embassy had established his guilt, questioning Maclean was essential to bring the whole affair to a conclusion. Venona needn't have been put at risk. Interrogation could have begun with the most damning Venona evidence—the late July 1944 Churchill cable to Roosevelt or the Anthony Eden cables to Lord Halifax in the March 8–16, 1945, Yalta series. The source could have been convincingly disguised, attributed to a Soviet defector in Washington or an MI5 or MI6 asset in place. Confronted with the precise dates and details, it is also difficult to believe Maclean, weakly vulnerable, wouldn't have broken down and confessed, finally ridding himself of the dirty trade he so despised. Had his confession been complete he might have incriminated Burgess and Philby, but even without his full cooperation his arrest and secret interrogation would have given MI5 a very powerful tool for questioning Philby and Burgess, his faithful courier.

Dick White evidently had already made plans for Philby's interrogation as a suspected Soviet agent. Not all of those detailed Philby files accompanied Sir Percy Sillitoe and Arthur Martin to Washington in early June to brief J. Edgar Hoover. Similar files had undoubtedly been prepared for Burgess.

But Maclean wasn't interrogated and we don't know the reasons. The most probable explanation is the simplest: something went disastrously wrong on May 25. Until then the operation had yielded everything expected of it; all had fallen into place, and the long-anticipated end was in sight. Perhaps too much success had encouraged too much confidence in the predictability of the coming days and weeks. May 25 was Maclean's thirty-eighth birthday; Melinda had prepared a special baked ham dinner at Beaconshaw, their house at Tatsfield. A visitor had arrived unannounced. His name was Roger Styles. Had MI5's installed devices picked up the name? If they had, it meant nothing. The MI5 team may have been convinced he would never have left his wife two weeks before she gave birth or that the second ticket Burgess had purchased for the SS *Falaise* wasn't for Maclean but for his homosexual companion. A few misjudgments, a mistaken assumption, a miscalculation, or a minor failure in communications or co-ordination, any of these could explain the lapses on May 25. But the two had fled and on Monday morning George Carey-Foster telephoned Dick White to tell him Maclean had disappeared. His wife had phoned to ask if the Foreign Office knew his whereabouts. White flew to Paris a few days later to consult with the French authorities on their investigation but without success.[8] With Maclean and Burgess gone, the only card left in his very weak hand was Kim Philby. The Philby file had already been assembled and his questioning planned, but for different circumstances. It was to have followed the Maclean interrogation.

In 1985, after Dick White's retirement, he offered a comment that explains something about the incidents of May 7–25, 1951. He believed Soviet intelligence had only "a limited measure of control" over the five Cambridge spies and was left "watching helplessly while all the golden rules were broken."[9] Referring to their clandestine tradecraft, perhaps their eluding surveillance as well, he might have included Yuri Modin and Nikolai Rodin. He characterized the Cambridge ring of five as "a bunch of interconnected amateurs" who presented the NKVD with "a kind of intelligence nightmare." So they evidently did. But the successful escape also proved to be a nightmare for MI5 and would haunt its ranks for years to come. The most enduring consequence was the forced fabrication of the September 1955 White Paper, a document that continued to haunt British intelligence in 1995.

Yuri Modin believed he knew very well what had happened and has recounted in detail how he brought off Maclean's escape those last weeks. He was successful because MI5 was in paralysis, or so he tells us.[10] With no reason to suspect Burgess and with MI5 incapable of any of the multiple counterintelligence techniques, except the most rudimentary visual surveillance by one watcher on foot, the conspirators had eluded detection. MI5 surveillance was rare but always conspicuous, he claims, conducted by inexperienced "greenhorns," as well as trainees. Easily dodging the clumsy novices, he met with Blunt, Burgess, and Cairncross in "streets, parks and squares well away from central London." He doesn't explain that conspicuous surveillance helps convince the subject of its predictably routine nature, as it also preys on the nerves of the accused. Watchers who come and go as visibly and reliably as Maclean's morning and evening train conceal more intensive and unobtrusive surveillance. Once a subject believes he or she has cleaned him- or herself of surveillance, as Modin is convinced he always did on his way to an assignation, he or she will safely resume his or her journey unaware of any far less visible surveillance now in place. Other forms of visual surveillance, including the use of multiple watchers, men and women, young and old, daily observation from static posts, and progressive surveillance along a suspect's usual route of travel using wired watchers on foot, in cars, on bicycles, even a woman pushing a pram, are ignored as the subject is passed from one watcher to the next. Modin also ignores the most important instruments of all, audio or electronic surveillance, the use of phone taps, surreptitious entry, the planting of listening devices, and black-bag operations leaving all evidence behind intact and undisturbed. As Dick White admitted years later, he knew the details of Burgess's conversation with Maclean at the Reform Club.[11] He would have left much more unsaid.

One incident in particular betrays the improbability of Modin's claims. He tells us MI5 hadn't searched Burgess's flat on New Bond Street after his flight because it had no reason to suspect Burgess until he disappeared. Once aware of his role, MI5 asked Blunt, Burgess's intermediary, to get a key to the flat through a third party. Modin believed "this breathtaking almost comical stroke of luck gave us several hours to tidy up after Burgess and destroy anything that might compromise us or one of our agents." Was it so simple? Not at all and here we confront the patchwork of fact, fancy, and official misinformation that so obscures those May events.

During an interview in 1982, Blunt disclosed that MI5 asked his help in gaining access to Burgess's flat to avoid the publicity of a search warrant. He found Philby's "Getting hot here" letter and removed it along with other incriminating documents.[12] According to an MI5 officer, however, MI5 and Special Branch officers soon followed and discovered the same letter Blunt insisted he had removed. Years later in Moscow Burgess denied he had left the letter behind. This farrago of contradictory claims defies all but the simplest answer. If MI5 knew of the Philby letter, as it obviously did, the letter had been either intercepted by a mail cover at MI5's Special Investigations Unit at the London Post Office or photographed earlier in Burgess's flat. The notion that MI5 would have required a warrant to search Burgess's apartment is as implausible as the idea the flat would not have been searched long before. Modin's pride is forgivable but he isn't to be believed.

He also tells us in his memoir, as noted earlier, that like Blunt he feared Maclean's interrogation "would wipe out our entire network." Maclean was never interrogated yet this is precisely what happened. In June 1951, a month after Burgess and Maclean fled, Modin found himself under surveillance as he was within a few hundred yards of meeting John Cairncross, the fifth member of the Cambridge Five spy ring. He broke off contact. Cairncross is said to have been incriminated by documents allegedly found by MI5 in Burgess's flat after his flight—another MI5 red herring.[13] On May 1, 1951, he had been transferred from Treasury to the Ministry of Supply on temporary loan, a relocation he didn't solicit but that gave him access to top-secret documents on British rearmament and weapons development. Despite Modin's awareness that Cairncross was under surveillance, during June, July, and August 1951, Cairncross passed innumerable secret documents to Modin. According to a KGB file examined by Nigel West, some of Cairncross's heist of 1,339 pages of British rearmament reports found their way to Stalin. In September and again in December, Cairncross was questioned by MI5. He supplied Yuri Modin with no more secret documents, was eventually dismissed, and ultimately relocated abroad.[14]

Cairncross doesn't concern us here, except for the circumstances of his case, notably his unexpected transfer to the Ministry of Supply, the British agency responsible for nuclear weapons and other weapons production. Two years earlier, in 1949, a British deception team began work with the Ministry of Supply in planning a disinformation operation to mislead Moscow on Britain's development of biological weapons.[15] Whether Cairncross's transfer was part of that operation or his pilfered documents included details on a bogus biological warfare scheme isn't known, but his unexpected move has all the familiar earmarks of a combined British intelligence disinformation operation. In any case, once Cairncross had completed his document deliveries to Yuri Modin, his espionage days were over and he was banished.

MI5's deception of Burgess indicates MI5 must have been well aware of Blunt's role. A few fragments from KGB files Nigel West examined in Moscow suggest as much, but Blunt doesn't concern us here.[16] He was unquestionably a unique case and would remain so for some years. With Blunt, Dick White's reach may have exceeded his grasp as well as his purpose. The king's royal servant and the surveyor of the king's pictures couldn't be treated as Cairncross was, brought in to be questioned, watched, and finally dismissed. Blunt had retired from government service in 1945, had no access to government documents, and was inactive except in times of special need and then as a kind of benign intermediary. Confronting or directly implicating Blunt would have served no purpose; the judgment would have violated not royal privilege but common sense. For MI5 to acknowledge his role even in secret would have been to admit more than it wanted known, as with Cairncross. He was also useful for MI5, as Cairncross had been those last eight months, which meant he could be continually monitored. In any case, with Burgess and Maclean eliminated, Blunt neutralized, and Philby soon to follow, all five members of the Cambridge spy ring had been removed from service. Neither Blunt nor Cairncross would be specifically named until years later.

Modin's network had been wiped out, just as he had feared, but not because of Maclean's interrogation. MI5 had been a step ahead of Maclean, Burgess, Philby, and the KGB from November 1950 until June 1951, and no doubt much earlier. That possibility has never been acknowledged or even suggested. When Modin left London in 1953, he was still persuaded he had never been exposed. Commentators agree. Virtually everyone has been quick to accept other versions, including Modin's, and believe the worst of British intelligence. MI5, of course, has had nothing to say.

Philby couldn't quite make sense of the events of those last weeks either. In Moscow, after sixteen years of pondering the mysteries as he composed *My Silent War*, he still couldn't fully sort it all out. He discussed those puzzles years later with Yuri Modin in Moscow. One question in particular he couldn't answer. Had MI5 and MI6 allowed all three to escape: Kim Philby, Donald Maclean, and Guy Burgess? The two men ruled out the possibility in Maclean's case, or at least Modin did. Maclean's arrest and interrogation by MI5 had been scheduled, his case was on the docket, Modin argued.[17] But then we remember that Modin was convinced Maclean's interrogation would have eradicated his entire network, all Cambridge Five: Philby, Maclean, Burgess, Blunt, and Cairncross. It would have been a bitter defeat for Moscow and for Yuri Modin, who seemed to have forgotten that his network had been wiped out.

Since Modin believed he had been indispensable in Maclean's escape, as he certainly was, we can forgive his reluctance to concede the point or admit he might have been duped, whatever Philby might have suspected. Vanity wasn't prominent in Modin's character, only pride of workmanship. The most engaging aspect of his memoir is its absence (he might have been a minor rural official we remember from one of Anton Chekhov's short stories). There are no heroics either, nothing to suggest he ever thought of himself as other than an average Russian efficiently carrying out routine responsibilities in a routine way, as methodical as a walkaround London postman, delivering and collecting his daily intelligence mail. Maclean's escape had been the triumph of his espionage career. But both men agreed that in Philby's case, "the British services had all but ushered him through the door."[18] Philby had implied as much in *My Silent War* in a curious incident some noticed but all wrongly dismissed. It was among the most unusual, revealing, and yet baffling vignettes in the entire book.

The incident occurred on June 6, 1951, in Washington after Maclean and Burgess had disappeared. In *My Silent War* Philby refers to a handwritten letter he received from Sir Jack Easton of MI6, his immediate superior in London. Easton told him he would soon receive a cable recalling him to London and that he should promptly obey. Without naming the letter carrier, Philby describes him as an "intelligence officer who specialized in the fabrication of deception material." The form, content, and message bearer puzzled him. Why should Easton tell him in a handwritten note about a cable soon to be sent through official channels? After thinking about it, he decided that it might be a signal that if he'd been considering escape, the time was now. He dismissed the idea. The London summons home arrived a few days later; he booked an airline flight and packed his bags. Easton met him at the air terminal, another cause for suspicion.[19] Handwritten letters carried by courier disappeared with the invention of the telegraph and the telephone, unless the sender was trying to elude both and leave no official record, as Easton obviously was. Although no MI6 documents ever see the light of day, Easton's letter wasn't intended to be seen by other MI6 officers at the embassy or to be read by anyone other than Philby. But that wasn't how he explained it thirty-five years later.

Easton is an enigmatic figure who, like Dick White, knew far more about the Philby case than he ever revealed. Like any memoirist, Philby is selective in relating scenes from his past. His short book rarely wanders; each event maintains the narrative line or makes a point, often to his advantage, but he also recalls incidents that serve no clear purpose except to suggest his awareness, however vaguely defined, that something curious was underway. His comments on Easton fall in that category. He is the only person named in his book who made Philby uneasy. His "rapier mind," according to Philby, was capable of "deeply subtle twists" and made "his stomach turn over." While Philby was aboard the SS *Caronia,* en route to New York, Easton called him on the ship's telephone and told him Dwyer, his predecessor, had resigned. Philby was puzzled as to why he had been warned. His meaning eludes us, but not his mistrust of Easton.[20] The same undercurrent of suspicion was apparent years later during his many hours of conversation with Genrikh Borovik. Those conversations took place in the late 1980s, forty years after; yet Easton was still very much alive in Philby's memory as he brooded over the past. Borovik concluded that Easton "was dangerously smart" and that Philby "was extremely careful talking to him." Borovik describes Easton's physical appearance, a rare departure for him. Easton had aroused his curiosity.[21]

Philby told Borovik that Easton signed the August 1949 MI6 cable he received in Istanbul offering him the Washington assignment, briefed him on Venona after his return to London in 1949, and interrogated him after his summons home in June 1951 before Dick White's questioning. He mentioned none of this in *My Silent War*, but there was nothing unusual in Easton's role. He was the MI6 officer responsible for liaison with the CIA and Philby was under his direction. What is unusual is that Philby should have been so wary or felt so threatened in dealing with him. Did he mean Easton was duplicitous? At MI6 Easton chaired the Defectors Committee in 1948 and worked with GCHQ and the London Controlling Section in search of deception opportunities, as did Dick White.[22] Philby perhaps knew or had deduced that Easton was involved in deception operations. His allusion to a mind capable of such subtle twists that his stomach churned might suggest that Easton had once proposed to him some hair-raising scheme that had frightening implications for Philby. We will never know what so aroused Philby's uneasiness but it is clear that Easton was singled out unlike anyone else.

Jack Easton shed some light on his June 1951 note thirty-five years later. In a 1986–1987 series of letters and interviews with Anthony Cave Brown, he identified his letter carrier to Philby as John Drew but offered no more.[23] Unknown to Cave Brown, there was much more. Then in retirement at Grosse Point, Michigan, Easton explained his letter had been written at the request of "C" and given to Drew, who happened to be leaving for Washington on official business. The purpose was to warn Philby of the coming cable recalling him to London so he could quickly pack up and hustle out of town before Percy Sillitoe arrived for his talks with J. Edgar Hoover. MI6 wanted to make sure Philby was beyond Hoover's grasp and unavailable for FBI interrogation. The choice of Drew was fortuitous, so Easton claimed. He happened to be leaving for Washington that evening. Moreover, if Philby viewed his message with suspicion, his own guilty conscience was responsible. He told Cave Brown that "anyone who tried that [disinformation] with him was a fool, for Kim had a quite remarkable sixth sense at detecting the lie in a report."

Easton's explanation isn't persuasive. If he was carrying out "C"'s instructions, a phone call would have been sufficient. If the substance of Sillitoe's brief on the Maclean and Burgess embarrassment was damaging enough to provoke Hoover's fury, Philby's diplomatic immunity would have kept him out of reach. To avoid difficulties, however, it would have been wiser to delay Sillitoe's trip until Philby left. Had Easton's note warning Philby to "obey the call promptly" suggested to him that danger was imminent, he might indeed have had reason to believe that Easton was showing him an open door.[24]

John Drew was an Air Ministry officer accustomed to carrying handwritten messages that left no documented record or retrievable traces. The mechanics of deception operations, especially in peacetime, more often employ oral instructions but if these aren't possible then a handwritten note must do. Drew was familiar with both as was Jack Easton. In June 1951 Drew led the Department of Forward Plans that succeeded the Hollis Committee's London Controlling Section in 1950 and was responsible for British deception operations centered in the Ministry of Defense. An experienced deceptions officer, in 1944 he was with Britain's Home Defense Executive and worked with British air intelligence to successfully deceive the Germans in targeting the V1 bombs on London. After the war, Drew was attached to the London Controlling Section while assigned to the Air Ministry. When the LCS was reorganized, he assumed command.[25] The handwritten note he carried to Washington on the heels of the disappearance of Maclean and Burgess was even more peculiar than Philby took it to be. As an officer of the old London Controlling Section and head of the new Department of Forward Plans, John Drew was the only person Easton knew he could trust with his note.

The absolute secrecy and the effort to avoid official cables, letters, or even any minutes that might record the discussion of deception plans is illustrated by a letter General Leslie Hollis wrote in Washington on Sunday, April 11, 1948. General Hollis was secretary of the British Joint Chiefs of Staff Committee and at the time headed the LCS. He had come to Washington to represent the British chiefs of staff at the U.S.-U.K.-Canadian meetings exploring prospects for an Atlantic defense pact. Discussions began at the Pentagon on March 22–23 (Donald Maclean sat in with the British embassy contingent). On that Sunday in April, Hollis had planned to fly to Ottawa, return to Washington the following Tuesday, and meet privately with Major General Alfred M. Gruenther, director of the U.S. Joint Staff, before traveling on to New York Wednesday to catch his boat for England.

Bad weather cancelled his Sunday flight to Ottawa and he found himself stranded in Washington, his plans to return scuttled as well. The previous Thursday, April 8, he had represented the British chiefs of staff in a top-secret Pentagon meeting with Gruenther and the U.S. Joint Chiefs of Staff to consider a top-secret memorandum Hollis had brought from London. No minutes were kept and General Hollis wanted to be certain he hadn't drawn the wrong conclusions from that April 8 meeting. This was the urgent subject he had intended to discuss personally with General Gruenther on Tuesday.

On that Sunday, with no other choice, General Hollis wrote a top-secret personal "My dear Al" letter to General Gruenther. His brief one-page letter explained his travel predicament, the value of his meeting with the Joint Chiefs of Staff, and the importance to him of setting out the broad conclusions they had reached. To his letter he attached a single-page top-secret summary outlining the unnamed "broad conclusions." The subject isn't mentioned in his letter or his memorandum. He then told Gruenther he had asked a British officer to get in touch with an American officer "on the matter we discussed." His letter resumes: "I am glad to hear that Dr. Bush is going to London shortly and will discuss deception with Lord Portal. I mentioned to you that one of Menzies' representatives, Easton (Air Commodore ret'd), will be here any day now. He can talk about deception in general terms as distinct from the particular aspect referred to by Bush at Mr. Forrestal's dinner."[26]

Lord Portal, formerly chief of the British air staff, was controller of atomic energy under the Ministry of Supply. Vannevar Bush was the scientific adviser on nuclear matters. Hollis then advised Gruenther that should he want to write to him privately, the letter would be forwarded in the British Joint Services Mission official bag to be "opened by nobody but myself."

One of the two conclusions Hollis believed had been reached at the April 8 meeting with the Joint Chiefs was an agreement "that following the visit of the British Planners to Washington, it might be desirable to reestablish some more permanent form of combined planning within the orbit of the Combined Chiefs of Staff Organization." The unnamed subject of Hollis's memorandum was the reestablishment of a combined U.S.-U.K. deception effort. During the war years, the London Controlling Section was represented on the British Joint Services Mission at the Pentagon.

Jack Easton was involved in British deception plans, worked with the LCS, and from time to time visited Washington, where he met with military officers as well as the CIA. We don't know what those plans were. Philby deeply mistrusted him for reasons that aren't clear except that he had too devious, too clever a mind. So did Philby. Yet, reading his comments, one might conclude that he was guileless compared to the cunning Jack Easton. Poor Philby. Marching heroically forward under the secret banner of Felix Dzerzhinsky, the great humanist, the knight of the revolution, he was ambushed by Jack Easton, whose Machiavellian twists of mind so frightened him his stomach turned flip-flops. Philby's pretense is as disingenuous as Easton's. His forbidding descriptions of Easton in *My Silent War* and his account of the handwritten letter delivered by the deception officer John Drew would have carried a message to those few in London who knew, as we don't, why he felt as he did.

We can only guess what Dick White thought when he read Philby's 1968 account of Easton's letter: disbelief, astonishment, perhaps followed by outrage. Years later, as he reflected on the past, White commented on Easton. "The art of intelligence missed him completely," he told Tom Bower.[27] Dick White and Jack Easton knew far more than anyone else in London about Philby and were virtually alone in their conviction that he was a Soviet agent. But it is a mistake to assume they agreed on how to use that knowledge or conviction to best advantage or that White was fully aware of Easton's activities in Washington.

On June 12, 1951, Sillitoe arrived in Washington on the instructions of Prime Minister Attlee to meet with Hoover to explain London's view of the Maclean-Burgess mess. Philby had just flown home. Sillitoe was accompanied by Arthur Martin, the MI5 case officer in the Maclean investigation, who was more familiar with the case than Sillitoe. We don't know what Sillitoe told Hoover but Martin met with FBI special agent Lamphere and told him Maclean was the British embassy spy. Asked where Philby fitted in, Martin said that most of what he had to tell him related to Philby. He gave Lamphere two MI5 memoranda that described the backgrounds of all three—Maclean, Burgess, and Philby—and why they were thought to be Soviet agents. A shorter memorandum summarized MI5's reasons for identifying Philby: (1) Philby, Burgess, and Maclean had all been Communists or left-wing socialists at Cambridge; (2) after Cambridge, Philby had become pro-German to build a cover story; (3) Philby had married Litzi Friedman, an Austrian Communist and a known Soviet agent; (4) former KGB agent Walter Krivitsky had pointed to a British journalist serving with the Franco forces as a Soviet spy; (5) Philby had been directly involved in the suspicious Konstantin Volkov affair (described below); (6) while posted to Turkey,

Philby was involved in an MI6 operation infiltrating Georgian agents into Georgia through Armenia;²⁸ (7) Philby was suspected of playing a part in the disappearance of Burgess and Maclean.²⁹

There was nothing new in these details. Except for the final two points, MI5 could have delivered a similar memo in 1946 before Philby's assignment to Istanbul. His leftist views were widely known in London for years and remembered by some with suspicion. The Krivitsky allegations had been made more than ten years earlier, in January 1940. The Volkov affair had occurred in September 1945, six years past. Philby had revealed his marriage to Litzi Friedman in 1946. These details may well have given MI5 grounds for suspicion but fell far short of establishing guilt. Until that June day in Washington, Lamphere had no reason to suspect either Maclean or Philby. Now the MI5 memorandum indicated that their espionage careers were, in his words, "intertwined." Lamphere was dumbfounded and angry as he belatedly discovered, like many, that he now hated Philby. His reaction went beyond the accumulated details that established nothing more than grounds for MI5 suspicion. Lamphere didn't ask, as he might have, how so comprehensive a dossier could have been so quickly compiled or how long the details had been dormant in the Philby file. But it wasn't improvised at all. It had been assembled in anticipation of Philby's summons home following Maclean's June 18–25 interrogation, as described earlier as part of the Maclean operation.

The Volkov affair is by far the most important episode mentioned by MI5 and the most serious for Philby. By having his exposure threatened, he realized the KGB was no less impregnable than the British services he had so easily penetrated. On September 4, 1945, the NKGB deputy chief in Istanbul, Konstantin Volkov, appeared at the British consulate. He had come in person because his August 27 letter to the British vice consul hadn't been answered. His business was brief, but astounding. He asked for political asylum and fifty thousand pounds in return for disclosing the names of nine British KGB agents whose identities he had learned during his earlier service at Moscow Center. He claimed the nine included two ranking Foreign Office officials, one head of section in British counterintelligence in London, and six others scattered elsewhere in British intelligence. He didn't divulge their names. The two most likely Foreign Office officials were Guy Burgess and Donald Maclean; the counterintelligence section head would have been Kim Philby. The British vice consul asked Volkov to return later and pouched the material to London as Volkov had requested, warning that his offer not be cabled to London: British diplomatic communications weren't secure.[30] Two weeks later London received the pouch and on September 19 Philby read the Volkov document. He was chief of IX, MI6's Soviet counterintelligence section. He quickly informed his Soviet control officer in London, or so one KGB file indicates. Other records in Moscow show that on September 20 Philby called on Burgess at the Foreign Office and gave him an envelope with "an exceptionally urgent message" to be delivered the same evening to his controller, Boris Kreshkin. Philby requested a meeting the following day. The envelope contained the account of Volkov's intended defection.[31]

Accounts vary as to why SIS chief Menzies decided to send Philby to Turkey to handle the Volkov case, just as they differ in describing the sequence of events once he was on the ground in Istanbul. The essential fact is the same: Volkov had disappeared. Either two days before or some days after Philby's tardy arrival in Istanbul from Cairo on September 26, an unconscious, heavily bandaged Volkov and his wife were trundled on litters aboard a Russian aircraft bound for Moscow. At Lubyanka Volkov confessed his intentions and was shot. After Philby's return to London, he explained the Volkov affair to "C" and others as best he could. He suspected Volkov's demand that his proposal be sent to London by diplomatic bag had brought about his downfall. During that delay, Volkov had unwittingly compromised himself. Whether everyone in London was equally convinced is open to question. In an interview with the London journalist Phillip Knightley in Moscow in the 1980s, Philby admitted that from September 1945 until he arrived in Moscow in 1963 he would never again feel secure in his work for the Soviets. His behavior thereafter suggests as much.[32]

Hugh Trevor-Roper mentioned the Volkov affair in his small book on Philby written with Dick White's encouragement in response to *My Silent War*. As described in chapter 4, he had hoped to include new information in his book but implied he was unable to do so because he would have violated the Official Secrets Act. The sensitivity of that detail indicated it came from Dick White and involved the Volkov case. Trevor-Roper touched on the subject but so discreetly as to frustrate interpretation without a clearer understanding of the differences that divided old enemies MI6 and MI5 on the Volkov bungling and Kim Philby. Dick White and others in MI5 suspected Philby had deliberately botched the Volkov defection to abort the possibility of his own exposure. Those suspicions were persuasive enough for Dick White to justify an MI5 "counter-espionage opportunity," as Trevor-Roper described it, that would "make a notable contribution to counter-espionage." In short, MI5 wanted to bait its hook and see if Philby swallowed it. White was confident he would and would be successfully netted by MI5—the "notable contribution to counter-espionage."[33]

But the old mandarinate at MI6, as Trevor-Roper contemptuously described them, didn't believe there was any reason to suspect Philby. And here we return to those differences between MI5 and MI6, or more particularly between Dick White and Jack Easton. Because of their access to GCHQ's broken Soviet cable traffic, both knew far more than anyone about Philby and both evidently agreed that he was a Soviet agent. But they wouldn't have agreed on how to use that knowledge. White was interested in opportunities for counterespionage, in identifying Soviet agents, networks, and their control. Deception was a means to that end. Easton was also interested in deception opportunities, but as a means of deceiving and misinforming the enemy. If Dick White hadn't known precisely what Jack Easton had been up to in Washington in 1949–1950, Philby's description of Easton's handwritten letter carried by John Drew would have told him that Easton had made a very serious blunder.

A year later, in the late summer of 1946, Philby finally confronted a problem he had refused to face for nine years. Since late 1939 he had been living with Aileen Furse, an Indian-born English woman he had met in September 1939. She had borne three children—a daughter born in 1941, two sons the following years—and was then expecting a fourth. Philby and Furse had been living as man and wife for seven years although he was still married to Litzi Friedman, the young Austrian divorcée Philby had met in Vienna in late 1933. Two years older, Friedman was more experienced than the recent Cambridge graduate and a member of the Communist underground. The two became lovers, the first of his many affairs. Through her, the illegal Austrian Communist Party recruited Philby as a courier. As a result of a February 1934 Austrian political crisis (Premier Dollfuss's police struck violently against the Austrian social democrats, the most venerable of all the European socialist parties), Litzi Friedman, identified as a Communist, was being sought by the Vienna police, or so it was claimed. On February 14, 1934, Philby married her at Vienna's city hall, although it isn't clear how a Communist fugitive might have appeared before an official magistrate.[34]

Years later Friedman would call her marriage part convenience, part love. Convenience was fulfilled on February 26 when she was issued a British passport at the British embassy in Vienna. In early May the couple returned to settle in London. In June of that year, Litzi Friedman's Austrian friend

Edith Suchinsky, now Edith Tudor Hart, introduced Philby to the OGPU agent who recruited him for Moscow. By 1937 romance had wearied and the couple parted, without a divorce, to lead separate lives. Litzi soon moved to Paris and became a courier for the KGB.[35]

In the summer of 1946 Philby met with Valentine Vivian, the MI6 deputy in charge of security, to belatedly admit his youthful fling in Vienna. His marriage, he explained, had enabled him to bring Litzi safely to England to rescue her from certain Nazi arrest and imprisonment. He asked permission to contact her to arrange for a divorce. Vivian consented and so did Litzi, then living in East Berlin with a Communist housemate. She met Philby in Vienna and agreed to petition for divorce on grounds of adultery. The divorce decree was issued and on September 17, 1946, Philby was free to marry Aileen Furse. Vivian may have been lenient in recognizing Philby's awkward predicament but he didn't let the matter drop. He asked for a records check. MI5, reportedly Dick White, told him Litzi Friedman Philby was a confirmed Soviet agent.[36] Gestapo documents gathered in Vienna after the war by British military intelligence might have disclosed her Communist Party membership (similar files had revealed that Klaus Fuchs was a member of the German Communist Party). As mentioned above, Friedman, under the Soviet codename MARY, had acted as a KGB courier in Paris in the late 1930s. MI5 wouldn't have known those details, which wouldn't emerge until the 1990s, however.

The Krivitsky claim dates to 1940. In October 1939, a former KGB agent who defected to the United States in December 1938 appeared before the House Un-American Activities Committee and named the chiefs of the GRU espionage network in the United States from 1924 until the day of his testimony, including the incumbent, Boris Bykov. He was Walter Krivitsky (born Samuel Ginsburg but also known by a number of cover names), who had once helped coordinate KGB and OGPU operations in Europe. The British learned through another source that Krivitsky knew of a Soviet agent in Foreign Office communications in London. The lead resulted in the October 1939 arrest of retired army captain John Herbert King, a fifty-five-year-old Foreign Office cipher clerk. A pitiful case, his arraignment and imprisonment were kept secret for seventeen years.

The circulation of Krivitsky's claim that he was aware of a well-born KGB agent in the Imperial Defense Council in London aroused British interest. He was summoned to London and arrived on January 19, 1940. During three weeks of interrogation he revealed the names of one hundred KGB and GRU agents throughout Europe. Of the thirty-five or more Soviet agents he identified in the United Kingdom, sixteen were British subjects, six in the civil service, two in journalism. Half the names were unknown to MI5; the remainder were on a MI5 watch list. Krivitsky also described several Soviet agents whose activities he recalled but not their names. One was a young English journalist sent to Spain with the Franco forces during the Spanish civil war. The description might have identified Philby. Krivitsky was similarly unable to recall the name of the Soviet agent of good family in the Imperial Defense Council; his Oxford background as recalled by Krivitsky didn't match Maclean's. Evidently neither of Krivitsky's leads was further explored.[37]

The significance of the Volkov and Litzi episodes mentioned by MI5 during those June 1951 briefings in Washington would have been known to MI5 and MI6 much earlier. In December 1946, more than a year after the Volkov incident and five months after Philby's admission of his marriage to Litzi and the MI5 notice to Valentine Vivian that she was a known Communist, Philby was relieved of his MI6 post as the head of Soviet counterintelligence and packed off to Istanbul as MI6 station chief.[38] After 1946 he began to pull in his horns and by 1947 had become dependent on Guy Burgess as his courier. In October 1947, months after Philby's arrival in Turkey, GCHQ upgraded its Istanbul intercept station, an upgrade that wouldn't have helped had an increased capability been its purpose.[39] Philby had no Soviet *rezidentura* control officer but used a courier route to Burgess in London. In Moscow years later he would admit to a visitor that he received each of his three subsequent recalls from Istanbul to London for consultations with suspicion and dread as to the reason for his summons.[40]

For Philby, Volkov's September 1945 offer to defect wasn't the only evidence of KGB vulnerability from within. That same month another Soviet defector, Igor Gouzenko, a GRU code clerk at the Soviet embassy in Ottawa, escaped from the shadows of the embassy code room to expose a number of Soviet espionage operations in Canada, the United States, and the United Kingdom. In September 1945 Philby had passed details of the Gouzenko debriefing, obtained because of his MI6 IX role, to his Soviet case officer in London. In November 1945 another defector from the KGB ranks, the American Elizabeth Bentley, began her clandestine cooperation with the FBI. On December 4, 1945, Philby supplied his Soviet handler in London with the names of the forty-one Soviet agents she had identified[41]

In August 1949, after seventeen months in Istanbul, Philby was unexpectedly offered the posting as MI6 station chief in Washington by Jack Easton, which meant curtailing his assignment. He accepted and returned to London. During his September predeparture briefing in London, Sir Maurice Oldfield of MI6 revealed a possible new betrayal that was the most frightening of all. Invisible on the streets, tirelessly unpredictable in its menace, there were no defenses against it, not even an unbreakable one-time pad. Oldfield briefly described a highly successful computerized U.S.-U.K. codebreaking operation that had exposed CHARLES (he didn't identify Klaus Fuchs), found an unidentified British embassy spy—the not yet identified Donald Maclean—and before long would expose others, perhaps even Philby.[42] This was undoubtedly the most burdensome baggage he carried with him when he boarded the SS *Caronia* with his family in late September bound for New York. In the 1980s in Moscow Philby admitted to Knightley he had worried about "radio traffic," meaning exposure by GCHQ intercepts.[43]

One defense against the Anglo-American codebreakers was to stand clear of any involvement with a Soviet embassy or mission and its KGB rezidentura. Philby did this in Washington (the Soviet rezidentura in Washington was also in very difficult straits). A second defense was to assign someone else to carry the intelligence baggage. This he also did, as he had been doing for two years. He supposedly sent messages to Burgess in London, who passed them on to Modin, although available KGB files contain no evidence that he did. Yet another defense was to work with a Soviet illegal based elsewhere who relayed the intelligence by a courier route or through a mail drop and rarely by radio transmission. In due time Moscow supplied Philby with a Soviet illegal.

In March 1950 Valeri Makayev arrived in New York from Poland on the *Batory*, a Polish vessel that should have been well known to the FBI, since it once spirited away a few American Communists fleeing the United States. Makayev, codenamed HARRY, was traveling on a falsely obtained U.S. passport under the name Ivan Kovalik. His bogus identity was borrowed from the real Kovalik. Born to Ukrainian parents in Chicago in 1917, he had returned with his parents to the Ukraine in 1930. After several years in Warsaw establishing his bona fides, Makayev renewed Kovalik's expired 1930 U.S. passport at the American embassy with the help of a blackmailed Polish visa clerk. Moscow bankrolled him with $25,000 to establish a new illegal KGB residency in New York with the help of two other KGB illegals. He was to rely on a circuitous mail or courier route in forwarding any of his agent's reports to Moscow: a mail route to London and a courier route through Finland using a Finnish sailor.[44]

Makayev dallied in setting up his New York apparatus. Something of a musician, he found a position at New York University as an instructor in musical composition and passed his time having an affair with a Polish-born ballerina with a studio in Manhattan. In November 1950 he evidently met in or around Manhattan with Burgess, who was acting as Philby's courier, a meeting documented by Mitrokhin's notes. It isn't clear how many times they met, although they did meet more than once, nor is it known what information was passed. In his 1994 memoir, Yuri Modin doesn't mention Makayev and he knew nothing of the Makayev network. Burgess's clandestine contacts with Makayev in New York, Philadelphia, or the immediate vicinity appeared to be functioning well enough to encourage Philby to finally agree to meet him. KGB files brought out secretly by Mitrokhin identified Makayev but say nothing about Philby meeting him until late in the Maclean investigation. Those two encounters have been described. The last was on May 23 or 24, 1951.

Useless to Philby, Makayev was a second-rater, not in the same class as Philby's earlier OGPU, NKVD and NKGB handlers. In 1951 he had been left $2,000 in a New York dead-letter box by the Soviet New York legal resident to deliver to Philby, presumably following his April or May appeal for help. He failed to retrieve it and the money was never delivered. Given another chance to improve his skills after Philby left Washington, he worked with Moscow's illegal network in New York, which included the best-known of all Russian illegals, Rudolf Abel. Makayev bungled that as well. He lost a hollow coin containing microfilm instructions for another agent (although not the hollow coin found in 1953 that helped compromise Abel, arrested in 1956). Makayev was summoned home to Moscow and fired. The FBI might have regretted he didn't blunder about New York a little longer.

Chapter
EIGHT

Dick White's dilemma.—Philby interrogated.—
Moscow to London cables.—GCHQ's breakdown.—
Unbelievable claims.—Disassociating Philby.—
Historical differences.—Shadowing Klaus
Fuchs.—Philby's London briefing.—Codebreaking
secrets.—Distortion and disinformation.—
Request for asylum.—Modin and Rodin at work.—
Burgess to London.—Conspiracy of dunces.

Guy Burgess's May 25, 1951, flight from Southampton had abandoned
Philby to suspicions that he too was a Soviet agent. Dick White was also
faced with a dilemma. Since at least the summer of 1950 he had misled the
Foreign Office, the FBI, and Philby about MI5's awareness of Maclean's guilt.
He knew far more about Philby than he had ever admitted and used that
knowledge to deceive Philby through his MI6 cipher with the reports he
sent to Hoover on the HOMER investigation. He had provoked Philby to send
Burgess to London to warn Maclean and mobilized the two-man Soviet apparatus in London in their support. Through Maclean he had planned to
expose Philby, whose interrogation would have followed Maclean's with or
without his confession. Philby's grilling would have been based on the file
White had been accumulating since the Volkov affair, when he had first
suspected Philby. But that plan had collapsed with Maclean's escape.

Jack Easton's problem was more difficult. He knew as much about Philby
as Dick White and had used that knowledge differently. At MI6 he was responsible for liaison with the CIA and had had a hand in Philby's assignment to Washington as MI6 station chief; he may even have recommended

him. Had Philby been identified as a suspected Soviet agent following the flight of Maclean and Burgess, the consequences would have been serious for Easton and MI6 but not irreparable. Much more shocking and far less forgivable would have been any evidence that Philby had been identified prior to his Washington posting. This was Easton's predicament. He and Dick White had known for some time that Kim Philby was a suspected Soviet agent. But for how long?

Philby had been identified by the same broken NKVD codebooks and cryptanalytic tools used by Venona at Arlington Hall Station. So had Guy Burgess. Their exposure by GCHQ's codebreakers wasn't revealed until a series of GCHQ cables was published with the fifth NSA release in September 1996. For more than forty-five years, none of the innumerable accounts of the Philby affair had ever mentioned the possibility or explored the likelihood that the same weapons that exposed Maclean had also exposed Philby. The NSA's Venona Historical Monograph no. 5 confirmed that identification but added several troubling caveats. "Only a small set of Moscow KGB messages to London were available for exploitation," the monograph noted, "mostly incoming messages from Moscow Center sent in September 1945." It explained that "this small opening, taken together with the exploitation of certain message [*sic*] of KGB New York and Washington assisted in the identification of important KGB agents Donald Maclean, Kim Philby and Guy Burgess."[1] Unlike Maclean, however, Philby and Burgess were exposed by GCHQ codebreakers in London at a later date, so the monograph concludes, meaning after the May 1951 conclusion of the Maclean case. Since those GCHQ cables, like Venona's Maclean cables, were under London's authority even more exclusively than the latter, no compromising or contradictory evidence from Venona penetrations at Arlington Hall Station could be turned up by curious analysts. The NSA historian also had no way of knowing their accuracy. Those cables were limited to whatever details British intelligence was willing to share. They didn't include the dates of the final or conclusive identifying recoveries because there were none. In fact, there was very little else in those GCHQ Philby and Burgess cables released in October 1996. London's intent in publishing them with the Venona releases was to disassociate Philby and Burgess from the Maclean case.

In Washington, after Burgess's disappearance with Maclean, Philby had two choices. He could bolt for Mexico or the Caribbean in an escape plan he claimed to have discussed with his Soviet handler in London or he could accept his recall to London and face the consequences.[2] Should he have fled, as he suspected Jack Easton had suggested, then his flight, like Burgess's, would have confirmed his guilt and ended the matter once and for all. Easton, he felt, seemed to be nudging him out the door. If Philby took to his heels, he would resolve Easton's more delicate personal problem of knowing Philby was a suspected Soviet agent before his posting to Washington. Dick White knew nothing of Easton's intentions. If Philby was in imminent danger, as Easton seemed to imply, it could only come from MI5, whose head, Percy Sillitoe, would soon meet with Hoover. The only way MI5 could legally establish Philby's guilt was by self-incrimination, either by flight or by confession. Easton had given MI5's game away.

Philby may have reasoned as much or Easton's note may have cited MI5; we don't know all the details. In any case, Philby had kept aloof from the official KGB apparatus in Washington, hadn't had any direct contact with a Soviet embassy handler since September 1949, and concluded there was no legally admissible evidence against him. He decided to return to England. On the bus from the aircraft, he was watched by an MI6 officer and met at the terminal by Easton, who presumably still wasn't sure of his intentions.

In London Easton questioned him first and sat in as Dick White continued at MI5 offices at Leconfield House. White pursued the line of inquiry prepared for Philby's interrogation following Maclean's questioning: his Cambridge political past, his marriage to a known Communist agent, the Krivitsky claims, his journalism in Franco Spain, and the Volkov affair. He went beyond the details given to the FBI and asked about Edith Tudor Hart, the Soviet agent who in June 1934 had introduced Philby to the OGPU illegal Arnold Deutsch, who had recruited him (MI5 had tapped Tudor Hart's phone before May 1951). He asked how Philby had financed his trip to Spain as a freelance correspondent before he had been hired by the *Times* (the OGPU had). Philby handled the questions well. White wasn't a forceful interrogator; accusation wasn't his style and if he didn't succeed, at least Philby realized White knew far more than was evident.[3] In Moscow years later he told Genrikh Borovik he believed White knew he was guilty.[4] But Philby stood his ground and the interview ended. Shortly afterward, CIA director Walter Bedell Smith informed MI6 that Philby was no longer welcome in Washington and that the CIA would no longer cooperate with MI6 as long as he remained in its ranks.[5]

In July, while the Philby problem was still unresolved, "C," the head of MI6, sent Easton across the Atlantic to explain MI6's assessment of the Philby case to the CIA. On July 13, he met with Smith and gave him the official line. In MI6's view, Philby had been guilty of nothing worse than boarding Burgess at his Washington residence. London was conducting an investigation to establish the facts. If more damaging information came to light, the CIA would be informed. The official MI6 response admitted nothing but Philby's indiscretion.

In 1986 Jack Easton explained that after his trip to Washington to meet with Smith, he was shown a long paper on Philby. Its origins were unknown, so he claimed, but its contents were so incriminating that he protested to "C" that his report to the CIA would have been quite different had he known of that intelligence before his trip. Some of the details were quite old and the dates proved MI6 was aware of them before Easton was dispatched to Washington. Two details mentioned GCHQ signals intelligence: the suspicious upsurge in Soviet wireless traffic from London to Moscow to Istanbul in the days after Philby had been informed of the Volkov offer in September 1945, and a similar surge in September 1949 after Oldfield had briefed Philby about the British embassy leak. In citing GCHQ, Easton suggested the slight possibility of a GCHQ intercept in the Philby case.[6] Easton's report to Cave Brown isn't credible. As we know, he was mentioned in a note from General Leslie Hollis to General Alfred Gruenther in April 1948 and would discuss deception "in general terms" with the Pentagon. He represented MI6 on the GCHQ Clandestine Committee or any similar unit in search of deception opportunities and would have known much earlier of the suspicious upsurge in wireless traffic out of and to London and no doubt what it had yielded. He was the only senior MI6 officer who, like Dick White, was convinced of Philby's guilt. Both were hobbled by the inadmissibility of their GCHQ evidence and the impossibility of disclosing they had known before Philby and Burgess were posted to Washington.

In late July, at Dick White's urging, Philby was reluctantly dismissed from MI6 by "C." In November the Philby interrogation resumed at Leconfield House. Helenus Milmo, an aggressive lawyer who had served with MI5 during the war, was brought in. His brief was prepared by Arthur Martin, the case officer in the Maclean investigation, who sat in and scrupulously noted Philby's every reaction during the interview. During questioning, Milmo demanded an explanation for the 1945 and 1949 signals anomalies described by Easton. Philby said he didn't know. Milmo's reference to signals traffic carried the unmistakable connotation that Philby was associated with the increase in Soviet traffic. Philby was no stranger to GCHQ codebreaking operations and knew that the most tangible evidence of his complicity would have been a broken London to Moscow cable that identified him as its source. His reply was truthful enough: he didn't know if such a cable existed, but that possibility must have lingered long in memory during his decades in Moscow. It was a question he could never answer.[7]

Milmo's interrogation failed. Philby continued to be questioned off and on during the months that followed by William Skardon, one of MI5's more experienced interrogators, but the intermittent interviews at Philby's house got no results. In September 1953, Dick White replaced the retiring Sillitoe as director of MI5 and in 1954 he ended the Philby investigation. Except for White and Jack Easton, by now the second in command at MI6, Philby's guilt was left ambiguous and would remain so for another twelve years.

The use of Soviet cover or codenames in the Venona decrypts made it extremely difficult for MI5 and MI6 to identify a Soviet agent unless very specific detail clearly and unmistakably established his or her identity. This was the case of the August 2–3, 1944, cables that named "G" as the officer who decrypted the Churchill-Roosevelt correspondence and unmistakably referred to Donald Maclean. Kim Philby's codename was STANLEY. That codename would have been even more difficult for MI5 since the number of possible suspects in London far exceeded the closed circle of Washington embassy diplomatic staff. Any mention of STANLEY in association with the London-Moscow exchanges on the Volkov defection, however, would have convincingly pointed to Philby. But absolute certainty was indispensable, especially to convince those MI6 seniors who never doubted Philby's loyalty. However strong Dick White's and Jack Easton's conviction that Philby was STANLEY, corroboration was essential and not merely because the Venona project was far too sensitive to be admitted to anyone except those who worked at or with GCHQ. Lacking that specific identifying detail, the distinction between a suspected agent and a known agent based on a broken Venona cable was blurred, regardless of how complete the Venona recoveries or how convinced the analyst that he or she had identified the source. This was why Maclean's and Burgess's interrogation was important for Dick White in indicting Philby.

The NSA's fifth release of Venona material in September 1996 contained a number of Moscow to London cables but only a few related to STANLEY and HICKS (Burgess). British jurisdiction had decisively curtailed their content. In examining those cables, we're confronted with the same interpretive problems that obscured Venona's Maclean archive. The difference between these texts and the recoveries by Arlington Hall is that with the latter we had the advantage of a few fragments that exposed Venona intelligence known to MI5 prior to April 1951, like the August 2–3, 1944, "G" cable reported by Meredith Gardner. All the Philby and Burgess cables released in September 1996 were penetrated and recovered by GCHQ in London. As a result, we have nothing to guide us except the KGB files seen in Moscow, analytical logic, and a little common sense.

The Venona successes at Arlington Hall Station show us the way. By 1946, as we know, Gardner's team had reconstructed the Soviet 1943–1946 codebooks and broken the spell table for converting Russian names to English. By 1947 he had broken Moscow-Canberra traffic sufficiently to identify the codenames of several of Moscow's Australian agents. GCHQ cryptanalysts should have had similar success with the Philby and Burgess cables; the recoveries of codenames and texts should have paralleled Gardner's successes. On that basis, MI5 would have begun to search for suspects by identifying those who had access to the intelligence being passed to Moscow. Access was the indispensable element. A Moscow to London cable that says, "S's report makes no sense; please clarify," is useless for MI5 analysts attempting to identify "S." An outgoing London to Moscow cable that passes on intelligence, as in "A Nov 8 meeting of the Foreign Office Russia Committee made the following decision," establishes the agent's access. Without those outgoing Canberra to Moscow cables, MI5 would have been unable to identify Moscow's Australian agents. Similarly, Maclean would never have been identified by MI5 without the outgoing Washington and New York to Moscow cables passing on the series of March 29–31, 1945, and the August 2–3, 1944, report on "G" 's decryption of the Churchill to Roosevelt telegrams.

And this is the rub. In the case of Philby and Burgess, the September 1996 NSA monograph tells us, "The small set of London KGB messages to London available for exploitation were mostly incoming messages from Moscow Center."[8] The claim is inexcusably inaccurate. None of the seven STANLEY (Philby) cables were outgoing London to Moscow messages. All of the October 1996 GCHQ Philby and Burgess releases were incoming, Moscow to London, except one HICKS (Burgess) cable too innocuous to matter. Lacking the outgoing STANLEY (Philby) cables and with no clue as to the intelligence he passed to his Soviet handler, GCHQ, MI5, and MI6 analysts would have been helpless, with no more idea who STANLEY was in 1945 than we would in October 1996.

Yet from Moscow's KGB files we know that in 1945, while Philby was chief of MI6's anti-Soviet section, he passed to Moscow details on the Gouzenko defection, on Allan Nunn May, the GRU's British agent betrayed by Gouzenko, and on the Elizabeth Bentley case in Washington.[9] Any one of those 1945 outgoing London to Moscow cables would have established STANLEY's access and helped identify Philby. They were all excluded. The Volkov cables were reportedly responsible for the upsurge in Soviet wireless traffic on or about September 17, 1945, as Jack Easton knew and Philby's interrogator, Helenus Milmo, had been told. Predictably enough, none of that Volkov traffic was included. In the case of HICKS (Burgess), one outgoing cable forwarded a Foreign Office document so vague it was meaningless. In June 1945 and again in August Burgess passed information to his Soviet control. In January 1947, he became personal assistant to Hector McNeil, the undersecretary at the Foreign Office, and in November and December 1947, he passed some 336 Foreign Office documents to his Soviet control officer in London. Again none was included in the October 1996 releases.[10]

Not only were outgoing London to Moscow cables excluded, but the incoming Moscow to London texts were worthless for counterintelligence purposes. Yet we are asked to believe that these Soviet texts were all GCHQ could supply MI5 and MI6 from September 1945 until the disappearance of Maclean and Burgess in May 1951. London's selectivity in releasing the STANLEY and HICKS cables is so disingenuous the question hardly need be asked: why, after fifty years, were those cables released at all?

By excluding all outgoing London to Moscow cables, by withholding the dates of GCHQ's recovery of the identifying detail, and by totally banishing other cables, such as the September 1945 Gouzenko and Volkov traffic, associating those cables with the NSA release of Venona returned one substantial benefit. On the basis of those fragmentary releases, analysts would conclude that the identifying detail from those cables wasn't recovered until some years later. Philby and Burgess, unlike Maclean, weren't identified until long after Venona's Maclean archive had been closed out in 1951. In short, the October 1996 releases suggest that both were demonstrably disassociated from the 1949–1951 Maclean case. That conclusion has successfully served London's purpose. Commentators agree with the NSA's Venona historian that Philby and Burgess were identified much later, but then what other conclusion could they draw?[11] None, not on the basis of the GCHQ evidence.

Common sense compels us to ask that if those broken Soviet cables identified Philby and Burgess much later than 1951, why suppress the dates or the identifying cables in 1996? The obvious answer is that they weren't broken after 1951 but before. London's official reply would be that Britain's Official Secrets Act prohibits full disclosure. But if that were truly the case, the prohibition would have applied to the scores of other GCHQ cables also released in September 1996. Just as unbelievably, GCHQ's failure to meaningfully penetrate those cables denies the success of the Venona cryptanalysts at Arlington Hall. Using the same 1943–1946 KGB codebooks, the same spell table, and the same analytical tools, they successfully broke into Soviet New York, Washington, and Canberra traffic and identified Soviet espionage networks in the United States and Australia. The conclusion that the identifying detail from those cables wasn't recovered until some years later isn't credible, not on the inadequate evidence on which it is based, most obviously the complete absence of any outgoing 1944–1945 London to Moscow cables. By late 1948, the Venona team at Arlington Hall Station had sufficiently broken into numerous March 1945 Washington to Moscow telegrams without the benefit of a crib to identify Foreign Office cables and the Washington embassy leak. Yet London, we're told, had no success at all using the same KGB codebooks. The claim isn't believable. The STANLEY and HICKS archive was opened only to the extent of telling us Philby and Burgess weren't identified as Soviet agents until after 1951 and thus had nothing to do with the Maclean affair.

At the time GCHQ released the Philby and Burgess cables to the Public Record Office at Kew in October 1996, unnamed British intelligence sources explained to the London press that the decision was forced on GCHQ by Washington's decision to declassify Venona.[12] In this way London justified its reluctant departure from the Official Secrets Act. It was also throwing a little dust in everyone's eyes. The claim that GCHQ had only a small number of incoming Soviet cables to work with is just as baseless. It might be more tolerable if we didn't know that there were more London to Moscow cables available in the case of Philby and Burgess than the October 1996 releases imply. They were identified in the 1990s from KGB files in Moscow.[13] Finally, it should be noted that all that was required for GCHQ and MI5 to identify Philby as STANLEY was a single London to Moscow cable that established his access. Yet not one London to Moscow STANLEY cable was released.

In the early 1990s Genrikh Borovik was granted access to numerous KGB files in Moscow containing intelligence Philby passed to his KGB handler and sent on to Moscow Center. A few early reports in the 1930s were sent by letter but most were 1945 cables. Borovik specifically identifies information cited in letters; reports means cable reports, as do documents unless otherwise identified, but the distinction isn't always clear. On August 29, 1944, Philby reported to his Soviet handler that fifteen GCHQ personnel were working on Soviet coded traffic and that Menzies proposed to add even more people (this report was by memo, presumably sent by pouch to Moscow).[14] In January 1945 STANLEY's handler reported that his wife had had another baby, who was desperately ill, and that they now had three children. In February 1945 STANLEY visited Paris and Rome and held talks with MI6 officers; in May he reported that the OSS had bugged the building of Togliatti, the leader of the Italian Communist Party; in June he was in Frankfurt for discussions with the Allied intelligence chief. An August 1945 report from London answered Moscow's question about whether the name "S" was known among his associates. Philby's London control replied that "Harold Adrian Russell Philby is known as Kim in his office" and that he was given this name, adopted from Kipling, as a boy. There were other STANLEY cabled reports as well.[15]

A September 1945 cable (the exact date isn't given) seen by Borovik passed on STANLEY's alert that he had learned details supplied by Gouzenko, the GRU code clerk who had defected in Ottawa that month. Philby also included excerpts from a letter written by MI6 chief Menzies to the chief of MI5 about the espionage case of James Klugmann, a known British Communist. No details are given but STANLEY's control noted he was agitated, and said he might have "information of extreme urgency" to pass on. STANLEY asked for another meeting in a few days; his control refused personal contact but did allow STANLEY to pass on the urgent material through HICKS (Burgess). The subject of such urgency was Allan Nunn May, the British nuclear physicist who had been betrayed by Gouzenko. In a follow-up report, STANLEY analyzed the evidence against May (he thought it inconclusive and legally baseless).[16]

In the September 1996 Venona GCHQ releases is an incoming Moscow to London cable that sheds light on the STANLEY report Borovik had seen in Moscow. On September 17, 1945, in a transmission of the highest urgency, a Moscow KGB cable (46[a]) questioned London about the accuracy of STANLEY's report. Since the report Borovik read in Moscow wasn't in the GCHQ September releases, the cable makes no sense to the reader. What STANLEY report was inaccurate? We don't know because that outgoing cable would have identified Philby. (The only event of any importance in Canada during the weeks before September 17 was the Gouzenko defection and Philby had access to those Royal Canadian Mounted Police [RCMP] reports.)

A day later, on September 18, the KGB in London reported its meeting with STANLEY (that cable is missing but was referred to in a Moscow to London cable, no. 54; most of the word groups were never recovered, or so GCHQ claimed). Moscow Center wasn't satisfied with the response and on

September 19 asked London in a one-sentence cable (no. 100) to expedite its reply to "KIM" 's cable. Because KIM was in quotation marks, British analysts deduced that KIM wasn't an acronym, as was customary in KGB texts, but a rare and accidental use of Philby's nickname. Moscow's reckless urgency in clarifying STANLEY's cable must have been responsible, evident as well in its brevity. It had been dashed off in such haste, security had been sacrificed for speed.

Moscow had every reason for alarm. STANLEY's first report to his Soviet control evidently identified Allan Nunn May but another passed on Gouzenko's erroneous date for meeting with his Soviet control after he returned from Canada to London. The date and place had been proposed by the GRU in Ottawa but were rejected in Moscow for another place and time. Philby had reported that earlier but wrong date from intelligence supplied to London by the RCMP. Moscow was alarmed at the error but was too late to the party. May was under MI5 surveillance in London, was later questioned, and soon confessed. The reference to KIM is the only one of the seven Philby cables of any counterintelligence value. If we are to believe the 1996 GCHQ Venona releases, GCHQ, MI5, and MI6 could make no sense of the reckless use of Philby's nickname for decades to come.

As noted above, the 1996 Venona releases omit Philby's London to Moscow traffic on the Gouzenko case as they do his reports on the Elizabeth Bentley defection. KGB files available to Weinstein and Vassiliev show his reports on both. The Gouzenko reports were sent from London to Moscow on November 26 and 28, and Bentley's list of the forty-one U.S. Soviet agents on December 4, 1945. (The authors refer to Philby's codename at the time as SOHNCHEN but correct the error in a footnote. Philby's Soviet codename was changed to STANLEY on August 16, 1944.) Both sets of cables would have revealed STANLEY's access at MI6, as would the Volkov cables that were responsible, so we're told, for the upsurge in London–Moscow wireless traffic. None was included in the 1996–1997 releases.

Gouzenko's defection troubled Moscow enough to warn the KGB rezidentura in London to take special precautions in meeting with British agents. Those September Moscow–London cables were included in the 1996 Venona release. A September 1945 GCHQ intercept from Moscow to London noted an important KGB espionage network in England that included STANLEY, HICKS (Burgess), and JOHNSON (unidentified but Anthony Blunt). A September 18 Moscow to London message (no. 47) included three English cryptonyms, the spy ring of STANLEY, HICKS, and JOHNSON. Those same names are again mentioned in a Moscow to London cable of September 21. GCHQ was now aware of the existence of the Soviet spy ring and the codenames of three of the Cambridge Five. The GCHQ Venona Moscow to London releases fail to identify Blunt as JOHNSON and don't mention John Cairncross, codenamed LISZT and MOLIERE. The reasons are apparent. Philby and Burgess were linked to Maclean and London's intent was to disassociate both from the Maclean case. Blunt and Cairncross weren't involved, although the May 1951 MI5 surveillance of Cairncross in London casts doubts on that conclusion.

The September 1996 GCHQ releases of the Philby and Burgess cables complemented London's effort to elude the consequences of the 1995 NSA decision to declassify Venona. To reiterate, those releases were intended to banish any suggestion Philby and Burgess had been identified as Soviet agents before the May 1951 flight of Burgess and Maclean. If London couldn't deny the NSA its declassification decision, it could tie its peddler's wagonload of pots and pans to the Venona carthorse for its own purposes. London did as much as it could but was compromised by the KGB files in Moscow, and even more decisively by the wealth of codebreaking secrets made public in 1995–1997 by the NSA and Meredith Gardner's October 1951 report disclosing Venona fragments recovered by his team at Arlington Hall. These London couldn't deny. The secrets were out and explained the broken codebooks, the English spell table, the duplicate KGB one-time pads, and the successful recoveries of Soviet cables from Moscow's U.S. and Australian operations. By October 1996 London was too late to the parade. It offered up a handful of pottage and a stew of Soviet cables that were as useless then as in 1945. We're asked to believe that these were the most authentic Philby cables GCHQ had to offer. We might as well have been told that fifty years ago every clock on the wall had stopped at GCHQ in London, where the best cryptanalysts in the world were still hopelessly struggling with a cargo of 1945 Soviet cables they couldn't master, not by 1948, 1949, 1951, 1965, or the decades that followed. Their secrets lay safely secure in the far, far, distant future. That conclusion isn't believable. In the October 1996 STANLEY and HICKS releases, British intelligence was practicing the same concealment pursued in the Maclean case and for identical reasons.

Curiously enough, the STANLEY cables released in September 1996 were among the Venona STANLEY cables MI5 officer Peter Wright had studied more than thirty years earlier, in 1962 and 1963, while they were stored in a secure office on the fifth floor at MI5 headquarters at Leconfield House. He mentioned those cables in his book published in 1987, when the Venona secrets were still considered impenetrable. He claimed GCHQ cryptologists had successfully broken into the Moscow–London circuit during a single seven-day period from September 15 to September 22, 1945. This is the exact time frame of the STANLEY cables released in September 1996. Wright's other claim, that he uncovered a Venona cable that would have identified Philby, is baseless.[17] His description, however, does indicate that many of the seven Venona STANLEY cables were stored at Leconfield House (he didn't mention the KIM cable) and therefore were not the most sensitive. The most sensitive would have been the outgoing London–Moscow cables. Whether Wright's well publicized book, which created a furor in Britain, guided GCHQ's decision on the release of the useless STANLEY cables is impossible to say.

Fifty years after the Maclean affair, Washington's decision to declassify Venona gave London a final opportunity to clarify the record. British intelligence might have admitted that he had been identified earlier than April 1951 and explained that his return to the Foreign Office in November 1950 was to place him under surveillance to identify his Soviet control. London could have collaborated in the 1995–1997 NSA release of the Venona archive by disclosing the complete texts of the Maclean recoveries as Arlington Hall did in publishing the Soviet cables that led to the FBI's identification of Klaus Fuchs, Judith Coplon, and Julius Rosenberg, among others. There was nothing unusual or extraordinary in MI5's 1949–1951 Maclean deception, which followed widely known counterintelligence practice. An agent of a foreign power was secretly identified and given access to official documents; counterintelligence officers monitored his movements to identify his foreign handler and any other agents under his control. Once that operation was concluded, the details could be disclosed at an appropriate time. After fifty years, there was no reason for Washington to suppress the dates or details of those incriminating Venona exposures and in 1995–1997 the NSA and the FBI had no hesitation in providing them. Full disclosure was the purpose of Venona's declassification. London might have followed suit, releasing the full texts of all twelve of GCHQ's final Maclean recoveries for publication with Venona.

But full and complete disclosure had different implications and more serious consequences for London than for Washington. Maclean wasn't MI5's only target. Philby and Burgess were part of the counterespionage operation designed to fully expose all three using Maclean as a stalking horse, an inclusion the Foreign Office and the foreign secretary weren't aware of. Both had been misled. So had the British government in preparing the 1955 White Paper. The MI5 and MI6 secrets and those at GCHQ remained securely under lock and key until the July 1995 decision to declassify Venona. The date of Maclean's conclusive identification as a Soviet agent was the rusty hinge that would reopen MI5's Pandora's box, sealed since 1949–1951.

That date wasn't April 1951 but a minimum of eight months earlier, more probably a year or even three years earlier. The sensitivity of the Venona Maclean texts when released would have refuted the notion of scores of suspects that required a long and protracted MI5 search for HOMER. The earlier identification of Maclean would have exposed the falsity of those periodic reports to Hoover through Philby's MI6 cipher from the early summer of 1950 through May 1951. Philby in particular, believed by so many to have gotten his crucial intelligence from Venona, had been deliberately misled by MI5. Since both Philby and Burgess were included in the Maclean deception, then both also had been suspected far earlier by GCHQ recoveries. When Roger Makins brought Maclean back to the Foreign Office, Philby and Burgess were posted to Washington. Not only had the Foreign Office been deceived but so had the FBI, the CIA, and Arlington Hall. In 1995, sustaining that fictitious April 1951 date and the pregnant wife cable seemed essential for London.

In their decision to declassify Venona in 1995, senior officials at the NSA, the CIA, and the FBI had assumed those GCHQ files were as obsolete as the NSA's. Assuming London had nothing to hide, they had little appreciation or understanding of British postwar intelligence operations using techniques that had been effectively utilized during World War II when the British joint staffs, MI5, MI6, and GC&CS at Bletchley Park, the Ultra decrypts, and the London Controlling Section had collaborated in identifying and exploiting opportunities for disinformation and deception. In 1947 the LCS had been reconstituted under the Ministry of Defense, in collaboration with MI5, MI6, and GCHQ, whose work on Soviet cable traffic was again available as needed for intelligence purposes.

At the time and for years to come, Washington had no comparable combined sigint, military, diplomatic, intelligence, and counterintelligence structure. Although there were serious disagreements between MI6 and MI5 or the Foreign Office and the service chiefs, nothing was as divisive as the intense bureaucratic warfare in Washington following the 1945 dissolution of the OSS. Until October 1950, when General Walter Bedell Smith took command, the CIA was a hapless fledgling and wouldn't begin to gain its feet until 1951. It was mistrusted by the service intelligence chiefs, by the

Joint Chiefs of Staff, by the State Department, and by the preposterous FBI director J. Edgar Hoover, who played his own squalid hand, interfering, undermining, leaking, and resisting any challenge to his power, his control of counterintelligence, and his secret access to congressional and newspaper vigilantes. In the vacuum, the CIA did little. The codebreakers at Arlington Hall went their own monastic way, translating obscure Cyrillic manuscripts from cipher and sharing their handwoven product with no one. In 1947–1948 it finally dawned on their military intelligence chief that codebreaking wasn't simply a peacetime intellectual exercise or a kind of acrostic macramé but might be put to practical use, as GCHQ had been doing for years. The FBI was invited to help in identifying Soviet codenames; the CIA was finally let in the door in 1952.

The identification of individuals in the FBI files whose activities or position matched the texts under those codenames led to dismissal, blacklisting, or, if possible, arrest and prosecution. Rarely did it serve any other purpose. In only one admitted case was a Soviet agent targeted in a deception operation. Judith Coplon was a political analyst in the Justice Department's Foreign Agents Registration Section evaluating FBI reports on Soviet agents and American Communists. She had been identified through a Venona decrypt, had been followed since January 1949, and was arrested by the FBI in New York on March 4, 1949, in the company of Valentin Gubitchev, a Russian agent at the United Nation. In her purse were a four-page memo and numerous data slips with memos from FBI files.[18] The FBI's Robert Lamphere wanted to keep her under surveillance to determine where the Coplon-Gubitchev trail would lead, a rare counterespionage opportunity, but was overruled by Hoover. Unwilling to allow a revolting Communist trollop in high heels to continue to pollute the halls of the Justice Department, he wanted the case quickly closed out.[19] That wouldn't have been MI5's decision.

FBI cooperation with the Venona project at Arlington Hall was defensive in nature, like its counterintelligence operations. Created by an inward-looking society separated by two oceans from political unrest, revolution, and subversion, the FBI is the agency for law and order, the legal and political status quo. Its technology and laboratory forensics are first-rate, but in defining and confronting subversion, which to the FBI means nothing more or less than an aberrant political belief, its judgments are often as primitive as the corporate-hired Pinkerton strike-and-skull breakers in the nineteenth-century Pennsylvania coal fields or Pittsburgh steel mills. This was so for decades with J. Edgar Hoover, it was especially true in 1945–1955, and it is true to a certain extent today.[20]

British intelligence and counterintelligence were trained in a more worldly-wise school and an older tradition. Both MI5 and MI6 were as offensive as defensive in their operations when need be, willing to take risks and dare the consequences if the occasion demanded, as it did in 1948–1950, when England was once again alone on the frontier, and as it had in 1939–1940, far more vulnerable than the United States to any Soviet thrust into Western Europe that would threaten Britain's security. A 1947 British Defense strategy paper addressed the problem: "A third major war within the next few years would be economically disastrous. The supreme object, therefore, of British policy must be to prevent war." As quoted earlier, the strategy document concluded that "the only effective deterrent to a potential aggressor is tangible evidence of our ability to withstand attack and to retaliate immediately."[21] And what would provide that "tangible evidence"? A nuclear deterrent. Prime Minister Attlee had decided to manufacture British nuclear weapons in January 1947.[22] This was among the subjects General Hollis raised in his secret talks with the Joint Chiefs of Staff at the Pentagon on April 8, 1948.

Maclean returned to the Foreign Office in November 1950 and was put under surveillance. Since both Philby and Burgess were included in that operation, they must have been suspected of being KGB agents by the summer of 1950, when Maclean was reassigned. Since London's guardians of an operation fifty years obsolete by Washington's clock were determined to conceal the truth, the question is, what other secrets was London also attempting to conceal? More specifically, what was Moscow's suspected agent, Kim Philby, doing in America all those twenty months?

Our point of departure is Maurice Oldfield's late September 1949 briefing of Philby before his sailing for the United States. Oldfield told Philby about the Anglo-American codebreaking secret and its exposure of two unidentified Soviet agents in the United States in 1944–1945, one at the British embassy in Washington, and the other, CHARLES, at Los Alamos. All three of Oldfield's disclosures would have been of urgent importance to Moscow, and Philby's response was completely predictable. He passed on the Oldfield intelligence, not to his Soviet contact Mikhail Shishkin, who had given him his final instructions, but to Guy Burgess at the Foreign Office. He reported that Anglo-American codebreakers had broken into Soviet wartime cipher communications and had been reading NKVD traffic, including one cable that had identified CHARLES, a Soviet agent for whom counterintelligence officers were now actively searching. He also claimed GCHQ had recently "achieved impressive results in its codebreaking operations" whereas the American success was "minimal."[23]

Soviet policy prohibited an agent's knowledge of another agent's operational codename. On the basis of KGB files in Moscow, Borovik claims that when Moscow Center changed Philby's codename from SOHNCHEN to STANLEY in August 1944, Philby wasn't to be told.[24] Philby had no more reason to know who CHARLES was in September 1949 than Fuchs would have known who STANLEY was. He didn't mention the codename in *My Silent War*, but as indicated above, KGB archives show he was given the codename in his MI6 briefing and passed it along to Burgess. By the time he wrote his 1968 account, he had identified CHARLES from newspaper accounts of Fuchs's arrest, trial, and conviction even without knowing the codename. But he was still confused about the sequence of 1949 events. He mistakenly placed Fuchs at Los Alamos, New Mexico, in 1949, probably because Oldfield had mentioned Los Alamos. In his 1968 account he also wrote that shortly after Fuchs was identified as a Soviet agent by Peter Dwyer at the British embassy, "he set sail for England on a routine visit" and "was arrested on arrival." His account is wrong in every detail. No less false are the innumerable tales about Philby's role in the Fuchs case and his warning to Moscow that enabled other KGB agents to go to ground. That warning came after Fuchs's arrest.

Fuchs wasn't at Los Alamos when Oldfield briefed Philby between September 22 and Philby's departure on September 28. He was in England, working at the U.K. Atomic Energy Research Establishment at Harwell in Berkshire. He was also under around-the-clock surveillance by MI5. On or about September 5, 1949, Dick White received word from the FBI passed through the Washington embassy that Fuchs was the Manhattan Project spy CHARLES. On September 9, MI5 officers convened at Leconfield House to plan the Fuchs investigation. Their purpose was "to obtain evidential proof" as to whether FUCHS "is or is not still a spy." The MI5 team included Furnival Jones, Arthur Martin, the HOMER case officer, James Robertson, William Skardon, and agents Collard and Read. The MI5 team planned to obtain "a Home Office Warrant for a mail cover on all correspondence to and from Fuchs at his home" and at Harwell, a "telephone check" at the Harwell switchboard, and a Special Facility operation installing a phone tap or microphone at the

Fuchs residence. He was kept under observation during any visits to London.

Initially MI5 surveillance at Harwell was thought to be "risky" in the small community and unlikely to produce results. Because of the sparse traffic on the local country roads, trailing Fuchs by car was deemed unsafe. MI5 watchers would instead pick up his car on the most likely trunk road. (James Robertson of MI5, who drafted the investigation plans, would argue in May 1951 that Maclean's surveillance at Tatsfield would be too risky for the same reasons.) In the MI5 periodic reports on the investigation, the source of the 1944 "leakage" pointing to Fuchs is never cited, although "the delicacy of the original information" meant that "no action could be taken which might in any way compromise the security of the sources involved." As the weeks passed, the investigation expanded and intensified. Coverage of Fuchs's movements at Harwell would be increased by extra War Department constabulary personnel; his visitors' bona fides were investigated, as were his fellow scientists at Harwell. He rarely left the facility and when he did, MI5 watchers were able to closely observe his movements, as they did on a September 22 visit to Wembley. A headquarters staff of selected watchers was maintained in permanent readiness in London.[25]

The MI5 investigation began on September 8, almost two weeks before Philby's final September 21 meeting with Mikhail Shishkin and three weeks before his September 28 departure from Southampton for New York. After Philby left for Washington, a new actor, Yuri Modin, stepped onto the London stage. On October 11 he met with Anthony Blunt, his mentor in eluding surveillance, to pick up the film Burgess had passed to Blunt containing Philby's message on CHARLES and the U.S.-U.K. codebreaking operation. Overexposed, the films were worthless. Modin met with Burgess on October 25 and again on December 7, when Burgess passed 168 documents of some 660 pages, but failed to include Philby's note. Modin and Burgess met again on February 10 and Burgess finally passed on Philby's intelligence note five months after Burgess had received it.

Fuchs's KGB control officer in London had last met him in April 1949. Fuchs failed to show up for a meeting scheduled for May 25 and the Soviet embassy had since lost contact.[26] Fuchs was one of Moscow's more important agents and Moscow Center was concerned about his possible compromise in New York by the American Harry Gold, a Soviet agent and sometime Fuchs courier (he had been questioned by the FBI). Had Burgess not delayed passing Philby's note to Blunt and had Blunt not butchered his camera work, the Soviet embassy might have attempted to reestablish contact with Fuchs. But Philby's note reached Modin too late. With the Soviet residency kept in the dark, MI5's unrelenting surveillance of Fuchs continued between October and December 1949 but without result. He was finally interrogated on December 21, December 30, January 13, and confessed on January 23, 1950.[27]

For six weeks following Fuchs's arrest, Moscow Center prohibited any contact with Burgess or Blunt. In March Philby was recalled to London to discuss the case with Valentine Vivian, the head of MI6 security. While in London he met with Burgess and passed on additional details about the U.S.-U.K. codebreaking operation. Burgess met with Modin on April 17 "without materials" and evidently passed the information orally. The description of the codebreaking operation Philby had given Burgess in late September and passed to Modin on February 10 and April 17 was sent by pouch from London to Moscow in April or May 1950. It reads in part:

> STANLEY (Philby) asked to communicate that the Americans and British had constructed a deciphering machine which in one day does "the work of a thousand people in a thousand years." Work on deciphering is facilitated by three factors: (1) a one-time pad was used twice; (2) our cipher resembles the cipher of a trade organization in the USA; (3) a half-burnt codebook has been found in Finland and passed to the British and used to decrypt our communications. They will succeed within six to twelve months.[28]

The KGB report is misleading enough to raise questions about the intelligence passed to Philby, his MI5 and MI6 sources, and their purpose. While GCHQ did use an upgraded version of the World War II Colossus computer, there was no new decryption machine.[29] The Anglo-American codebreaking success was a purely analytical and intellectual triumph using classic cryptanalytic techniques. The KGB messages were laboriously hand-broken one fragment at a time, "sweat of the brow," as the NSA monograph explains, by book, not machine decipher. Although new IBM machine sorters were used at Arlington Hall to segregate messages, they would play no part in breaking out message fragments. The successful decryption wasn't a matter of a single one-time code pad used twice by mistake but thirty-five thousand pages of duplicates printed and bound in one-time pads used by Soviet code clerks. The Finnish codebook played no role in the 1944–1946 recoveries, although it later proved useful.[30] The KGB trade message function (from the Soviet Amtorg Trading Company in New York, among others) was misunderstood, and Arlington Hall, not GCHQ in London, made the Fuchs identification and the first Maclean recoveries.

By 1949 Moscow already knew about Venona and had known for some time. Philby had known since August 1944 that more than a dozen GCHQ cryptologists were working on Soviet coded traffic and that more would be added. He had learned as much from Felix Cowgill, his MI6 colleague. After he had been appointed head of Section IX in October 1944, he would have known of GCHQ decryption operations.[31] In 1946 Moscow Center had concluded that New York and Washington to Moscow enciphered traffic was being closely monitored by U.S. intelligence and cautioned both stations to reduce their volume, not because Moscow knew its traffic was being decrypted but out of concern that it would betray unusual or espionage activity. Moscow learned of Venona in 1947 or 1948 from William Weisband, an Arlington Hall Russian linguist who wasn't a cryptanalyst and didn't know why the cables were vulnerable. (In 1950 Weisband was under FBI surveillance in Washington and would be questioned, albeit inconclusively.)[32] By the time the KGB recognized the flaw, virtually all the corrupt pads had been used by Soviet code clerks, whose transmissions had been intercepted and were awaiting analysis at Arlington Hall.

In giving up the Venona secret, or at least what Philby was wrongly told of Venona, his sources were yielding knowledge of an intelligence asset Moscow was aware of, one that Soviet code clerks no longer used and that had no further value. Moscow could do nothing about the backlog of Soviet cables gathered by Arlington Hall and GCHQ made vulnerable by the flawed one-time pads except wait helplessly, like Philby and Burgess, as they were attacked by Anglo-American codebreakers. For more than forty years it was believed Philby's knowledge of the Venona secret had compromised one of the most sensitive of all Anglo-American intelligence operations. Yet Philby's betrayal was of far less value than has been extravagantly claimed. The passing of that distorted information also served more important purposes.

The KGB report to Moscow on U.S.-U.K. codebreaking operations raises a number of intriguing questions. Philby's September 1949 briefing in London was intended to set the stage for his Washington assignment. The HOMER investigation was then eight months underway and in 1950 Philby would begin receiving reports on its progress. By the time of Burgess's August arrival, Philby had received "dozens of reports" on the investigation. The U.S.-U.K. codebreaking success evidently was raised by Oldfield in explaining how the 1944–1945 Washington embassy leak was discovered.

The intelligence he gave Philby appears reasonable enough as preparation for his Washington arrival, but not his mention of the unidentified CHARLES. The Fuchs investigation wasn't an MI6 matter and wasn't relevant to Philby's duties in Washington. At the time of Oldfield's meeting with Philby, moreover, MI5 not only was deploying every instrument at its command against Fuchs, but was anticipating some form of clandestine contact between Fuchs and the Russians. His watchers had been warned that Fuchs, if still active as a spy, "must at some stage pass documentary material to the Russians, whether direct or through a cut-out or through a series of cutouts." The "cutout or cutouts could be any person whom Fuchs meets for any purpose," including "a waiter in a restaurant or a servant at Harwell itself." His movements were monitored twenty-four hours a day, his visitors were listed and investigated, his mail was read at the Newbury Post Office and treated chemically for traces of invisible ink, his Harwell phone was bugged, a microphone was installed in his Harwell office and in his home (he had no home phone), and he was successfully shadowed during each trip to London by MI5.[33]

In light of what we now know about Venona, its methodology and techniques as explained in 1995 by the NSA, Cecil Phillips, and others, the most ominous detail Philby passed to Moscow was either false or falsely distorted. There was no miraculous new computer able to do "the work of a thousand people in a thousand years." Venona recovered 49 percent of the 1944 New York to Moscow traffic, many only in fragments, 15 percent of the 1943 cables, and a mere 1.5 percent of the Washington to Moscow traffic.[34] Even when analysts were attacking potentially exploitable messages encrypted with the thirty-five thousand pages of additives erroneously printed in Moscow and bound on Soviet one-time pads, some cables or passages "remained unexploitable after 37 years of effort."[35] This was hardly the success that would fully unlock all Soviet coded encryptions "within six to twelve months." Philby's note to Burgess on Anglo-American codebreaking also wrongly emphasized the achievements of GCHQ operations in the United Kingdom at the expense of the Americans, whose own success was dismissed as "minimal," as if to suggest that any threat of exposure came from the GCHQ codebreakers on England's side of the Atlantic. At the time, Philby was outward-bound for New York and Washington.

It is difficult to believe Oldfield knew the full details of the intelligence given in his briefing. He must have been briefed by others before his meeting, including Dick White. Jack Easton also supplied Philby with details on U.S.-U.K. codebreaking. But there is no question that the most threatening particulars in the KGB report sent to Moscow were untrue. Deliberately falsified intelligence designed to mislead and deceive is called disinformation. It is unthinkable, of course, that the cleverest and most successful spy of his era was given false intelligence on the eve of his departure for the most important assignment of his career, yet the detail given Philby on U.S.-U.K. codebreaking methods, technique, and anticipated success was false. He was given disinformation.

Some of the details in the KGB report to Moscow had been passed by Philby to Burgess during his March 1950 visit to London. After Philby arrived in Washington in October 1949, he was apparently given a tour of Arlington Hall Station, presumably under the auspices of GCHQ's liaison officer. Had Philby visited Arlington Hall as frequently as some have imagined, or had he stood watching at Meredith Gardner's shoulder as he broke the Venona cables word group by word group, as others have absurdly claimed (Yuri Modin and Peter Wright among them), he would have recognized something was very seriously wrong. He might even have concluded that someone was lying to him, either Meredith Gardner at Arlington Hall by a very artful performance or Oldfield by his grandiose fables. But he didn't draw either conclusion.[36]

The intelligence he received on the 1944–1945 leak at the British embassy established the groundwork for the HOMER reports later sent to Washington through his MI6 cipher, another disinformation operation but one that served a counterespionage purpose. We don't know whether Oldfield claimed CHARLES was still at Los Alamos or Philby inferred as much. Like the codebreaking disclosures, however, the CHARLES intelligence was intended to provoke Philby and the Soviet embassy to action. The plan succeeded in the first leg—Philby immediately reported it to Burgess—but because of Burgess's and Blunt's bungling, it failed in the second.

If MI6 and MI5 cooperated in furnishing the detail in Oldfield's briefing, then in the classic sense they were working at cross-purposes. On one hand the briefing served Dick White's counterespionage intent—baiting a hook for Philby—and on the other it fulfilled Jack Easton's MI6 misinformation purpose, although both the codebreaking and the CHARLES secrets would have prompted Philby to immediate action, as they indeed did. But they were unsuccessful. No Soviet embassy officer or Soviet illegal who handled Klaus Fuchs or Philby was exposed, only Burgess, had he been under surveillance. Had Philby immediately contacted Mikhail Shishkin and had the MI5 watchers been as well organized in his pursuit as the team tracking Fuchs, then the Philby affair might have ended quite differently there on MI5's London turf. But Philby's only contact was with Guy Burgess and shortly thereafter he left London and sailed away to New York and Washington. He was now beyond Dick White's reach and would soon land in Jack Easton's MI6 territory. Were Dick White and Jack Easton collaborating after Philby arrived in Washington? Most probably no, not at all.

Once at post in Washington, Philby bypassed the Soviet embassy and by his own admission remained out of contact with any Soviet control for nine or ten months, although KGB files indicate it was much longer. According to Modin, any intelligence he had obtained in Washington was sent to Burgess in London. His Soviet contact, when it finally came after almost eighteen months, was with a Soviet illegal based in New York. In March 1950, six months into his posting, Philby was recalled to London to discuss the Fuchs affair, apparently with Colonel Valentine Vivian, chief of MI6 security. The KGB report pouched to Moscow forwarding Philby's detail on the U.S.-U.K. codebreaking miracles also indicated Vivian "considers that STANLEY's past is not entirely clear. A role in establishing STANLEY's past may be played by his first wife who is somehow connected to the CHARLES case. STANLEY [Philby], PAUL [Burgess], and YAN [Blunt] consider that the situation is serious."[37] While in London, Philby had also asked Burgess to "communicate to us [the KGB residency] his personal request for granting him political asylum in the USSR in case of obvious danger."

It isn't clear why Philby would be summoned to London to discuss the Fuchs affair in which he played no part—except as an MI5 ploy to renew surveillance—or why he might be asked about Litzi, his first wife, perhaps MI5's justification for his summons. But he had again met with Burgess, his courier, who didn't pass his request for political asylum to Modin when he met with him on April 17 nor at their next meeting, on May 15. On May 9 the Foreign Office unexpectedly approved Burgess's assignment to the British embassy and on May 17 informed him that the internal investigation into his scandalous behavior had been dropped. On June 4 he met with Nikolai Rodin in a suburban London park. During their prolonged six-and-a-half-hour conversation the Russian attempted to calm his fears about U.S.-U.K. decryption capability, explained that Moscow had made a few wartime errors but those had been corrected, and assured him there was no supercomputer able to break Soviet codes. At this meeting Burgess passed on Philby's request for asylum in case of danger.

On June 25 the Korean War exploded, as unforeseen by the Foreign Office in London as by Washington. At the Foreign Office Burgess was assigned to the Far East division, as he would be in Washington, and his assignment quickly took on new meaning: unknowingly the Foreign Office personnel office had set the fox among the chickens. He had at least two more meetings with his Soviet handlers in London, on July 1 and July 8, presumably with Modin. At the second meeting he passed on a film of Foreign Office documents and was told how to initiate contact with the Russians in Washington. He would be leaving for the United States on July 28.[38]

Since the MI6 briefing of Philby in London in September 1949 contains all the elements of both a counterespionage and a disinformation initiative, it helps confirm that MI5 and MI6 knew a great deal about both Philby and Burgess at the time. But to what purpose? Better to ask Jack Easton why Philby was posted to Washington in the first place. He had barely managed to elude Volkov's probable incrimination in September 1945 when the increase in cable traffic from the Soviet embassy in London had aroused suspicion; he had admitted his first marriage to a woman who was a known Soviet agent; he had been relieved as chief of MI6's IX anti-Soviet section in December 1946 and packed off to Istanbul. And his past still wasn't "entirely clear," as Vivian is said to have told him in March 1950, most probably at MI5's behest. But it didn't matter what MI6 or MI5 might have suspected. His services were highly valued by Moscow Center, which believed, or so Yuri Modin tells us, that in due time he would be named "C," the chief of MI6. The intelligence Maurice Oldfield shared with him in September was proof enough that he was trusted with the most sensitive intelligence MI5 and MI6 had to offer. Moscow was of the same mind, even if Burgess had disastrously bungled the CHARLES note and Nikolai Rodin was forced to scale down the threat of an omniscient supercomputer.

During Rodin's protracted tête-à-tête with Burgess in the reassuring solitude of a suburban park on June 4, Burgess assured him that he saw no signs of danger ahead and was ready to resume passing documents. In his report to Moscow, Rodin remarked agreeably that Burgess had come to their meeting "sober" and suggested that meetings with Blunt and Burgess continue. After studying his report, Moscow Center agreed and approved the residency's continuing to meet with Burgess and Blunt.[39] The KGB archives indicate in his report to Moscow Nikolai Rodin mentioned the absurdly amateurish length of his heart-to-heart talk with Burgess. Had Yuri Modin's MI5 greenhorns been watching from the shrubbery, they might have concluded they were dealing with a conspiracy of dunces.

Burgess was very much part of the Philby story, so much so that Philby admitted in Moscow that if it hadn't been for Burgess's flight from Southampton with Maclean, he could have worked for MI6 for another ten years.[40] If MI5 hadn't known of his integral role, those many London meetings with Nikolai Rodin and Modin would have made it obvious. Accordingly, suitable advance accommodations were soon made in Washington. By the time Philby's dutiful courier had joined him in Washington, a special position had been created for a British army officer to keep Burgess under observation. The intelligence was tracked down by Chapman Pincher, who attributed it to one of his many confidential sources.[41] Pincher doesn't explain why an army officer was given the assignment but had little doubt that MI6 or MI5 was responsible. His conclusion might appear a little odd until we know more about what went on with the Royal Air Force in Washington. He doesn't pursue the instant importance of Burgess's assignment to the embassy's Far Eastern Department now that the Korean War was underway. But Burgess didn't stay long. The department head refused to have Burgess on his staff and he was soon moved to another section.[42] Secrets given in confidence, like Pincher's, are suspect, especially when cited to corroborate questionable assumptions or conclusions. What makes Pincher's note mildly credible is that he hadn't the slightest suspicion that MI5 and MI6 were capable of a deception operation or indeed much of anything except gross incompetence. Yuri Modin and Rodin were obviously of the same mind.

Chapter
NINE

Misplaced in time.—The CIA orphan.—U.S.
military weakness.—London's Russia Committee.—
Secret USAF-RAF cooperation.—U.S. war plans.—
The Soviet specter.—Searching for a strategy.—
Political and psychological warfare.—The
Berlin crises.—The bomb as a deterrent to war.—
The Foreign Office rebuffs the military.—The
threat to Western Europe.—Philby's unlimited
potentialities.

By the 1970s and 1980s Philby had gained enough notoriety to emerge from the intelligence shadows and be embraced by popular culture. In the United States his renown is based on his well-publicized 1949–1951 penetration of the CIA, a penetration that spoke for itself. The consequences must have been calamitous for Washington's reclusive intelligence giant, or so it was assumed. In *My Silent War*, Philby mentioned a few of his espionage triumphs but official secrecy obscured the details of those episodes until years later. His other betrayals were left to imaginations richly stimulated by the events of the 1960s, including the Bay of Pigs, the Cuban missile crisis, and especially the Berlin Wall, the sinister presence that divided East from West and that only spy novelists could penetrate. Ian Fleming's novels were soon replaced by John le Carré's grimly ambivalent moral fables that seemed more authentic even if they depicted shadows far more than substance. But they were enough to retire James Bond to Hollywood, where Fleming's celluloid fantasies found a permanent home.

It didn't matter that Philby no more belonged to that era than General George Patton's armored divisions did to the rice paddies of the Vietnam

War, an equally preposterous misplacement in time and space. Nevertheless, pernicious conclusions weren't difficult to come by, even if his widely heralded espionage triumphs had another flaw: they were assumptions based on his access and little more. There were no documents that enabled outsiders to assess their importance; the episodes cited in his memoir were of less consequence than his claims.

The Philby case had its origins in the late 1940s, during the uncertain dawn of the Cold War. Not until twelve years after he left the United States and defected to Moscow, in June 1963, did he come under intense scrutiny. The significance of his defection remained a mystery until late 1967, when his MI6 role was clarified by the London journalist Phillip Knightley. Philby had been head of IX, MI6's anti-Soviet operations. That revelation, publicized eighteen years after he was posted to Washington, made the affair a cause célèbre in England and Philby a household name, so Oxford Regius Professor of History Hugh Trevor-Roper wrote in beginning his slight 1968 book on Philby.[1]

During the years that followed, as more books appeared, Philby's reputation flourished. His importance was amplified not by new details about his MI6 career—none was officially offered except his own—but by the explosive growth of the espionage marketplace, the fact, the fiction, and the myths generated. With the radically transformed Cold War, espionage was now in vogue, more mysterious, more sensational, and more popular than ever. Philby was accepted as a true authentic, his name and notoriety instantly identifiable. He was a celebrity.

In the transposition, his twenty months in Washington were misplaced, enlarged through the distorting lens of those turbulent intervening decades that gave such major significance to his espionage, even if far removed from the 1946–1949 period when London and Washington struggled secretly, anxiously, and indecisively with problems of a different character. Those examining his long career ignored that battleground, not only because it was far less dramatic, less sensational, and less chilling but because it was less accessible. The most important official documents, few of which were directly related to the Philby case, weren't available in the 1960s and 1970s. They were still hostages to the Cold War and wouldn't begin to be released for another decade. The neglect was unfortunate. The relevance of the closing years of Philby's espionage career can't be measured without some understanding of that era.

Had official documents been available in 1949, they would have revealed the CIA as a small untested intelligence agency under poor leadership with trifling resources and an ambiguous mandate. The CIA deeply involved in clandestine operations, which had organized coups in Iran (1953), Guatemala (1954), Indonesia (1954), and the disastrous Bay of Pigs invasion of Castro's Cuba (1961), was light years removed from the CIA in 1948–1950. The latter no more resembled the secret sprawling bureaucratic colossus of conspiracy, deceit, popular fantasy, and lunatic suspicions than President William McKinley's buggy whip White House resembled President Kennedy's overstaffed executive establishment in 1961–1963. The CIA's total operational personnel in 1949 was less than a thousand, although the precise numbers are impossible to determine. The numbers would increase six-fold by 1952 but that increase is small when measured by the baseline: the Central Intelligence Group (CIG) began in 1946 with fewer than a hundred officers. Those numbers exploded by the early 1960s, when CIA staff at the Miami base alone totaled more than eight hundred. But this was another era and another CIA, not that of Philby's Washington.[2]

Created in 1947, the CIA orphan had been governed since its inception by a custodial circus at the National Security Council that had no clear idea of its role apart from espionage and intelligence collection abroad. Until late 1950 the CIA remained in transition, struggling to find itself and fully define its mission while facing serious leadership, organizational, and personnel problems. The mistrust of other well-established and more powerful agencies unwilling to yield their authority or prerogatives to the new intelligence foundling compounded and prolonged its difficulties. The chiefs of the three service intelligence agencies—the army, the navy, and the air force—the Joint Chiefs, and the State Department were the principal culprits.[3] The CIA also lacked the statutory authority for covert operations, which didn't begin until late 1949 and then insignificantly and unsuccessfully.

Until the outbreak of the Korean War in June 1950, the American military establishment was also in difficult straits, underfunded and underequipped for the challenges abroad. By 1947 demobilization had left the United States, the most powerful nation on earth, incapable of fighting a conventional war with conventional military forces in Western Europe or elsewhere. President Roosevelt hadn't expected U.S. troops to remain more than two years in Europe after 1945 and so informed both Churchill and Stalin at Yalta. President Truman's crippling budget limitations didn't permit even the minimal increases the armed services now required. The troops available couldn't carry out the existing war plan; only one division was ready for combat and any larger deployment anywhere would require partial mobilization.[4] Neither a Republican Congress nor Truman, who was facing reelection in 1948, would support a renewal of the draft or compulsory universal military training.

Other official documents prepared and circulating in secrecy in 1947–1950 would have described the desperation of Anglo-American military and air force war planners. Fearful of Soviet intentions in Western Europe, their plans prepared in response to Russian military aggression were premised on limited and imaginary resources. There was no hydrogen bomb, no intermediate or long-range ballistic missiles. Massive retaliation and Mutually Assured Destruction (MAD) were not yet Cold War strategies. Until 1949 the United States had sole possession of the atomic bomb, the most devastating military weapon then devised, but it was just beginning to be developed as an efficiently manufactured weapon rather than the complex and somewhat clumsy rudimentary devices used at Hiroshima and Nagasaki. Its awesome power and the staggering responsibilities it posed, morally and technically (would its secret ever get out?), had created a continuing debate about its future. As late as 1948 Truman hadn't ruled out the possibility that it might come under international control through the United Nations. The lack of new long-range strategic bombers neutralized the bomb's military value except in theoretical planning exercises or as an intimidating psychological weapon, a tool the Joint Chiefs' strategists—but not the U.S. Air Force—were slow to recognize. At a National Security Council meeting in February 1948, Secretary of State George Marshall best expressed the limitations a diminished U.S. strength in conventional forces imposed on the conduct of foreign policy. He noted ruefully that on every explosive front from Greece and Palestine to China the United States was "playing with fire and had nothing with which to put it out."[5]

In Great Britain the war's end had brought national reconstruction and a marginally better life as the effect of diminishing monetary reserves hadn't yet forced the devaluation of the pound sterling. The armed forces had been drastically reduced and could expect no relief from Prime Minister Attlee's Labor government, intent on restoring Britain's global leadership not by military strength but by the ideals of democratic socialism. Labor's socialist state and planned economy would be free of the inequities and social injustices of America's remorseless capitalism and the USSR's repressive Marxist imperialism. England would stand apart from the two dominant powers and offer a third way, providing the "spiritual lead"—or so a Foreign Office paper would claim—with the help of the "material resources in the Colonial Empire." Great Britain would prove "that we are not subservient to the

United States or to the Soviet Union."[6] The most doctrinaire socialists among Attlee's Labor Party ministers and parliamentarians and Foreign Secretary Bevin himself opposed any belligerent anti-Soviet policy. If the tightening noose on Eastern Europe seemed to Washington to keep its leaders dangling at Stalin's will on Moscow's gibbet, left-wing Laborites regarded the ties as benignly reasonable: the USSR was establishing friendly nations along its western frontiers.

The same socialists on the extreme left rejected Britain's too exclusive identification with the United States and dismissed Britain's joining any future Atlantic pact. Bevin advocated a propaganda (i.e., information) offensive emphasizing England's example for European social democracies. The correct response to Communism wasn't vehement anti-Communism but vigorous promotion of the virtues of democratic socialism. As Bevin described Britain's future foreign policy in a cabinet memo in January 1948 (drafted by a civil servant), "What we have to offer in contrast to totalitarian Communism and *laissez-faire* capitalism are the vital and progressive ideas of the British Social Democracy." He scorned "American propaganda which stresses the strength and aggressiveness of Communism, tends to scare and unbalance the anti-Communists, while heartening the fellow travelers and encouraging the Communists to bluff more extravagantly." British propaganda, with its emphasis on Russia's poverty and backwardness, would "relax rather than raise the international tensions."[7] Such was socialist England's initial promise under Prime Minister Attlee and Foreign Secretary Bevin. The British chiefs of staff believed they were whistling past the graveyard. Since 1947 they had urged review of the political warfare machinery under the control of the Foreign Office and initiation of "certain 'black' secret operations."[8] Later events in 1948 proved them right.

In April 1946 the Foreign Office created the Russia Committee and began to plan a Soviet strategy of sorts, analyzing and evaluating Moscow's initiatives and recommending appropriate countermeasures, all of them relatively benign. The chiefs of staff of the three British services—the Royal Navy, the Royal Air Force, and the Army—not only were excluded from the committee but weren't told of its existence until two years later.[9] Foreign Secretary Bevin was determined to keep Soviet policy firmly under their control and away from the more belligerent service chiefs, who were as disdainful of the Foreign Office dabblers as the U.S. Air Force was of the State Department's forbidding USAF reconnaissance flights over the USSR or Eastern Europe (the Royal Air Force took on the job). Britain's service chiefs pressed for more aggressive political warfare against the USSR, employing "black" or secret operations, tactics more suitable to wartime, when the military played the dominant role.[10] The latter was precisely what Bevin and the Foreign Office wanted to avoid.

Unknown to the foreign secretary or the cabinet, the Royal Air Force had allied itself with American war planners and begun secret collaboration in mid-1946 with the U.S. Air Force in anticipation of conflict with the USSR. Although there was no formal or written policy guidance, the two channels of exchange were through the Air Force Staff at the British Joint Services Mission and the USAF staff in Washington and between the British Air Ministry and the USAF attaché in London.[11] The staffs also exchanged USAF and RAF intelligence officers. Rear Admiral Tom Inglis of naval intelligence, a bothersome nuisance for everyone at the Pentagon and the CIA, threatened to suspend passing naval intelligence to the air force as long as an RAF officer was assigned to USAF intelligence. General Charles Cabell, director of USAF intelligence, successfully ignored him.[12]

In June 1946 General Carl Spaatz of the U.S. Air Force arranged with Britain's air marshal Sir Arthur Tedder, the Royal Air Force chief of staff, to prepare five air bases in East Anglia for emergency use by the USAF, including two storage sites configured for handling U.S. nuclear weapons.[13] All of the many post-1946 U.S. Joint Chiefs' war plans required RAF cooperation and the request may have followed completion of Harrow, the USAF nuclear annex to Pincher, the Joint Chiefs' secret war plan. Pincher was completed on June 18, 1946, and Harrow the following autumn, calling for the atomic destruction of thirty Soviet cities, including Moscow, Leningrad, and Gorki.[14] General Spaatz, who had advocated a new U.S. strategic air policy centered on the atomic bomb long before the strategy had been accepted, had worked closely with Tedder, Eisenhower's deputy supreme commander in Europe during World War II. Only General Eisenhower, army chief of staff, his chief of staff General Walter Bedell Smith, U.S. secretary of war Robert Patterson, and a few others were aware of the 1946 U.K. storage arrangements. The British cabinet wasn't informed. In Washington the Joint Chiefs' war plans were never shared with civilian agencies, not the National Security Council, the State Department, or the CIA.

The U.K. storage arrangements were as theoretical as war plans Harrow or Pincher. At the time neither Spaatz nor Tedder knew how insignificant the U.S. atomic stockpile was. Always spoken or whispered, the numbers were never committed to paper. Until 1947 President Truman had been as oblivious as the Joint Chiefs of Staff, whose ignorance hadn't dulled its imagination in dreaming up U.S. war plans based on a nuclear arsenal just as imaginary. The Atomic Energy Commission, not the Pentagon, had custody of the atomic bomb. David Lilienthal, the chairman, was the only one in Washington who knew the ugly secret. In early 1947 while inspecting Los Alamos, where the unassembled bombs were stored, he discovered in a basement a crude chicken-wire enclosure that held the entire U.S. nuclear arsenal. Inside was one bomb. He describes the moment as "one of the saddest days" of his life. The twenty-four-man team required two days to assemble the components for more bombs and all had been demobilized to return to civilian life.[15] The secret was disclosed to Truman and the Joint Chiefs on April 16, 1947. The usually imperturbable Truman was shocked beyond belief. Undaunted and undeterred, the Joint Chiefs went back to the drawing board. By the end of 1947, they still lacked a realistic operational war plan to deter Soviet aggression in Western Europe based on any existing or foreseeable nuclear arsenal or adequate strategic air power delivery capability.

Unknown to Washington, Moscow had reason to believe otherwise. In an ironic espionage quirk that strengthened rather than exposed the enemy's weaknesses (the intent of all deception schemes; this one was fortuitous), the Kremlin was given a much higher estimate of the diminutive U.S. nuclear arsenal based on an impeccable source. In October 1947 Moscow received by diplomatic pouch a detailed account of the atomic spy Klaus Fuchs's September 27 meeting in London with Alexander Feklisov, the deputy resident at the Soviet embassy responsible for scientific intelligence. A month earlier, Feklisov had been briefed in Moscow by a Russian nuclear scientist who had supplied a list of technical questions for Fuchs's response, proof enough of Moscow's desperate anxiety about U.S. and U.K. nuclear capability. Fuchs estimated the U.S. stockpile at 125 atomic bombs with a production of fifty a year (he also gave Feklisov a sketch of the mechanism for a hydrogen bomb under theoretical development in the United States).[16] According to a "veteran of Soviet atomic espionage" quoted by a Russian historian, Vladimir Zubok, in September 1945 Fuchs had passed to Moscow the U.S. monthly production of uranium-235 and plutonium, enabling Russian scientists to calculate the annual production of atomic bombs, which they concluded was too small for an atomic blitzkrieg of the USSR. Curiously enough, Zubok's source was a Russian article written by the same Alexander Feklisov who had handled Fuchs in London.[17]

The 1947 Fuchs figure was higher than the existing U.S. nuclear arsenal, although the components for additional bombs were available. Lilienthal later mentioned a 1947 inventory of no more than a dozen bombs, none ready for immediate use, and a production rate of two additional weapons per month, only slightly less than Fuchs's annual estimate. Even if the U.S. nuclear stockpile had increased substantially by mid-1948, few serious U.S. military planners believed that a U.S. strategic air offensive would win a war with the Soviet Union.

In June 1947 General Kenneth Strong, the head of the new Joint Intelligence Bureau (JIB) in the Ministry of Defense, supplied the U.S. Air Force with target intelligence on Russian towns to be used by the USAF in nuclear targeting.[18] Strong had been Eisenhower's chief of intelligence during World War II and together with Tedder was the British military officer most respected by U.S. officers. He was also a trusted friend of General Walter Bedell Smith. The two men began working closely together during the Allied offensive in North Africa in 1943. In August of that year, the two had flown from Algiers to Gibraltar and on to Lisbon disguised as commercial travelers (Smith on a British passport) to begin secret negotiations with the Italians that led to Italy's formal surrender in Sicily on September 3. When Eisenhower was named supreme commander of Allied forces in Europe, he asked that Strong be assigned as his G-2. General Sir Alan Brooke, chief of the Imperial General Staff, refused. Some English officers thought that Strong had become a bit too American in his ways (the same criticism leveled at Sir Dick White). For many American officers, Brooke was insufferably British in his ways. The denial led to an angry exchange with the easily aroused General Smith, the recriminations so bitter that Brooke protested to Eisenhower, who ignored him and appealed his request for Strong directly to Churchill. Brooke was overruled and Strong was Eisenhower's intelligence chief throughout the European campaign; Dick White was his deputy for counterintelligence. Strong was invaluable in helping arrange the German high command's Rheims and Berlin surrenders. Air Marshal Tedder was with him. One American military historian called Strong "as shrewd an intelligence analyst as the Allies had."[19]

Strong's duties often brought him to Washington and in early October 1950, immediately after Smith took up his post as CIA director, he asked Strong if he would consider joining him as his deputy. Strong had resigned his commission after the war and in January 1946 was named director general of political intelligence at the Foreign Office before moving on to the Defense Ministry. Although tempted, he declined Smith's offer. He was reluctant to surrender his British citizenship and didn't believe a foreigner could work successfully at the agency. He would later decline General Eisenhower's 1951 request, made over dinner in London at Claridge's, that he rejoin him at NATO as chief of intelligence. Smith had to be satisfied with using Strong as his model in reorganizing the CIA as Strong had organized the North African and SHAEF intelligence staffs. Both men scorned decision by committee and relied almost uniquely on individual judgment, initiative, and responsibility.

After Philby's dismissal from MI6, Strong was a familiar figure at Smith's CIA headquarters at 2430 E Street in Washington, although his presence is never mentioned by the most garrulous CIA officers of the period. One retiree who recalled his prolonged presence—a reliable CIA officer, not a fantast—believed General Strong was temporarily transferred from the Ministry of Defense as MI6's liaison with the CIA in Washington, where he remained until August. There's no doubt Strong was trusted by Smith and trusted absolutely.

Strong's Joint Intelligence Bureau was helping Commonwealth nations set up similar agencies combining air, naval, and military intelligence. Evidently the JIB was also working in association with the secret Commonwealth Sigint organization established in 1946–1947 for the pooling of wireless intelligence. In 1949–1950 Australia was reorganizing its intelligence agency after the Venona decrypts passed to Canberra revealed extensive Soviet penetration of the Ministry of External Affairs and the weakness of the Australian security service. Strong's senior staff at the JIB included intelligence officers he had worked with during World War II, as familiar as he had been with strategic and tactical deception. The London Controlling Section that ran Britain's postwar deceptions was under the Ministry of Defense and would have been in liaison with Strong's bureau. As early as July 1946 General Strong had urged the Attlee government to set up a peacetime psychological warfare unit but Foreign Secretary Bevin had rejected the notion.[20]

In late 1947 fear of Communist subversion in Western Europe finally drove the Washington policy establishment to begin thinking seriously about covert operations for political and psychological warfare. London's Foreign Office was well ahead of the State Department in creating the Russia Committee in April 1946. In Washington Secretary of Defense James Forrestal was also searching for a strategy. He had played a leading role in creating the CIA and was the most ambitious and tireless member of the Washington policy clique from 1947 until months before his death in May 1949. He was just as forceful in planning, prodding, cajoling, and intriguing for a more aggressive CIA role in political warfare and covert operations. A September 1947 CIA legal opinion concluded that black propaganda, primarily designed for subversion, confusion, and political effect, as well as certain special operations were not within the authority Congress granted the CIA. The door was held open for funding resistance movements in Western Europe "in the event of further extension of Communist control" but only with congressional approval.[21]

Forrestal had asked for a CIA legal opinion on covert action in the hope of covertly aiding the Italian Christian Democrats (he turned to his well-heeled Wall Street friends instead). British historian A. J. P. Taylor faults him for playing a large part in inventing the Cold War, a memorable quip, like many in Taylor's too brief reviews, but no more accurate than crediting George Marshall with singlehandedly inventing the 1947 Marshall Plan.[22] As early as 1945 Forrestal was haunted by the specter of Soviet ideological and military power; his obsession is evident in his diaries, in which he copied confidential and secret reports on the USSR. He was among the first to point out the contradictions between U.S. military resources and foreign-policy objectives, warning that military limitations (Truman's budget restrictions) were crippling U.S. foreign-policy goals. In 1945 and 1946, during a period of indecisive drift, he was one of the few in Washington searching for a coherent and comprehensive national strategy. He found one in February 1946 in American diplomat George Kennan's long telegram from the U.S. embassy in Moscow analyzing Soviet power. Then secretary of the navy, Forrestal reproduced the cable and made it required reading for hundreds of officers in the armed forces.[23]

He was also responsible for Kennan's September 1946 assignment to the faculty of Washington's think tank of the times, the National War College, and his later selection by Secretary of State Marshall to head the Policy Planning Staff, a new State Department unit to replace in part the War Department's Division of Plans and Operations. While at the War College, Forrestal asked Kennan to comment on a paper prepared by his staff on Marxism and Soviet power. Kennan preferred to draft his own analysis and did. The paper was later published as "The Sources of Soviet Power" in the July 1947 issue of *Foreign Affairs* and would help form the basis of U.S. strategic doctrine for containment of the USSR. Kennan urged the patient but firm containment of Russian expansionist tendencies. In 1976 he would insist that his intention was to persuade Washington to deal realistically rather than naively with Moscow and disabuse Stalin of any notion the USSR could pursue its own ambitions in Europe or elsewhere at the expense of American national interests. He was later "shocked" by the narrowness of its interpretation by

U.S. policymakers and their erroneous conviction that Soviet hostility was so great only overwhelming military power could induce the Russians to behave responsibly.[24]

In the autumn of 1947, among the more ominous events that drew the attention of Washington as well as the Soviet policy planners of the Foreign Office's Russia Committee was the creation of the Cominform, seen as the newest and latest instrument of Communist subversion in Western Europe. On September 22–27, 1947, nine leaders of the European and Eastern European Communist parties met at Szklarska Sereba, Poland, to launch a new information bureau to coordinate party activities. The Cominform was believed to be a recreation of the old subversive Comintern abolished four years earlier during the war. In London the Foreign Office's Russia Committee reached the same erroneous conclusion: the Cominform was Moscow's recreated instrument for subverting the European democracies. For Washington, it was another straw in the wind, another reason for establishing a covert operations counterweight at the CIA. The facts were otherwise.[25]

Creation of the Cominform was a defensive tactic designed to mobilize resistance to the Marshall Plan, frustrate the creation of an anti-Soviet coalition in Western Europe, and consolidate Moscow's control of Eastern Europe. Limited in scope, in no sense did it revive the old Comintern, an international alliance of Communist parties formed in 1919 to promote socialist revolution throughout the world and dissolved by Stalin in 1943. (In 1934 Philby apparently believed he had been recruited by a Comintern agent.) The new Cominform was organized at Stalin's direction to bring into line the nine European Communist parties, not to coordinate revolutionary action, but to accuse, lecture, and reeducate on political correctness, Moscow style. The intent was to unite Communist leaders in repudiating the 1947 Marshall Plan, the imperialist plot designed to enslave European economies. Originally planned to force Czechoslovakia to resist joining the Marshall Plan, it had been postponed after Prague rejected association. When finally held, it proved to be a failure. The leaders of the Italian, French, and Yugoslav Communist parties—Togliatti, Thorez, and Tito—didn't even attend. The Cominform failed its first and only test when Tito refused to submit to its arbitration in resolving his differences with Moscow. On June 28, 1948, Yugoslavia was expelled from the Cominform. In November 1949, at a Cominform meeting in Budapest, the Yugoslav Communist Party was condemned as murderers and spies. Stalin's faithful flock had done its work and he lost all further interest. The Cominform's brief fire had burned out and the ashes were abandoned years later to the Kremlin's potter's field.[26]

The Cominform was insignificant except as an instrument of Stalinist discipline and conformity. Those subverted weren't the European democracies but the leaders of the European Communist parties and the East European Communist satellites (the French Communist Jacques Duclos, who did attend, sat on a park bench afterward and wept bitter tears). Washington's alarm betrays the apprehension, fear, and confusion that marked many policy decisions. Against that confused background, Kennan's earlier long 1946 telegram from Moscow's impenetrable shadows would have seemed a brilliantly conceived solution to Washington's dilemma, whatever its relevance to Soviet intent. The perception of the Cominform as Moscow's subversive instrument was no less a failure in intelligence gathering and analysis.

In November 1947 a joint state-army-navy-air force committee agreed on a "black" (covert) and "white" (overt) information program for the CIA. The NSC debated the issue but Secretary of State Marshall and the armed services objected, reluctant to give the CIA authority for covert action without outside control.[27] The NSC resolved the impasse by sanctioning a CIA role in covert psychological operations "consistent with U.S. foreign policy and overt foreign information activities." This meant that the CIA's covert political warfare or propaganda voice was to sing as sweetly as *The Voice of America* from which it would take its weekly song sheets, as it in fact did. The formula wasn't dissimilar from British foreign secretary Bevin's insistence on propaganda as education, not deceit or dissimulation, although the American model wasn't democratic socialism.

To carry out the NSC directive on covert psychological warfare (that is, offensive action against the enemy by means other than military force), the CIA set up a special unit within the Office of Special Operations (OSO).[28] Few were satisfied with the speed or the results of the effort and none less than Forrestal. On March 26, before the April Italian elections, he wrote to the NSC director, Admiral Sidney Souers, pointing out that the "international situation has become more critical" and that "our foreign information activities" must be developed and coordinated with "our foreign and military policies." He asked for a review of CIA progress.[29] Forrestal was not only registering his unhappiness with the speed of the CIA execution but the military and the Joint Chiefs' disgust with the CIA/State conception of psychological and political warfare, which they believed demanded more extreme measures. The survey, concluded in April, merely chided CIA director Hillenkoetter for not moving more quickly. He was instructed to work with "anti-Communist democratic forces in foreign countries, particularly those politically left of center." The State Department's Policy Planning Staff under Kennan was also frustrated by the CIA performance.

George Kennan's views on political warfare were given in a May 4, 1948, Policy Planning Staff memorandum sent to the NSC and elsewhere. The preamble was typically Kennan: "Political warfare is the logical application of Clausewitz's doctrine in time of peace. In broadest definition, political warfare is the employment of all the means at a nation's command, short of war, to achieve its national objectives." The cornerstone of Kennan's plan was the creation of a public U.S. liberation committee to sponsor political refugee committees to revive "among political refugees from the Soviet Union a sense of national hope and purpose." The committees in turn would inspire "continuing popular resistance within the countries of the Soviet World." In case of war they would serve "as a nucleus for all-out liberation movements." The national movements would be led by "outstanding political refugees from the Soviet World, such as Mikolajczyk and Nagy" (respectable nationalist social democrats and moderates).[30]

Kennan believed his project "in the traditional American form [of] organized public support of resistance to tyranny in foreign countries. Throughout our history, private American citizens have banded together to champion the cause of freedom for people suffering under oppression." He noted contemptuously that "the Communists and Zionists have exploited this tradition to the extreme, to their own ends and to our national detriment, as witness the Abraham Lincoln brigade during the Spanish Civil War and the current illegal Zionist activities." He proposed the American "tradition be revived specifically to further American national interests in the present crisis." The plan was noble in the abstract, but naively oblivious to the ugly realities that awaited its realization in Europe, the recruitment of the nameless political rabble, mercenary riffraff, and extremist ex-Nazi thugs from the German displaced persons camp. For other reasons as well it proved a disaster for the CIA and an eventual embarrassment for the United States when its details were disclosed years later. (Dean Acheson, Truman's secretary of state, who valued Kennan's counsel, also wrote that Kennan "mingled flashes of prophetic insight and suggestions of total impracticability.")[31]

Kennan recommended the prompt creation of a directorate of political warfare operations under the cover of the NSC. The director would be chosen by and be responsible to the secretary of state. The CIA was ignored. Kennan insisted that unless covert political warfare was carried out under the direction and control of the State Department, the idea should be abandoned. A directorate is not what Kennan got, but enough of his plan remained intact to set a course for the CIA's new Office of Policy Coordination (OPC), created by the NSC in June 1948. The CIA director in cooperation with State and Defense would ensure that covert operations were consistent with U.S. foreign and military policies, which meant the OPC would be under State Department and military control. The NSC, which had created the unit to operate independently of the CIA, didn't consider the OPC an intelligence operation. Nevertheless, a covert operation unit was finally established within the CIA but only nominally under CIA control. This was far from what the Joint Chiefs wanted.

The OPC, as it developed, expanded, and ultimately spiraled out of control over the next five years, wasn't as Kennan, George Marshall, and others had originally conceived it. Testifying before the Senate Church committee in October 1975, Kennan explained that the primary purpose was to counter Moscow's well-funded subversive operations in France and Italy, which were attempting to gain control of "key elements" of public life as Communist fronts: the publishing industry, the press, labor, student, and women's organizations, and so forth. The limited OPC covert operations would fund similar democratic organizations. In supporting the oppressed peoples of Eastern Europe, Kennan intended that they be given recognition and a reason for hope, not air-dropped émigrés with guns and grenades to spark a rebellion. He meant that "when and if the occasion arose," meaning a civil uprising that might be years away, an OPC covert operations team would be ready to support this "nucleus for all-out liberation movements." If his expectations were naive, so was his understanding of the reckless military amateurs and adventurous dilettantes in the CIA and the Pentagon who would seize their opportunity and gallop off with it Wild West fashion. The OPC's covert operations under director Frank Wisner far exceeded Kennan's intent.[32]

In the spring of 1948, while the CIA dawdled in setting up a unit for covert political and psychological warfare operations and the State Department was pondering Clausewitz and sending scholarly essays about it to NSC colleagues, the armed services and the Joint Chiefs were fed up. They believed the CIA should be a JCS subordinate, as had the OSS during World War II. Limited to a wartime responsibility for psychological and political warfare, annoyed by State's high-minded pieties, dubious about CIA competence and impatient for action, the Joint Chiefs proposed the immediate creation of a psychological warfare agency responsible to the NSC to begin operations "at the earliest possible moment."[33] The Joint Chiefs' hostility to the CIA and the State Department in their conception, design, and execution of political and propaganda warfare was similar to the conflict in London between the civil servants of the Foreign Office's Russia Committee and the more aggressive chiefs of the British services over the same issues. The U.S. Joint Chiefs' ambitions for a greater peacetime role and more hard-hitting tactics in political and psychological warfare were the British service chiefs' ambition as well but denied by Bevin's Foreign Office. The Joint Chiefs' proposal was made on or about April 1, 1948, the day the first Berlin crisis erupted.

The future of Germany was the continuing destabilizing threat to Western Europe's precarious equilibrium. Berlin was the tinderbox that could ignite the explosion. In 1948 few would predict Germany would remain divided as it did for more than forty years. Most analysts assumed that the country would ultimately become a unified nation. The unpredictable factor was the means, whether by mutual concessions and agreement among the four occupying Allied powers or by Soviet aggression.[34] Berlin also most troubled the Joint Chiefs by fully exposing U.S. military vulnerability. But the larger issue would define American and British strategic war plans, determine U.S. and U.K. nuclear policy, and embitter Allied-Soviet relations for years to come. As John Lukacs explained it some years later, the Soviet-American crises in Europe "might have been due to a fundamental mutual misunderstanding: Washington presupposing that the immediate Russian aim was to upset and conquer Western Europe, Moscow presupposing that the American aim was to upset and reconquer Eastern Europe."[35] Both assumptions proved wrong. Allied war plans in 1948–1950 based on that hypothesis had implications for Philby's 1949 posting to Washington. Not until the outbreak of the Korean War in June 1950 would those narrower strategic premises be reexamined.

Since the Communist coup in Prague in February 1948, Foreign Secretary Bevin had been rethinking the Foreign Office's Soviet strategy. In early March he advocated the creation of a Western European defense agreement. The Brussels Defense Pact was signed on March 17 but without the military capability to achieve much of anything. Three days later, the Soviet Union's representative on the Allied Berlin Control Council walked out. In the meantime, Bevin flew to Washington to successfully persuade the Americans to join. On March 31 the Soviets notified the U.S. commander in Berlin, General Lucius Clay, that they were imposing road and rail restrictions on traffic into West Berlin, a signal that Moscow wouldn't tolerate a strong, economically autonomous Germany in the now united British and U.S. zones. Truman rejected the suggestion that he warn Stalin the interception of U.S. military convoys might provoke a war. The Russians soon relaxed the Berlin restrictions, and traffic began to move again. Fears were diminished but not forgotten.[36] The air force, which had disagreed with an April 2 CIA estimate that there was no imminent threat of war, was impatient with the bureaucratic impasse and began to consider a propaganda and psychological warfare campaign of its own.

On April 8, 1948, General Hollis, the secretary of the British Joint Chiefs of Staff Committee, met with General Gruenther and the U.S. Joint Chiefs of Staff at the Pentagon to consider a British proposal so secret no formal minutes were kept or issued.[37] As described in chapter 7, the purpose was to consider a British chiefs of staff memorandum dealing with our "desirable strategic objectives and the planning work which should be undertaken." Although the subject wasn't identified in the Hollis memo or his covering letter to General Gruenther, there is no doubt that the subject was deception operations and the British Joint Chiefs' proposal to reestablish a combined deception effort as had existed three years earlier when the London Controlling Section was represented on the British Joint Services Mission. In his letter to Gruenther, Hollis had mentioned Jack Easton's coming visit to Washington and the opportunity to discuss deception "in general terms as distinct from the particular aspect referred to by Bush at Mr. Forrestal's dinner."

U.S. Air Force chief of staff General Carl Spaatz was a member of the Joint Chiefs and heard Hollis's April 8 presentation. (Spaatz was retiring at the end of April to be replaced by General Hoyt Vandenberg.) The Joint Chiefs' decision on the proposal isn't known. There were serious divisions within the Joint Chiefs, particularly between the navy and the air force on the control of the atomic bomb and the responsibility for strategic bombing warfare. On May 12, 1948, General Spaatz and USAF Major General R. C. Lindsay met in London with Air Marshal Tedder; Air Marshal Sir James Robb; Air Commodore Mills, director of plans; and chief of air staff Marshall of the Royal Air Force. The meeting was held "Pursuant to the Provisions of JSPC" (the Joint Strategic Planning Committee chaired by General Gruenther) and agreed in a memo of understanding that (a) the atom bomb would be used at the onset in the event of war; and (b) as a deterrent to war, appropriate propaganda measures would be taken to publicize the bomb's use.[38] Several aspects of the USAF-RAF top-secret May 12 memorandum make it unique. It was outside any of the required Washington and Pentagon executive channels of agreement and preceded the NSC policy decision on the use of nuclear weapons, which were still under civilian control. The participants were part of an informal collegial network of U.S. and British air force professionals bound together by their wartime service and years of mutual cooperation and trust. All shared a common understanding of strategic preparation, covert operations, and the value of strategic deception, an abiding suspicion of the Soviet Union, a frustration with peacetime London and Washington, and the interminable compromises, delays, and meddlesome intrusion of civilian and bureaucratic oversight. That common concern ignored the more formal proprieties of national agreement.

In April 1948 negotiations began for a formal U.S. Air Force–Royal Air Force target intelligence agreement.[39] A Joint Chiefs' committee also met secretly with British officers to discuss the transfer of U.S. bombers to Britain as part of war plan Broiler, an update of the earlier U.S. Pincher. U.S. B-29s would be flown against Russian cities from British bases in England, Egypt, and India.[40] Apart from direct talks with Ministry of Defense or Air Ministry officers in London, U.S.-U.K. military coordination was managed through the British Joint Services Mission in Washington established during World War II, presumably General Strong's Washington base as well.

General Hoyt Vandenberg, the former director of the Central Intelligence Group who succeeded Spaatz as air force chief of staff, favored a more dynamic and sustained effort to publicize the devastating consequences of atomic warfare. He had spent several months in the USSR in 1943–1944 as chief of an air mission to Moscow and later commanded the Ninth Air Force in Europe, where he had worked closely with General Walter Bedell Smith, Air Marshal Tedder, and Major General Kenneth Strong. He concluded that the Cold War and the atom bomb had created such new and intractable problems that they required different and unusual methods. He believed the air force should create its own Psychological Warfare Air Command equal in importance to the Strategic Air Command. The new command would bring in experts to exploit greater awareness of the devastative capacity of nuclear weapons as a deterrent to war. With far less psychological subtlety than Vandenberg might have preferred, General George Kenney, commander of the Strategic Air Command, gave a blustering speech in May insisting that peace with the Soviet Union was little more than "a superficial armistice," a belief shared by many on both sides of the Atlantic. The May

17, 1948, edition of *Newsweek* reported the remarks and described the planned destruction of the USSR with atomic weapons should the Russians suddenly go "berserk" and overrun Western Europe.[41]

Kenney's blunt warning came a few days before the May 6 completion of the Joint Chiefs of Staff new top-secret war plan conceived in response to Forrestal's prodding. Codenamed Halfmoon, the plan targeted fifty atomic bombs on twenty key Soviet political-military centers, provided "authority to employ atomic bombs has been obtained" (it hadn't).[42] The general's salvo was also part of an air force campaign on behalf of the new B-36 strategic bomber as well as a crude sortie in psychological warfare. It soon drew an angry response. On June 6, in a note to the State Department, the Soviet ambassador in Washington vehemently denounced the speech as an example of "unbridled propaganda for a new war against the Soviet Union" in violation of the U.N. General Assembly's resolution condemning "all forms of propaganda designed to encourage any threat to the peace." The Soviet note deplored the plan "to use American air forces, air bases and atomic bombs against the destruction of Soviet cities such as Moscow, Leningrad, Kiev, Kharkov, Odessa and others" and the plan's strategy for "closing the circle of air bases around Russia until Russians are throttled."[43]

Although in the spirit of the secret agreement signed at the May 12 London meeting between Royal Air Force and U.S. Air Force officers—the value of the atom bomb as a psychological deterrent to war—Kenney's buccaneering speech was an empty threat. The Soviet Union lay beyond the strike capability of the U.S. Strategic Air Command. One historian asserts that only 319 aging Boeing B-29s were available; air-refueling capability by tankers was still being developed. General Gruenther had never believed an air offensive from the United Kingdom was an acceptable concept but had proposed it as the only alternative allowed under Truman's budget ceiling.[44] The possibility of a U.S. air strike nevertheless worried Moscow. A secret March 1948 Moscow cable to the Soviet embassy resident in Washington opened to Western scholars by the KGB years later requested his assessment of reports describing urgent U.S. military preparations for an offensive against the Soviet Union. The cable was never broken by Venona.[45]

On June 24, 1948, the Berlin standoff again erupted when the Russians blockaded West Berlin, cut electricity, and halted all land and water traffic, isolating two million Berliners. Two days later Truman, the Joint Chiefs of Staff, and the National Security Council rejected General Clay's call to defy the blockade with military force. On his own initiative Clay had launched U.S. air transport to resupply the city and Washington wisely expanded the

Berlin airlift. On June 28 Truman approved the transfer of two additional B-29 squadrons to Germany. Within three weeks he sent four squadrons of B-29 bombers to Lincolnshire, England.[46] The news releases accompanying their arrival claimed the ninety or so B-29s were capable of carrying nuclear weapons. The claim was another thrust in air force psychological warfare, a deception on the cheap achieved with nothing more than a press release and a copy machine, but designed to trouble those who knew nothing of the bombers' nuclear capability or the Lilliputian U.S. nuclear arsenal and lacked the means of verification. At least one Russian military observer in the USSR drew the most ominous conclusion: the ninety B-29s with one or two bombs aboard meant two hundred Hiroshimas.[47]

The deduction was what the U.S. and Royal Air Forces intended but was far from the truth. The B-29s weren't fitted for atomic weapons. Not until early July 1950, following the outbreak of the Korean War, would President Truman allow the stockpiling of nonnuclear components of nuclear bombs at forward bases in England. The United States may have had fifty nuclear weapons in the stockpile, a questionable number supplied by one expert years later, but certainly not two hundred. The Atomic Energy Commission, not the Pentagon's military chiefs, retained custody. Forrestal had been unsuccessfully badgering Truman to transfer the weapons to the Pentagon, but not until September 13, 1948, did he agree that only if necessary he would do so.

The Berlin crises succeeded in bringing the atomic bomb to the center of U.S. strategic planning even if the Pentagon didn't yet have custody and no decision had been made as to whether it would be used. In June the Senate adopted the Vandenberg Resolution supporting Truman's plans to enter into a European collective defense agreement. In July, talks opened in London on establishment of the "Western Union" defense pact. In its July 16 instructions to the U.S. representatives, the JCS told them to "avoid discussing with any of the foreign conferees the policy or the plans of the United States with respect to the employment of atomic weapons in warfare." Those instructions were adopted from a report to the NSC by the secretary of defense and circulated as NSC-9/4.[48]

The limited atomic stockpile had fueled intense competition between the air force and the navy over the allocation and delivery of atomic weapons (the U.S. Air Force had collaborated more successfully with the Royal Air Force than the U.S. Navy). Relief came in April and May 1948 after new tests had shown that atomic bombs with twice the awesome destructive power of the Hiroshima and Nagasaki bombs could be built with far less fissionable material. The conclusive top-secret nuclear tests were held at Eniwetok in the U.S. Pacific Proving Grounds in the Marshall Islands, a U.S. Trust Territory. Operation Sandstone proved the value of improvements made in the design of nuclear weapons. X-Ray, a thirty-seven-kiloton bomb, was tested on April 15; Yoki, forty-nine kilotons, was tested May 1; and Zebra, an eighteen-kiloton bomb, was tested on May 15, 1948. Because the Sandstone tests required a sizable flotilla of ships and ten thousand men, the secret tests could hardly be concealed. A Soviet warship standing some twenty miles from Eniwetok Atoll observed the detonations. Moscow was less informed about the results. The tests demonstrated a 75 percent improvement in the yield of fissionable material, which meant that far more bombs for the stockpile could be produced with less material. An atomic weapons scholar noted that Sandstone "marked the end of the era of the atomic device as a piece of complicated laboratory apparatus rather than a weapon."[49]

At the Naval War College meeting at Newport, Rhode Island, on August 20–22, 1948, the Eniwetok success was celebrated. There were now enough atomic bombs to go around—perhaps as many as four hundred by 1950. The Newport conference could now agree that the air force would have interim operational control of atomic weapons but would use to advantage any strategic bombing ability developed by the navy in developing new aircraft carriers. The USAF rift with Naval Aviation had been resolved, but the $14.4 billion U.S. defense budget limited the air force to Britain in carrying out an air offensive against the USSR. There were other problems. In October General Vandenberg sent Lieutenant General Curtis E. LeMay to Offutt Air Force Base in Nebraska to overhaul the Strategic Air Command and establish it as the major instrument of deterrence. That same year, the SAC flew a mock air raid against Dayton, Ohio, in what was called a maximum effort mission. Not a single bomber completed its mission.[50]

As noted earlier, in 1948 the Soviet Union lay well beyond the strike capability of the U.S. Strategic Air Command except by one-way or kamikaze missions. Even as late as 1953, a B-50 crew targeted against Tula, a Soviet city near Moscow, was instructed to turn southwest after its mission "in the hope of a successful bailout" somewhere in the Ukraine, where they were told they might encounter "friendly natives." The pilot, Colonel Walter Boyne, wasn't optimistic.[51]

As inadequate as the SAC B-29, B-36, and B-50 strategic strike force, and as limited as the U.S. atomic arsenal, U.S. Air Force senior officers and their

Royal Air Force counterparts were convinced that in the absence of sufficient military forces for the United States and the United Kingdom to fight a conventional war in Europe, the surest and most effective deterrent was in persuading the Kremlin of the deadliness of Allied intent and its overwhelming nuclear and strategic air capability. Moscow had to be convinced that Soviet military aggression in Western Europe would be met by atomic devastation. The persuasion problem was twofold: overcoming Moscow's skepticism as to whether the United States would actually use the bomb and removing any doubt about its decisive or war-winning power, the size of the U.S. nuclear arsenal, and its strategic air capability.

In September the NSC had finally and formally agreed on U.S. nuclear policy. In NSC-30, "Policy on Atomic Warfare," the premises were set forth: the atomic bomb "offers the present major counterbalance to the ever-present threat of Soviet military power." It also advised against any public declaration that the United States was willing to use nuclear weapons in the event of war. The logic appeared to be that in the debate that followed, U.S. public opinion might be so violently opposed that Moscow might question U.S. nuclear resolve and move more aggressively, "which it is fundamentally U.S. policy to avert." The Russians, it concluded, should "never be given the slightest reason to believe the United States would even consider not to use atomic warfare against them if necessary."[52] The language was clumsily left-footed in making a sensible point ("We're not war-mongering"), but the meaning was evident enough even if hidden in secrecy and intended only for the highest executive councils. The nuclear bomb was the sole guarantee of European security in the face of Moscow's massive superiority in military manpower. If NSC-30 implied that the nuclear threat was a psychological deterrent to Soviet aggression, it wasn't clear how that warning might be delivered to Moscow. U.S. Air Force and Royal Air Force senior officers had recognized its deterrent value much earlier.

In September the British chiefs of staff were also stirred to action. Earlier in the year, General Leslie Hollis, Stewart Menzies of MI6, and William Hayter of the Foreign Office attempted to create a mechanism that would give the chiefs participation in the planning and execution of the Foreign Office's propaganda offensive against the USSR. The idea was rejected.[53] During a September conference with the minister of defense, Air Marshal Tedder resumed the offensive. He criticized the Foreign Office's Cold War counteroffensive as totally insufficient and called for the government to commit every resource to more aggressive countermeasures to deter Soviet expansion. The chiefs of staff and their services intelligence chiefs weren't merely displeased but disgusted, like the U.S. Joint Chiefs, with the entire thrust of Britain's lethargic Cold War offensive. They wanted operations to be directed and controlled by an interagency staff able to deploy all available means, including executive action or covert political warfare. The recommendations were passed to Bevin and led to further discussions with the chiefs of staff. The Foreign Office insisted that its Russia Committee was in fact Great Britain's Cold War planning staff, brushed the rest aside, but agreed that Tedder should join the committee.[54]

On November 12, 1948, in London, Secretary of Defense James Forrestal listened as former prime minister Churchill also deprecated the "dangerous tendency to write down the atomic bomb in its effect on Russia and on Western Europe." Churchill was preaching to the choirmaster. Six days later, Forrestal met with Tedder and the other two British chiefs of staff. Tedder pointed out that the strategic war plans in which "the two countries are engaged" were "utterly unrealistic because they do not include in sufficient detail the planning for atomic warfare." Forrestal's reply didn't address Tedder's specific concern, at least in the sanitized version made public in 1951, which omitted detail on Anglo-American war plans or a combined U.S.-U.K. covert operation. Tedder's comment also referred to the inadequacy of the Joint Chiefs' plans for the defense of Europe. Forrestal would have told him a new plan was on the drawing board. The British chiefs of staff also made it clear that "they considered it essential that the United States sign a pact to support the Western European powers in the event of hostilities." (In April 1949, the North Atlantic Treaty Organization [NATO] was formally established; twelve nations led by the United States and the United Kingdom signed the constituting treaty. For several years it remained merely a paper military force.) On his flight back to Washington, Forrestal dictated a memo to President Truman describing the lessons he'd learned from his talks with the British chiefs of staff and others that reinforced his own beliefs. The atomic bomb's advantage as a policy weapon "should not be deprecated" as a deterrent to Soviet aggression. He reported that throughout his European trip he was "increasingly impressed by the fact that the only balance that we have against the overwhelming manpower of the Russians, and therefore the chief deterrent to war, is the threat of immediate retaliation with the atomic bomb." U.S. Air Force officers and the British chiefs were of the same mind.

At Tedder's first meeting with the Foreign Office Russia Committee on November 25, he suggested there should be "a small permanent team which would consider plans which would subsequently be executed by ourselves and the Americans." He also advised that "unless we reformed our present machinery for conducting the 'cold war,' we might lose it." A subcommittee was formed for long-range planning but the plan for immediate action was shelved. The meeting also took up a possible Albanian operation. Tedder was skeptical of its value unless followed up by military action and "likened it to a barrage laid down before attack by troops; if it was laid down too far ahead your friends were simply annihilated." His words proved prophetic, although no one appeared to recall his warning later.[55]

Tedder's description of "a small permanent team" to prepare plans to be executed by the British and Americans resembled the small joint team led by Spaatz and Tedder that had agreed to the USAF-RAF memorandum of May. The Russia Committee accepted the recommendation for a small permanent planning section but it was placed under the Foreign Office to avoid any peacetime revival of wartime agencies for executive action dominated by the service chiefs of staff.

U.S. and Royal Air Force collaboration continued in secret. The British were concerned about the effects of the transfer of American bombers to England. A secret cipher message of January 20, 1949, sent by Air Marshal Charles Medhurst from the Air Ministry in London to the British air force staff in Washington answered a USAF proposal to send the 509th Medium Bomber Group to the United Kingdom. The British chiefs of staff agreed but only if the transfer wasn't publicized. The 509th Bomber Group had obliterated Hiroshima and Nagasaki. During World War II Medhurst was director of air intelligence at the Air Ministry and later assistant chief of air staff intelligence. He worked with Ultra and British "Y" or communications intercepts at the Air Ministry and dealt with Moscow on intelligence exchange, including codebreaking operations.[56] By November 1949 Medhurst was assigned to the British Joint Services Mission in Washington with offices in the Main Navy building. In November, talks were underway for the Royal Air Force to incorporate thirty-two U.S. B-29 bombers in its operational wings by July 1, 1950.[57] At the time, Philby was in Washington and the Korean War was still seven months away.

The earlier Halfmoon war plans and their modification as Fleetwood and Trojan hadn't included plans for the defense of Western Europe. In February 1949 a fourth Joint Chiefs war plan, codenamed Offtackle, was underway. Initiated by General Eisenhower and submitted to the Joint Chiefs in November 1949, Offtackle could now assert that "atomic weapons will be used by the United States." Like the other plans, Offtackle considered strategic air power the only means of blunting the Soviet advance in Western Europe. The objective was to drive Russian forces back to their pre–World War II borders but assumed that Soviet superiority in ground forces would yield quick successes in Western Europe. A year of mobilization would be needed to build forces sufficient to recapture any lost territory. Bases in England, Okinawa, and Cairo-Suez would be staging areas for the air offensive and were to be secured from Soviet attack. Offtackle called for plans "to secure the United Kingdom against invasion, and defend it against air attack to the degree necessary to insure its availability as a major base for all types of military operations." Other objectives were to maintain Allied control of the Western Mediterranean–North African area and the Cairo-Suez area.[58]

As the Pentagon, the Joint Chiefs, and the Royal Air Force knew full well, the doubts were in the details. Offtackle intended an immediate nuclear attack on the USSR should Moscow launch a ground offensive. Even had the entire U.S. stockpile of Hiroshima-type bombs been delivered as planned—and the air force doubted that this could be done—once the air strikes were over, the United States would have exhausted its arsenal of atomic weapons and aircraft. The U.S. strategic bomber force consisted of some 250 or more obsolescent B-29s and a handful of not wholly dependable B-36s. At a May 1996 ceremony in honor of SAC's fiftieth anniversary, an SAC pilot whose B-29 was based in the United Kingdom in 1950 recalled that his Russian target city, Gorki, would have been reached with only enough fuel to fly another sixty miles, a suicidal ending that evokes the final scene of Stanley Kubrick's film *Dr. Strangelove*.[59]

Offtackle also called for a prolonged conventional bombing campaign after the atomic attacks. As several study groups showed, however, the air force hadn't the planes, crews, forward bases, or special equipment required for a conventional bombing campaign. Finally, the war plans assumed a long and protracted struggle that could be won only by an immense ground campaign slogging through Europe and on into the USSR, where the plan would disappear in the snow and ice of a distantly interminable future, far beyond the imaginative grasp of the Joint Chiefs' planning staff or indeed anyone else.

By February 1949 Foreign Minister Bevin had yielded considerable ground in his opposition to clandestine warfare. Still adamant in denying the British service chiefs or the Defense Committee a role in determining anti-Soviet policy, he proposed that the Foreign Office's Russia Committee work with the United States to aid Greece, encourage Yugoslav's Tito, and detach Albania from the Soviet orbit.[60] In March the chiefs of staff forwarded to Prime Minister Attlee a proposal by Air Chief Marshal John Slessor for "a counter-offensive employing all appropriate economic and political weapons under the control of a specially qualified staff." William Strang of the Foreign Office was asked to review his refusal to relinquish control of anti-Soviet operations to any group or body independent of the Foreign Office, the British chiefs of staff in particular. He proposed to Bevin "a small secret committee" for political warfare that would include Sir Maurice Dean of the Ministry of Defense and give the service chiefs a role. Instead, Bevin established a Permanent Undersecretary Department at the Foreign Ministry that fully controlled British foreign-policy initiatives, including clandestine operations. The British services had only minimal representation.[61]

The British chiefs of staff pleas for a much more active role in planning anti-Soviet counteroffensives not only were ignored but were effectively neutralized. They were advocating a Cold War reestablishment of the same extreme measures adopted in World War II, in which they had all participated and which was still very much alive in memory. Operations would be conducted in absolute secrecy and with maximum flexibility using all necessary tactics and resources. The Foreign Office would have none of it. The Soviet offensive remained under Foreign Office control. Had the British service chiefs decided informally to launch their own counteroffensive operations using their own intelligence assets at the Ministry of Defense, they would have been well equipped to do so with the same secrecy that obscured their collaboration with the U.S. Air Force. The London Controlling Section would have been the instrument for deception operations. MI5 and MI6 officers who had collaborated with the W Board in World War II would have supplied the opportunities.

In March the Joint Chiefs of Staff briefed the House Armed Services Committee on its strategic war plans listing seventy strategic targets in the USSR within range of the B-36s. The details were leaked to the press and drew a stern rebuke from the committee chairman, Carl Vinson, who demanded an explanation from Stuart Symington, secretary of the air force. Symington claimed the leak wasn't officially inspired, although there is little doubt that it was. In March or April 1949, strategic air command officers met with the Royal Air Force to complete pre D-Day plans for a strategic air offensive from the United Kingdom as called for by U.S. Air Force war plan Trojan. The U.S. strategic air force plan, an ambitious if entirely theoretical operation, was designed for an all-out obliteration of Russian industry and cities by B-29s and B-50s flown from European and U.K. airfields, and B-36s from U.S. airfields. Three hundred atom bombs would be delivered in the initial attack, seventy more in the following wave, with the remainder held in reserve.[62] The U.S. Air Force lacked both the nuclear bombs and the long-range strategic bombers to carry out such an assault. Similar U.S.-U.K. collaboration continued with the Joint Chiefs' war plan Offtackle. In the meantime the Pentagon's propaganda machine continued to rumble.

This was the background in August 1949 when Jack Easton sent a telegram to Philby in Istanbul offering the post of MI6 station chief in Washington. The Anglo-American codebreakers had achieved significant success in penetrating Soviet codes, although the extent of that success is still concealed by GCHQ. The British Russia Committee and the CIA's OPC were planning covert operations in Albania and the Soviet republics to the disdain of the service chiefs; both were sideshows, irrelevant to the real threat. In Western Europe, twelve ill-equipped Allied divisions with little or no air support faced twenty-seven Soviet divisions backed by more Red Army divisions in reserve, supported by sixty thousand East German military police. The American forces were occupation troops and would have proved as inadequate, ill trained, and ill prepared as they were in Korea in June and July 1950. In London and Washington, U.S. and British military and Royal Air Force officers were secretly collaborating on forward preparations for an atomic blitz of the Soviet Union and groping for the most effective means of driving home that warning to Moscow as a deterrent to war.

Philby was delighted with Easton's offer. The "lure was irresistible," as he said. If "lure" seems ambiguous, depending on which end of the fly rod you're struggling with, it wasn't for Philby. The new assignment in Washington offered "unlimited potentialities," or so he imagined.[63] He accepted. In London during his September briefing by Sir Maurice Oldfield, he learned of a remarkable new "deciphering machine which in one day does the work of a thousand people in a thousand years." Those unlimited potentialities were now measurably constrained and so must have been his enthusiasm. But his final instructions from his handler Mikhail Shishkin preceded his briefing by Oldfield. Once in Washington, he was out of touch with his Soviet illegal for more than a year and perhaps eighteen of his twenty months.

Chapter
TEN

The CIA in transition.—Censure and scorn.—

Admiral Hillenkoetter.—Philby and Angleton.—

Delusional rubbish.—Albania and the Ukraine.—

Displaced persons camps.—"A horrible mistake."—

A pint-sized opportunity.—Philby's reports.

In October 1949, when Philby arrived at the British embassy, the CIA was scattered about in some twenty-eight buildings in Washington. The largest group of offices was located at 2430 E Street in four yellow brick buildings on Navy Hill, as it is now called as a State Department annex, overlooking the Lincoln Memorial and the Potomac River. Four temporary buildings stood nearby. Somewhat secluded by Washington street-front or walk-in standards, the gated and fenced compound was occupied by the Office of Strategic Services (OSS) during the war. Isolated from the main complex, down the hill and across Independence Avenue near the Reflecting Pool, were other temporary buildings, I, K, and L among them, where the Office of Special Operations (OSO) and the Office of Policy Coordination (OPC) were housed. Other units were located elsewhere in transient quarters.[1]

Whatever its reputation after Philby gained his notoriety, the CIA wasn't an effective intelligence agency in 1949–1950. The dispersal of offices during those early years reflected its organization. Until October 1950, when General Walter Bedell Smith took command, the agency was still loosely scattered, loosely organized, and judged by all those familiar with its operations incompetent and unproductive. Despite these weaknesses, the CIA of this period has been consistently misread and wrongly described in both the United States and the United Kingdom. British journalists in particular exaggerated CIA operations and relevance to show the importance of Philby's liaison responsibilities. Some writers were evidently misled by similarly uninformed American journalists.[2] One British account claims that from the onset the Central Intelligence Group (CIG) showed a "ruthlessness and hunger for power," that it "seized control" of military and naval intelligence organizations and the State Department, and "uncovered" and "wiped out" a War Department "secret intelligence service," presumably the Strategic Services Unit (SSU). These claims have absolutely no basis in fact.[3]

The evolution of the CIA is a complicated tale of bureaucratic ambition, jealousy, bitterness, suspicion, and confusion among Washington's competing executive agencies and military commands. Our interest is simpler. The OSS was dissolved by a presidential order signed on September 20, 1945, that took effect on October 1, 1945. Its clandestine services were transferred to the War Department as the SSU and research and analysis were moved to the State Department. To maintain an intelligence capability while the formation of a national intelligence service was debated, the CIG was created on January 22, 1946. In April 1946 the SSU was liquidated and over the next six months or so its personnel, foreign stations, and foreign assets (agents) were acquired by the CIG. On July 26, 1947, the National Security Act became law and the Central Intelligence Agency was formally established.[4]

All of the first CIG and CIA directors were drawn from the armed forces. All were experienced military officers, some more familiar with intelligence operations than others, and all had served in World War II. The first two CIG directors recruited or brought with them military, War Department, and OSS intelligence professionals who had also learned their trade during World War II. Their presence in the CIA's senior ranks also corrects the notion that the agency was early dominated by the Eastern Establishment's old boy network, whose era came later. They also fetched along inexperienced and incompetent officers with little imaginative cunning, poor political judgment, and the rigidity of a chain of command culture.

Admiral Roscoe Hillenkoetter, the first CIA director in 1947, was a kindly man and a capable naval officer, but inadequate at the helm of the CIA. He relinquished much of his daily command of CIA activities to his deputy, Colonel Edwin Wright, and dealt instead with the many external problems arising from the agency's precarious position among competing executive agencies. In advancing agency interests through the Washington brokers' bazaar, he relied on caution, accommodation, and compromise rather than a talent for leadership. He was also hobbled by his poorly defined statutory authority, often challenged by his more combative service peers who usually outranked him. The gentlemen diplomats at the State Department were another intrusive nuisance; their talent for lofty principle and protecting their policy turf wasn't helpful.[5]

Awareness of CIA drift, disarray, and indecisiveness under Admiral Hillenkoetter was made categorical in January 1949, the year of Philby's arrival. After an intensive twelve-month effort, a survey group submitted a three-hundred-page report on the CIA to the National Security Council. The final report was devastating in its critique of every phase of agency operations. The NSC had requested the study in January 1948 as a comprehensive survey but after a few months' work, the executive secretary in despair told the three group members that "dissatisfaction with CIA is so widespread throughout the government and some of the internal problems of CIA seem so acute," he doubted the review would be soon concluded.[6] It wasn't. Although the study was finally released in January 1949, the recommended changes did not begin to be implemented until October 1950, after Smith assumed directorship.

The study was also called the Dulles report, although Dulles's interest was confined to prying into clandestine operations, the only intelligence activities he truly cared about, and one reason Smith mistrusted him. He officially joined the CIA as deputy director of plans in January 1951. Even though Smith valued Dulles's intelligence experience, he lacked confidence in both Dulles and the OPC's Frank Wisner, suspecting that neither was entirely honest with him but that both were pursuing their own personal policy goals. (In August 1951, Dulles was made Smith's deputy and Wisner replaced him as DDP.) He was also wary of Dulles's unrestrained enthusiasm for covert operations and believed that unless he was closely controlled, he might lead the CIA one day into "some ill-conceived and disastrous adventure," as he inevitably did. For that reason Dulles wasn't Smith's choice as his successor. The Bay of Pigs operation was the waiting disaster. Dick White also disdained the adventurism of both Dulles and Wisner. After taking command of MI6 in 1956, he decided to end collaboration with the CIA in clandestine warfare.[7]

The study censured Admiral Hillenkoetter and Colonel Wright not only for failing to understand the CIA's mandate but for incompetence in carrying it out. Agency shortcomings couldn't be blamed entirely on the admiral.

The faults could by shared by many in Washington, especially the service intelligence chiefs, the Joint Chiefs, and the State Department, although the need for strong leadership was essential for creating a strong CIA, as General Smith would prove when he swept aside bureaucratic roadblocks by ignoring them or issuing orders and defying challenge from any quarter. The survey concluded that intelligence coordination and planning could only be effective with a strong director and CIA; both were absent in 1948–1949. It called on the director to exert "forthright leadership," an exertion only a top-floor boardroom of Wall Street lawyers might believe could be achieved by simple fiat. Washington's bureaucracy doesn't work that way. The three survey members knew the admiral was the wrong man for the job. They reproached him for lacking sufficient day-to-day contact with the work of the CIA offices and recommended he reorganize his office to include on his immediate staff the heads of the CIA's component operations.

Although the NSC found the criticism of Hillenkoetter and the CIA "too sweeping," a benign pardon for Admiral Hillenkoetter as not wholly responsible for the mess, it accepted the report's basic findings.[8] The Dulles group wasn't alone in faulting the agency's weakness. In a November 1948 report, the Hoover Commission's Eberstadt Committee censured the CIA failure in scientific and technical intelligence collection. The report warned that the failure "to appraise the extent of scientific development in enemy countries may have more immediate and catastrophic consequences than failure in any other field of intelligence." It cited the failure of conventional intelligence in estimating Soviet development of an atomic bomb. In September 1949 the assistant director for scientific intelligence advised Hillenkoetter that the OSO's deficiencies continued. "OSO has failed completely to discharge its responsibility for covert collection of scientific and technical intelligence, including atomic warfare, guided missiles, and electronics." The "rate of Soviet production of atomic bombs must be determined accurately" and OSO collection failures "had made this impossible."[9]

Internal memoranda provide a closer look at the performance of two of the most important CIA positions in 1948–1949. After the departure on May 1, 1947, of General Hoyt Vandenberg, the most effective of the first CIG and CIA directors, Admiral Hillenkoetter had retained Vandenberg's deputy, Colonel Wright, an army mustang up from the ranks with no intelligence experience. Wright, later promoted to brigadier general, is described as a kind of éminence grise who kept both Vandenberg and Hillenkoetter jealously secluded from officers serving below. While the admiral managed relations with other agencies from high on the bridge and was constantly outflanked, outmaneuvered, outgunned, or run aground on the Potomac mud banks, Wright ran CIA operations after his own sergeant-major military fashion. The admiral's abdication was condemned by the Dulles report in concluding the tail was wagging the dog: CIA operational policy was determined more by administrative than intelligence considerations.[10]

In 1948 the Office of Special Operations, led by Colonel D. H. Galloway, was more or less the backbone of the agency's clandestine intelligence operations, although it would soon be elbowed aside by the adventurers in the OPC who were stealing away OSO officers and funds. Galloway, who had helped create the OSO's Soviet Division, was equally hapless. A Vandenberg West Point classmate, the only obvious reason for his assignment, he had been brought in on July 11, 1946, as assistant director of the OSO, which also included the deputy chief for counterespionage, the deputy for plans and projects, and the geographical offices. Descriptions of both Wright and Galloway from within the CIA were harshly derogatory.

In January 1948 a former OSS officer who had transferred to the CIA as an OSO deputy resigned in disgust along with three other officers. He wrote bluntly of Colonel Galloway's performance:

> Special Operations is headed by an officer known among his Army friends as "Wrong-Way" Galloway. Their doubtful esteem of him is more than matched by that of his associates and subordinates within his office and by that of the heads of other branches within CIA. Colonel Galloway has little comprehension of the real nature of secret operations, and is so irascible and dogmatic that he discourages any efforts to discuss technical details with him. For his technical and organizational advice he is accustomed to call upon subordinates like William Tharp, Chadbourne Gilpatrick, or Harry Rositzke, who although they have been in the organization for some time, have had practically no real operational experience. Their freely offered operational theories appear to be acceptable to Colonel Galloway at the same time that they are the despair of their more experienced associates.[11]

Frank Wisner, who headed the CIA's first covert-action arm, the Office for Policy Coordination (OPC), was equally scathing in his criticism of General Wright. On April 15, 1949, in a memo to the State Department counselor, he complained of what he called the "military mind" and "having to deal with such unenlightened and unsympathetic individuals" in CIA intelligence operations. "As a concrete illustration of what I mean, the present chief of this service had already designated General Pinkie Wright as the top

CIA representative upon the Western Union Clandestine Committee, and this would have become effective but for the fact that General Wright was 'rotated' to some relatively minor duty in Japan. In a word, however, he is the Regular Army top-sergeant type, the smallness of whose knowledge and comprehension of foreign affairs and foreign personalities is matched only by his certainty that he knows these and all the other answers."[12]

Wisner was a sophisticated Mississippi gentleman from the Old South and a New York law firm by way of the University of Virginia. What he meant was that Wright, the Oregon-educated army mustang, was a crudely incompetent dunderhead. He would have disgraced the CIA and no doubt humiliated Wisner had he represented the agency at meetings with the Foreign Office gentlemen from the Russia Committee. But then Wisner was writing to the counselor of the State Department, Charles Bohlen, a diplomat of the old school, and restrained his expletives, although referring to Wright as "Pinkie" conveyed his meaning. Fortunately or unfortunately, the OPC under Wisner was only nominally a CIA component. Hillenkoetter had yielded operational control to State and Defense and Wisner escaped Wright's crude grasp. Wright left the CIA on March 9, 1949, for the Far East. Hillenkoetter selected a replacement who declined after a Department of Defense insider told him that the admiral's ship was sinking, if not already on the bottom. Wright was never replaced. Galloway was relieved earlier, in December 1948, seven long months after his dismissal had been raised on May 28.

Another indication of Hillenkoetter's indifferent control was CIA communications. In 1946 the CIG had inherited the SSU communications section intact, its equipment, codes, and ciphers. Communications between the SSU at the War Department and its field stations had been handled by U.S. military installations or the State Department using a special cipher system. Under Hillenkoetter, CIA cables from the field were sent to the OSO and OPC. A cable secretariat wasn't established in the director's office until Smith took command in 1950. Not long after he arrived in Washington, Philby evidently offered the CIA use of MI6 communications at the embassy, supposedly much faster than the CIA's own communications. CIA cables from U.S. embassies at the time would have been patched in cipher through the State Department. This clumsy procedure together with the dispersal of CIA offices may account for the delays. The Defense Department maintained the quickest worldwide communications network.[13]

State Department and Foreign Service intransigence hobbled the CIA further in effectively carrying out intelligence collection abroad by its reluctance to assign CIA officers to diplomatic and consular missions. In April 1948 Admiral Hillenkoetter complained that for more than a year he had been attempting without success to enlarge the OSO staff overseas, the workhorses of CIA intelligence collection. He was notified that by January 1, 1948, the CIA would have to reduce its staff to no more than two hundred officers at U.S. missions, totally inadequate to the CIA's responsibilities.[14] The State Department's miserliness in accepting CIA officers at its foreign missions remained a problem for years and had nothing to do with the quality of the officers. As a rule, their quality was consistently high compared with the best Foreign Service officers and far superior to those who staffed the military, air, and naval attaché ranks.

The NSC asked the secretaries of Defense and State to review the survey group's recommendations and on July 7, 1949, adopted the second group's proposals for CIA reorganization and reform. The details don't concern us here. More important is that from July 7, 1949, until Walter Bedell Smith reluctantly agreed to be named director (he had been approached by Truman the previous May) and assumed office on October 7, 1950, only nominal changes had been made. A thirty-year CIA veteran who had joined the CIG in 1947 wrote of the 1947–1950 period that CIA "shortcomings extended beyond the inadequate flow of sensitive information." Much had been expected of the Dulles report "but little or nothing was done to implement the recommendations . . . we bumbled along in 1949 and early 1950 much as before." An even more damning comment was made by one of the most able and distinguished Washington professionals. In January 1949 former undersecretary of state Robert Lovett, who had returned to Wall Street that month, advised an officer in the State Department that he had better intelligence from his Wall Street firm than the CIA during his years at State. CIA operations were "lousy" and Hillenkoetter a "very ineffective and pedestrian officer."[15]

Until the reorganizations began, the CIA remained the same ill-led, ill-functioning intelligence organization the Dulles report had sweepingly criticized. Hillenkoetter didn't replace Wright and remained without a deputy director until he too left the CIA. He had requested sea duty in June 1950 after the outbreak of the Korean War and departed in October to eventually command a destroyer in the Far East. The problems the CIA had been struggling with were still unresolved.

This was the fabled CIA Philby was introduced to in October 1949, the same CIA whose mythical fame, based on its 1950s and 1960s clandestine operations, both successful and disastrous, would add much to the Philby legend. After all, he successfully penetrated the citadel, the embodiment of all that was most clandestine, most successful, and most secret of U.S. intelligence agencies. The CIA's true secret in 1949–1950 was its rudderless drift. At that point, the CIA's reputation would have been better given to Arlington Hall Station, about which few knew anything, and whose operations would later be absorbed by the NSA, an agency whose budget, personnel, and successful worldwide operations in association with the United Kingdom's GCHQ would ultimately dwarf the CIA.

Had the CIA been more responsibly organized, it might have participated in the Venona operation at Arlington Hall Station. But it knew nothing about Venona, although a few CIA officers were aware of its existence. In 1948 they were given access to certain Venona material but liaison was discontinued after Arlington Hall couldn't identify either a satisfactory channel or a proper office at the CIA that might best use the intelligence material.[16] The suspension says a great deal about CIA disarray. Not until 1952 would the CIA share in the Anglo-American Venona project. In 1948 the CIA was developing its own "effective method of penetrating the Iron Curtain"—not new agents, new intercept capabilities, or new spy satellites, but "high-level balloons." Embarrassing letters were sent to the chief of naval operations and the air force asking for technical help. The plan was to float hundreds of balloons carrying propaganda leaflets across the Iron Curtain. It was eventually carried out.[17] One such blizzard of leaflets so covered an Albanian hillside where émigrés were hiding that they might have thought the winter snows had come.[18] In the meantime Arlington Hall was successfully decrypting thousands of KGB coded messages plucked from the wires or the atmosphere. In that effort there was only the slightest inkling of the new technological revolution that would transform worldwide intelligence collection.

No matter how poorly organized or badly directed CIA headquarters and how hapless its clandestine intelligence chief in the Office of Special Operations, diplomats as well as CIA officers overseas are often unaffected by the disorder. Washington leadership or its absence is never an accurate measure of competence in the field. Officers serving in U.S. diplomatic missions and U.S. army installations abroad define their own purpose and generate their own energy whether they're acting under important or inane instructions from Washington. More often than not, their lonely enthusiasm is provoked rather than stifled by Washington's indifference or neglect. So they set about doing what they were sent out to do, discovering subjects of interest and importance and proving their worth to themselves and others—the ambassador, the station chief, and any idly useless desk or incompetent division officer back at State, the CIA, or the Pentagon. The most powerful example that comes to mind is the Iranian revolution of late 1979. Any number of Foreign Service and CIA officers at the embassy in Tehran or the consulates at Tabriz and Isfahan were well aware that changes were in the wind. Their warnings were ignored.

In any event, in 1949–1951 there were undoubtedly secrets to be collected in Washington from CIA operations overseas and Philby collected them, although what he did with them is open to question. In one of the temporary CIA offices near the Reflecting Pool, Philby would have met James Angleton, the executive assistant to the CIA's assistant director for special operations, who was responsible for clandestine intelligence collection. Angleton had returned to Washington from Italy in November 1947 as special assistant to the previously scorned Donald Galloway.

He was the CIA's liaison with other intelligence agencies, including MI6, and the French and Israeli intelligence services. Angleton no doubt escorted Philby to the CIA administration building at 2430 E Street NW to meet Admiral Hillenkoetter. In *My Silent War* Philby describes him as "an amiable" sailor and says no more. He claims Angleton was "the driving force" of the OSO, an exaggeration Angleton would have proudly welcomed. He wasn't among the more prominent CIA officers at the time. Philby also misidentifies the acronym as the "Office of Strategic Operation." The two errors are repeated in many books about Philby and indicate how poorly he served their authors as a guide to the CIA.[19] He inflates Angleton's importance most probably because he was so voluble in his own cause. Angleton's notoriety, like his internal mischief, would come after December 1954, when he became chief of the counterintelligence staff under the directorate of plans. His later legend owes much to his 1949–1951 relations with Philby.

During Philby's Washington tour the two men often met, lunched, and drank together. Angleton, an unusual man in unusual ways, would have valued Philby's bibulous company. He was a prattling windbag with a genius for bewitching many with his obsession for intelligence gossip, conspiratorial theory, and intellectual enigmas, like Ezra Pound's *Cantos,* more impressive in piecemeal fragments than the full text that crumbles with age into incoherence. So have all of Angleton's theories. Among Angleton's Mad Hatter notions was his belief that the Sino-Soviet split was a deception; that British prime minister Harold Wilson was a Soviet agent; that CIA director William Colby's profile was that of a KGB sleeper; and that the Church Committee's

1975 investigation of the CIA was a plot masterminded from Moscow by Kim Philby. Paraphrasing A. J. P. Taylor's remark about diplomats, Angleton's career supports the theory that the intelligence profession not only attracts neurotics but produces them. Dick White mistrusted Angleton, who, in his words, couldn't distinguish between "the substance and the shadows."[20] If his delusional rubbish is remembered now, it's only because of its absurdity. In Moscow years later Philby told Yuri Modin that Angleton was "off his head."[21] This was before CIA director Colby reached the same long overdue conclusion and retired (fired) Angleton in December 1974.

Did Angleton boast of a few OSO secrets? Most probably. By Philby's own account he was more engaged with Wisner's Office of Policy Coordination, the most active CIA operation at the time but not under CIA control. The OPC was just beginning its pursuit of lost causes in Albania and the Soviet republics. Perhaps Angleton described a few OSO clandestine agents in Europe under CIA control. Were they important? Probably not. The OSO had few secrets to give up and no intelligence assets in the so-called denied areas or behind the Iron Curtain. There were no Colonel Penkovskys in Moscow in those days, no CIA agents in Moscow like those betrayed by Aldrich Ames in the 1980s.[22] Even as late as 1958 the agency had no assets in the USSR. We don't know what Philby and Angleton discussed. Did Philby record their conversations for eventual posting to Burgess? Evidently not. Angleton did. He kept his own journal. He made a written record of every conversation the two had ever had, whether in his office or during lunch, all to be dutifully typed up by his secretary. Not a single memorandum was ever found.[23] Years later he admitted burning them out of embarrassment and shame. He was surely the most indelibly marked of Philby's Washington victims. Long after Philby surfaced in Moscow, Angleton was still proclaiming his perfidy, a new Moscow plot masterminded by Kim Philby. Banished from the CIA, he was by then merely a deranged voice left behind in the wilderness, a ghost-haunted soul, like so many other chroniclers of the Philby legend.

Meeting on November 25, 1948, the Russia Committee considered a suggestion that "offensive operations might be best started in a small area" and offered Albania for consideration. "Would it not be possible to start a civil war behind the Iron Curtain and, by careful assistance, produce a state of affairs in Albania similar to the state of affairs that the Russians had produced in Greece?" Civil discontent, internal confusion, and possibly armed conflict within the Soviet satellites would bring in Soviet armies of occupation and drain Moscow's manpower and financial reserves. Some were doubtful but the committee decided that "our aim should certainly be to liberate the countries within the Soviet orbit short of war."[24] (At the meeting, Herbert Morrison predicted war with Russia by the summer of 1949.)

The meeting had raised the question of a planning staff but the idea was rejected by Bevin, who had no intention of reviving the old wartime Special Operations Executive (SOE) or giving the military an operational role. In February 1949 Bevin's private secretary briefed the Russia Committee on Bevin's three decisions. He agreed to "detaching Albania from the Soviet orbit," encouraging greater U.S. support on behalf of Greece, and discreetly backing Tito. He didn't submit his proposals to the Defense Committee but intended to move ahead on his own once he had been given the authority by Prime Minister Attlee.[25]

The 1949–1951 British and American operations in the Soviet republics and Albania were inspired by postwar developments in the Soviet Union and the Balkans. Tito's break with Moscow offered an example that might be duplicated in Albania while in the USSR continuing partisan warfare in the Ukraine presented an opportunity that might also be exploited with men and arms. The official rationale for both concealed a somewhat simplistic determination to do something to discomfit the Soviet Union and prove to the Foreign Office architects that the covert struggle with the Soviet Union was joined but not so joined as to provoke Moscow to war.

In April 1945 Yugoslavia had been the first country to sign a treaty of friendship, aid, and mutual cooperation with the Soviet Union. Over the next two years, Yugoslav relations with Moscow steadily deteriorated. Apart from Albania, Yugoslavia was unique in Eastern Europe as the only country to liberate itself without direct military help from the Red Army. Although closely bound ideologically to Moscow, that independence of spirit asserted itself as Yugoslavia began to resist subordinating its policy interests to the USSR. In defying Soviet hegemony, Tito's heresy fractured and finally broke Stalin's edict that the world was divided into two opposing camps, Western imperialism against the Communist or progressive bloc, principally his submissive East European satellites. Stalin's imperative was the cornerstone of Soviet propaganda and Tito's defection crumbled its walls. In 1948 Yugoslav treachery was condemned and Stalin withdrew Soviet military advisers, renounced the treaty of friendship, and broke off diplomatic and economic relations.

Anti-Soviet partisans in the Soviet republics began their resistance in 1944–1945 after the retreat of the German armies. Well-armed local units in the Western Ukraine, Byelorussia, Latvia, and Estonia continued to battle the Red Army reinforced by troops brought in by the Soviet Ministries of the Interior and Security (NKVD). Partisan warfare was especially intense in the Western Ukraine. Some of those guerrilla bands had been organized by the Germans as SS units to fight local partisans harassing the Germans. An April 1946 Kremlin report to Stalin claimed that in March more than eight thousand guerrillas in the Western Ukraine were killed or captured, among the latter, local leaders of the Ukrainian Nationalist Formation. The March fighting in Lithuania resulted in fewer than two hundred killed but more than fifteen hundred captured. Partisan warfare would continue in the Ukraine until 1950, five years after the end of the war.[26]

In 1947 Albania and Yugoslavia had agreed in principle to unite (a large ethnic Albanian population had long been settled among the Serbs in the Kosovo region of Yugoslavia). Belgrade was helping Albania in a number of ways at some sacrifice to its own people and to Moscow's annoyance. Although the anti-Serb faction in Albania rejected unification in 1948, Tito wouldn't have ignored a civil war in Albania, the intent of the Anglo-American OPC operation. He was a heretic but he remained a dedicated Communist, as did the unified Yugoslav leadership. They had resisted the hegemony of the Soviet system and rejected Stalin's methods, not Communist ideology. What had offended them most was what Milovan Djilas called the "insatiable demands of the Soviet political bureaucracy" (he meant Stalinism) that had nothing to do with Communist unity. They loathed "the spiritual extinction" Djilas had witnessed among Stalin's dinner and drinking colleagues at Kuntsevo, Stalin's dacha outside Moscow. The same extinction was evident among the supine East European Communist leaders in whom the fires of revolution had long died out.[27]

In 1948 the CIA also began to ponder ways of exploiting the Yugoslav-Moscow split. A June 30 internal memo concluded that "The Cominform denunciation of Marshal Tito and his firmly defiant stand constitutes [sic] the first major open break in the satellite front which the Soviet Union has established in Central Europe. The situation arising there from," it continued, "tends to arouse dissension and confusion in the world structure of Communism and invites exploitation by prompt, effective propaganda measures through every available medium, with the idea of achieving a lessening of Moscow control over satellite governments." There was no suggestion as to the means by which this might be achieved (apart from the research then underway on high-altitude balloons to float millions of propaganda leaflets, brochures, and books across the Iron Curtain).[28]

A month later, Frank Wisner was named director of the CIA's OPC and immediately set to work concocting plans for covert operations. A year earlier, as the deputy at the State Department's Office of Occupied Territories, he had toured displaced persons camps in Germany, where some seven hundred thousand refugees from Eastern Europe were awaiting resettlement.[29] In September 1948, as OPC director, he asked for Kennan's help to overcome a major obstacle to their possible use in OPC operations, U.S. Army cooperation in Germany, the collection point for ex-prisoners of war and displaced persons. Kennan appealed to Acting Secretary of State Lovett, who wrote to Secretary of Defense Forrestal urging "the whole-hearted cooperation of the United States military authorities in Germany" in support of political action among refugees from the Soviet Union and the "handling of *bona fide* political refugees and deserters from the Soviet Union."[30] Were they truly bona fide? Questions should have been asked but weren't, because no one cared. Among the refugees were members of German SS units who had fought with the Germans against the Soviet army.[31]

On October 13 Forrestal assured the State Department that the U.S. army command in Germany would support the OPC and so notified General Lucius Clay in Germany. The OPC began preparing a list of projects for Kennan's approval. In January 1949, a list was submitted. Kennan declared it the minimum required. In March 1949, members of the Russia Committee arrived in Washington to request U.S. participation in a joint operation intended to destabilize Albania. The British met Frank Wisner and others from the Pentagon's OPC advisory staff who agreed to participate. The OPC set up its working staff and the director sent an officer to Europe to organize and train an Albanian émigré force.[32] The CIA had at last embarked on covert operations, although only nominally under CIA control. In a May 1949 memo to the Pentagon, Wisner requested military support for OPC covert operations. There was no immediate response from Secretary of Defense Johnson, who had replaced Forrestal. Johnson was totally out of his depth in the position and among Truman's worst appointees (Secretary of State James Byrnes was another). Johnson's actions sometimes so defied common sense that Dean Acheson, by then secretary of state, thought him mentally unbalanced.

The State Department was impressed enough by the Russia Committee's plan for action to adopt it as its own. On September 14, 1949, State submitted to the NSC a paper calling for action to "reduce and eventually cause the elimination of dominant Soviet influence in the satellite states of Albania, Bulgaria, Czechoslovakia, Hungary, Poland and Romania."[33] Kennan's Policy Planning Staff helped draft the document, which had no practical value. Years later Kennan would insist that the United States should never take part in any effort to overthrow the Soviet regime. On September 29, he asked to be relieved as director of the Policy Planning Staff and announced his intention of leaving government service at the end of June 1950. In a diary passage on November 19, he confided that his planning staff had been a complete failure.

In October 1949, Secretary Johnson finally answered Wisner's request, a delay that may have been caused by the Joint Chiefs' doubts about yielding autonomy to the OPC and its mistrust of the CIA. (The documentary record also suggests there were serious high-level differences at the State Department on OPC operations but those don't concern us here.) The Pentagon agreed to support covert operations if they weren't inconsistent with the Joint Chiefs' military policies, and weren't undertaken if disapproved by the Department of Defense. The CIA would fund the operations, the equipment required would be available, but the details had to be arranged with each U.S. military commander of the area.[34] The Pentagon could control the weapons and combat equipment available and in so doing control the level of insurgency. On October 7 Johnson designated Brigadier General John Magruder, retired from the U.S. Army, as his special adviser on OPC activities. Magruder had headed the old Strategic Services Unit at the War Department (the remnants of the disbanded OSS) before it became the basis for the CIA's OSO in 1947. In August 1946, SSU headquarters under General Magruder had cabled the SSU unit in Munich warning that their Russian émigré sources weren't worth the effort and that their target should be Soviet intelligence personnel and organizations. He was evidently against the Albanian operation; had he been adamantly opposed and informed the Pentagon, it is difficult to understand how the operation would have gone forward.[35]

Wisner's OPC now had in hand what was required. In Germany, the OPC could begin recruiting Ukrainians, Letts, Poles, Byelorussians, anti-Stalinist Russians, mercenaries, and any other political rabble out of the displaced persons camps to form the cadres for the liberation of their Soviet homelands. Many were former Nazi collaborators and thugs, members of SS brigades admitted through American army lines and into camps posing as escaped prisoners of war. In some instances, Ukrainian and Byelorussian brigands, extortionists, and ex-Nazi goons were already in control of their camps. At Regensburg, Michelsdorf, and Osterhofen, they employed the same brutality they had shown when organized by their German occupiers as special SS antipartisan units.

Those displaced persons camps must have been a nightmare for Kennan's bourgeois social democrats and political moderates, huddled in silence as they submissively awaited deliverance and their escape abroad to Canada, Australia, and the United States, where the immigration barriers were coming down. Among the OPC's associates was Radislaw Ostrowsky, leader of the Byelorussian Central Council organized by the Germans when they occupied Byelorussia. Stephan Bandera's Organization of Ukrainian Nationalists (OUN) was another OPC accomplice. The OPC planned to reestablish Ukrainian and Byelorussian underground networks, and through them supply arms and equipment to partisan units. Bandera's OUN had also collaborated with the Nazi SS. OPC support for Bandera would soon sour and it attempted to distance itself from the OUN.[36]

American and former Wehrmacht instructors trained the recruits in guerrilla operations, hand-to-hand combat, map reading, two-way radio transmissions, and enciphering and deciphering signals. They would be flown at low altitude into the western Ukraine and Byelorussia by OPC chartered aircraft to be dropped by parachute with forged papers, arms, rubles, and portable radios to establish contact with local agents. The first flight into the Carpathians was made on the night of September 5, 1949. Most of the Ukrainians were caught and arrested; some were turned by their Russian captors and sent false radio transmissions back to their bases to decoy even more. The OPC operations in the Ukraine would continue for several years. None accomplished much of anything at all. "It was a horrible mistake," said one American who directed the air drops. "None of them survived."[37]

The Albanian operation originated by the Foreign Office's Russia Committee mixed caution, limited finances, the success of Britain's World War II guerrilla operations in Albania, which were now irrelevant—there would be no collapsing German front and no advancing Allied armies as there had been in 1945—and a similar misreading of Soviet and Yugoslav policy. Pint-sized Albania was chosen as a target because its size suited Britain's pint-sized resources. The operation had to be large enough to win internal support but not of such a scale as to dangerously provoke Moscow. The consequences should have been obvious: it was too small to do anything but fail. MI6 ran the initial operation under Foreign Office direction with former SOE officers as advisers. They had operated successfully in Albania during the war, knew the region as well as the various émigré factions, but lived in a kind of historical vacuum that romanticized their World War II Albanian adventures when the German military collapse was inevitable. Since they seemed not to have the slightest notion of the events of the past three years, the call to high adventure must have been a compelling motive. Footloose Serbs, Croats, and Corsicans once joined the French Foreign Legion for the same reason. One British adviser claimed Moscow was being paid in kind for supporting the Greek Communist insurrection.[38]

Stalin had relinquished his interest in Greece after August 1946 when warned by the United States that any Soviet attempt to move against the Turkish straits would be met by force. Stalin wasn't supporting the Greek insurgents. In February 1948 he told a Yugoslav delegation in Moscow that "the uprising in Greece . . . must be stopped as quickly as possible." The United States and the United Kingdom would not permit any break in the "line of communication in the Mediterranean."[39] Tito had supported the insurgency but he had closed his border with Greece in mid-1948.

The Albanian operation was an open secret even before it began. In preparing the political groundwork by bringing the Albanian émigré factions together, the British MI6 advisers traveled openly about the Mediterranean. They held meetings in Rome with Albanian émigrés who could no more keep secrets than their Italian hosts, in Athens with Greek officials who couldn't keep secrets either, and in Alexandria, where King Zog the royalist pretender was holding court and no one knew what a secret was. In August 1949, the formation of the Albanian National Committee was announced in Paris. On September 14, even before the first MI6 landings, the London *News Chronicle* warned that Albania was about to explode. Cyrus Sultzberger of the *New York Times* reported in March 1950 before the first U.S. airdrops that the West had plans to destabilize the Hoxha regime in Albania.[40]

By the time Philby arrived in Washington, the British contingent that had established an Albanian émigré training camp at Malta under MI6 was already in action. On October 3, 1949, a British schooner landed a nine-man Albanian émigré unit on the Albanian coast. After two days the unit divided. The four-man team was soon ambushed; three were killed, and the fourth disappeared. Unable to arouse local supports, the other, five-man team escaped into Greece. A second group of eleven émigrés landed October 10, roamed the mountains uselessly and ineffectually, and later crossed into Greece. Albanian security forces were constantly on the prowl and the émigrés were far too few in number to convince the Albanian villagers that rebellion was possible. The British wisely dropped out of the operation in 1951. Whatever the design or intent, the plan was as ill conceived as any notion that Tito would have watched impassively as a monarchist pretender like Zog or a regime of Albanian ex-German and Italian collaborators was installed in Tirana. The Albanian operations never reached even that level of success. The only observers who took it seriously were its British and American planners and the luckless Albanian émigrés who had joined the cause.[41]

Nevertheless, it is too easy to condemn covert operations fifty years in the past with the cynicism of hindsight and the judgment time alone makes obvious. The hopes and fears that inspired them, whether in Albania or the Soviet republics, are now almost impossible to imagine. The imminent possibility of a European war would have persuaded the U.S. military of the advantages of the Ukrainian operation. Some participants commenting on those operations years later differ on their purpose. If the Albanian goal was to separate that country from the Soviet orbit, as first suggested by the Foreign Office, then it was a failure. If the purpose was to determine whether such a limited operation might provoke an Albanian insurrection, as one American believed, then it wasn't a total loss. The British were wise enough to recognize its impossibility and withdrew.

For some in London and Washington, the Albanian operation served the need for action more than any expectation of decisive consequences, which were beyond reach, given the resources committed. Those benefits were psychological and if they inspired the Albanian operation's British and American architects, the call to action fell on deaf ears among the Albanian mountain populations. The trifling puniness in arms and men gave no heart whatsoever to those shrewd Albanian mountaineers who were supposed to be inspired to rebellion. To that extent in the end both proved to be exercises in vanity and self-delusion. The Albanian operation is similar in that respect to the 1983 American invasion of pint-sized Grenada. That diminutive Caribbean nation offered the first opportunity to overthrow a so-called Communist regime after the Vietnam debacle and the Iran crisis had paralyzed the national will, or so its champions declared. It enabled President Reagan's supporters and Reagan himself to declare that "our military forces are back on their feet and standing tall," by which he meant standing tall among runts, midgets, and dwarfs.[42] Grenada was in part a fraud inspired in part by fraudulent intelligence claiming the coming of a "Soviet-Cuban dominated State," an inflated Cuban military force and a Soviet and East German presence that was largely imaginary.[43] Its benefits too were psychological, but that only confirms the character of those invigorated by its success. Albania and the Soviet republics belong in the same category except that both failed.

Philby is believed by some to have compromised British-American covert operations in the Soviet republics and Albania.[44] In Washington he was a member of the four-man British-American team that ran the Albanian operation out of the OPC office at the Pentagon. Others are deeply skeptical that Philby was responsible for the failure. American CIA officers who participated in both the Ukraine and Albania operations believed both were compromised by others or fell of their own weight. Philby wasn't yet in Washington when the first British landings took place and there is no evidence MI6 had told him of them in London in September. Although he knew about the later operations, he was out of touch with a KGB control officer for more than a year and lacked the means of quickly passing that intelligence to London, except by mail through Burgess, until Burgess arrived in Washington in August 1950.

The infiltration of Albanian émigrés either by sea or by air followed a loosely reckoned timetable. Weather conditions often delayed the landings and the airdrops. The U.S.-trained émigrés were often parachuted far from the intended drop zone near their remote native villages where they were to rally local support. If the Albanian security police were nearby at the time, their presence might have been explained by a general awareness of the locale of émigrés opposed to the Tirana regime. It is impossible to believe Philby had the means for any timely disclosure of OPC individual operational plans or that he would even have found it necessary. The ultimate failure would have been as self-evident as the futility of their numbers and purpose.

The OPC's paramilitary staff had made plans for a much larger Albanian operation that went far beyond a handful of Albanian émigrés dropped by air or infiltrated by sea and amounted to a full-scale invasion by thousands of men. The project study was found in a file by Richard Bissell before he left the CIA in 1962 and was described to Thomas Powers in the late 1970s. The invasion force evidently dwarfed Bissell's own Bay of Pigs operation of 1961.[45]

Yuri Modin wrongly claims Philby passed a great many details about the OPC operations in Albania, the Ukraine, and the Baltic. Those messages would have been sent to London by mail, not courier, not a timely channel for passing on the dates and times for ongoing operations. But as appendix B makes clear, Modin was compiling much of his detail on those operations from various published sources available years later and hopelessly confused the results. Notes brought out by Mitrokhin indicate that Philby did betray the geographical coordinates for a U.S. and British airdrop into the Ukraine.[46] It is impossible to explain how he could have passed that detail or maintained a steady flow of up-to-date reports from Washington by mail or courier. That intelligence would have been useful only had it been timely, passed directly to a KGB control or cutout, and reported just as quickly. The only such opportunities would have been during Philby's visits to London, a March 1950 return when he met with Burgess, an August–September 1950 trip to discuss the Albanian operation, or January 1951, when he listened to Dick White's report on the Maclean investigation.

Chapter ELEVEN

Moscow and the bomb.—Deterrent to war.—Black operations.—A basis for deception.—The forgotten chiefs of staff.—Finding an agent.—General Sibert.—The British fly solo.—Only in memory.—Unresolved ambiguities.

Stalin's attitude toward American nuclear capability and its effects on his political and military decisions from 1945 through 1951 is a complex subject that defies categorical assumptions. Interpretations are best left to Russian scholars who are still considering the subject. It also goes beyond our purpose except in a general sense. In his memoirs Khrushchev recalled that Stalin was terrified to the point of cowardice by the American atomic bomb, but his claim should be interpreted as part of his continuing efforts to debunk the Stalin myth. Between 1945 and his death in 1953, he gave only two speeches and no personal interviews, in part to conceal his declining health, but he sometimes responded to written questions. In a 1949 written response to a Western correspondent, he expressed no fear of atom bombs, which he believed were designed to scare those with weak nerves. He claimed they couldn't decide wars because "there are not enough of them." He agreed the U.S. atomic monopoly was a threat but thought it wouldn't last and that use of the bomb would be forbidden.[1] His dismissal of the bomb was intended for an international audience and he could hardly have spoken otherwise, but his comment that there weren't enough atomic bombs would have been closely read in Washington and London. In August 1949 the Soviet Union exploded its own atomic bomb.

Work had begun in late 1942, before the recruitment of the atomic spies in 1943–1945, and soon began exploiting the technology obtained from Los Alamos to duplicate the Alamogordo-type atomic bomb exploded in the New Mexico desert in 1945. Russian physicists were more advanced than has been recognized in some phases of the processes required for atomic fission. The problems Russian physicists and technicians encountered might have persuaded Stalin that mass production of atomic bombs was improbable. The Russian effort was hampered by the low productivity of scientific and industrial forced labor; many of the most prominent Soviet nuclear scientists were serving ten-year sentences; some one thousand prisoners were working on scientific research in Siberian prison camps, living in makeshift tents behind barbed wire.[2] Soviet strategic doctrine explicitly rejected the proposition that the atomic bomb could by itself win a war, but the doctrine may have been dictated as much by Stalinist conformity as nuclear inadequacy. It was revised after Stalin's death.[3]

A former Russian general with access to Soviet archives insists that in 1949 the Soviet leadership believed that plans were being made in the Pentagon for the nuclear bombardment of the USSR and credited Stalin with pursuing a cautious policy to avoid any provocation with his former ally.[4] More than twenty-two years after the 1948 war scare, Viacheslav Molotov, Stalin's foreign minister and among his intimates until 1949, when he fell from favor, would vividly recall American war plans for those years when two hundred Russian cities would be subject to simultaneous bombing. Molotov's reminiscences suggest U.S. war plans had made a lasting impression, although the source of his numbers isn't clear. Transcribed in 1970–1971, long after the Stalin era and a decade before extensive details of U.S. nuclear targeting were published during the Reagan years, his remarks cast no suspicion on the inadequacy of U.S. nuclear weapons. Molotov too recognized that in consolidating its wartime gains in Eastern Europe and East Germany, Moscow had to know "when and where to stop."[5] U.S. military planners and others misunderstood or failed to realize Stalin's respect for the United States as the strongest nation on earth.

In early 1950, Stalin created a Council of Ministers Directorate to plan for Moscow's defense against an American nuclear attack. Worried that a few American nuclear-armed bombers could obliterate Moscow as they had Dresden during World War II even without atomic bombs, Stalin warned that "they [the Allies] have more planes, a sufficient number of atomic bombs, and they are nestled practically next to our door." The construction of two concentric rings of radar and missile units around Moscow didn't begin until 1952–1953.[6]

Whatever Moscow truly believed, what mattered was what Washington and London thought the Kremlin believed. In 1948–1949 many in Washington, including Forrestal and General Vandenberg, were troubled by the apparent Russian dismissal of the atom bomb's war-winning power and U.S. willingness to use it. In London the British chiefs of staffs were less troubled by what Stalin may or may not have believed than the threat of Soviet military power that endangered Western Europe—whose collapse had far more drastic consequences for England than the United States. In 1946–1947 Prime Minister Attlee wasn't fully convinced he could depend on the United States to defend the British isles and believed the manufacture of a British nuclear bomb "was essential to our defence."[7] In January 1947 Attlee held a secret meeting with a group of cabinet ministers and made the decision to manufacture the bomb. In 1947 British defense planners wrote that "the supreme object of British policy must be to prevent war" and that "the only effective deterrent to a potential aggressor is tangible evidence of our intention and ability to withstand attack and to retaliate immediately." The chiefs of staff believed the best deterrent against a future attack would be "our known preparedness to defend ourselves and to hit back."[8] The emphasis on "tangible evidence" and "our known preparedness" in a top-secret military document indicates that Britain's retaliatory capacity had to be known to the potential aggressor.

An aggressive counteroffensive would have called on U.S. and British intelligence services to remove any Soviet doubt on both points: Allied intent to use the bomb and the bomb's devastative capacity, meaning both the number of bombs available and the capacity for delivery. A covert propaganda or psychological warfare campaign similar to General Kenney's blustering speech of May 1948 or leaks from the Joint Chiefs' congressional briefing in 1949 might have reached its target within the Kremlin, but it would have been insufficient. What Moscow lacked and what the Anglo-American military planners needed was a wholly credible means of verification or corroboration.

What other options were available? In Washington the CIA had been granted more autonomy for covert action by the NSC in June 1948, but its covert OPC arm was only nominally under the CIA and monitored by military officers. The NSC directive had specifically excluded "cover and deception for military operations," a signal that the Joint Chiefs didn't want CIA amateurs mucking about on its terrain.[9] The OPC turned to the State Department's preference for supporting indigenous guerrilla movements, far afield from George Kennan's original intentions or the U.S. Air Force's needs of the moment, and instead was concocting plans for promoting civil disorder in Albania and rebel cells in the Ukraine. In London the Foreign Office's Russia Committee had ignored the service chiefs' call for more aggressive anti-Soviet measures to be led by a small, experienced, select group who would control secret operations and fight Britain's Cold War in ways similar to those in World War II. They had looked to the past, as Englishmen do, and found their predicament similar to those perilous years in 1939–1941 when British military weakness was exposed to superior German strength. British and American weaknesses in conventional military forces in Western Europe in 1948 and 1949 were similar to those British deficiencies. The British service chiefs had advocated a Cold War reestablishment of the same extreme measures adopted in that war, in which they had all participated and which was still very much alive in memory. Those operations would be conducted in absolute secrecy with maximum flexibility, using all necessary tactics and resources.

In 1948–1949 the possibility of Soviet aggression in Western Europe had more immediate consequences for Britain than for the United States. Lord Tedder, Air Marshal Sir James Robb, and General Hollis believed that the threat of nuclear retaliation was the most effective weapon the Allies possessed as a deterrent to war in Western Europe. The British chiefs of staff, all experienced in the deceptions of World War II, had sought a more active role in planning and implementing the British counteroffensive against the USSR. In November 1948, Tedder had suggested to the Russia Committee the creation of a "small permanent team" to consider Cold War plans to be executed by "ourselves and the Americans." The chiefs of staff had suggested "black," secret operations. Hollis had urged more aggressive psychological warfare, another term for deception. Air Marshal Slessor had recommended a counteroffensive using all appropriate weapons by a "specially qualified staff." Those many appeals had been denied by Foreign Secretary Bevin. In the meantime the Foreign Office, which controlled Britain's Soviet policy, was planning a very porous and limited Albanian operation.

Having been rejected, Tedder, Robb, and Hollis might have considered turning to the London Controlling Section deception team in the Ministry of Defense. Bound together in secrecy by their wartime service, their years of cooperation and trust, and their conviction that the threat of atomic devastation was the most potent weapon to deter Soviet aggression in Western Europe, where Allied military weakness was all too obvious and Soviet superiority in conventional forces all too ominous, those few British officers might have considered such an initiative with no official sanction, no official oversight, and without the knowledge of the Foreign Office, the Joint Intelligence Committee, or any other cabinet authority. From 1946 through 1949, a credible basis for the British deception had already been established in the continuing exchanges between the U.S. Air Force, the Strategic Air Command, and the Royal Air Force.

In July 1947, when the Ministry of Defense began providing the U.S. Air Force with Russian target intelligence, as described earlier, General Leslie Hollis's team of deception experts conceived a deception operation, Atomic Scientific Research and Production, intended to mislead Moscow on Great Britain's nuclear weapons capability. At the time, England had no nuclear capability. Hollis's deception operation also lacked a credible candidate, an identified Soviet agent to deliver its message to Moscow. Fearing failure and that Soviet agents had sufficiently penetrated British nuclear and weapons development to enable Moscow to identify the bogus intelligence, namely that Britain had no atomic weapons, the Hollis Committee shelved the plan until more was known about Soviet penetration.[10] Better scrub the project entirely rather than have Moscow discover the bogus operation and suspect that their duped agent had been identified by British intelligence.

By 1949, collaboration between the USAF and the Royal Air Force on Allied war plans and the use of British bases provided an alternative to London's earlier deception scheme based on a nonexistent nuclear weapon. USAF Strategic Air Command bombers began a continuous rotation in and out of British air bases in July 1947. In April 1948, General Hollis visited Washington to brief the Joint Chiefs on the British chiefs of staff memorandum proposing joint deception operations. Three months later, in July, Air Ministry officer John Drew visited Washington and discussed deception procedures with the Orange team, a U.S. equivalent of the London Controlling Section. (The London report on his visit noted that whereas in Britain military policy was the servant of foreign policy, that wasn't true in Washington.)[11] As Anglo-American military planners knew well, the threat of nuclear retaliation was more psychological than real, whatever the identification of targets scattered far and wide across the USSR by Allied war plans or however inadequate the number of atomic bombs and strategic bombers able to carry out such strikes. War plans Pincher, Halfmoon, Trojan, and Offtackle would have been powerful psychological weapons, exaggerating both the awesome power of the U.S. nuclear arsenal and the number of B-29, B-36, and B-50 bombers available to the U.S. strategic air command. The U.S. Joint Chiefs had belatedly recognized the importance of nuclear strength as a purely psychological rather than a strictly military advantage, long after U.S. Air Force and the Royal Air Force chiefs had reached that conclusion. In January 1950, in urging the development of the hydrogen bomb after the Russians had acquired an atom bomb of their own, the Joint Chiefs concluded the hydrogen bomb would be a decisive factor "to grossly alter the psychological balance" between the United States and the USSR.[12] It mattered less that the hydrogen bomb's destructive power was so enormous that its military value was questionable.

In planning a deception operation, the controlling officers would have known that the two essential factors were credibility and verification, what the cruder U.S. Air Force broadsides from Washington had lacked. A doctored top-secret Joint Chiefs' war plan covertly passed to a Soviet military attaché in Washington, say, by one of the fifty or so officers on the Joint Chiefs' planning staff, might have seemed believable but would have failed the test. Ideally the source would be a proven Soviet agent so well placed and whose credibility was so well established that in Moscow his intelligence would be accepted as authentic. As described earlier, in 1947 the LCS abandoned a deception operation for lack of a Soviet-controlled conduit for delivering its message to Moscow and uncertainty about Soviet penetration of Britain's weapons agency.

A strategic deception operation using Anglo-American war plans and bombers as a deterrent to Soviet aggression in Western Europe required a suspected or known Soviet agent of proven credibility whose long loyalty to Moscow and unique access to official secrets amounted to verification. Was one available? Evidently he was. What better candidate than the officer so trusted by British intelligence that he'd been briefed on U.S.-U.K. codebreaking secrets in revealing knowledge of two still unidentified Soviet agents at Los Alamos and in Washington? His name was Kim Philby.

In 1976 an experienced and respected U.S. army intelligence officer then in retirement disclosed that Philby had been used in Washington "to pass fictitious information about the effectiveness of the Strategic Air Command and the size of the U.S. atomic arsenal at the time of the Korean War." The comment was made by General Edwin L. Sibert during a series of conversations with Anthony Cave Brown, an English writer researching a book on Sir Stewart Menzies, "C," the chief of MI6. Cave Brown included the remark in his Menzies biography published in 1988.[13] Sibert didn't disclose who had originated the plan or who carried it out, named no names, and claimed no success, but simply and plainly asserted its fact. In 1976 little was known about the Joint Chiefs' 1948–1951 war plans, U.S. and Royal Air Force collaboration, the U.S. nuclear arsenal, GCHQ and Arlington Hall's Venona operation, World War II's LCS, the Foreign Office's differences with the British chiefs of staff, or the CIA's 1949–1950 internal problems. Although much more had been made public in recent years, the Sibert comment has been ignored and never explored within the background of those very difficult years.

Cave Brown repeated Sibert's remarks in his 1994 book, *Treason in the Blood*, on the Philbys, father and son, but added more details. He writes that while an assistant director at the CIA, Sibert learned that Philby had been used as a conduit for disinformation. He implies that Philby was given details of the war plan codenamed Trojan and insists that "the highest level consultation concerning the Anglo-American aspects of Trojan passed through Philby's office in Washington to 'C' in London."[14] His 1994 embellishments include several jarring discrepancies that don't annul Sibert's original statement but do make Cave Brown's interpretation problematic. He doesn't challenge the Philby legend but raises a few inconclusive questions in pursuing the many allegations, possibilities, probabilities, and contradictions that complicate the Philby case. Among them is General Sibert's comment, obscured in his book by the lumber-room clutter of detail and debris of claims and counterclaims.

A similar allegation that Philby had been used to misinform the Soviet Union was made a year later. In 1977 William Corson suggested that Donald MacLean, Guy Burgess, and Kim Philby had all been identified as Soviet spies through an "American-Israeli secret intelligence connection" long before their flights to Moscow and manipulated accordingly. He claimed a small band of unnamed CIA professionals played on the personal, physical, and moral weaknesses and vanities of all three and were able to use them to CIA advantage, including "providing them with intelligence disinformation to mislead the Soviets." He also claims that CIA awareness of their espionage enabled the same CIA officers to discover the identities of other Soviet agents in the United States and "thwart Soviet subversive initiatives" throughout the government, private business, and scientific community.[15] Corson doesn't identify his source or the nature of the disinformation and gives no details to support his bizarre claims. Instead they are offered as a kind of impenetrable riddle that arouses our curiosity yet when approached more closely vanishes like a morning mist here in the Virginia countryside.

Its vaguely mysterious wording—"the CIA's small band of secret intelligence professionals"—has all the suspicious earmarks of secondhand rumor circulated by its promoters to mystify, confound, and deceive. This isn't unusual among intelligence officers who cloak their claims in a surpassing but inadmissible secrecy after they've been publicly swindled. Its consoling fiction could have originated as idle fantasy within the CIA but that's doubtful. More probably it was one of James Angleton's many post facto absurdities, a harebrained fabrication to ease his own humiliation at being taken in (the British writer Andrew Boyle was similarly hoodwinked by Angleton).

General Sibert's detail is more credible. His background alone makes his comment worth serious consideration. An experienced intelligence officer, he was one of the casualties of the CIA's 1948 disorder. A West Point graduate, like his father before him and his brother as well, he had served during the European war as General Omar Bradley's Twelfth Army Group's intelligence chief and had worked closely with Generals Walter Bedell Smith, Kenneth Strong, Hoyt Vandenberg, and others. As General Bradley's G-2, he received the British Ultra intercepts of German communications.[16] In March 1944, Bradley established a Special Plans Section to prepare and carry out deception and cover plans for all U.S. forces in the United Kingdom. Sibert was involved in those operations. He was known and respected by Strong, who defended him against unfair charges that Sibert's intelligence failure as Bradley's G-2 was responsible in part for the successful German offensive in the Ardennes on December 16, 1944.[17]

In July 1946, the month following his appointment as director of the Central Intelligence Group, Vandenberg sent his acting deputy, Kingman Douglas, and William H. Jackson to Frankfurt to recruit General Sibert for the CIG. Sibert was then chief of intelligence for U.S. forces in the European theater. Jackson had served on Sibert's intelligence staff during the war and would later become a member of the NSC survey group and the principal drafter of the Dulles report; General Walter Bedell Smith named Jackson his CIA deputy in October 1950. In the Cold War annals written years later, Sibert's most notable feat—for better or for worse—was in bringing to the War Department's attention Major General Reinhardt Gehlen, the former Wehrmacht chief of the Intelligence Section Foreign Armies East. This tale doesn't concern us here.

Vandenberg followed up his offer to Sibert with a personal visit to Frankfurt. Sibert accepted his invitation and on September 13, 1946, reported for duty as head of the Office of Operations (OO), which handled overt collection. Vandenberg had planned to put him in charge of all CIG intelligence collection but abandoned the idea because of the opposition of General Edwin Wright and Colonel D. H. Galloway, director of special operations— the same two officers who were the despair of others at the CIA in 1947– 1948. Sibert, who had expected more, had to be satisfied with far less. Disappointed, he left the CIA in June 1948 and returned to active duty.[18] In the 1951–1953 CIA history declassified in 1990, a footnote explaining Sibert's return to regular army duty was deleted. His onward assignment isn't clear. From 1948 until 1950 he was evidently staff director at the Inter-American Defense Board in Washington, presumably under General Matthew Ridgeway. He was chief of staff of the Far East Command in 1950 during the Korean War. After thirty-four years in the military, he retired in 1954 as a major general and died of an aneurysm in 1977 at Vinson Hall in Maclean, Virginia.

And here we confront the discrepancies in Cave Brown's book.[19] For reasons best known to Cave Brown, he was attempting to put Sibert's remark in the context of the outbreak of the Korean War rather than the 1948–1950 period and in so doing made several serious errors. General Sibert left the CIA in June 1948, sixteen months before Philby arrived in Washington and seven months before the Joint Chiefs' planning staff completed war plan Trojan. Sibert couldn't have known of Trojan while an assistant director at the CIA. Trojan was abandoned a year before the Korean War erupted. Predicated on the first year of a global war beginning in Europe in early 1950, the air force annex or Trojan called for three hundred atomic bombs to be dropped on Russian cities by B-29s, B-50s, and B-36s in the first wave and seventy more in the second. The massive air assault was so unrealistic and other aspects of Trojan so beyond Allied capability that the Joint Chiefs abandoned it and began work on a new plan. The result was Offtackle. The JCS discussed the plan with British and Canadian chiefs of staff in Washington September 26 through October 4, 1948, which delayed final approval. After final revisions, Offtackle was approved on December 8.[20] Although Trojan was shelved, its massive air attack on the USSR retained a psychological value that could have been exploited.

Never widely known, Sibert's comments about Philby have been ignored or dismissed as another unlikely claim by those attempting to salvage CIA honor by showing the agency wasn't so gullible after all. The Philby legend was too strongly established to be compromised by unverified hearsay—never mind that hearsay built it from the ground up—especially when so little was known about the London and Washington 1948–1950 background or Sibert. The general wasn't among those who trafficked in Philby memorabilia but was a highly regarded military and intelligence officer with nothing to gain by his assertion. If there is no reason to believe it was intended to deceive, it is possible he was misinformed by those who had other purposes in mind, but just as certain that an officer of his integrity would never have volunteered the comment unless he was convinced of its authenticity and the reliability of his source. His remarks have never been explored against the 1948–1950 background. Instead Philby's Washington service has become entangled with James Angleton, his CIA liaison officer, whose name became widely known much later and whose comments were different in character and purpose. Both the Angleton and Philby legends have been sustained by the same apocryphal litter of hearsay, rumor, anecdote, and conjecture that makes any reasonable clarification difficult.

But apart from his professional reputation and his specific reference to a U.S. war plan, perhaps Trojan or a facsimile thereof, Sibert gives us no reason to accept his word, nor does Cave Brown, who only confuses the issue, even though Philby's use as a channel for strategic disinformation, if true, helps clarify many contradictions that have obscured the affair since 1951. Such an operation or an attempt at a deception operation helps explain a few of his more cryptic comments in *My Silent War* or offered gratuitously to his visitors during his 1980s Moscow reminiscences.

In July 1963 Harold Wilson, later the British prime minister, may have drawn a similar conclusion. The Macmillan government was in crisis following Philby's defection to Moscow, which had created an uproar in the press and outrage in the House of Commons. As leader of the opposition, Wilson had appealed to Prime Minister Macmillan for answers to calm the clamor and was invited by Macmillan to meet in secrecy with "C," the head of the SIS, by now Dick White. As Wilson would later write in his memoirs, one simple fact he was given by "C" made sense of the entire Philby story. That fact was never disclosed in public or private, but enabled Wilson to close ranks with the Macmillan government and quiet but not silence the commotion.[21] If Wilson was satisfied with Dick White's simple fact, it must have assured him that British security interests hadn't been seriously compromised to the extent many claimed. Possibly he told him that any information to which Philby had access was controlled by MI6, another way of describing disinformation. But we don't know what White said and the mystery leaves unresolved the question of Philby's use in 1949–1951 as an unknowing disinformation agent under British control.

Evidently Sibert didn't give Cave Brown details as to who was responsible for the deception or who was its agent; he may have been reluctant to compromise military friendships, embarrass others still in responsible positions, or touch on subjects too sensitive to discuss in 1976. It is doubtful that he played a role in any deception or knew how or when Philby was identified as a Soviet agent. Mere suspicion of Philby wouldn't have been enough for those who conceived the operation. Much more had to be known than had ever been disclosed and the source would have had to be trusted absolutely. If General Sibert was correct, then the planners knew far more than we know even today. The evidence identifying Philby would have included everything known to GCHQ, General Hollis, and his London Controlling Section. If there was a Philby deception, it would have originated with an incriminating GCHQ recovery of the 1945 KGB Moscow–London traffic, most probably between 1946 and 1948 when Meredith Gardner was successfully penetrating Soviet coded communications of 1944 and 1945.

In the abstract, General Sibert's deception plan is plausible in value but questionable in execution, particularly in its use of Philby. Ignoring the fact that not one shred of documentary evidence has yet been found nor is ever likely to be found to support it, its probability can be considered by asking how such an operation could have successfully escaped disclosure. Secrecy is too easily mandated in Washington to succeed unless bonded by absolute silence. The union of secrecy and silence is the rarest of all covenants in a capital where the controlled leak is a tactical tool among executive agencies, policymakers, congressional watchdogs, and anonymous White House insiders to advance agendas, slander reputations, wreck judicial appointments, and slough off responsibility for failure.

To this must be added the problem of sheer numbers—too many people knowing far more than those in authority recognize. Before the first U-2 was shot down over Sverdlovsk in the Ural Mountains on May 1, 1960, U-2 flights were known to many in Washington, including a few of my middle-grade colleagues working at State's Intelligence and Research Bureau. They had seen the maps of the USSR and knew the routes over the test range at Tyuratam and Plesetsk where the first Russian intercontinental ballistic missiles were located. The Bay of Pigs operation was so tightly held at the CIA that many senior officers were unaware of the plans, although it was widely recognized on the Miami street that something was afoot. David Martin publicized a partial version of the Venona secret in his 1980 book, *Wilderness of Mirrors*. Although mistaken and incomplete in many details, his account was accurate enough to trouble NSA officials.

Carrying the question even further increases our skepticism. If General Sibert was correct in his belief, asserted as fact, not theory, how could the operation have escaped disclosure for more than fifty years? Few Washington secrets have. Many NSC executive sessions for the same period have been released; so have State Department top-secret cables and memos. CIA officers have disclosed some details about the operations in Albania and the Ukraine. The agency has declassified a 370-page report on the Cuban missile crisis, including original agents' reports, intelligence dissemination, and a performance critique. Many of the Joint Chiefs' 1948–1951 war plans are available for review in the National Archives. Why not some stray document that verifies Sibert's assertion of a deception operation?

One immediate although not entirely persuasive answer is that only a very few senior U.S. military officers, two or three at most, knew of it and left no paper trail. But even the best-kept secret of the Truman years, the size of the U.S. atomic arsenal, was eventually made public, even though the exact numbers are still debatable. Moreover, why wouldn't those responsible have acknowledged the existence of a U.S. intelligence operation that turned the Philby myth on its head and eased CIA embarrassment at his too often proclaimed success in penetrating the agency? The most obvious answer is that the CIA didn't know. If it had, one of those many retired case officers of whatever importance who decades later seemed so well informed on so many clandestine operations would have proudly proclaimed the secret years ago. CIA officialdom often finds a way to let its muzzled dogs loose in the streets and would have had good reason to restore agency dignity and honor after having been outrageously duped by Kim Philby.

But the CIA would have had no role: strategic deception is a military, not a civilian, intelligence operation. It would also have been excluded because in 1949 it hadn't the organization, the resources, or the access to military plans required by the deception. The Joint Chiefs of Staff consistently refused to share its war plans or its intelligence with the CIA or any other civilian agency. Although the service intelligence chiefs relented after General Smith took command in 1950, as late as February 1951 the Joint Chiefs gave instructions that no Joint Chiefs paper or operational cable should be given to the CIA, despite Smith's request that they were needed in planning covert action.[22] The exclusion of the CIA accounts for the bewilderment about the Philby affair professed by so many CIA officers and the confusion of those who offered their own interpretations. It also explains the understandable reaction of the very able former (and now deceased) CIA director Richard Helms when another retired CIA officer told him of my suspicions and admitted he too found them credible. "Impossible," Helms scoffed. "I would have known." Precisely: he didn't know because he wouldn't have known.

Finally and most decisively, the scheme would have escaped disclosure only if it weren't an American operation at all, but a British one—British in origin, British in execution, and British in closure. If there was a disinformation operation in Washington using Philby, as General Sibert maintained, then a GCHQ recovery of a STANLEY cable inspired it, the Hollis Committee's LCS planned it, and British Royal Air Force officers in Washington carried it out. These possibilities alone would have kept its secret buried in silence, never committed to paper, and never released to the dusty archives of the British Public Records Office, securely safe from disclosure for more than fifty years.

The probability defies belief, of course: a British intelligence operation carried out on our very soil in Washington D.C.? "Impossible!" howl those retired CIA civilian warriors who were too long denied their revenge only to discover they've not only been ignored but trumped by the same London incompetents who sent Philby and Burgess to Washington. "Under our very noses? It would have been catastrophic! Unthinkable!" The intelligence sophist—he's often written about Philby with bewildering results and after forty years still doesn't know what he believes—might snort that it would have been contrary to every written or unwritten agreement that bound the intelligence services of both countries. Had that trust been violated, the consequences would have been infinitely more damaging to Anglo-American relations and British interests in particular than any possible gains.

Well, yes—maybe. But it was far from unthinkable. The U.S. Air Force and the Royal Air Force had been closely cooperating in secret since 1946 and in some instances without the knowledge of their senior civilian officials in London and Washington. Even if very few in Washington knew about the Venona operation at the time—and very few did—when Philby arrived in 1949, U.S. and British intelligence were cooperating at Arlington Hall and had been for several years in the joint codebreaking operation that pooled the resources of GCHQ and the Armed Forces Security Agency (as the ASA was renamed in 1949 and put under the authority of the Joint Chiefs of Staff). British liaison was maintained through an office established by the British as a result of the U.S.-U.K. Sigint agreement, the Senior United Kingdom Liaison Office—and, by the way, who knew precisely what that community of conspiratorial GCHQ and Royal Air Force intelligence officers was up to? Very few are aware even today, yet we do know that one was coordinating Sigint intercept operations with the U.S. Air Force chief of intelligence.

A deception scheme in Washington using Philby would have been unworkable except as a British operation. Its secret could never have been kept inviolable as a joint U.S.-British chiefs of staff operation similar to those of World War II. At that time, control was centered in wartime London, not in peacetime Washington. The Pentagon, the service intelligence agencies, and the CIA knew no more about Philby than did any other U.S. intelligence agency, which seemed to be little at all, and certainly nothing to identify him as a suspected Soviet agent. An American plan would have been impossible to originate, impossible to conceal, and impossible to execute. Any deception would have had to be managed within the context of his official duties. He had no reason to meet with the U.S. military except those few assigned to the OPC Albanian operation or as part of his liaison with Arlington Hall Station under U.S. military intelligence, but his so-called liaison officer would have been British, not American.

British military planners and the Royal Air Force had more reason to initiate such an operation than their American counterparts. In 1948–1949, with the future of NATO still an open question, the outbreak of war in Western Europe had more serious consequences for Britain than the United States. There was also the matter of honoring secret agreements. There were far too many players on Washington's stage, too many executive agencies, too many prima donnas, too many meddlesome politicians, as Prime Minister Attlee knew full well, too many quarrels within the Joint Chiefs of Staff, and too many ways for secret agreements to go public and go disastrously wrong. The Attlee government had been both shabbily treated and weakened in trusting Truman to carry out the secret provisions for cooperation on atomic energy as agreed to by Roosevelt and Churchill in the 1943 Quebec agreement and the 1944 Hyde Park memorandum. Truman and his advisers had known nothing of the agreement. When finally given a photocopy by the British, it was denounced by General Leslie Groves as a fraud. In 1945 Truman had refused to help Britain build a nuclear plant, forcing the Attlee government to go it alone. As we know, Britain had been dealt a further blow by the August 1946 McMahon Act forbidding formal agreements on atomic energy.[23]

Lord Tedder, Vice Chief of Air Staff Robb, or General Hollis would have faced none of these problems had any or all decided to go it alone. (Tedder was replaced by Air Marshal Sir John Slessor as air force chief of staff on

January 1, 1950, and was subsequently lured from retirement to command the British Joint Services Mission in Washington. But his presence wasn't related to any deception operation. Far more important military issues between London and the Pentagon brought him to Washington.) With a British operation, there would have been no risk of exposure. Part of its appeal must have been its simplicity. It would have been a very modest, very simple, and very brief operation, quickly executed and quickly over. It would have been totally different from the complex operations of World War II that required long and well-coordinated plans and exchanges between the planners and the participants, between the LCS, the various theater commands, MI5 and MI6 in many cases, and British GCHQ at Bletchley Park.

Once Hollis and the LCS approved the plan, no more than one or two Royal Air Force officers posted to Washington would been required to carry it out. The action officer could have been drawn from the RAF staff at the British Joint Services Mission where Air Marshal Sir Charles Medhurst was assigned. Before his 1949 posting to Washington, Medhurst was with the Air Ministry in London, where he dealt with the transfer of USAF bombers to British airfields. In November 1949 in Washington he participated in plans to incorporate thirty-two U.S. B-29 bombers in British Royal Air Force operational wings by July 1, 1950. Colonel Marr-Johnson of the Royal Air Force intelligence staff was a GCHQ liaison officer with Arlington Hall under the cover of the British Joint Services Mission in the Old Navy building.

And then there is Jack Easton, the retired air commodore, as General Hollis described him in his introductory letter to General Gruenther in April 1948. Easton was in the Air Ministry during World War II, was on the Royal Air Force intelligence staff, and had participated in SIS operations. He had close ties to the RAF, had served with Charles Medhurst at the Air Ministry, and undoubtedly played a role in any 1949–1950 deception operation. But it is as impossible to know his role as it is to confirm the operation. He might have helped conceive it in partnership with the London Controlling Section or he could have been persuaded by Hollis and senior air force officers to help position its essential component, Philby's posting to Washington. If so, then he had made an unforgivable error in yielding his intelligence priorities to those of the military.

Dick White made that point in his conversations with Tom Bower in the 1980s. In commenting that "the art of intelligence missed [Easton] completely," he said Jack Easton and John Sinclair were "weak and ineffectively no good. Despite being staff officers of the best tradition, they bowed to the [military] chiefs." After taking over from Sinclair as "C," head of MI6, White wanted to end MI6's relations with the military in anti-Soviet operations and soon did. The military, he said, "still had not mastered the transition from war to peace." Although his remarks were made in the context of events in the mid-1950s, they would have applied equally to 1949–1951.[24] Any 1949–1950 deception operation in Washington was a very small page torn from the still secret book of much larger World War II operations.

Technically such a deception could be considered purely British, forwarding details on Royal Air Force preparations for the deployment of U.S. atomic bombs and U.S. bombers at bases under U.K. control as called for by Trojan and other 1949–1950 USAF war plans. While General Hollis and senior RAF officers conceived the operation, they might have asked for the approval of a like-minded senior U.S. Air Force officer. The unwritten assent of the air force's General Vandenberg would have been sufficient; he might have agreed to a British operation run by experienced British officers with absolutely no possibility of disclosure. His consent would have been appropriate, but not essential, although it is difficult to understand how General Sibert would have known of the operation otherwise. He was Vandenberg's close personal friend. When he raised the deception with Cave Brown in 1976, Vandenberg had long passed from the scene (he retired in June 1953 and died in April 1954).

The London Air Ministry sent its cipher messages to the British air force staff through a Joint Communications Office but it isn't clear whether that office was at the British embassy or the Royal Air Force offices in the Old Navy building on Constitution Avenue.[25] Another communications channel was also available, MI6's special cipher at the British embassy, said to be the most secure at the mission. The MI6 cipher was apparently used to transmit all of the embassy's most secret political and military intelligence, including atomic weapons data. It evidently transmitted information gathered by Dr. Wilfred Mann, the British embassy attaché assigned by MI6's Scientific Intelligence Service in London (although this seems doubtful in view of the McMahon Act), as well as plans for the Strategic Air Command's use of British airfields and the storage of nonnuclear assemblies.[26] As we know, from October 1949 until June 1951 the MI6 cipher and cipher clerk were under Philby. Had the Joint Communications Office been attached to the Joint Services Mission and not the embassy, the use of the embassy MI6 channel by Royal Air Force intelligence officers would have been difficult to justify. An RAF officer could have used the embassy cipher and passed to the Air Ministry the USAF details of the Trojan war plan, as General Sibert believed.

A deception operation working through a known agent returns benefits that go beyond misinforming the enemy of capability and intent, as was practiced in the double-cross system in England during the war in using MI5-controlled German agents to misinform their German commands. In the British double-cross system, the Abwehr codes given to the German double agents controlled by MI5, like Dick White's agent SNOW, enabled the British to break other German codes. This more complex advantage would have benefited the Arlington Hall Anglo-American codebreakers: signals intercepts, cryptology, and codebreaking technique. It also returns us to Maurice Oldfield's September 1949 briefing in London before Philby's arrival in Washington. The U.S. codebreaking effort was downplayed with the claim that it had managed only minimal success despite years of effort in decrypting Soviet codes. As noted earlier, this suggested that any codebreaking threat came from GCHQ in London, not the AFSA in Washington, and therefore Philby had nothing to fear from the far less successful American effort.

A plain text copy of an original message is helpful as a crib in penetrating a coded message even without a codebook. In 1948 FBI agent Lamphere gave Gardner the original plain texts of Soviet coded messages the FBI had photographed in a black-bag operation at the Soviet trade mission in New York in 1944 and evidently helped Gardner recreate the code.[27] Details on USAF war plans passed through Philby's MI6 cipher to the London Air Ministry and relayed by Philby to his KGB case officer at the Soviet embassy would have been of similar value to U.S. and GCHQ codebreakers. Intercepted by the AFSA signals station at Vint Hill Station near Warrenton, Virginia, and analyzed by the Anglo-American team at Arlington Hall or Eastcote in London on the basis of the original text, they might have proved helpful in breaking a KGB code.

If this was the suggestion MI6's Oldfield or Easton intended in Philby's London orientation—namely, that Washington's codebreaking capability was deficient or minimal—it failed. There would be no sudden upsurge in signals traffic from the Soviet embassy in Washington as a result of any urgent message Philby passed to his case officer. There would be no coded text of any military cable obtained through the MI6 cipher. Philby completely bypassed the Soviet embassy. A long and time-consuming courier and mail route sent any secret messages. What they were, we don't know except that there were very few.

Philby's account of his Washington years in *My Silent War* includes only one reference to war plans. He describes a meeting with Walter Bedell Smith at his CIA office to discuss a document of some twenty-odd paragraphs detailing war plans. Philby had spent the morning studying the paper and was amazed at Smith's recall of every detail without as much as a glance at the document.[28] Philby's anecdote, besides citing a penetration of CIA secrets (the CIA knew nothing about the Joint Chiefs' war plans), was intended to briefly characterize Smith as Philby had others in Washington, often sympathetically. The general was an exception; their meeting was less than warm. Philby recalled his cold eye and "his machine-tool brain." In a 1988 interview with Phillip Knightley in Moscow, Philby further described the document, claiming it was a detailed account of how MI6 and the CIA would cooperate in the event of a war with the Soviet Union. Philby said he immediately passed it on to his Soviet control, dictating the entire text from memory.[29]

This is unlikely. The meeting undoubtedly took place between November 1950 and February 1951. MI6's deputy General John Sinclair visited Washington in December 1950 to discuss MI6 and CIA plans for wartime cooperation; a memo of understanding was agreed to in February.[30] Philby didn't meet with his illegal Soviet control officer any earlier than April 1951. Philby also claims he received other information he couldn't use because so few people had access that had Moscow acted, the CIA would have been suspicious. He told Knightley he didn't pass on some intelligence because he wouldn't have been believed. Genrikh Borovik also claims that during their 1980s conversations Philby told him that in Washington he had heard "heated words" about dropping the atomic bomb on the Soviet Union and the possibility of a Soviet retaliatory strike on the United States or the Soviet occupation of Western Europe. According to Borovik, Philby regretted he couldn't report those Washington discussions to Moscow because he had no Washington KGB contact for his first nine to ten months.[31]

Philby was assigned to Washington in 1949, when the war fears of 1948 were very much alive. The Korean War was nine months away and the Korean peninsula was far from the minds of Allied military planners. Fear of Russian aggression in Western Europe in 1948–1950 was the justification for USAF war plans and would have been the basis of any British deception operation (by the early summer of 1950 there were more than ten thousand U.S. Air Force personnel in England, 180 U.S. warplanes and fifteen hundred U.S. Navy personnel.)[32] Allied weakness in conventional forces in Western Europe was the primary concern; atomic bombs delivered by strategic air power was the only deterrence available in the face of Russian military superiority. In wartime, strategic and tactical deception for a well-defined military purpose is a continuous series of operations as new offensives are planned across a widely scattered front. Any 1949 peacetime deception would not have been continuous but carried out during a respectable interval following Philby's October arrival. It could have been executed by the air force annex to Trojan, which had just been abandoned by the RAF and USAF, or a similar USAF-planned atomic blitz. Intended to warn Moscow against aggression in Western Europe, once that material had been transmitted disclosing the overwhelming power of the U.S. nuclear arsenal and the strategic bomber delivery capacity, the mission would have been accomplished. It would have been a modest effort, quickly executed and quickly concluded—not much more than a well-aimed shot in the dark. Further reports incrementally updating U.S. retaliatory strength would have been pointless.

If the deception hadn't been carried out by June 15, 1950, the Korean War would have reduced its relevance. The U.S. psychological advantage had first been diminished in late August 1949, when Russia had unexpectedly exploded its own atomic bomb; Philby had already been offered the Washington post. The U.S. atomic bomb and the possibility of a massive nuclear strike against Moscow hadn't deterred the North Korean military offensive. The Korean War also reduced that advantage further by exposing the defects of too great a reliance on massive nuclear retaliation as a psychological deterrent to aggression. U.S. nuclear capability and its strategic bomber capability were no longer enough. The Korean War transformed U.S. military strategy, reduced the primary emphasis on strategic air power, and concentrated instead on vastly increasing American conventional force strength, as was now possible under Truman's enormously expanded defense budget.[33] A strengthened NATO would eventually emerge. Communist China's November 1950 entry into the Korean War also raised a completely new and different set of diplomatic and military problems between London and Washington. The Korean War thus reduced the significance of any deception operation in Washington. Philby's usefulness had run its course—unless Jack Easton, as Philby's immediate superior, foolishly attempted to play his own card.

In early October 1950 during General Smith's first week or first days as CIA director, General Strong called on him at CIA headquarters. Strong doesn't explain the purpose of his visit nor whether it was at his suggestion or at Smith's invitation. It was a difficult time for Smith. A brilliant officer, organizer, and planner, he hadn't sought the CIA job, didn't want it, and had refused it until President Truman convinced him he had no choice but to accept. He was tough, demanding, quick-tempered, feared, and difficult to work with. His confidence wasn't easily or quickly earned. He knew the CIA needed to be drastically reorganized and better understood the necessity and requirements for sound intelligence operations than any of his predecessors, but General Strong knew more. During that meeting Smith asked Strong to be his deputy. It was an extraordinary offer, but Smith trusted Strong absolutely. Smith also knew more about Allied deception operations during World War II than any American officer. With General Strong he had managed deception operations in the North African, Mediterranean, and European campaigns and understood their methods, their value, and the absolute secrecy they required.

At the time of this October meeting, the Foreign Office Promotions board in London had already met and Roger Makins had arranged for Maclean's return to the American desk after the end of his convalescence in early November. Dick White's counterespionage operation had begun. In *My Silent War* Philby claims that by August 1950 he had seen numerous reports on the MI5 HOMER investigation passed to J. Edgar Hoover through his MI6 cipher. General Strong's Joint Intelligence Bureau was established under the minister to integrate army, air, and navy intelligence gathering, handling, and analysis. The bureau had assisted the U.S. Air Force in its targeting of Russian cities under the various war plans. The London Controlling Section and the Department of Forward Plans were at the Ministry of Defense; both would have been known to General Strong.

Admiral Hillenkoetter, the CIA director Smith replaced, didn't belong to that close-knit community of Allied officers who had served together at SHAEF headquarters and in the field during World War II. They included General Smith, Lord Tedder, General Strong, and Dick White, who had been Strong's deputy for counterintelligence at SHAEF, as well as General Bradley, General Spaatz, General Vandenberg, and others. Jack Easton wasn't a member of that group either. Once Smith took up his duties in October 1950, relations between the CIA director and British military and intelligence officers would have changed significantly. Smith's offer to General Strong indicates the uncommon bond that existed between the two men. The reciprocal trust, frankness, and loyalty that gave such integrity and strength to their long friendship were in the balance in early October 1950. In the broader sense so were British-American intelligence relations.

For those reasons, it is altogether probable, if not certain, that at their first meeting Strong told Smith everything that he and Dick White of MI5 knew about Kim Philby. The two were Smith's closest associates in British intelligence; they had both worked closely with him, and they both knew him intimately. They would also have known the terrible costs of not dealing frankly and openly with him. There are many reasons for believing Smith knew nothing about Philby. But in this instance Strong's integrity and character and the absolute trust and honesty between the two men, as well as General Strong's concern for the future of British-CIA relations, are simply too powerful not to believe that all that Strong knew about Philby was also known to Smith. Whether Strong went beyond telling Smith that Philby was strongly suspected of being a Soviet agent is another question. At the time Smith was worried about the wider implications of the Korean War; in recruiting old associates to join him at the agency, he'd told them, as he did General Strong, that it might be a prelude to World War III. If Strong obscurely mentioned a deception operation, no more would have been necessary; Smith would have understood.

In June 1951 Smith banished Philby from Washington as quickly as he could and reportedly told "C" that the CIA wouldn't cooperate further with MI6 until Philby was shown the door. The uncompromising severity of Smith's ultimatum is convincing evidence that he knew far more than mere suspicion that Philby was a suspected Soviet agent. After Philby's dismissal, Strong was a familiar figure at CIA headquarters at 2430 E Street in Washington as MI6's temporary liaison. Had Smith the slightest suspicion that the general hadn't told him everything he knew, Strong's effectiveness in Washington and their relationship would have ended. But it didn't and Strong's relations with the CIA and the Pentagon grew even stronger in the coming years.[34] In his book written years later, Strong mentions Philby's name in a curious aside. He emphasizes the importance of intelligence secrecy and security, even if the notoriety given individuals like Philby cast doubts on both the discretion of intelligence agencies and their security. He expresses his conviction that the Philbys of this world are far less important than the claims made for them; he also insists he didn't believe for a moment there was "ever the slightest chance" that Philby would become head of MI6. (With more concealed disdain, he failed to include Philby's name in the book's index.)[35]

Military and intelligence operations that leave no paper behind don't exist except in memory. And after the memories have perished, nothing is left. Since the most sensitive intelligence operations are never committed to paper, material evidence will never be found confirming General Sibert's claim. It probably doesn't exist. There were no cabinet meetings, no executive conferences, no official minutes or memoranda of agreement. The few in London who conceived the operation and the one or two in Washington who executed it acted on their own initiative without official sanction and outside official channels. Secrecy was as much a part of the deception as the design.

Few vital secrets would have been put at risk by the British initiative and none was truly sacrificed. If so, they were of lesser importance. The Albanian operation was well publicized before it began. The intent to destabilize the Hoxha regime had been reported in the London press before those first October 1949 incursions got underway. Philby's disclosures didn't first reveal the operation and wouldn't have ended it. Nevertheless, lives were lost even if American and British officers weren't among them. In November 1948 a skeptical Lord Tedder had warned the Russia Committee of its unrealistic design. Like an artillery barrage laid down too far ahead of a military offensive, he predicted, "Your friends were simply annihilated."[36] In the classic deception operations of World War II, moreover, lesser operations were sometimes sacrificed so that more important initiatives would succeed. The plan's architects were playing for higher stakes. Any Anglo-U.S. war plans passed were largely illusory and required a nuclear arsenal and a strategic strike force that would be inadequate for years to come. The so-called codebreaking secret was known to both Philby and Moscow, although inaccurately and incompletely. The distorted detail he was given served another purpose.

If it's impossible to verify General Sibert's 1976 comment, we can judge its plausibility. His claim is credible in all its parts: origin, purpose, design, secrecy, and execution. In 1949–1950 a few British military senior officers in London had the will, the secrecy, and the Royal Air Force officers in place in Washington to execute a simple deception intended to deter a possible war in Western Europe. They believed the retaliatory atomic threat with its strategic air force delivery capability was the most effective deterrent in the Allied arsenal. RAF collaboration with the Strategic Air Command and the U.S. Air Force, including the USAF's war plan Trojan, provided the material; and the embassy's MI6 cipher a channel of communications. A British RAF officer could have executed the plan with virtually no possibility of compromise.

But now we've left the thin ice we have been wandering and are out in open water, far from shore. If a British deception plan as cited by General Sibert is plausible, would it have been successful? The logical answer is that we'll never know; the speculative answer is, probably not. Philby was out of contact with any Soviet handler, legal or illegal, for most of his twenty months.

From KGB files opened in Moscow we know that during a March 1950 visit to London, six months after Philby's arrival in Washington, he told Burgess to ask Moscow to give him political asylum if the danger grew too great. His fear may have been the threat of a GCHQ intercept, as he told Knightley in Moscow, or the fact that some in MI5 and MI6 were still troubled about his past. His appeal may suggest that an incident out of the ordinary had occurred between his October 1949 arrival and the message to Burgess. For some unknown reason, he might have realized he was then under suspicion. Since he was out of contact with the KGB during the six months before his request, an incident or a provocation at the British embassy or elsewhere in Washington might have been responsible.

In *My Silent War* and during his 1980s Moscow recollections, Philby hints that he recognized something unusual was afoot in Washington. And here we return to his odd characterization of Jack Easton and the handwritten letter delivered by John Drew after the disappearance of Maclean and Burgess. The incident is as curious as Philby took it to be. Other incidents that aroused his mistrust may have preceded it. In the 1980s he admitted to his Russian admirer, Genrikh Borovik, that in Washington he was out of contact with his KGB control for nine or ten months or until after the Korean War erupted. This is an oddly gratuitous admission for a spy of Philby's reputation. Washington was Moscow's prime intelligence target. For the KGB's most successful agent to freely admit that he was out of contact for more than half his time in Washington is difficult to explain. To volunteer his inactivity is out of character for a man who elsewhere boasted of small triumphs that never happened.

Those comments, like Philby's mistrust of Easton in his memoir, would have sent an implied message of recognition back to London: if deception had been the purpose—and use of his embassy MI6 cipher to pass details of Trojan's atomic blitz of the USSR to the Air Ministry would have qualified— he hadn't been deceived. He had been out of touch with the KGB for those first nine to ten months. By 1993, when Borovik's book was published, most of the principals were dead, including Philby. There were few around who still remembered and fewer who even cared. In any case, the ambiguity of any such attempt at deception may have haunted Philby, as did the purpose of Jack Easton's note. Both implied that London knew far more about his past than was ever revealed. If so, it was a mystery he could never solve and carried with him to his grave.

Chapter
TWELVE

Old myths revisited.—Why legends survive.—
Field of vision.—Hijacking history.—Counterfeit cards.—No more to be learned.—The wartime
generation.—The pygmy plan.

Washington's decision to declassify Venona attracted widespread publicity when announced on July 11, 1995, at CIA headquarters in Langley, Virginia. The ceremonial opening promised even more to the assembled journalists, scholars, intelligence officers, and other prominent guests in disclosing the secrets of the most celebrated American espionage cases of the 1940s, some hidden for almost fifty years. In the First Release, issued that day, little was found to contradict the traditional version of the Maclean affair. Newspapers repeated the same shopworn anecdotes and the same tired recollections that had been repeated endlessly over the years regarding Venona and the three Cambridge spies. Misleading and incomplete, they added nothing new.

The *Washington Post* reported on July 30, 1995, that Kim Philby "visited the Venona site and received summaries of Venona translations." On October 2, 1996, after the Venona cables were released by the Public Record Office, the London *Times* claimed Philby was given regular reports "on the progress of the Venona project." On September 29, the eve of a three-day intelligence conference in Washington and two days after the Fifth Venona Release, the *Sunday Telegraph* reported that Philby told the KGB that Meredith Gardner "had decrypted a cable which identified the Soviet agent HOMER as the British diplomat Donald Maclean." But the American and British commentators could be excused. Still captive to the legends that had prevailed for decades, there had been little time to closely study the Venona archive.

Following the publication of the complete Venona archive, several American scholars studied the cables for years and subsequently published the results of their exposure of scores of Soviet agents in the United States. Yet no questions were raised about the true extent of British participation in Venona or the reliability of cables that told us only what London wanted us to know about Maclean and nothing about Philby or Burgess. The reference to the Washington conference in the September 29 *Telegraph* should have raised a few eyebrows. The commentator noted that "Sadly, no British intelligence veterans have been authorized to speak." A skeptic might have asked, Why not? Why not indeed? London was content to let stagnant water stand.

Intelligence legends endure because the writers, journalists, and historians who helped establish them are comfortable with the results and have no compelling reason to modify their contribution, certainly not after thirty or forty years. The Philby, Maclean, and Burgess legends were among the most durable. New evidence may improbably appear, as it did in the Venona archive, but in such complex, obscure, or ambiguous form as to be imperceptible. If suspicions are somehow aroused by new material, exploring them further seems hardly worth the effort. The obsequies are long over, the books are on the library shelves, the crowd has moved elsewhere, like the publishing houses, and the money is in the bank. Why bother?

Apart from a few unofficial leaks intended to support its 1955 White Paper fiction, British intelligence services have never contributed one iota of official or documentary evidence in support of the prevailing popular legends that now entomb the three spies. Lacking that contribution, common sense must tell us that Philby's career in particular must have been reconstructed with very flimsy material. Indeed it was. Anecdote, hearsay, and conjecture were the straw, bricks, and mortar that built on Philby's solid enough 1940–1945 MI6 foundation. Much of the reconstruction of his postwar career is no more substantial than a house of cards. Yet it continues to stand.

In England and America, the Philby canvas was never stretched to full size to include the very complex 1948–1949 historical landscape that is essential to identifying the soil in which the Philby case had its roots. When he arrived in Washington in October 1949, the deceptions of World War II still cast a long shadow over British intelligence planning. Anglo-American military vulnerability in Europe wasn't a topic of popular concern in either England or the United States. The diminutive U.S. nuclear arsenal and the deficiencies of the Strategic Air Command were well-kept secrets, as were U.S. war plans and the close cooperation between the USAF and the RAF. The differences that alienated the British service chiefs of staff from the Foreign Office over Soviet policy wouldn't be known for several decades. The absence of that background obscured the logic of the Maclean and Philby affairs as it did any deception gambit in Washington designed to warn Moscow against aggression in Western Europe.

Philby's 1947–1951 espionage career was interpreted against the backdrop of the more highly visible Cold War drama of later years, principally the 1960s and 1970s. Framed within a narrow lens by those with a limited field of historical vision and reported by headline journalism, slipshod analysis, obsessed conspiracy theorists, and blinkered intelligence dogmatists, Philby's accomplishments were elevated far beyond reason. Assumptions were made about his successful penetration of an effective CIA colossus that didn't exist in 1949–1950. He is believed to have stood at the shoulder of an American cryptologist at Arlington Hall as he broke into Venona's encrypted Soviet traffic word by word and enabled Moscow "to monitor the precise progress that was being made." Never mind that this was a physical impossibility or that he was gullible enough to believe that the Americans and British had constructed a new deciphering machine that in one day did the work "of a thousand people in a thousand years."[1] Writers, journalists, and KGB memoirists alike have repeated these and other fictions. They've also described for us a clumsy, incompetent MI5 and were aided in no small part by MI5's and MI6's silence except for the foolishly conceived 1955 White Paper. As a result, at least one long chapter recording forty years of Anglo-American intelligence success has been lost to history.

With all of the Venona releases now in the public domain, London's sleeping dogs at GCHQ, never having barked, never having been fully awakened, only mildly stirred enough to dig up a few meatless bones for our inspection, will continue to sleep and the Maclean, Philby, and Burgess affairs will remain buried in secrecy and silence. The book has again been closed on the three and will remain closed, even if any such London counterespionage or a relatively unremarkable Washington deception operation would have been to the credit of a very few, very close-mouthed British military and intelligence officers. The much-maligned British intelligence services deserve far better. After fifty years, the audacity of their initiatives would undoubtedly excuse their secrecy and silence, even in official Washington—which in its present confusion and disorder would need another fifty years to understand what exactly had been going on—but it won't happen. London still plays out the counterfeit cards it dealt fifty years ago.

The definitive answer to the possibility of a Washington military deception will never be known, however credible in time, place, and circumstance. The effort at concealing the Maclean cables and the 1945–1949 GCHQ London to Moscow STANLEY cable recoveries are evidence enough that the circumstances of Philby's posting to Washington were never as simple or unambiguous as has been assumed; his troubled behavior further suggests something was amiss. London's motives in releasing selective cables may arouse our contempt and strengthen our suspicions, but our questions will go unanswered. The dates those KGB cable fragments were fully penetrated will remain concealed. The most that can be asserted beyond any doubt is that Maclean, Philby, and Burgess were the objects of an MI5 counterespionage deception from November 1950 until May 1951. London's 1995 determination to conceal the details of Maclean's exposure and Philby's involvement remains steadfast.

In the United States the Philby affair has also suffered from later CIA officers' superior belief that an operation like the Philby deception would never have escaped their notice, least of all if conducted by the military. Certainly not. The military would have been too clumsy or inept to bring off an adventure of such daring. Yet if there was a deception operation in Washington, the Royal Air Force carried it out. These self-serving CIA analyses are identical to the equally foolish frames of analysis that led the Russia Committee and the CIA during this same period to the adventures in Albania and the Ukraine.

The British principals have all since passed from the scene, a generation of men created by World War II who in 1948–1949 still lived in its shadow, men for whom another war in Europe was beyond Britain's strength but not their imagination. They borrowed a page from the past to preserve the future, not as a certainty but merely as a possibility. Sir Arthur Tedder, Sir Charles Medhurst, Sir Kenneth Strong, General Leslie Hollis, and Sir Dick White were of that generation. Silent to the end, they defied an ineffectual Foreign Office and dared something more. If silence is the most powerful expression of contempt for the traitorous as well the clamorous Grub Street crowd in their pursuit, they were well served. And then there is Major General Edwin Luther Sibert, whose solitary word is the only testimony we have that a military deceit existed even if the complexities of time and circumstance in 1948–1949 confirm its plausibility. But in the absence of proof, which we will never have, more anecdotes and hearsay will be circulated. The chronicles of the newest espionage case as reported by another generation's journalists will continue to contain references to H. A. R. Kim Philby, the legendary KGB spy who brilliantly penetrated MI6, the CIA, and the Anglo-American codebreakers' inner sanctum, betrayed their secrets to the shame of all, and was rewarded with a KGB generalship. Why would we expect more? As we were warned by the English poet and critic William Empson, who was also a Cambridge lad in the late 1920s but is remembered for more respectable reasons,

The pygmy plan
Is one note each and the tune goes out free.[2]

The Maclean Cables—Third NSA Venona Release, February 27, 1996

The Venona archive contains twelve Maclean telegrams. Several consist of separately numbered sections that were transmitted individually by Soviet code clerks. Six of the cables were sent from New York to Moscow between June and September 1944 and six from Washington to Moscow in March 1945.[1] It is believed that all were first recovered in 1947–1948 but only partially, in scattered fragments. Those initial recovery dates can be determined or inferred from Meredith Gardner's periodic listing of Russian cover names between September 1947 and August 1948 and his final comments in October 1951. All were originally gathered by Arlington Hall Station beginning in 1947.

NEW YORK TO MOSCOW MACLEAN CABLES

1. June 28, 1944. New York to Moscow 915

Heading: To VIKTOR.[2] Preface: Your 2712.

The only meaningful fragment describes "SERGEJ's meeting with GOMMER" on June 25 and his coming travel to TYRE (New York) "where his wife is living with her mother while awaiting confinement."

This is the first Maclean cable in terms of chronology and is claimed to have identified Maclean as GOMMER (HOMER) as a result of his New York visits. The cable fragment had been in the Arlington Hall archive since August 1948 at the latest and is mentioned in Meredith Gardner's 1947–1948 list of cover names. In October 1951 Gardner reported that "the contents were totally unknown until recently." On March 30, 1951, an English member of Gardner's Venona team (his name was blanked out) transmitted to England the suggestion that G. was HOMER (GOMER) and GOMMER. Gardner added that "This identification, if true, allowed the placing of G. in New York in June 1944."

The GOMMER cable was broken by the GCHQ Venona cell at Eastcote. Quite likely it was already in the GCHQ inventory prior to March 30, 1951, and had been broken much earlier.

2. August 2–3, 1944. New York to Moscow 1105–1110

Heading: None. Preface: None.

The first 149 word groups of this six-part cable were "unrecoverable." The two superimposed titles—"Intelligence from Source H" and "H's Work for a Committee"—were undoubtedly added later, by either Arlington Hall or GCHQ.

In early August 1950, Mrs. Gray, an American analyst with the Gardner team, decrypted two fragments of this cable, which read "work including the personal telegraphic correspondence of Boar [? Churchill] with Captain [Roosevelt]" and "weeks ago G. was entrusted with deciphering a confidential telegram of Boar's [?] to Captain." According to Meredith Gardner, Gray's recoveries "were communicated to the British 11 August 1950, who thereupon set up worksheets for further recovery work. The suspicion that 'G.' was the source of material 'G' occurred to people at AFSA immediately upon seeing Mrs. Gray's work, and this suspicion was suggested to the British at the same time."[3]

The Churchill to Roosevelt cable wasn't copied but was briefly described as an attempt to persuade Roosevelt to change Allied invasion plans from the south of France (ANVIL) in favor of a massive offensive through northeastern Italy, Venice, and Trieste on north through the Ljubljana Gap to Austria. Roosevelt and "his Generals" were opposed. The cable begins with a reference to an upcoming meeting of the European Advisory Commission (EAC) in SIDON (London). The fragment continues: "is/are taking part in the work of the Committee. Almost all the work is done by H. [G.] who is present at all the sessions. In connexion with this work H. [G.] obtains secret documents [6 groups unrecovered]." This section should also have identified Maclean, who represented the British embassy in Washington consultations for the EAC meeting in London.

British names or entities mentioned include (General) Wilson, Richard Law, the Foreign Office, and the War Office. They should have alerted the British liaison officer at Arlington Hall Station in 1947–1948.

3. August 10, 1944. New York to Moscow 1146

Heading: [B to VIKTOR]. Preface: None.

The cable addresses KGB internal affairs and describes various transfers of Soviet agents from one handler to another. The final paragraph refers to Moscow cable 3608, which the transmitting officer is evidently answering. It reports that "HOMER's information was transmitted in a condensed form word for word without personal conclusions." The comment could have referred to the very long, six-part August 2–3 New York to Moscow cable.

4. September 5, 1944. New York to Moscow 1263

Heading: To VIKTOR. Preface: None.

The title of this very brief cable—"HOMER Reports Future Meeting of Roosevelt and Churchill in Quebec"—was added by Arlington Hall. The text reports that "According to information from HOMER, CAPTAIN [Roosevelt] and BOAR will meet about September 9 in Quebec to discuss the impending occupation of Germany. A detailed account of HOMER's report will follow."

In October 1951 Gardner explained that there "was nothing in the message to connect it with the Washington material of the following year." But here once again Churchill's name should have drawn the attention of the British at

Arlington Hall when first penetrated by mid-1947, most especially when viewed with the August 2–3 cable and the promise of more to come on the Quebec meeting.

5. September 7, 1944. New York to Moscow 1271–1274

Heading: To VIKTOR. Preface: [3 groups unrecovered] followed by "report of 2 September" (the verbatim quotations from the report are in inverted commas). The title of this four-part message—"HOMER's report of Sept 4. Rebuilding England. Occupation of Germany"—was added by Arlington Hall.

The cable contains direct quotations from HOMER on Anglo-American economic talks and the occupation of Germany, citing "the STRANG documents, which you know." Sir William Strang was the British representative on the European Advisory Commission created to prepare plans for the surrender, occupation, and control of Germany.

Also mentioned by HOMER are internal American disagreements on postwar German policy, and British plans for Greece. British names mentioned besides Strang are Churchill, Reginald Leeper, the British ambassador in Athens, the Foreign Office, and the British chiefs of staff.

6. September 23, 1944. New York to Moscow 1352

Heading: To VIKTOR. Preface: A report from Muza.

HOMER, "G," or "H" isn't mentioned in this brief cable (most word groups were unrecovered). It does cite Roosevelt's codename and the problems of postwar Germany. Nevertheless, in a list of Soviet cover names first prepared in 1947–1948 and supplemented in the years that followed, this cable is included under the GOMER and G (HOMER) inventory. The Venona text released in 1996 contains no reference to HOMER, "G," or "H" nor any other designation that might link it to Maclean. Possibly the "G" or GOMER designation was excised from the final text (the NSA Historical Monograph lists it as a possible Maclean cable). In any case, this cable is an enigma.

WASHINGTON TO MOSCOW MACLEAN CABLES

7. March 29, 1945. Washington to Moscow 1788

Heading: Material from "H" in one release (July 10, 1965) and Material of "G" in another release (October 13, 1965). Preface: "I am transmitting [1 group unrecoverable]."

This is the Russian translation of a March 8 cable from Ambassador Clark-Kerr in Moscow to London, repeated by the Foreign Office to Ambassador Halifax. Probably a cipher cable, it cites a March 8 cable in Washington to Moscow, as does 1791. This "Material from 'H' [G]" cable had first been penetrated by Arlington Hall in 1947.

Meredith Gardner believed "G" or "H" was an arbitrary code designation and had "no reason to connect 'G' with a person's name or cover name." Not until June 1951, after the flight of Maclean and Burgess, did he learn that HOMER referred to Maclean. The cable comment by the GCHQ Venona analyst explains that "H" (G) "is certainly an abbreviation for GOMER [HOMER], the cover name for Donald Duart Maclean, who was 1st Secretary at the British Embassy, WASHINGTON, at this time." Oddly enough, the copy of this cable on file at the Public Record Office at Kew omits this explanatory reference and merely identifies "G" as HOMER (GOMER), Donald Maclean.[4]

Two hundred and eighty-three word groups, or most of the text, was unrecoverable despite the fact that GCHQ would have obtained the original cable.

8. March 29, 1945. Washington to Moscow 1791

Heading: Material from "H" [G]. Preface: "I am transmitting cipher telegram no. 95 of 8 March 1945 from the ISLAND's [Britain's] Embassy in SMYRNA [Moscow] to the POOL [British embassy in Washington]."

This telegram is from the British ambassador Clark-Kerr in Moscow to the Foreign Office and repeated to Washington. The subject is Ambassador Harriman's recommendation to the State Department on the Polish commission. More than two hundred word groups were unrecoverable. The British copy at the Public Record Office includes an attachment recovering scores of word groups not decrypted in the "NSA version."

9. March 29, 1945. Washington to Moscow 1793

Heading: Materials of "G." Preface: "I am transmitting a telegram of the NOOK [Foreign Office] no. 2535 of 16 March this year to the POOL [British embassy in Washington]."

This is a cable from Foreign Secretary Anthony Eden instructing Lord Halifax to see Secretary of State Stettinius as soon as possible, "and after that, if you can, the President and show them [two groups unrecovered but obviously Clark-Kerr's draft note] to Molotov." It references Roosevelt's cable to Churchill (719) and Churchill's answer (912), neither of which is in the Venona archive. The purpose was to coordinate the U.S.-U.K. response to Molotov on the Polish issue. The NSA 1996 release identified it as a cable from Foreign Secretary Eden but not the British version in the Public Record Office. Fifty-five word groups were unrecovered.

The Public Record Office version of this cable includes an attachment that recovers a dozen or so word groups that weren't broken at Arlington Hall.

10. March 30, 1945. Washington to Moscow 1808–1809

Heading: Material from "H." Preface: "I am transmitting telegram 2212 of 8 March 1945 from the NOOK [Foreign Office] to the POOL [Ambassador Halifax]."

This cable begins with the drafter's preface "Supplementary to my telegram no. 1018 to Moscow." Paragraph 1 begins with the comment "The rapid deterioration of the situation in ROUMANIA." It mentions the Polish commission. The

Russian translation was sent to Moscow in two parts, as designated in the Venona cable. Three hundred and seventy-four word groups in the cable were unrecoverable. The original March 8 cable was in the first person—both "we" and "I" are found in the text—which meant it was either from Foreign Secretary Eden or sent on behalf of Prime Minister Churchill. It was sent on the same date as Churchill's personal and top-secret telegram to Roosevelt (905) which also begins with Churchill's comment on Romania. The March 30 Venona cable received in Washington on March 8 is similar to the opening of the March 8 Churchill to Roosevelt cable, which reviews the situation in the Balkans before beginning his more personal appeals to Roosevelt. It is possible that those opening paragraphs were in a Foreign Office circular telegram sent to the addressees on the prime minister's instructions as his own personal tour d'horizon reviewing alarming developments in the Balkans and Eastern Europe for the addressees, including the British embassy in Washington. This is merely a supposition.

11. March 30, 1945. Washington to Moscow 1815

Heading: None. Preface: None.

Chronologically this is the first in the Venona series of six March 29–31 cables. It is a Russian translation of telegram 1517 of March 7, 1945, from Lord Halifax to the Foreign Office responding to Foreign Secretary Anthony Eden's request that he review with the State Department a proposed U.K.-U.S. draft note to be sent to Molotov, which he'd sent earlier in London's 2078. (Eden's cable isn't in the Venona series.)

There are several peculiarities in this cable. It omits both the heading and the preface, indicating seventy-five groups were unrecoverable, begins abruptly with a few brief sentences, then claims another forty-six groups were unrecoverable. In every other instance the March Maclean cables are prefaced by the transmitting officer's identification of the material and source. Because that routine heading was omitted here, the GCHQ analyst was obliged to hedge: "This is probably material from 'H'/HOMER, i.e., a telegram stolen by Maclean." A further note explained that "The 75-group gap presumably contains the introductory remarks by the WASHINGTON MGB officer and the beginning of the text of the stolen telegram." The less familiar word groups in his comment might have been unrecoverable, but it is far less plausible that the GCHQ cryptologists would have claimed that the same repeatedly used and repeatedly recognized word groups that preface the other Venona March "G" and "H" cables would be "unrecoverable." Just as incomprehensible is the GCHQ failure to recover the opening sentences of paragraph 2, which should have been broken, as were parts of the remainder of the cable, had GCHQ used Halifax's original telegram as a crib.

The GCHQ assumption about "introductory remarks" by the MGB officer raises further suspicions. In forwarding Maclean's copies of British telegrams to Moscow, the transmitting officer usually reproduced the full text without personal comment. In only two of the twelve Maclean cables did the transmitting officer inject explanatory remarks. In a New York to Moscow cable of August 2–3, 1944, he mentioned G's marital status. As we know, that remark wasn't included in the February 1996 Venona release of the same cable. He also described two of G's embassy responsibilities but these couldn't be entirely suppressed because the Arlington Hall recovery was quoted word for word by Meredith Gardner in October 1951.

The Venona cables released in February 1996 exclude any of the transmitting officer's explanatory remarks that might have identified Maclean any earlier than the April 1951 recovery of the GOMMER cable. The original Halifax cable was dated March 7 and was the first in the six-cable March series. It is reasonable to assume that the transmitting officer commented on his embassy source, "G," as he did in the August 2–3, 1944, cable, as well as London's addressee, Foreign Secretary Anthony Eden.

12. March 31, 1945. Washington to Moscow 1826

Heading: Materials of "G." Preface: "I am transmitting a telegram of the NOOK [Foreign Office] no. 2536 of 16 March to the POOL [British embassy].

This cable from Foreign Secretary Eden to Lord Halifax supplements his cable of the same day instructing Halifax to see Secretary of State Stettinius as soon as possible. It offered more advice to Halifax for his conversations with Stettinius and the president. Two hundred and thirty-one groups were unrecoverable.

The GCHQ release to the Public Record Office doesn't identify it as a cable from Foreign Secretary Eden.

Modin's Mistaken Memoirs

Yuri Modin's account of his KGB service is an interesting, readable, but un-reliable memoir that proves the pitfalls of attempting to reconstruct the Philby, Burgess, and Maclean cases from secondary sources.[1] Modin's memory serves him reasonably well in relating events in which he participated, but he loses his way when describing other events. Nevertheless, his memoir shouldn't be regarded as a deliberate attempt at misinformation, deceit, or fal-sification. He relied on previously published accounts available to him in re-constructing details of 1949–1951 events in London and Washington of which he had no direct knowledge and improvised in his attempts to patch together a coherent narrative. The most engaging aspect of his memoir is the absence of vanity. Nothing in his book suggests he ever thought of himself as other than an average Russian carrying out routine responsibilities in a routine way. He might have been a walk-around London postman, delivering and collect-ing the daily mail.

Modin first began working for the KGB at Lubyanka in Moscow not as an intelligence officer but as an English-language translator in the principal foreign intelligence unit's British section. In 1944 he was given some responsibility for the Cambridge Five, evidently in translating their enciphered messages sent from London. In June 1947 he was posted to London as a code clerk at the Soviet embassy. In February 1948 he began to handle John Cairncross and later became Burgess's handler, apparently in the autumn of 1949. He also met with Anthony Blunt, who had left KGB active service in 1945 and served as Burgess's inter-mediary. In his memoir Modin emerges as a likable KGB officer who was genu-inely fond of the three British agents he handled.

Burgess, Blunt, and Cairncross were totally different in personality and char-acter and Modin handled each with tact and understanding quite apart from his remarkable ability to elude MI5 surveillance for so many years, although it is doubtful that he did escape surveillance in 1949–1951. To his credit, he is unable to explain Burgess's assignment to Washington except in terms of "a somewhat warped sense of humor," similar to allowing "Maclean to be named head of the American section at the Foreign Office." What both men needed, he believed, was serious medical treatment. Curiously enough, he tells us noth-ing about his intelligence training in Moscow before departing for England. He seemed unfamiliar with any but the most primitive methods of identifying sur-veillance and explains that he was advised by Blunt, who had been trained by M15, in ways of eluding surveillance. When describing his many London meetings with any of the three, he appears reliable. But when he strays from London, he becomes much less accurate and often errs.

He writes that Maclean resumed work at the Foreign Office in June 1950; Maclean returned in November 1950. He twice tells us Burgess was assigned to Washington as a first secretary in August 1950; Burgess was assigned in May as second secretary. He claims Philby's position as MI6 chief in Washington was unoccupied until he arrived. MI6's Peter Dwyer was chief when Philby took up his post. He recalls Philby's departure from England to Washington by plane; yet he left by boat, the SS *Caronia*. He identifies James McCarger as an MI6 officer; he was with the CIA. He notes Geoffrey Patterson was in charge of the HOMER investigation, which is inaccurate. He claims that in September 1949, before Philby departed for Washington by plane (*sic*), he sent Burgess to him to pass on intelligence about the U.S. codebreaking effort. KGB files in Moscow show Philby's September 1949 contact was with MAX (Mikhail Shishkin), not Modin. He claims Philby took part in planning the Albanian coup, but there was no such coup. He writes that Philby sent details to Burgess in London of the first MI6/CIA Albanian incursion in December 1949. The first Albanian émigrés were put ashore in October 1949 by MI6, not by the CIA. He alleges the CIA and MI6 recruited Ukrainian émigrés in the United States for the OPC operations in the Ukraine. This is false. He states that beginning in 1951 MI5's Peter Wright orchestrated witch hunts in searching for KGB agents recruited by Burgess; Wright didn't join MI5 until 1955. Until then he was a technical adviser, not an investigative officer. Modin asserts that during World War II the GC&CS computer Colossus cracked the Enigma code. Colossus cracked the German Fish code.

He is wildly inaccurate in describing Philby's September 1949 Oldfield briefing in London, passed to Burgess by Philby in London. He claims the details were in a report to MI6 by the Army Security Agency's William Weisband, who told MI6 that a brilliant American intelligence analyst named Meredith Gardner was attempting to decode KGB traffic from Moscow Center. Weisband was the KGB agent at Arlington Hall familiar with Gardner's work who had reported the breakthrough to his controller in Washington in 1947 or 1948. None of the details released in the 1990s from Moscow's files describing the KGB rezidentura courier report on Philby's Oldfield briefing even vaguely resembles Modin's version.

His account of Philby's Washington years is another puzzle, pieced together from fact, fancy, and authorial improvisation. If a Soviet case officer who worked so closely with Guy Burgess and Anthony Blunt can botch many 1949–1951 events, there is little hope that those working wholly from secondary and hearsay sources can do much better. Modin notes that Philby never had the "least contact with any KGB contact based in the United States," an assertion refuted by the Mitrokhin archive notes on Makayev, who arrived in New York in March 1950 to establish an illegal network to handle Philby, among others. Modin claims Philby's contact with the KGB would be to the London residence through Burgess, but that this was rare, "for the very act of sending a letter or a telegram was liable to put the network at risk." Yet he declares that soon after Philby's October arrival he sent a message in the autumn of 1949 to "our services in London" (which suggests Modin didn't see it) with passages from a newly deciphered message between Churchill and Truman. As we know, there were no Churchill to Truman cables in the Venona inventory. Modin borrowed this error from Western writers and journalists, most probably David Martin's *Wilderness of Mirrors* and Robert Lamphere's mistaken comments on those same cables in his own book.

Modin doesn't disclose how Philby's message was passed to London. He alleges the cable Philby cited included the name HOMER but "Philby had no idea who lurked behind this pseudonym." By his own account in *My Silent War* Philby realized in September 1949 that Maclean was the unidentified Soviet agent. According to Modin, the Truman message had been shown to Philby by Meredith Gardner, with whom Philby had "carefully nurtured a friendship" and that "a few months later," during the autumn or early winter of 1949, the unsuspecting Gardner told Philby that HOMER was in the Foreign Office. Gardner didn't know the two Venona cable fragments citing HOMER referred to Maclean. Moreover, "several months" is less than a year and Maclean didn't return to the Foreign Office until November 1950. Modin also tells us Philby was standing at Meredith Gardner's shoulder during the HOMER decrypts and was able to follow the progress "on a day to day basis." The claim is false in numerous ways as well as a physical impossibility. Modin has evidently embellished a questionable account in Peter Wright's *Spycatcher*, published in 1987.

In any event, Modin asserts that after Philby passed this message, he quickly followed with a second, which "after decoding, read: 'I think it's Maclean.' " Modin tells us the KGB knew HOMER was Maclean but decided "to keep Philby in the dark." He also keeps the reader in the dark as to how the KGB knew about HOMER if Philby didn't know. In fact Moscow knew nothing about HOMER or the search for the embassy spy until the spring of 1951. In Philby's "next dispatch" the KGB was reassured that HOMER's identity was still vague enough for any one of "hundreds of people" to have access to the "secret transatlantic communications channel of 1945 to be a potential suspect."

Modin tells us he and the KGB station chief in London, Nikolai Rodin, sent Philby's reports to Moscow Center, whose quick response was "Maclean must be kept in place for as long as possible." Modin has borrowed these words from Philby's *My Silent War* in claiming he was told as much by his KGB "friends" after they discussed the Maclean case at a meeting outside Washington. Modin, of course, has already told us that "for reasons of security neither Burgess nor Philby maintained any direct contacts with KGB agents in Washington." This denies Philby's self-described meeting with his friend outside Washington in *My Silent War*, a book Modin professes to have helped edit. If the meeting did take place, which is as doubtful as the advice he received, it would have been no earlier than April 1951.

As usual, Modin ignores the discrepancy in dates and passes on to January 1951, when he claims the field of suspects was reduced to four: Gore-Booth, Roger Makins, Michael Wright, and Donald Maclean. The names are partially correct but there were nine suspects at the time, not four, and the dates are wrong. The names weren't given to Philby by MI6 until late April or early May, after he had suggested MI6 explore the 1940 Krivitsky allegations. Modin also denies Philby was responsible for the Krivitsky suggestion despite Philby's own claim in *My Silent War* that he wrote the Krivitsky memo to MI6. With Gore-Booth eliminated (for reasons Modin couldn't discover), the list of names was reduced to three, including Maclean. Philby and Burgess decided it was time to act. Yet Modin's numbers are off; there were five remaining suspects, not three.

The London residence was the KGB's "only link" to Philby, Modin purports, and a telegram would be too risky "because the FBI knew quite well that Philby had been informed of the HOMER suspects." With Maclean now one among three suspects, Burgess suggested he should get himself sent home and warn Maclean. Burgess carried out his plan in February and got himself arrested. On April 7 Ambassador Franks consulted his superiors and "nine days later," on his return from the weekend, Burgess was sacked. Philby and Burgess worked out the details and Burgess left for London. Burgess's May 1 departure was three months after a plan plotted in February, two months prior to Maclean's inclusion on the list of five names.

Modin also blunders in citing two more Philby disclosures that display him at his improvisatory best. In March 1951, he claims, Philby gave Burgess the names and arrival points of three groups of six men who were to be parachuted into the Ukraine. At the time, Modin says, Burgess was "heading home." Burgess didn't head home until May 1, and then on the *Queen Mary*. Modin insists he had made good use of the Ukraine intelligence, passed to him through Blunt. If true, then the intelligence reached Modin two months after the Ukraine drops.

He gives his even more muddled interpretation of the Venona secret. "It was now known for certain," Modin informs us, "that the analyst Meredith Gardner had discovered a blunder in a telegram sent from New York to Moscow." The blunder isn't immediately described, presumably because Philby, who evidently was its source, didn't know any more than Weisband knew when he had passed the same sketchy intelligence to his KGB handler two years earlier. Nevertheless, on the basis of the revelation passed to Modin and on to Moscow, the KGB deciphering specialists at Lubyanka immediately set to work.

They eventually uncovered two KGB messages revealing an error by an encryption clerk at the Washington embassy. Having exhausted his inventory of one-time pads, he had used the same pad twice. In precise detail Modin attempts to fully clarify the chain of events responsible for the error. A diplomatic bag forwarding the one-time pads to Washington was delayed en route. The Soviet ship carrying the bag was delayed because its prudent captain had decided to stay in port in Britain longer than usual. He had decided to remain in port because of "intense submarine activity in the North Atlantic." Intense submarine activity was taking place in the North Atlantic because a war was going on. Modin doesn't need to remind us that the same war had been going on since 1939, as had the intense submarine activity in the North Atlantic. Modin assures us "The authors of the error [the two-time use of one-time pads] were severely punished." Modin should be punished for thinking we could believe this nonsense. There were thirty thousand flawed KGB one-time pads and the error belonged to Moscow, not any dilatory encryption clerk in Washington, Modin's scapegoat.

The string of causal connectives shows Modin at his most desperate if not the Soviet deductive machine mechanically stamping out such rubbish. The error is reported, the objective cause identified, the objective reasons traced back, the objective source found. Modin's version is a fiction, but one doesn't have to know the entire truth to understand he is dissembling; it is logically and objectively reasonable. In such analyses did Moscow's KGB phalanx march to the Marxist-Leninist drumbeat.

Modin's chaotic account of the HOMER episode in Washington, his random patchwork from published sources, and his confused date lines show he was only generally informed of Philby's activities. He was critical of the KGB resident in London, Nikolai Rodin, whose negligent tradecraft (using a Soviet embassy limousine for transport to a clandestine meeting) offended his own prudence and jeopardized his own security, but he was powerless to change Rodin's ways. He may have been ignored as a result of Rodin's assuming a greater role in the Burgess-Philby network after the September–February debacle that delayed notification of Klaus Fuchs's identification. Left out in the cold, Modin didn't quite know what was going on and had to patch and piece together as best he could. Once Burgess was back on Modin's home turf in London in May 1951, he no longer had to improvise on the basis of whatever covert or popular accounts, fictions, and fables he could dig up in Moscow. As an active participant in the last weeks of the Burgess-Maclean affair as well as Cairncross's final months in 1951, he could finally rely on his own memory, but that too was sometimes faulty.

Modin claims that John Cairncross gave him NATO's plans for nuclear arms in Germany. No date is supplied. NATO was established in April 1949 but the transfer of nuclear arms to West Germany would not even be considered for years to come, and certainly not during Cairncross's position at Treasury or the Ministry of Supply. Either Modin is lying or Cairncross was being duped by a British intelligence deception operation during his final months at his Ministry of Supply posting in 1951. By the end of 1951, Cairncross was finished as a Soviet agent.

After arriving in London, Burgess alerted Blunt, who subsequently met with

Modin. Blunt told him Maclean was about to be arrested. Blunt couldn't have known Maclean was to be arrested because the decision wasn't made until May 25. Yet later in his memoir Modin says the May 25 date was entirely fortuitous.

In his memoir, Modin writes that he first met Philby in Moscow years after his 1963 defection. During a trip to Washington in the early 1990s, however, he told Cave Brown he met with Philby in London in 1949 but they "spent not a second more than necessary in each other's company." He also claims he met with Philby again in London in 1952. Cave Brown asked him how he knew Maclean's May 25 arrest and interrogation were imminent. Modin refused to say except that he "acted from information received." Cave Brown concluded that Modin's informant "was probably the Fifth Man," a KGB agent "never identified but who was thought to be alive in 1992."[2] In such ways do the ghosts and goblins multiply for those many wanderers lost in the dark, dense Philby woods. Modin was often among them.

Notes

PREFACE

1. Robert Louis Benson and Michael Warner, eds., *Venona: Soviet Espionage and the American Response, 1939–1957* (National Security Agency, Central Intelligence Agency, Washington, D.C., 1996), p. xxvii.
2. Anthony Cave Brown, *Treason in the Blood: H. St. John Philby, Kim Philby, and the Spy Case of the Century* (Houghton Mifflin, Boston, 1994), pp. 406–417.

CHAPTER ONE

1. The limited surveillance on Maclean was disclosed in the text of the September 23, 1955, Foreign Office White Paper, *Kessing's Contemporary Archives* (Kessing's Publications, London, October 1–8, 1955), pp. 14457–14459.
2. Richard J. Aldrich, ed., *Espionage, Security and Intelligence in Britain, 1945–1970* (Manchester University Press, Manchester, 1998). Aldrich cites a document from the Morrison Papers, British Library of Political and Economic Science: "Foreign Office to Herbert Morrison, 19 July 1963, with enclosed memorandum," Burgess and Maclean file, 8/5.
3. The Soviet Union's intelligence service was popularly known as the KGB, although the name wasn't adopted until 1954. Earlier acronyms were the OGPU (1923–1934), the NKVD (1934–1941), the NKGB (February 1941–July 1941), the NKVD (July 6, 1941–April 1943), the NKGB (1943–1946), the MGB (1946–1953), the MVD (1953–1954), and the KGB (1954–1991). To avoid confusion, in many instances I have used the better-known acronym KGB. In this instance MGB is appropriate.
4. This account of the Modin/Burgess/Blunt meetings is drawn from the Russian viewpoint as found in Yuri Modin, *My Five Cambridge Friends* (Farrar, Straus, Giroux, New York, 1994), pp. 200–209. Although Modin is often reliable in describing his own involvement, he is also undependable and frequently wildly off the mark. (See appendix B.) Modin's account strongly suggests Moscow wasn't aware of the danger to Maclean until so informed by London the second week in May. Modin's account, if true, contradicts every published version, including Philby's.
5. Nigel West and Oleg Tsarev, *The Crown Jewels* (Yale University Press, New Haven, 1999), p. 182.
6. Robert Cecil, *A Divided Life: A Personal Portrait of the Spy Donald Maclean* (William Morrow, New York, 1989), p. 143. Cecil was Maclean's younger contemporary at Cambridge and served with him in Washington and at the

Foreign Office in 1950–1951. Reliable, intelligent, and well informed, he is as sympathetic to Maclean as he is contemptuous of Philby—"a born spy who reveled in deception and had no compunction about sending agents to their deaths"—and to a lesser extent Burgess—"a juvenile lead running out of roles" (p. 132).

7. "Foreign Office to Herbert Morrison, 19 July 1963," in Aldrich, p. 142.

8. Modin, p. 208.

9. Christopher Andrew and Vasili Mitrokhin, *The Mitrokhin Archive* (Penguin Books, London, 1999), p. 209.

10. Modin, p. 187.

11. The complete White Paper text from which the following quotations are drawn is found in *Kessing's Contemporary Archives*, pp. 14457–14459. The White Paper was provoked by a leak to the press reporting the defection of a KGB officer in Australia, Vladimir Petrov, who revealed that Maclean and Burgess were both Soviet agents now living in Moscow. On February 11, 1956, Maclean and Burgess officially surfaced in a joint press conference in Moscow.

12. Anthony Glees, *The Secrets of the Service* (Carroll and Graf, New York, 1987), pp. 10–11. Professor Glees's very useful book has been unaccountably overlooked.

13. Tom Bower, *A Perfect English Spy: Sir Dick White and the Secret War, 1935–1990* (St. Martin's Press, New York, 1995), p. 154.

14. The 1963 Beirut episode has been reconstructed by many Philby commentators, including Phillip Knightley, *The Master Spy* (Alfred A. Knopf, New York, 1989); Anthony Cave Brown, *Treason in the Blood: H. St. John Philby, Kim Philby, and the Spy Case of the Century* (Houghton Mifflin, Boston, 1994); Peter Wright, *Spy Catcher* (Viking, New York, 1987); and Genrikh Borovik, *The Philby Files* (Little, Brown, Boston, 1994). Philby evidently admitted he had warned Maclean through Burgess that "the security services were about to take action against him." Peter Wright, a retired MI5 officer, was not involved in the Philby case in 1950–1951 but in 1963 listened to the tapes of Philby's Beirut interrogation. In his book, Wright errs on several major points; one is his false claim that Yuri Modin traveled to Beirut to warn Philby of Elliott's coming interrogation. His claim was intended to complement his obsessive but fallacious insistence that Sir Roger Hollis of MI5 was a Soviet agent. Wright isn't a wholly dependable analyst; many of his observations, along with his reconstructed dialogue, are palpably false.

15. Alistair Horne, *Macmillan, 1957–1986*, vol. 2 (Macmillan, London, 1988), p. 687. On November 7, 1955, Macmillan told the House of Commons that Philby had carried out his official duties ably and conscientiously and that he had no reason to conclude Philby was the so-called Third Man.

16. *Kessing's Contemporary Archives* (Kessing's Publications, London, August 24–31, 1963), p. 19597.

17. Rebecca West, *The New Meaning of Treason* (Viking Press, New York, 1964), p. 364.
18. Mikhail Lyubimov, "A Martyr to Dogma," in Rufina Philby, *The Private Life of Kim Philby* (Fromm International, New York, 2000), p. 284. Lyubimov first met Philby in Moscow in January 1975, p. 274.
19. Kim Philby, *My Silent War* (Ballantine Books, New York, 1983), p. 109.
20. Ibid., pp. 153, 169.
21. West and Tsarev, pp. 180–182.
22. Moscow had learned of the U.S. codebreaking success from William Weisband, a Russian-born ASA clerk, probably in 1947 or 1948. Allen Weinstein and Alexander Vassiliev, *The Haunted Wood: Soviet Espionage in America—The Stalin Era* (Random House, New York, 1999), pp. 286, 291–293; Robert Louis Benson and Michael Warner, eds., *Venona: Soviet Espionage and the American Response, 1939–1957* (National Security Agency, Central Intelligence Agency, Washington, D.C., 1996), p. xxviii. Weisband was not a cryptologist nor was he active in the ASA codebreaking effort. It is questionable whether he knew the mechanics of the Venona recoveries. John Earl Haynes and Harvey Klehr, *Venona: Decoding Soviet Espionage in America* (Yale University Press, New Haven, 2000), pp. 48–49.
23. Lyubimov, pp. 284–285.
24. K. Philby, p. 153. He repeatedly claimed the FBI played the major role in the Maclean investigation (pp. 166, 175, 179) and insisted he refrained from discussing the case with the CIA because "it was an FBI case" (p. 185). His many assertions on this point are incorrect.
25. Patrick Seale and Maureen McConville, *Philby: The Long Road to Moscow* (Simon and Schuster, New York, 1973), pp. 195–214. Seale and McConville's work is an admirable reconstruction of Philby's career and is even more impressive in view of the limited intelligence available at the time. But when they touch on the most sensitive intelligence issues, they are at the mercy of unattributed sources, unidentified MI5 and MI6 officers who were either ill informed or engaged in disinformation or damage control. One obvious error is their claim that a Soviet agent in the Justice Department, Judith Coplon, enabled Moscow to follow the FBI Maclean investigation. Coplon was arrested in New York in early 1949, during the first months of MI5's Maclean investigation.
26. See chapter 3.
27. David Martin, *Wilderness of Mirrors* (Harper and Row, New York, 1980), pp. 39–50. The title of his book is often credited to James Angleton, who in fact borrowed it from T. S. Eliot's *Gerontion*. Eliot adapted the phrase from Elizabethan dramatist Ben Jonson's play *Volpone*. The three meanings derive from three different dramatic contexts.
28. Third NSA Venona Release (February 27, 1996).
29. Those who believe Sir Roger Hollis was a KGB agent include Wright, *Spy*

Catcher, and Chapman Pincher, *Too Secret Too Long* (St. Martin's Press, New York, 1984). Wright was the source of some of Pincher's confidential information.

30. Cecil James Phillips, "What Made Venona Possible?" in Benson and Warner, p. xv; Haynes and Klehr, pp. 28–35.

31. Meredith Gardner, "Development of the 'G'–HOMER [GOMER] Case" (October 11, 1951), p. 1. Records of National Security Agency Public Release, Copies of Records Relating to Project Venona 1941–1947, National Archives, RG 457, Box 4, Top Secret. When the first penetrations were made, Gardner believed that the "Materials 'G' " preface was an arbitrary code designation, not a reference to the source's cover name. GCHQ analysts at Eastcote in London established the GOMER (HOMER) codename connection by 1949 at the latest. Meredith Gardner's Special Report, a two-page summary of the Maclean case, is cited repeatedly in the notes that follow. It is unquestionably the most important document declassified by the NSA. Without it, London's version of the Maclean case would have gone unchallenged. An internal AFSA report, the British had no control over its release. The last cat out of the NSA bag, it wasn't published until September 1997, at the end of the NSA project and after GCHQ had released its own Venona cables to the British Public Record Office in 1996. The delay raises several puzzling questions. Had the report been issued promptly in July 1995, at the onset of the NSA declassification project, it would have drawn far more attention than it has.

32. A brief description of the background leading to the decision to declassify Venona is in Haynes and Klehr, pp. 4–7. Senator Daniel Moynihan played a leading role in the decision. His views on the damage done to American foreign and domestic policy by withholding secret material are described in his 1998 book *Secrecy: The American Experience* (Yale University Press, New Haven, 1998). A shorter version is his article "Secrecy as Government Regulation" *Political Science and Politics* 30 (June 1997), pp. 160–165.

33. Andrew and Mitrokhin, p. 26.

34. *The Mitrokhin Archive* is invaluable in its notes on Philby's Washington posting. Weinstein and Vassiliev in *The Haunted Wood* deal primarily with Soviet espionage in the United States. West and Tsarev in *The Crown Jewels* focus more on Burgess, Blunt, and Cairncross than on Philby but clear away much of the rubbish associated with the Cambridge spies.

35. Andrew Boyle, a British biographer, was an exception. He called Philby "a pseudo-hero" committed to the "perpetuation of his own legend" among "the immortals of the spy cult." Boyle, *The Fourth Man* (Dial Press, New York, 1979), pp. 444–445. Boyle was evidently infected by the Angleton conspiratorial virus during his Washington research. While denigrating Philby, he offered up another English spy at the Washington embassy as the fourth man. His claim, probably suggested by Angleton, is without substance.

Philby casually disclaimed "the gratifying exaggeration of my own importance" in his memoir, p. 7.

CHAPTER TWO

1. Christopher Andrew and Vasili Mitrokhin, *The Mitrokhin Archive* (Penguin Books, London, 1999), p. 76; Genrikh Borovik, *The Philby Files* (Little, Brown, Boston, 1994), pp. 38–39. The cipher cable from London to Moscow reporting Philby's recruitment in June 1934 was seen by Borovik in Moscow. Borovik is a valuable source despite his occasional errors. He assembled some five hundred pages of transcripts gathered during his conversations with Philby in Moscow from 1985 until Philby's death in 1988. In 1987 he arranged Graham Greene's trip to Moscow to meet Philby. After Philby's death, Borovik was uncertain how to proceed with the voluminous material he had collected. A few years later, Greene suggested that Borovik amplify his notes with material from the KGB archives. To his surprise, Borovik received permission in the early 1990s and wrote his book in 1993. He didn't have the opportunity to discuss those KGB revelations with Philby, which was probably a blessing in disguise.
2. *Newsweek*, January 1, 1968, pp. 32–33.
3. Oleg Kalugin, *The First Directorate* (St. Martin's Press, New York, 1994), pp. 134–135. Kalugin is an authoritative source on Philby's years in Moscow. He retired from the KGB in February 1990, joined the democratic reform movement, and was elected to the Soviet Congress of Peoples Deputies. Christopher Andrew and Oleg Gordievsky, *KGB: The Inside Story of Its Foreign Operations from Lenin to Gorbachev* (HarperCollins, New York, 1990), pp. 4–7; Anthony Cave Brown, *Treason in the Blood: H. St. John Philby, Kim Philby, and the Spy Case of the Century* (Houghton Mifflin, Boston, 1994), pp. 514–517.
4. Nigel West and Oleg Tsarev, *The Crown Jewels* (Yale University Press, New Haven, 1999), pp. 160–165. Moscow's suspicions were documented in the KGB archives.
5. Andrew and Gordievsky, p. 5.
6. Andrew and Mitrokhin, p. 537.
7. The figures on the Cambridge spies' intelligence yield are drawn from documents counted by West and Tsarev in the Moscow archives, pp. 170–171, 214.
8. Philby's failure to meet with any Soviet control officer at the KGB residency in Washington is cited in Andrew and Mitrokhin, p. 204. Mitrokhin's notes don't conclusively establish whether Philby's lack of contact was immediate or later. In his own 1994 memoir, however, Yuri Modin, the former KGB officer who served as Burgess's handler in London, insists Philby had no contact with a KGB officer, either legal or illegal, while in Washington.

Modin, *My Five Cambridge Friends* (Farrar, Straus, Giroux, New York, 1994), pp. 186–187, 197. Philby's Moscow recollections support the lack of any immediate contact. In the 1980s he told Borovik he had no contact with any Soviet agent for nine to ten months. Borovik, p. 178.

9. Kim Philby, *My Silent War* (Ballantine Books, New York, 1983), p. 174; Modin, p. 197. Philby gives few dates in his account of his Washington posting. Taken in the context of his memoir, his meeting with his Russian friends and the decision that Maclean should stay at his post was made between November 1950 and April 1951, while Maclean was acting head of the American section at the Foreign Office. Modin claims that Maclean was not to be contacted during that period, pp. 181–182.

10. West and Tsarev, pp. 294–345.

11. This same interview appeared without attribution in *Newsweek*, January 1, 1968, p. 33. A footnote to the article briefly describes Felix Dzerzhinsky, the founder of the Soviet secret police.

12. Robert C. Tucker *Stalin in Power* (W. W. Norton, New York, 1950), pp. 364–365.

13. Rufina Philby, *The Private Life of Kim Philby* (Fromm International, New York, 2000), pp. 59, 63–69.

14. Kalugin, pp. 132–135.

15. James Bamford describes Walker's espionage in *Body of Secrets: Anatomy of the Ultra-Secret National Security Agency from the Cold War through the Dawn of a New Century* (Doubleday, New York, 2001), pp. 244–245; 276–277. Also Andrew and Gordievsky, pp. 525–531. Oleg Kalugin, who handled Walker in Washington but never met him, describes the origins of the case, pp. 83–90. Aldrich Ames's espionage exploits have been gathered in monotonous detail in several books. The essentials are in Andrew and Mitrokhin, pp. 287–288.

16. R. Philby, pp. 24–83.

17. Mikhail Lyubimov, "A Martyr to Dogma," in ibid., p. 274.

18. K. Philby, "Lecture to the KGB, July 1977," in ibid., pp. 244–258.

19. Philby's touchy insistence on the importance to Moscow of his CIA insights is in Phillip Knightley, *The Master Spy* (Alfred A. Knopf, New York, 1989), p. 226.

20. Graham Greene's comments on *My Silent War* are in "The Spy," *Collected Essays* (Penguin Books, London, 1970), pp. 310–314. The same essay appears as a foreword to the Ballantine edition of *My Silent War.*

21. Greene's tribute to Robert Southwell is in Graham Greene, *Reflections* (Penguin Books, London, 1991), p. 270. An account of Southwell's arrest appears in Hugh Trevor-Roper, "Twice Martyred," *Men and Events: Historical Essays* (Harper and Brothers, New York, 1957), pp. 114–115.

22. The Orwell comment is in a review of Greene's novel *The Heart of the Matter.*

See *The Collected Essays, Journalism, and Letters of George Orwell*, vol. 4 (Secker and Warburg, London, 1969), p. 441.

CHAPTER THREE

1. Robert Louis Benson and Michael Warner, eds., *Venona: Soviet Espionage and the American Response, 1939–1957* (National Security Agency, Central Intelligence Agency, Washington, D.C., 1996), p. xiii.

2. James Bamford, *The Puzzle Palace* (Penguin Books, New York, 1983), pp. 391–410. Bamford updated his account in his *Body of Secrets: Anatomy of the Ultra-Secret National Security Agency from the Cold War Through The Dawn of a New Century* (Doubleday, New York, 2001), p. 394. The Benson and Warner monograph and the NSA Historical Monographs accompanying the 1995–1997 Venona releases aren't helpful in elaborating on U.S.-U.K. cooperation on Venona, constrained as they were by London's evident refusal to supply details.

3. The Soviet text of the Philby message is in Genrikh Borovik, *The Philby Files* (Little, Brown, Boston, 1994), p. 235.

4. Bradley Smith, *Sharing Secrets with Stalin* (University Press of Kansas, Lawrence, 1996), p. 254.

5. Details on the SSA intercept operation, the ASA, and Operation Shamrock are drawn from the "Supplemental Detailed Staff Reports on Intelligence Activities and the Rights of Americans," *Final Report of the Select Committee to Study Governmental Operations with Respect to Intelligence Activities* (Government Printing Office, Washington, D.C., 1976).

6. Government Code and Cipher School, Series details for HW 17, Decrypts of Communist International (Comintern) Messages 1930–1945, Public Record Office. Desmond Ball and David Horner, *Breaking the Codes: Australia's KGB Network, 1944–1950* (Allen and Unwin, St. Leonards, New South Wales, 1998), p. 197; Bamford, *The Puzzle Palace*, pp. 171–172; Christopher Andrew, *Secret Service: The Making of the British Intelligence Community* (Hodder and Stoughton, London, 1986), pp. 517, 635. Presumably Tiltman had senior GCHQ liaison responsibility with Arlington Hall Station during his Washington years. Nigel West describes his role in helping the ASA reconstruct Russian one-time pads in *Venona* (HarperCollins, New York, 2000), pp. 14–15. Tiltman's name is never mentioned in the 1995–1997 NSA Historical Monographs.

7. "Copy of an Undated Report of Meredith Gardner," Records of National Security Agency Public Release, Copies of Records Relating to Project Venona 1941–1947, National Archives, RG 457, Box 4, Job NN3–457–98–001, Top Secret. Also Venona Historical Monograph no. 6, *New Releases, Special Reports, and Project Shutdown* (September 1997).

8. Government Code and Cipher School and Government Communications Headquarters, Venona Project Records 1940–1949, Series details for HW 15, Public Record Office.

9. Ball and Horner, p. 198. Meredith Gardner told the authors that Sudbury headed the GCHQ Venona operation.

10. Ibid. The authors cite an interview with Renee Frank of the NSA.

11. West, pp. 95–120; Ball and Horner, pp. 191–193, 274–275. The NSA Venona Historical Monographs fail to mention the War Cabinet documents.

12. Memorandum for the Secretary of the Air Force from Major General George C. McDonald, USAF, Director of Intelligence, Office of the Deputy Chief of Staff, Operations dated January 2, 1948, National Archives, RG 263, Hqs. USAF, Air Force Plans Project Decimal File, 1942–1954, Box 741A, Top Secret. Subject: Conversations with British Representatives Concerning British Collaboration with Australia and New Zealand on Communications Intelligence Activities. General McDonald's memo distributed within USAF senior and operational channels indicates that USAF intelligence maintained liaison with Royal Air Force officers in Washington assigned by GCHQ. Travis agreed to a written interpretation limiting British freedom of action in sharing signals intelligence with Commonwealth nations.

13. GC&CS and GCHQ, Venona Project Records 1940–1949, Series details for HW 15.

14. Ball and Horner, p. 274; West, p. 95.

15. Third NSA Venona Release (February 27, 1996), accompanied by Venona Historical Monograph no. 3, *The 1944–1945 New York and Washington–Moscow KGB Messages*. The Maclean cable recoveries were not grouped separately but were scattered among the five hundred or so translations. Records of National Security Agency Public Release, Copies of Records Relating to Project Venona 1941–1947, National Archives, RG 457, Box 4, Top Secret.

16. Venona Historical Monograph no. 6 explains that eleven, possibly all twelve, Maclean cables date from 1944, six from New York to Moscow and six from Washington. In fact the New York cables date from 1944 and the Washington cables from 1945.

17. Meredith Gardner, "Additional Cover Names and Related Information in Diplomatic Traffic." The ASA interoffice routing memo is dated September 26, 1947. National Archives, RG 457, Box 4, Job NN3–457–98–001, Top Secret.

18. Meredith Gardner, "Development of the 'G'–HOMER [GOMER] Case" (October 11, 1951), p. 1. Records of National Security Agency Public Release, Copies of Records Relating to Project Venona 1941–1947, National Archives, RG 457, Box 4, Top Secret.

19. GC&CS and GCHQ, Venona Project Records 1940–1949, Series details for HW 15.

20. Ball and Horner, p. 199.

21. Evidence of the transfer to GCHQ is found in the attachments added to two cables by GCHQ cryptologists amending the Arlington Hall recoveries by identifying word groups previously "unrecovered" in the "NSA version" (Washington to Moscow 1791 and 1793 of March 29, 1945).

22. Ball and Horner, p. 198. As noted above, the authors cite a 1997 interview with Renee Frank of the NSA.

23. Gardner, "Development of the 'G'–HOMER [GOMER] Case," p. 2. In passing a broken fragment from a "G" telegram "to the British," he comments that they set up "work-sheets" for further decryption, which indicates direct personal contact. His "rigid safeguards" note is in his "Covernames in Diplomatic Traffic" (August 30, 1947), Records of National Security Agency Public Release, Copies of Records Relating to Project Venona 1941–1947, National Archives, RG 457, Box 4, Top Secret.

24. Gardner, "Covernames in Diplomatic Traffic." Colonel Marr-Johnson was listed on the distribution of "I.D. Special Analysis Report no. 1." Captain P. Marr-Johnson led a team of GC&CS cryptanalysts to Singapore in 1941 but it isn't clear if he was the same officer. Richard J. Aldrich, *Intelligence and the War against Japan* (Cambridge University Press, Cambridge, 2000), p. 40.

25. Richard J. Aldrich, ed., *Espionage, Security, and Intelligence in Britain, 1945–1970* (Manchester University Press, Manchester, 1998), pp. 45–46. Aldrich published a memorandum: "British Proposal for Liaison on Noise Investigation." National Archives, Director of Intelligence USAF Headquarters Files, File 2-1102/2-1199, RG 341, Box 40. Colonel Marr-Johnson also received a copy of a supplemental Gardner report.

26. Third NSA Venona Release (February 27, 1996), Washington to Moscow 1788, March 29, 1945. The telegram contains the text of a cable from Sir Archibald Clark-Kerr, the British ambassador in Moscow, to the Foreign Office and was repeated to Lord Halifax, the British ambassador in Washington. (See appendix A.)

27. Kim Philby, *My Silent War* (Ballantine Books, New York, 1983), p. 153.

28. Nigel West and Oleg Tsarev, *The Crown Jewels* (Yale University Press, New Haven, 1999), p. 182.

29. Borovik, p. 259.

30. Gardner, "Development of the 'G'–HOMER [GOMER] Case," p. 2.

31. Ibid., p. 1.

32. West, pp. 134–135.

33. John Earl Haynes and Harvey Klehr, *Venona: Decoding Soviet Espionage in America* (Yale University Press, New Haven, 2000), pp. 91–115, 150–151.

34. Benson and Warner, p. xxii.

35. Robert Lamphere and Tom Shachtman, *The FBI-KGB War* (Random House, New York, 1986), pp. 128–131. The many references and quotes from Lamphere that follow are drawn from these pages. Lamphere's anger at MI5 isn't fully reflected in his book. He told others privately that he had been

"double-crossed" by MI5. Chapman Pincher, *Too Secret Too Long* (St. Martin's Press, New York, 1984), p. 174.

36. Lamphere and Shachtman, p. 86.

37. Peter Malone, *The British Nuclear Deterrent* (St. Martin's Press, New York, 1984), pp. 2–5. Sir John Cockcroft, "The Miracle of Atomic Energy," an address before the Empire Club of Canada, November 12, 1959, in *The Empire Club of Canada Speeches, 1959–1960* (Empire Club Foundation, Toronto, 1960), pp. 82–89. In 1944–1946 Cockcroft had led a group of British, French, and Canadian scientists at Chalk River, Ontario, working on plutonium production, so it isn't clear to the layman precisely what technical information the British were lacking. John Newhouse, *War and Peace in the Nuclear Age* (Alfred A. Knopf, New York, 1989), p. 26.

38. *Foreign Relations of the United States, 1945*, vol. 2, *General Political and Economic Matters* (Government Printing Office, Washington, D.C., 1967), pp. 63–75; Leslie R. Groves, *Now It Can Be Told: The Story of the Manhattan Project* (Harper, New York, 1962), pp. 402–404; Dean Acheson, *Present at the Creation: My Years in the State Department* (W. W. Norton, New York, 1969), p. 164–167.

39. Groves, pp. 405–406.

40. H. Montgomery Hyde, *The Atom Bomb Spies* (Atheneum, New York, 1980), p. 61. May was identified as a Soviet agent in September 1945. Sir John Cockcroft was quickly told of his identification by the RCMP and asked about the importance of his nuclear work. May returned to England in October and was under surveillance by MI5. He was first questioned by MI5 in February 1946.

41. The description of Maclean's CPC role and the Tube Alloy file is in Robert Cecil, *A Divided Life: A Personal Portrait of the Spy Donald Maclean* (William Morrow, New York, 1989), p. 70. Cecil's source was George Carey-Foster.

42. Bevin's doubts are described in Alan Bullock, *The Life and Times of Ernest Bevin, Foreign Secretary, 1945–1951* (Heinemann, London, 1983), p. 216.

43. Cockcroft, p. 84.

44. *Foreign Relations of the United States, 1948*, vol. 1, pt. 2, *General United Nations* (Government Printing Office, Washington, D.C., 1976), pp. 679–688. Undersecretary of State Robert Lovett chaired the meeting. Secretary Forrestal attended, as did David Lilienthal, chairman of the Atomic Energy Commission, the British ambassador, Roger Makins, and Donald Maclean. See also Walter Millis, ed., *The Forrestal Diaries* (Viking Press, New York, 1951), pp. 336–339. Acheson, p. 168, credits Lovett with negotiating the modus vivendi. See also Newhouse, p. 60.

45. *FRUS, 1948*, vol. 1, pt. 2, pp. 721–723; Millis, pp. 471–473.

46. *Foreign Relations of the United States, 1949*, vol. 1, *National Security Affairs and Foreign Economic Policy* (Government Printing Office, Washington, D.C., 1977), pp. 443–459; Acheson, pp. 314–321.

47. In 1984 Chapman Pincher, the British journalist, alleged that the Attlee government considered suppressing the May case in the "national interest." The suppression would have been to avoid the negative repercussions in Washington at the time of debate on the McMahon Act, although Pincher ignores that issue. Chapman Pincher, *Too Secret Too Long* (St. Martin's Press, New York, 1984), p. 156. Pincher based his claim on confidential information. On March 21, 1946, the *New York Times* reported Groves's letter to Senator Hickenlooper on May and his access to U.S. atomic secrets. (Groves's information most probably came from the FBI.) Hickenlooper read the letter in the Senate on March 20. Gregg Herkin, *The Winning Weapon: The Atomic Bomb in the Cold War, 1945–1950* (Random House, New York, 1982), pp. 133–134.

48. Klaus Fuchs, FO 493/2334, PFY. 62551, Top Secret, British National Archives and Public Records Office.

49. Percy Sillitoe, *Cloak without Dagger* (Cassell, London, 1955), p. 110.

50. Anthony Glees, *The Secrets of the Service* (Carroll and Graf, New York, 1987), pp. 359–362. Sir Patrick Reilly wrote to British historian Glees in July and August 1986 setting down his recollections of the Maclean affair, including his explanation of Sillitoe's messages to Hoover through the MI6 special cipher. Reilly's letter to Glees reads in part: "Sir Percy Sillitoe was absolutely determined not to put a foot wrong with Hoover. . . . He kept Hoover informed with messages which were sent over for special security (!) through MI6 and therefore of course through Philby." The purpose of the latter, so Reilly believed, was to mollify Hoover after his outrage in early 1950 at the British magistrate's refusal to allow FBI agents to interview Fuchs until after his sentencing. Since MI5, not the Foreign Office, was responsible for the reports to Hoover, Sillitoe probably told Hoover that they were intended for the FBI director personally and not to be shared, either within the FBI or with the CIA. In the latter case, Hoover would have welcomed the caveat. Hoover and his deputy Mickey Ladd, who served as Philby's principal FBI contact, did not inform Lamphere of those messages.

51. In 1960 Herbert Morrison, the retired foreign secretary, wrote that only "myself and one or two very high officers of the Foreign Office and no one else" knew of the Maclean case, but he wasn't aware that Maclean was the prime suspect until he signed the interrogation order in late May, or so he claims. *An Autobiography by Lord Morrison of Lambeth* (Odhams Press, London, 1960). Sir Patrick Reilly and George Carey-Foster drafted the document, and Sir William Strang approved it. Glees, p. 360; Cecil, p. 135. Barrie Penrose and Simon Freeman identify the same three individuals in *Conspiracy of Silence: The Secret Life of Anthony Blunt* (Farrar, Straus, Giroux, New York, 1987), p. 342.

52. Philby wrote that "In communicating to us their conclusions, MI5 informed us that Maclean would probably be approached when the case against him

was complete. Meanwhile, certain categories of foreign office paper would be withheld from him, and his movement would be put under surveillance." Philby, p. 177. Borovik also reported that in Washington Philby was the first to learn of Maclean's surveillance and personally handed that information to the FBI. Borovik, p. 281. He was referring to the Sillitoe report to Hoover. Sir Patrick Reilly also described Sillitoe's April and May messages to the FBI to keep Hoover informed. Glees, pp. 360–361.

53. Anthony Cave Brown, *Treason in the Blood: H. St. John Philby, Kim Philby, and the Spy Case of the Century* (Houghton Mifflin, Boston, 1994), p. 417.

54. At the State Department and overseas, my responsibilities sometimes gave me access to top-secret NSA codeword SPOKE and ULTRA material but never to codeword intelligence not part of my duties.

55. West, p. 29.

56. Philby evidently called at Arlington Hall and met Meredith Gardner. Peter Wright, *Spy Catcher* (Viking, New York, 1987), pp. 184–185. Wright claims that during a visit to London in the late 1960s, Gardner told him Philby regularly visited Arlington Hall Station and peered over his shoulder in admiration "of the progress he was making," meaning progress on "the extent of the Venona leak." Wright contends Philby was able to inform Moscow of the "breadth of their disaster," i.e., the consequences of Russian code clerks' use of the flawed duplicate codebooks. One such Philby visit might have been useful to authenticate his London predeparture briefing by Oldfield on the Anglo-American codebreaking operation, but never on a regular basis. Wright is not only an unreliable source but a weaver of crazily patched quilts from a few random threads. Those hoping to credit Philby's access to the Venona secrets have seized on his Gardner anecdote. Common sense alone should have told Wright his claim was physically impossible. In one of the rare photographs of Arlington Hall and Meredith Gardner at work, he is shown seated at a long table among numerous women cryptanalysts in a large room filled with similar tables and cryptanalysts, all busily and laboriously working out their cryptanalytic puzzles. The work was long and progress very, very slow. The room resembled a very large, very busy insurance actuarial office filled with clerks and accountants. It was far different from the several isolated individual analysts' cubicles I visited during a day at the NSA at Fort Meade in the winter of 1978. (At the time, I was on detached duty from the State Department to the Department of Defense.) Even assuming Philby was a regular visitor, which is totally improbable, to imagine that intelligence of great moment could be learned from standing at Gardner's shoulder at the precise moment of a new breakthrough or that the Russians through Philby could precisely measure Venona's day-by-day progress is utter nonsense. As far as Venona's Maclean cables are concerned, all had been passed to GCHQ before Philby arrived in Washington; Eastcote, not Arlington Hall, had responsibility.

57. Phillip Knightley, *The Master Spy* (Alfred A. Knopf, New York, 1989), pp. 132, 151, 170.
58. Borovik, pp. 260, 265, 273. Borovik also claims that at the FBI offices Philby had been working on the Soviet agent at Los Alamos. The Fuchs case had been solved before Philby arrived in Washington; he was then under surveillance in England. Philby was completely confused when it came to Fuchs even in 1968.

CHAPTER FOUR

1. Dwight D. Eisenhower, *Crusade in Europe* (Doubleday, Garden City, 1948), p. 320.
2. Detail on British deception operations during World War II is drawn from Michael Howard, *Strategic Deception in the Second World War* (W. W. Norton, New York, 1995), pp. 3–6, 16, 24–28; and J. C. Masterman, *The Double Cross System* (Yale University Press, New Haven, 1972), pp. 1–35.
3. Howard, pp. 25–27; Anthony Cave Brown, *Bodyguard of Lies* (William Morrow, New York, 1975), pp. 2–4, 7–8.
4. Howard, pp. 89–93. "Special means" is described in technical terms based on a British Cabinet document in Howard, p. 253. Also Cave Brown, *Bodyguard of Lies*, pp. 279–280, 282–290.
5. Even though Sillitoe's book was censored by Dick White, his choice of anecdotes in telling us how he quickly taught himself the mysteries of the intelligence trade is evidence enough of the quality of his mind (he explained to his readers the chemical secrets in compounding invisible inks). Percy Sillitoe, *Cloak without Dagger* (Cassell, London, 1955), pp. 163–164. Decades later Dick White remembered him as "vapid and shallow." Tom Bower, *A Perfect English Spy: Sir Dick White and the Secret War, 1935–1990* (St. Martin's Press, New York, 1995), p. 138.
6. Biographical details on Dick White, his role in the 1939–1940 MI5 deceptions, his service at SHAEF headquarters, and his later years at MI5 and MI6 are drawn from Bower, pp. 6–23, 38–46, 57–72. Much of Bower's detailed narrative is based on innumerable interviews with White. See also Barrie Penrose and Simon Freeman, *Conspiracy of Silence: The Secret Life of Anthony Blunt* (Farrar, Straus, Giroux, New York, 1987), pp. 244–247.
7. The SNOW operation is described by Masterman, pp. 36–45. Also Howard, pp. 3–6.
8. Cave Brown, *Bodyguard of Lies*, pp. 729–730.
9. Bower, p. 68.
10. Cave Brown describes in an author's note to *Bodyguard of Lies*, pp. 823–827, his twelve years of attempting to penetrate London's wall of secrecy that concealed World War II deception operations.
11. Bower, pp. 73, 367.

12. Ibid., pp. 366–368. Bower's account is based in part on interviews with Dick White.
13. Hugh Trevor-Roper, *The Philby Affair: Espionage, Treason, and the Secret Service* (William Kimber, London, 1968), pp. xii, 48–49, 55.
14. Bower, pp. 367–369.
15. War Cabinet and Cabinet Office, Correspondence and Papers 1940–1978, Series details for CAB 154, Public Record Office. Also Richard J. Aldrich, *The Hidden Hand* (Overlook Press, Woodstock, 2002), pp. 256, 372–373. Aldrich identifies the LCS as the Hollis Committee.
16. Julian Lewis, *Changing Direction: British Military Planning* (Sherwood, London, 1988), p. 320.
17. Howard, p. 56.
18. Dennis Wheatley, *The Deception Planner: My Secret War* (Hutchinson, London, 1980), pp. 227–228.
19. Aldrich, pp. 272–273. Aldrich was citing a Ministry of Defense document of July 1, 1946, DEFE 2/1252.
20. Stephen Dorril, *MI6: Inside the Covert World of Her Majesty's Secret Intelligence Service* (Simon and Schuster, New York, 2002), p. 145.
21. Peter Wright, *Spycatcher* (Viking, New York, 1987), p. 75.
22. Sir Patrick Reilly wrote to Anthony Glees that "we at first expected to find the spy among cipher officers, clerks, etc." Glees, *The Secrets of the Service* (Carroll and Graf, New York, 1987), p. 359. Carey-Foster, the Foreign Office security officer, declared that it was inconceivable "that any senior member of the service could be a traitor." Bower, p. 91. "I just can't believe it," Sir William Strang exclaimed when told Maclean had become the prime suspect. Robert Cecil, *A Divided Life: A Personal Portrait of the Spy Donald Maclean* (William Morrow, New York, 1989), p. 117.
23. Bower, pp. 88–89.
24. Those September 1945 GCHQ intercepts are found among the Fourth and Fifth NSA Venona Releases (July 17 and September 27, 1996). (1) September 12, Moscow to London, no number: "Dzhen (JANE)," "Perry," "Ellen," "Kanati." Latter is cited in October 19 cable. (2) September 17, London to Moscow, no. 36: "Eduard." Kanati had served in Washington from 1939 until February 1945. (3) September 17, Moscow to London, no. 41: "Manya," "Willow," "Lister," "Fer," "Bordeaux," "Sergej." (4) September 18, Moscow to London, no. 47: "Johnson," "Stanley," "Hicks." (5) September 20, Moscow to London, no. 198: "Simpson." (6) September 20, Moscow to London, no. 199: "Jack" and "Rosa." (7) "Rosa" is also cited in an October 9 Moscow to London cable, no. 1315. (8) September 20, Moscow to London, no. 1223: "Ket (KATE)," "GRIP."
25. Detail on GCHQ's internal organization in 1942–1951 is extremely sketchy, not surprising for an operation so secret that few were aware of its very existence until the 1980s. Assigned to the GCHQ directorate were officers

representing the London Signals Intelligence Board, established in 1942 to follow GCHQ operations, and the London Signals Intelligence Committee, a defense committee. Desmond Ball and Jeffrey Richelson, *The Ties That Bind: British Intelligence Cooperation between the U.K.-USA Countries* (Allen and Unwin, Boston, 1995), pp. 20–21, 28. Colonel Marr-Johnson of the LSIC was attached as liaison officer to Arlington Hall in 1947, if not earlier. Evidently the Maclean or HOMER cell at Eastcote was even more secluded than many GCHQ operations. Nigel West, *Venona* (Harper Collins, New York, 2000), p. 29. The GCHQ Counter-Clandestine Committee is described by John Sawatsky, *For Services Rendered* (Penguin Books, New York, 1983), p. 25.

26. Maclean's importance to Moscow is indicated in a November 1945 cable from Moscow Center to its U.S. chiefs of station uncovered in the KGB archives in Moscow by Allen Weinstein. Following the defection of Elizabeth Bentley, all contacts with Maclean were to be suspended to avoid his exposure. Allen Weinstein and Alexander Vassiliev, *The Haunted Wood: Soviet Espionage in America—The Stalin Era* (Random House, New York, 1999), p. 107.

27. Foreign Relations of the United States, 1945, vol. 3, The Yalta Conference (Government Printing Office, Washington, D.C., 1967), p. 980.

28. Winston Churchill, *Triumph and Tragedy* (Houghton Mifflin, Boston, 1953), pp. 399–401.

29. Martin Gilbert, *Winston C. Churchill: The Road to Victory, 1943–1945*, vol. 3. (Houghton Mifflin, Boston, 1986), p. 1237; Herbert Feis, *Churchill-Roosevelt-Stalin*, rev. ed. (Princeton University Press, Princeton, 1967), pp. 573–574.

30. *FRUS, 1945*, vol. 3, p. 989.

31. Harriman cable to the Secretary of State, Moscow, March 4, 1945, in *FRUS, 1945*, vol. 5, *Europe* (Government Printing Office, Washington, D.C., 1967), pp. 141–142.

32. Warren F. Kimball, ed., *Churchill and Roosevelt: The Complete Correspondence*, vol. 3 (Princeton University Press, Princeton, 1984), pp. 547–551.

33. In the absence of the foreign secretary (or the secretary of state), the ranking officer would have been guilty of an unpardonable breach of protocol were he to adopt the imperious "I" as signatory on outgoing cables. At an embassy, however, in the absence of the ambassador the chargé d'affaires can and does use the signatory "I."

34. Kimball, pp. 551–559.

35. In Hiss's presentation before the House Un-American Activities Committee, he indicated that he had helped draft the Declaration on Liberated Europe, but didn't mention the Declaration on Poland, no doubt because it was so controversial. Allen Weinstein, *Perjury: The Hiss-Chambers Case* (Alfred A. Knopf, New York, 1978), p. 353.

36. Kimball, pp. 560–561; Gilbert, pp. 1247–1248.

37. Kimball, pp. 564–565.

38. Ibid., pp. 560–561; Gilbert, pp. 1249–1250.

39. Gilbert, p. 1252; Kimball, pp. 571–572.

40. Harry Hopkins, Roosevelt's emissary, told Anthony Eden and Lord Halifax that "few of the President's messages after Yalta were his own." He made no changes in the State Department texts of his March replies to Churchill. Kimball, p. 566.

41. *FRUS, 1945*, vol.5, pp. 189–190.

42. Feis, pp. 574–575.

43. Ibid., p. 636.

44. *An Autobiography by Lord Morrison of Lambeth* (Odhams Press, London, 1960), p. 276.

CHAPTER FIVE

1. Government Code and Cipher School and Government Communications Headquarters, Venona Project Records, Material from "H" (Donald Maclean), HW 15/32, Public Record Office.

2. Anthony Glees, *The Secrets of the Service* (Carroll and Graf, New York, 1987), p. 359.

3. Sir William Strang, "War and Foreign Policy, 1939–45," in David Dilks, ed., *Retreat from Power: Studies in Britain's Foreign Policy of the Twentieth Century*, vol. 2 (Macmillan, London, 1981), pp. 90–95; Herbert Feis, *Churchill-Roosevelt-Stalin*, rev. ed. (Princeton University Press, Princeton, 1967), p. 358.

4. State Department serial files and microfilms for this week in March 1945 at the National Archives contain nothing on the State Department exchanges with the British embassy. A few are still classified.

5. Glees, p. 171.

6. Allen Weinstein and Alexander Vassiliev, *The Haunted Wood* (Random House, New York, 1999), pp. 290–291.

7. Allen Weinstein, *Perjury: The Hiss-Chambers Case* (Alfred A. Knopf, New York, 1978), p. 357.

8. Robert Cecil, *A Divided Life: A Personal Portrait of the Spy Donald Maclean* (William Morrow, New York, 1989), pp. 91–107. Cecil describes in detail Maclean's disintegration in Cairo as well as his often bewildering behavior after his return to London. He dates the boating party incident to the summer of 1949. Rebecca West writes that it took place in March 1950. West, *The New Meaning of Treason* (Viking Press, New York, 1964), p. 221. Cecil, a Foreign Office diplomat, was extremely well informed about the Maclean case, received information from his Foreign Office colleagues not released elsewhere, and was on good terms with Maclean's friends and family. West's early account is overlooked as outdated but she brings a shrewd eye to several of the absurdities of the Maclean case.

9. Christopher Andrew and Vasili Mitrokhin, *The Mitrokhin Archive* (Penguin Books, London, 1999), p. 202.
10. Cecil, p. 110.
11. Genrikh Borovik, *The Philby Files* (Little, Brown, Boston, 1994), pp. 258–262.
12. Nigel West and Oleg Tsarev, *The Crown Jewels* (Yale University Press, New Haven, 1999), pp. 180–183; Yuri Modin, *My Five Cambridge Friends* (Farrar, Straus, Giroux, New York, 1994), p. 184.
13. An excellent account of Maclean and Philby and their years at Cambridge is found in Patrick Seale and Maureen McConville, *Philby: The Long Road to Moscow* (Simon and Schuster, New York, 1973), pp. 19–53. They are particularly comprehensive in establishing the social, political, and intellectual temper at Cambridge 1929–1933. Robert Cecil's account of Maclean's family and student days is memorable as well. Cecil, pp. 22–31.
14. Cecil, p. 77.
15. Noel Annan, *Our Age: Portrait of a Generation* (Weidenfeld and Nicolson, London, 1990), pp. 225–227. He also called Burgess a "monster of improbability."
16. The Tangier incident is briefly described by Modin, pp. 180–181; also West and Tsarev, p. 180. Gladwyn Jebb's comments are in *Memoirs of Lord Gladwyn* (Weidenfeld and Nicolson, London, 1972), p. 101. The "most brilliant undergraduate of his day" description is from Goronwy Rees, *A Chapter of Accidents* (Chatto and Windus, London, 1971), pp. 110–111. The "dirty, drunken, sexual inebriate" epithet was delivered in the House of Lords by Viscount Astor, later to play party host to John Profumo and Christine Keeler, as Anthony Glees points out. Glees, pp. 10–11.
17. On two different occasions in the 1930s Arnold Deutsch, the OGPU agent who had recruited Philby, had told Moscow he was indecisive. Borovik, pp. 55, 148.
18. Ibid., p. 274.
19. Sir Patrick Reilly's letters to Anthony Glees describe the MI5 reports to FBI director J. Edgar Hoover through Philby's MI6 cipher on the progress of the HOMER investigation. Reilly specifically mentions the May 23 or 24, 1951, report that Maclean would be detained and interrogated but the April 17 message that Maclean was now under surveillance is implied. Glees, pp. 359–361. As noted earlier, however, Philby confirms that he received a report from MI5 (undoubtedly in mid-April) that Maclean was under suspicion, that he would "be approached when the case against him was complete," and that in the meantime "certain categories of foreign office paper would be withheld from him, and his movement would be put under surveillance." Kim Philby, *My Silent War*, (Ballantine Books, New York, 1983), p. 177

1. Sir Patrick Reilly gave Anthony Glees the number of thirty-five original HOMER suspects (no names) in a July 10, 1986, letter. Glees, *The Secrets of the Service* (Carroll and Graf, New York, 1987), pp. 359–360. Robert Cecil also cites a figure of thirty-five suspects by the end of 1950, subsequently reduced to nine late in the investigation, but doesn't reveal his source. Cecil, *A Divided Life: A Personal Portrait of the Spy Donald Maclean* (William Morrow, New York, 1989), p. 118.

2. Based on an interview with George Carey-Foster, Tom Bower writes that Maclean had drunkenly confessed to being the English Hiss to a secretary at an unnamed British embassy, who reported it in a letter to the head of Foreign Office personnel in London. The letter was found in the Maclean file by Arthur Martin, who showed it to Carey-Foster. Bower, *A Perfect English Spy: Sir Dick White and the Secret War, 1935–1990* (St. Martin's Press, New York, 1995), p. 103. John Costello claims Maclean made the remark to Cyril Connolly in London. Costello, *Mask of Treachery* (William Morrow, New York, 1988), p. 548. Robert Cecil says Maclean made the remark to his friend Phillip Toynbee in a London nightclub incident described by Toynbee in an article he wrote. Cecil, p. 121. The multiple sources indicate how difficult it is to separate fact from fiction in the London gossip bazaar.

3. Philby's failure to meet with any Soviet control officer at the KGB residency in Washington is cited in Christopher Andrew and Vasili Mitrokhin, *The Mitrokhin Archive* (Penguin Books, London, 1999), p. 204. See also Yuri Modin, *My Five Cambridge Friends* (Farrar, Straus, Giroux, New York, 1994), pp. 186–187, 197.

4. Modin, p. 187.

5. Genrikh Borovik, *The Philby Files* (Little, Brown, Boston, 1994), p. 178.

6. Mitrokhin's KGB notes smuggled out of Russia confirm Burgess's courier role after he arrived in Washington in August 1950. Andrew and Mitrokhin, pp. 204, 207–209.

7. The Burgess assignment to Washington has remained a puzzle to every Philby commentator. Phillip Knightley wrongly concludes Burgess may have maneuvered for the posting to help Philby cope with the extra work brought on by the Korean War. Knightley, *The Master Spy* (Alfred A. Knopf, New York, 1989), pp. 163–164. The assignment was made in May 1950, a month before the war began. Anthony Cave Brown can't solve the mystery either, except to suggest that an unknown Soviet agent high in the Foreign Office sent Burgess to support Philby should Maclean be exposed. Cave Brown, *Treason in the Blood: H. St. John Philby, Kim Philby, and the Spy Case of the Century* (Houghton Mifflin, Boston, 1994), p. 417. This is more or less consistent with Cave Brown's penchant for explaining one mystery by introducing another. Yuri Modin can't explain the posting either except as an

example of "a somewhat warped sense of [English] humor." Modin, p. 182. Others have found the assignment equally "incomprehensible." Barrie Penrose and Simon Freeman, *Conspiracy of Silence: The Secret Life of Anthony Blunt* (Farrar, Straus, Giroux, New York, 1987), pp. 326–328; Verne Newton, *The Cambridge Spies* (Madison Books, Lanham, N.Y., 1991), pp. 268–269. Patrick Seale and Maureen McConville speculate that the Foreign Office believed that in Washington Burgess's oddities would be less conspicuous at a large diplomatic mission. Seale and McConville, *Philby: The Long Road to Moscow* (Simon and Schuster, New York, 1973), p. 208.

8. Andrew and Mitrokhin, pp. 204–206.

9. Meredith Gardner, "Development of the 'G'–HOMER [GOMER] Case" (October 11, 1951), p. 2. Gardner's comment on the British setting up "work-sheets" suggests that the British analysts at Arlington Hall had their own work section set apart from the Venona team. That may also explain his observation that "the British surround the handling of [blanked out] material with rigid safeguards." Gardner, "Covernames in Diplomatic Traffic," Records of National Security Agency Public Release, Copies of Records Relating to Project Venona 1941–1947, National Archives, RG 457, Box 4, Top Secret.

10. Sixth NSA Venona Release (September 1997).

11. Robert Louis Benson and Michael Warner reported that "British liaison officer Kim Philby received actual translations and analyses [of the Venona messages] on a regular basis after he arrived for duty in autumn 1949." The footnote refers the reader to Genrikh Borovik, an unreliable source on Venona. Benson and Warner, eds., *Venona: Soviet Espionage and the American Response, 1939–1957* (National Security Agency, Central Intelligence Agency, Washington, D.C., 1996), p. xxvii. There are other errors. Both seem to have been unfamiliar with Meredith Gardner's October 1951 report when they wrote their monograph.

12. Cecil, p. 117.

13. Glees, p. 363. This intelligence was contained in a November 1, 1985, letter from Lord Sherfield (Roger Makins) to Glees.

14. *Foreign Relations of the United States, 1947*, vol. 1, *General, the United Nations* (Government Printing Office, Washington D.C., 1974), pp. 785–789.

15. Chapman Pincher, *Too Secret Too Long* (St. Martin's Press, New York, 1984), p. 175. Pincher cites the Foreign Office lists on the date and a Cyril Connolly conversation for Maclean's drunkenness. He also claims any notion that Maclean was given his post on the advice of MI5 so that he could be watched "was not the case." His source was confidential. The best that can be said for the latter is that Sir Roger Makins is more reliable.

16. Bower, p. 102.

17. Modin, pp. 181–182.

18. There are innumerable accounts of Burgess's drunken antics, mishaps, and buffoonery in Washington, New York, and elsewhere during his final

months, February through April 1951. The most complete, interesting, and well documented is in Newton, pp. 305–324.

19. James Bamford, *Body of Secrets: Anatomy of the Ultra-Secret National Security Agency from the Cold War through the Dawn of a New Century* (Doubleday, New York, 2001), p. 28.

20. An interesting behind-the-scenes account of Washington's reaction to the Chinese entry is in Walter Isaacson and Evan Thomas, *The Wise Men* (Simon and Schuster, New York, 1986), pp. 235–243.

21. Dean Acheson, *Present at the Creation* (W. W. Norton, New York, 1969), pp. 478–480; Clement Attlee, *As It Happened* (Heinemann, London, 1954), pp. 199–201.

22. Ibid., pp. 481–486. Knightley claims Truman's assurance to Attlee that he "did not want to use the atomic bomb in Korea" was an enormous advantage to Moscow. Knightley, p. 173. Modin claims that on his own initiative Maclean passed him documents prepared for Attlee's December 1950 Washington visit as to the U.S. use of the atomic bomb in Korea as well as Attlee's reassurance by Truman. Modin, pp. 181–183. It is impossible to understand why Moscow would have been reassured. Of course Truman didn't want to use the bomb. Only a lunatic would. But he gave no assurances he wouldn't use it if required.

23. Julian Lewis, *Changing Direction: British Military Planning* (Sherwood, London, 1988), pp. 319, 332.

24. Richard J. Aldrich, ed., *Espionage, Security, and Intelligence in Britain, 1945–1970* (Manchester University Press, Manchester, 1998), pp. 142–143. Aldrich copies a Foreign Office memo to Herbert Morrison, July 19, 1963, with enclosed memorandum, Burgess and Maclean file, 8/5, Morrison Papers, British Library of Political and Economic Science. Tom Bower's version of the Strang meeting puts Dick White in control. He also dates the Sillitoe messages to Hoover from that April meeting. His source was evidently Carey-Foster. Bower, pp. 104–106.

25. Aldrich, p. 142. Sir Patrick Reilly recalled that Maclean was to be put under surveillance, which meant "full observation" both at work and at home. Glees, p. 364.

26. Kim Philby, *My Silent War* (Ballantine Books, New York, 1983), p. 177.

27. Borovik, p. 281.

28. Philby, p. 175. Borovik expands on Philby's motives. Borovik, p. 276.

29. Andrew and Mitrokhin, p. 207.

30. Philby, p. 176.

31. Newton, p. 413. Newton interviewed Mackenzie.

32. Glees, p. 361. Reilly's recollections were in a letter to Glees.

33. Andrew and Mitrokhin, p. 209. In this instance Mitrokhin's KGB notes supply a precise date that coincides more or less with the Sillitoe message to

Hoover informing him of the arrest and interrogation order to be submitted to Foreign Secretary Morrison on Friday, May 25.

34. Cecil, p. 137. Cecil's informant was Anthony Blunt.

CHAPTER SEVEN

1. Robert Cecil, *A Divided Life: A Personal Portrait of the Spy Donald Maclean* (William Morrow, New York, 1989), p. 135.
2. Anthony Glees, *The Secrets of the Service* (Carroll and Graf, New York, 1987), pp. 359–361.
3. Rebecca West, *The New Meaning of Treason* (Viking Press, New York, 1964), p. 364.
4. Yuri Modin, *My Five Cambridge Friends* (Farrar, Straus, Giroux, New York, 1994), p. 190.
5. John Earl Haynes and Harvey Klehr, *Venona: Decoding Soviet Espionage in America* (Yale University Press, New Haven, 2000), pp. 33–36.
6. STANLEY and HICKS are included among the Venona cables released in October 1996. The Cairncross and Blunt codenames have never been identified by GCHQ in any official release despite the fact that they were known.
7. Peter Wright, *Spy Catcher* (Viking, New York, 1987), pp. 128–138.
8. Tom Bower, *A Perfect English Spy: Sir Dick White and the Secret War, 1935–1990* (St. Martin's Press, New York, 1995), pp. 112–113.
9. Ibid., p. 300.
10. Modin, p. 208.
11. Bower, pp. 134–135.
12. Cecil, p. 137.
13. Bower, pp. 134–135. According to Bower, papers in Burgess's flat examined by Jane Archer, a longtime MI5 analyst, revealed official documents written by John Cairncross and resulted in MI5's surveillance. Cairncross was summoned for interrogation but MI5 "failed to get the evidence" necessary for prosecution. The source evidently did not explain why Cairncross papers would have been found in Burgess's flat. There is no reason they would have been there.
14. Nigel West and Oleg Tsarev, *The Crown Jewels* (Yale University Press, New Haven, 1999), p. 225.
15. Richard J. Aldrich, *The Hidden Hand* (Overlook Press, Woodstock, 2002), pp. 373–374. Aldrich's source was LCS (49)1, "Review of Overall Deception Policy," CAB 81/80, January 7, 1949, Public Record Office.
16. In 1948 Blunt reported to his KGB handler that MI5 told him it was unable to break any "Soviet cyphers" or open foreign-embassy diplomatic bags. The same year Guy Liddell of MI5 told him of a secret committee, presumably at the Ministry of Supply, created "to develop bacteriological weapons." In

January and again in May 1949 MI5 asked his agreement to use the Courtald Institute of Art to meet with agents recruited from East European embassies in London. Blunt agreed and gave MI5 the key to a room on the ground floor. According to KGB files, by September 1949 "at least one meeting with a Foreign MI5 agent had been conducted at the Courtauld." West and Tsarev, pp. 176, 186. All of the above invite suspicion. The codebreaking assertion was false, as no doubt was the inability to open diplomatic bags. In 1949 the LCS planned a disinformation operation based on Britain's development of biological weapons. Blunt's permission for MI5 to use the Courtauld Institute is as extraordinary as Blunt's explanation to his handler that MI5's first-floor room wouldn't interfere with his top-floor Leica camera work photographing documents supplied by Burgess, as he did in September 1949 with the notes given to Burgess by Philby (which Blunt overexposed). With access to the first floor, MI5 and its Special Facility crew could have roamed the Institute at will after hours with access to whatever room was needed to install its devices. It is also difficult to believe that Blunt or Moscow was gullible enough not to suspect something was going on, as it indeed was.

17. Modin, pp. 262–263.
18. Ibid., p. 263.
19. Kim Philby, *My Silent War* (Ballantine Books, New York, 1983), pp. 186–187.
20. Ibid., pp. 120, 151–152, 154.
21. Genrikh Borovik, *The Philby Files* (Little, Brown, Boston, 1994), pp. 257–258.
22. Stephen Dorril, *MI6: Inside the Covert World of Her Majesty's Secret Intelligence Service* (Simon and Schuster, New York, 2002), p. 145.
23. Anthony Cave Brown, *Treason in the Blood: H. St. John Philby, Kim Philby, and the Spy Case of the Century* (Houghton Mifflin, Boston, 1994), pp. 432–435.
24. Philby, p. 186.
25. Michael Howard, *Strategic Deception in the Second World War* (W. W. Norton, New York, 1995), pp. 171, 177; Aldrich, pp. 179, 372, 504; Dorril, p. 171.
26. Navy Historical Archives, Washington Navy Yard, no. 171, Papers of Admiral William D. Leahy, Box 8, Joint Chiefs of Staff Miscellaneous Memoranda. The file includes three documents: the Hollis top-secret and personal letter to Gruenther, Hollis's top-secret memo on the April 8 meeting with the JCS, and Gruenther's March 24 memorandum for Admiral Leahy with a four-page summary of the first two meetings of the U.S.-U.K.-Canadian conferees on March 22 and 23. The document in the JCS file is a typewritten copy made at the Pentagon of the Hollis original, which was on British Joint Services Mission letterhead. The Pentagon secretary had typed in "/s/ J. O. Hollis," but the written signature was undoubtedly "Joe Hollis," as he was known by his English and American friends. His attached memo is signed L. C. Hollis. In Dennis Wheatley's account of his war years with the LCS when he worked with Hollis, he often refers to him as Joe. Wheatley, *The Deception Planner: My Secret War* (Hutchinson, London, 1980).

27. Bower, p. 178.
28. Two agents were killed; the third disappeared. In his talks with Borovik in Moscow in the 1980s, Philby suggested he had initiated the operation. Responsibility has never been clarified.
29. Robert Lamphere and Tom Shachtman, *The FBI-KGB War* (Random House, New York, 1986), pp. 232–237.
30. The Volkov affair has been described with some variation in every account of Philby's MI6 career. See Christopher Andrew and Oleg Gordievsky, *KGB: The Inside Story of Its Foreign Operations from Lenin to Gorbachev* (Harper-Collins, New York, 1990), pp. 371–372; Christopher Andrew and Vasili Mitrokhin, *The Mitrokhin Archive* (Penguin Books, London, 1999), pp. 182–183. Others provide more detail as well as a touch of narrative drama. Cave Brown, pp. 363–366; Patrick Seale and Maureen McConville, *Philby: The Long Road to Moscow* (Simon and Schuster, New York, 1973), pp. 179–181; Phillip Knightley, *The Master Spy* (Alfred A. Knopf, New York, 1989), pp. 135–139.
31. Andrew and Mitrokhin, p. 182. The Mitrokhin note doesn't identify the means of communication. KGB files seen by West and Tsarev indicate he passed a note to Burgess. West and Tsarev, p. 174.
32. Knightley, p. 139. Seale and McConville reached the same conclusion as a matter of common sense. Seale and McConville, p. 183.
33. Hugh Trevor-Roper, *The Philby Affair: Espionage, Treason, and the Secret Service* (William Kimber, London, 1968), pp. xii, 48–49, 55.
34. Philby's Vienna period is in Seale and McConville; Knightley; and Cave Brown. Seale and McConville supply material on Aileen Furse, pp. 112–114.
35. Andrew and Mitrokhin, p. 110.
36. Seale and McConville, p. 181. They cite Vivian as their source. Bower reports that in 1946 Dick White was told by an informant that Litzi Philby was a Communist agent, but that it "hadn't been held against Philby." Bower, p. 172.
37. The Krivitsky conundrum has been rediscovered by every journalist who has ever written about Soviet espionage in the United States circa 1935–1945. No new facts have ever been added to that tattered dossier. A reliable account appears in Gordon Brook-Shepherd, *The Storm Petrels* (Ballantine Books, New York, 1982), pp. 165–166. See also Seale and McConville, p. 89; David Martin, *Wilderness of Mirrors* (Harper and Row, New York, 1980), pp. 1–10.
38. Philby was summoned and told of his Istanbul assignment by SIS deputy Major General John Sinclair. He insisted the posting came as no surprise. Philby, p. 135. Accounts by various writers differ as to the circumstances of his transfer. Most agree that the Istanbul posting was intended to give him SIS field experience (Seale and McConville, p. 184); others suggest the posting was necessary for his rise to the top ranks of MI6; (Knightley, pp. 140–

141). Cave Brown gives the posting a curious but plausible twist and suggests MI6 wanted Philby out of London and beyond the grasp of MI5, still disturbed by the Volkov incident. In Istanbul Philby was authorized by "C" to "trail his coat" as a disillusioned MI6 officer and attract Soviet notice as a potential recruit, or so Cave Brown claims (p. 369). He provides no evidence in its support. He later suggests Philby was scheduled to become the third-ranking SIS officer in London after his Washington assignment (p. 426). Trevor-Roper is of a different mind and believed Philby was destined to become "C," head of MI6, if only because of the lack of better-qualified candidates (p. 42). As much as anything, Trevor-Roper's judgment indicates his contempt for the quality of ranking MI6 personnel.

39. John Sawatsky, *For Services Rendered* (Penguin Books, New York, 1983), pp. 23–25. Sawatsky, a Canadian journalist, doesn't reveal his source; he was probably Leslie James Bennett, a Welshman and former GCHQ official who immigrated to Canada in 1954. He was later hired by the Royal Canadian Mounted Police's security unit. Sawatsky describes in detail the many RCMP counterintelligence operations targeting Soviet espionage in Canada. For rather preposterous reasons, Bennett was later thought to be a Soviet agent and left the service in 1972. Sawatsky's book is an indictment of the competence of the Canadian security service.

40. Borovik, p. 254.

41. Philby's report on the Gouzenko case as well as Elizabeth Bentley's list of forty-one Soviet agents were uncovered in Moscow by Allen Weinstein and Alexander Vassiliev, *The Haunted Wood: Soviet Espionage in America—the Stalin Era* (Random House, New York, 1999), pp. 104, 108.

42. West and Tsarev, p. 182.

43. Knightley, p. 186.

44. Andrew and Mitrokhin, pp. 205–206.

CHAPTER EIGHT

1. Robert Benson, "KGB Messages to the London Residency," Fifth NSA Venona Release (September 27, 1996), p. 2.

2. Philby, *My Silent War* (Ballantine Books, New York, 1983), p. 179.

3. Genrikh Borovik, *The Philby Files* (Little, Brown, Boston, 1994), p. 301; Phillip Knightley, *The Master Spy* (Alfred A. Knopf, New York, 1989), p. 181; Anthony Cave Brown, *Treason in the Blood: H. St. John Philby, Kim Philby, and the Spy Case of the Century* (Houghton Mifflin, Boston, 1994), p. 440. Tom Bower says MI5 had tapped Tudor Hart's phone. Bower, *A Perfect English Spy: Sir Dick White and the Secret War, 1935–1990* (St. Martin's Press, New York, 1995), p. 131.

4. Borovik, p. 299.

5. Christopher Felix, *A Short History in the Secret War*, 4th ed. (Madison Books,

Lanham, N.Y., 2001), p. 281. Felix is the pseudonym of James McCarger, a former CIA officer, active during the years under review.

6. Easton's explanation is in Cave Brown, pp. 438–443.
7. The events that followed Philby's dismissal, including the Milmo interrogation, are described in numerous accounts. See Bower, pp. 128–138.
8. Benson, p. 2.
9. Allen Weinstein and Alexander Vassiliev, *The Haunted Wood: Soviet Espionage in American—the Stalin Era* (Random House, New York, 1999), pp. 104–107.
10. Nigel West and Oleg Tsarev, *The Crown Jewels* (Yale University Press, New Haven, 1999), p. 178. Since those Foreign Office documents were passed to his Soviet control during a four-power meeting in London attended by Molotov, they may not have been put on the embassy cipher wire to Moscow, although Moscow Center would have been interested in those papers.
11. Christopher Andrew and Vasili Mitrokhin, *The Mitrokhin Archive* (Penguin Books, London, 1999), p. 800: "They [the Philby STANLEY cables] appear not to have been decrypted until some years later." Nigel West, *Venona* (HarperCollins, New York, 2000), p. 139: "The certainty that STANLEY was Philby emerged only after his defection."
12. An article by Michael Smith published in London's *Daily Telegraph* after the October 1, 1996, GCHQ release to the Public Record Office claimed the decision was forced on British intelligence by the NSA's decision to put the Venona transcripts on its Internet Web site. An October 2 *Manchester Guardian* article also claimed the GCHQ release was forced by Washington's decision to publish Venona. Any such claims by British intelligence were intended to suggest that GCHQ was obliged to empty its cupboard. The released cables make it clear GCHQ didn't comply.
13. In 1994 Richard Aldrich wrote that unconfirmed reports indicated that in 1993 London had approached Moscow requesting that Soviet archives relating to Britain remain closed. Aldrich, "Never-Never Land and Wonderland?" *Contemporary Record* 8, 1 (summer 1994), pp. 132–150.
14. Borovik, p. 235.
15. Ibid., pp. 240–243.
16. Philby's comments on the Gouzenko and May case are found in his "Unpublished Memoirs and Articles," in Rufina Philby, *The Private Life of Kim Philby* (Fromm International, New York, 2000), pp. 262–266. He also updated his comments on the Fuchs case in the same series after having totally botched his description in *My Silent War*.
17. Peter Wright, *Spy Catcher* (Viking, New York, 1987), pp. 182–183, 187, 195–196. Wright is frequently unreliable but in this case his detail is credible enough to consider. He describes, but doesn't identify, one of the cables citing the STANLEY, HICKS, and JOHNSON cryptonyms; it was London to Moscow no. 47 of September 18, 1945. He subsequently visited GCHQ, discussed Venona, found its old-fashioned methods too slow, and decided to locate a

computer capable of attacking the Venona traffic. He found one at the "Atomic Weapons Research Establishment (AWRE)" and for three months it labored away on Venona cables "six hours a night." The computer eventually disgorged the STANLEY cryptonym in the context of an already broken Moscow to London cable citing a KGB problem in its "Mexican Affairs." Since Wright wrongly insists that in September 1945 Philby was head of the Iberian section of MI5 (he wasn't but left to become chief of IX in October 1944), he claims that his discovery was "categoric proof" that Philby was STANLEY. It was a "bitter moment" and a hollow triumph for Wright, despite the falsity of his assumptions and conclusions: Philby had fled Beirut a few months earlier.

18. Allen Weinstein, *Perjury: The Hiss-Chambers Case* (Alfred A. Knopf, New York, 1978), p. 402.
19. Robert Lamphere and Tom Shachtman, *The FBI-KGB War* (Random House, New York, 1986), pp. 104–110.
20. As a young draftee just out of college, after sixteen weeks infantry training I was assigned to U.S. Army Counterintelligence (CIC) and trained at the CIC School at Fort Holabird, Maryland. FBI agents from Washington sometimes lectured and spoke from notes that dated from the McCarthy era. I subsequently spent the hottest summer of my life at U.S. Military Intelligence Headquarters (G-2) Central Records Center in Baltimore. There I analyzed and evaluated classified documents gathered from foreign and domestic intelligence sources, many dating back to the 1930s. FBI field reports on so-called subversives were the most useless, so much so that analysts could draw no credible conclusions. Most frequently they were ignored.
21. Julian Lewis, *Changing Direction: British Military Planning* (Sherwood, London, 1988), pp. 318–320.
22. Ibid., p. 319.
23. West and Tsarev, pp. 180–181. All of the incidents described by West and Tsarev are based on KGB documents, sometimes paraphrased, sometimes quoted.
24. Borovik, p. 234.
25. Klaus Fuchs, FO 953/2334, PFY.62551; also KV 2/1237–1270, Top Secret; British National Archives and Public Record Office.
26. West and Tsarev, p. 247.
27. Ibid., p. 181.
28. Ibid., p. 182.
29. GCHQ's Colossus computer was the world's first large electronic-valve programmable logic calculator. It was designed and built at the Dollis Hill Post Office Research Laboratories in North London in 1943 by a team led by Dr. Tommy Flowers to help Bletchley Park decode intercepted German telegraphic traffic enciphered using the Lorenz SZ42 cipher machine. Ten were built and operational in Bletchley Park during World War II. Not a stored-

program computer, Colossus was hard-wired. The intercepted message, punched onto ordinary teleprinter paper tape, was read at five thousand characters per second. The existence of Colossus was a secret until 1970. The decryption algorithms remain a secret today.

30. Second NSA Venona Release (October 26, 1995), p. 5.
31. Borovik, pp. 235–236.
32. Weinstein and Vassiliev, pp. 286, 291–293. They cite documents discovered in the KGB archive in Moscow on Weisband's work.
33. Fuchs, FO 953/2334, PFY.62551.
34. John Earl Haynes and Harvey Klehr, *Venona: Decoding Soviet Espionage in America* (Yale University Press, New Haven, 2000), p. 35. GCHQ has volunteered nothing about its rate of success or its methodology.
35. Cecil James Phillips, "What Made Venona Possible?" in Robert Louis Benson and Michael Warner, eds., *Venona: Soviet Espionage and the American Response, 1939–1957* (National Security Agency, Central Intelligence Agency, Washington, D.C., 1996), p. xv.
36. David Martin, "The Code War," *Washington Post Sunday Magazine*, May 10, 1998, p. 27. Martin wrote that "Philby and Gardner actually met briefly in the Mansion at Arlington Hall and even shook hands" before going their separate ways. (The Mansion was the main building and entrance.) His account was evidently based on interviews, Cecil Phillips among them, and is far more reasonable.
37. West and Tsarev, p. 182.
38. Ibid., pp. 182–185.
39. Ibid., p. 184.
40. Borovik, p. 280.
41. Chapman Pincher, *Too Secret Too Long* (St Martin's Press, New York, 1984), p. 178.
42. Cave Brown, pp. 418–419.

CHAPTER NINE

1. Hugh Trevor-Roper, *The Philby Affair: Espionage, Treason, and the Secret Service* (William Kimber, London, 1968), p. 15. Trevor-Roper also warned that Moscow would deliberately build up the Philby legend; pp. 19, 226. English and American journalists and writers, not Moscow, were responsible for its growth.
2. In June 1946 the CIG had fewer than 100 officers. Six months later, the total was 1,816, about half in support positions. By 1949, among the two CIA operational units, the Office of Special Operations (OSO) had approximately 400 to 500 officers abroad whereas the Office of Policy Coordination (OPC) had 302. This leaves aside the nonoperational and support personnel. By 1952, after Philby left Washington, the OPC had grown to 2,812 employees.

These figures are cited in the "Supplemental Detailed Staff Reports on Foreign and Military Intelligence," *Final Report of the Select Committee to Study Governmental Operations with Respect to Intelligence Activities* (Government Printing Office, Washington, D.C., 1976), pp. 31–37. See also Thomas Powers, *The Man Who Kept the Secrets: Richard Helms and the CIA* (Alfred A. Knopf, New York, 1979), p. 48. Details on the number of OSS officers transferred to the War Department's Strategic Services Unit (SSU) and subsequently to the CIA's OSO are found in the Memorandum by the Director of the Strategic Services Unit, Department of War (Magruder), Washington, February 14, 1946, National Archives, RG 263, Records of the Central Intelligence Agency, Troy Papers, Box 11, Folder 78, Secret. See also Memorandum from the Fortier Committee to the Director of Central Intelligence (Souers), Washington, March 14, 1946, National Archives, Central Intelligence Agency Historical Files, HS/CSG-1808, Job 83–00036, Box 12, Folder 11, Top Secret.

3. Examples of the other executive agencies' frustration of the CIA can be found in the Minutes of the Ninth Meeting of the National Intelligence Authority (NIA), Washington, February 12, 1947, Central Intelligence Agency Historical Files, HS/HC-245, Top Secret.

4. Walter Millis, ed., *The Forrestal Diaries* (Viking Press, New York, 1951), pp. 374–377. On February 18, 1948, General Alfred M. Gruenther briefed President Truman at the White House on the woeful state of U.S. troop readiness and warned that the overseas deployment of more than one division would require partial mobilization.

5. Ibid., p. 573.

6. W. Scott Lucas and C. J. Morris, "A Very British Crusade," in Richard Aldrich, ed., *British Intelligence Strategy and the Cold War, 1945–1951* (Routedge, New York, 1992), pp. 95–99.

7. "Future Foreign Publicity Policy," by E. Bevin, Foreign Office, January 4, 1948, cited in Lucas and Morris, p. 95.

8. Ibid., p. 94.

9. Richard J. Aldrich, *The Hidden Hand* (Overlook Press, Woodstock, 2002), pp. 150–152; Stephen Dorril, *MI6: Inside the Covert World of Her Majesty's Secret Intelligence Service* (Simon and Schuster, New York, 2002), pp. 40–43.

10. Lucas and Morris, p. 94.

11. Letter to Air Marshal Sir Victor Goddard, British Joint Services Mission, Pentagon, April 27, 1948, with attached staff paper memorandum, National Archives, Air Force Plans Decimal File 1942–1954, SG 581 (TS), Box 96, Secret. The staff memorandum dates USAF-RAF collaboration to mid-July 1946. The Royal Air Force asked for "a much wider and freer exchange of military information." The request was under consideration.

12. Charles P. Cabell, *A Man of Intelligence: Memoirs of War, Peace, and the CIA*, ed. Charles P. Cabell Jr. (Impavide Publications, Boulder, 1997), p. 254. In Jan-

uary 1953 Smith asked Cabell to accept appointment as CIA deputy director. He served from April 20, 1953, until January 1962.

13. Alex Danchev, "In the Back Room: Anglo-American Defence Cooperation, 1945–51," in Aldrich, *British Intelligence Strategy and the Cold War, 1945–1951*, p. 227; John Newhouse, *War and Peace in the Nuclear Age* (Alfred A. Knopf, New York, 1989), p. 46.

14. War plan Pincher is described by Steven T. Ross, *American War Plans, 1945–1950* (Frank Cass, London, 1988), pp. 25–49; Gregg Herkin, *The Winning Weapon: The Atomic Bomb in the Cold War, 1945–1950* (Random House, New York, 1982), pp. 219–221, 376–377.

15. Lilienthal made his remarks during a 1979 interview with the historian Gregg Herkin, p. 196. On February 15, 1946, Lilienthal visited Los Alamos for the first time. In his journal the following day he described it as "one of the most dramatic and deeply moving experiences" of his life. He didn't disclose what he was shown at Los Alamos the previous day. "Top Secret limitations" barred further detail. *The Journals of David Lilienthal*, vol. 2, *The Atomic Energy Years* (Harper and Row, New York, 1964), p. 20.

16. Nigel West and Oleg Tsarev, *The Crown Jewels* (Yale University Press, New Haven, 1999), pp. 242–243.

17. Vladimir M. Zubok, "Stalin," in John Lewis Gaddis, ed., *Cold War Statesmen Confront the Bomb: Nuclear Diplomacy since 1945* (Oxford University Press, London, 1999), pp. 54, 72.

18. Richard J. Aldrich, ed., *Espionage, Security, and Intelligence in Britain, 1945–1970* (Manchester University Press, Manchester, 1998), pp. 91–92, 97. Aldrich found the June 1947 JIB document in USAF files at the National Archive in Washington. It is possible the JIB began supplying similar documents earlier.

19. The many details about Major General Kenneth Strong and General Walter Bedell Smith are taken from Strong's book, *Intelligence at the Top: The Recollections of a British Intelligence Officer* (Doubleday, New York, 1969). Russell Weigley, an American military historian, lauds him in his account of General Eisenhower's command, *Eisenhower's Lieutenants* (Indiana University Press, Bloomington, 1981), p. 701. Strong as Smith's model in reorganizing the CIA is described by Ludwell Montague, *General Walter Bedell Smith as Director of Central Intelligence* (Pennsylvania State University Press, University Park, 1992) pp. 58, 59, 64.

20. Dorril, p. 72.

21. The legal opinion is in a Memorandum from the General Counsel of the Central Intelligence Agency (Houston) to Director of Central Intelligence Hillenkoetter, Washington, September 25, 1947, National Archives, Central Intelligence Agency Historical Files, HS/HC-805, Item 12, Secret. Subject: CIA Authority to Perform Propaganda and Commando Type Functions.

22. The comment is in A. J. P. Taylor's "The Cold War," *From the Boer War to the Cold War: Essays on Twentieth Century Europe* (Penguin Books, London, 1996), p. 391. He adds that Forrestal "drove himself mad by reading the works of Marx and Lenin and ended up throwing himself from a high window." For a historian who scorns psychoanalytical judgments, as Taylor does, his comment is unusual but in his short essays he often indulges himself with memorable if strained generalizations.

23. Townsend Hoopes and Douglas Brinkley, *Driven Patriot: The Life and Times of James Forrestal* (Random House, New York, 1992), pp. 270–280. Also Millis, pp. 135–140. His search for a coherent national policy is in Millis, p. 114. A brief but excellent description of Kennan's frustrations in Moscow as well as the immediate impact of his telegram in Washington is found in Walter Isaacson and Evan Thomas, *The Wise Men* (Simon and Schuster, New York, 1984), pp. 352–362.

24. George Kennan never believed Stalin to be an enigma nor doubted his 1945 ambitions. They remained "simple and clear": the extension of Soviet political and military power in Eastern Europe and the Balkans, the same 1939 demands Stalin had made of Hitler during their Nonaggression Pact. Kennan, *Russia and the West under Lenin and Stalin* (Little, Brown, Boston, 1960), p. 351. Kennan's "shock" at the emphasis given U.S. military power in interpreting his containment policy was uttered some forty years later during his extensive comments on the Soviet Union. G. R. Urban, ed., "From Containment to Self-Containment," in *Stalinism: Its Impact on Russia and the World* (Wildwood House, Aldershot, 1985), pp. 348–414. His dissatisfaction with the growing emphasis given NATO led to his resignation from the State Department in early 1950. Walter LaFeber, *America, Russia, and the Cold War, 1945–1971*, 2d ed. (John Wiley and Sons, New York, 1972), pp. 82–83.

25. Millis, pp. 326–327. The Cominform's purpose is described in Adam Ulam's *The Rivals: America and Russia since World War II* (Viking Press, New York, 1971), pp. 130–134. See also Isaacson and Thomas, p. 426.

26. Dmitri Volkogonov, *Stalin: Triumph and Tragedy* (Grove Weidenfeld, New York, 1988), p. 534. Accounts of the Cominform's creation are found in Adam Ulam, *Stalin: The Man and His Era* (Beacon Press, Boston, 1973), pp. 660–661. See also Ulam, *The Rivals*, pp. 130–134. Milovan Djilas supports Ulam's interpretation. Djilas, *Conversations with Stalin* (Harcourt, Brace and World, New York, 1962), pp. 128–129.

27. Memorandum from the Secretary of the State–Army–Navy–Air Force Coordinating Committee (Moseley) to the Undersecretary of State (Lovett), Washington, October 15, 1947, National Archives RG 353, Records of Interdepartmental and Interdepartmental Committees–State Department, Records of the State–War–Navy Coordinating Committee, Box 55, File 304, 381, Psychological Warfare, Pt. 1, Secret. Subject: Proposal for a National Psychological Warfare Organization.

28. The CIA covert psychological program was created in a Memorandum from Director of Central Intelligence Hillenkoetter to the Assistant Director for Special Operations (Galloway), Washington, December 22, 1947, Central Intelligence Agency Historical Files, HS/CSG-917, Job 83–00036, Box 6, Folder 11, Top Secret.

29. Memorandum from Secretary of Defense Forrestal to the Executive Secretary of the National Security Council, National Archives, RG 59, Records of the Department of State, Policy Planning Staff Files 1947–1954, Lot 64 D 563, Political and Psychological Warfare 1948–1950, Box 11, Top Secret.

30. Policy Planning Staff Memorandum, Washington, May 4, 1948, National Archives, RG 273, Records of the National Security Council, NSC 10/2. Subject: The Inauguration of Organized Political Warfare. George Kennan presented the paper at a meeting of NSC consultants.

31. Dean Acheson, *Present at the Creation* (W. W. Norton, New York, 1969), p. 446. Kennan disagreed with the increasing emphasis given to NATO, the militarization of containment, which Acheson firmly endorsed. Kennan was an extraordinarily complex individual who inspired trust as well as disdain among his contemporaries. See Isaacson and Thomas, pp. 421–438.

32. Senate Select Committee on Government Operations with Respect to Intelligence Activities, *Covert Action Report* (Government Printing Office, Washington; D.C., 1975), pp. 31–35.

33. The Joint Chiefs' plan is described in a Memorandum from the Assistant Secretary of State for Public Affairs (Allen) to Acting Secretary of State Lovett, Washington, March 31, 1948, and a Memorandum from the Director of the Office of Information and Educational Exchange (Stone) to Acting Secretary of State Lovett, Washington, April 1, 1948, National Archives RG 59, Records of the Department of State, Records of the Executive Secretariat, NSC Files, Lot 63 D 351, NSC 4, Box 4205, Top Secret.

34. The German problem in 1948 has been analyzed by many Cold War historians Adam Ulam is among the most lucid. Ulam, *The Rivals*, pp. 148–151. The April 1948 crisis as it occurred is in Millis, pp. 407–408.

35. John Lukacs, *A New History of the Cold War*, 3d ed. (Anchor Books, New York, 1966), p. 82.

36. The evolution of the 1948 Berlin crisis is documented in a study released by the CIA in 1999, "On the Front Lines of the Cold War: Documents on the Intelligence War in Berlin, 1946 to 1961." CIA intelligence analysts discounted the possibility that Moscow intended to go to war over Berlin.

37. Navy Historical Archives, Washington Navy Yard, no. 171, Papers of Admiral William D. Leahy, Box 8, Joint Chiefs of Staff Miscellaneous Memoranda.

38. The May 12, 1948, bilateral London discussions between the USAF and the Royal Air Force are found in the National Archives. "Pursuant to the Provisions of JSPC Paragraphs 10, 11, and 12 of JSPC S 77/4," May 12, 1948,

National Archives, RG 341, Air Force Plans Project Decimal File 1942–1954, SG 581, Entry 335, Box 742, Top Secret.

39. Between April and November 1948 numerous letters and memoranda were exchanged between the U.S. Air Force and the Royal Air Force in negotiating the agreement. Joint Agreement on Target Intelligence, October 28, 1948, To Air Vice Marshal L. F. Pendred, CB, MBE, DFC, Assistant Chief of Air Staff, Air Ministry, from C. A. Cahill, Major General, USAF Director of Intelligence, National Archives, RG 341, Control and Cables Section, General File July 1945–December 1954, Box 743, Top Secret. Richard Aldrich cites a November 1948 letter from Cabell to Pendred notifying him that the USAF-RAF agreement had been approved. Aldrich, *Espionage, Security, and Intelligence in Britain, 1945–1970,* p. 97.

40. Herkin, pp. 251–252. He cites U.S. JCS Records, JCS History II, pp. 120–122, in the National Archives.

41. *Newsweek,* May 17, 1948, pp. 30–32.

42. Records of the Joint Chiefs of Staff, "Brief of Emergency Short Range Emergency War Plan (*Halfmoon*)," May 6, 1948, CCS 381 USSR (3–2-46) s 13 JCS 1844/4, Box 73, National Archives.

43. *Foreign Relations of the United States, 1948,* vol. 4, *Eastern Europe; the Soviet Union* (Government Printing Office, Washington, D.C., 1974), pp. 851–854.

44. Millis, p. 505.

45. Allen Weinstein and Alexander Vassiliev, *The Haunted Wood: Soviet Espionage in America—the Stalin Era* (Random House, New York, 1999), p. 290.

46. Ulam, *The Rivals,* pp. 148–151; Millis, pp. 451–462; Hoopes and Brinkley, p. 374; Newhouse, p. 65; Herkin, pp. 256–261.

47. The Russian military observer was interviewed by John Newhouse years later. Newhouse, p. 65. The B-29s weren't capable of delivering atomic weapons nor would President Truman permit nonnuclear components to be moved to England. Herkin, pp. 256–261. The U.S. 28th Bomb Group flew to Scampton in Lincolnshire on July 17 and was followed on July 18 by the 2d Bomb Group at Lakenheath. Two squadrons from the 307th Bomb Group arrived at Marham on August 8.

48. *Foreign Relations of the United States, 1948,* vol. 3, *Western Europe* (Government Printing Office, Washington, D.C., 1974), pp. 188–193.

49. Details of the April–May 1948 nuclear tests in the South Pacific are described in Kenneth W. Condit, *History of the Joint Chiefs of Staff, The Joint Chiefs of Staff and National Policy, 1947–1949* (Office of Joint History, Office of the Chairman of the Joint Chiefs of Staff, Washington, D.C., 1996), p. 283; Richard Rhodes, *Dark Sun: The Making of the Hydrogen Bomb* (Simon and Schuster, New York, 1995), pp. 320–321; Thomas Saffer and Orville Kelly, *Countdown Zero* (G. P. Putnam, New York, 1982), pp. 66, 95–111. According to a Soviet document, Beria was so doubtful the Soviet Union had exploded its own bomb that he phoned a Russian observer of the Eniwetok detonations to

ask if the mushroom cloud was identical. Christopher Andrew and Oleg Gordievsky, *KGB: The Inside Story of Its Operations from Lenin to Gorbachev* (HarperCollins, New York, 1990), p. 378.

50. The Newport discussions are reported in Hoopes and Brinkley, pp. 410–414; Millis, pp. 476–478. The SAC's shortcomings, including the failure of the mock air raid, are in Curtis E. LeMay and MacKinley Kantor, *Mission with LeMay* (Doubleday, New York, 1965), pp. 429–433. LeMay wrote that the once mighty USAF had gone to "utter hell" by the autumn of 1948.

51. Walter Boyne, *Beyond the Wild Blue: A History of the U.S. Air Force* (St. Martin's Press, New York, 1997), pp 40–41.

52. Herkin, p. 268.

53. Lucas and Morris, p. 101.

54. Aldrich, *The Hidden Hand*, pp. 149–151. Aldrich writes that until then the service chiefs were unaware of the Russia Committee's existence.

55. Aldrich, *Espionage, Security, and Intelligence in Britain, 1945–1970*. Aldrich includes a page of minutes from the Russia Committee meeting of November 25, 1948.

56. Cipher from Air Ministry in London to B.F.A.S. Washington, Message for Nowell from Medhurst, MSX 808, National Archives, RG 341, Air Force Plans Project Decimal File 1942–1954, SG 581 (TS), Box 743. Air Commodore H. E. Nowell was with the air force staff. Medhurst's World War II duties are mentioned in Bradley Smith, *Sharing Secrets with Stalin* (University Press of Kansas, Lawrence, 1996), pp. 56, 62; F. W. Winterbotham, *The Ultra Secret* (Dell Publishing, New York, 1974), pp. 37–38, 43–44, 92, 131.

57. Vandenberg letter to Major General Johnson, USAF, November 28, 1949, National Archives, RG 341, Air Force Plans Project Decimal File 1942–1954, SG 581 (TS), Box 743.

58. Records of the Joint Chiefs of Staff, Brief of Joint Outline Emergency War Plan (Offtackle), May 26, 1949, CCS 381 USSR (3-2-46) s32 JSPC 877/59, Box 78. Offtackle wasn't given JCS approval until December 1949. Herkin, p. 297; Steven T. Ross, *American War Plans, 1945–1950* (Frank Cass, London, 1996), p. 111.

59. Similar 1948–1949 conjectural fantasies of Pentagon staffers are also evident in a March 22, 1948, Joint Intelligence Report claiming 35 percent of the American population was vulnerable to Communist infiltration and subversion. Ross, p. 105.

60. Lucas and Morris, p. 103; Aldrich, *The Hidden Hand*, pp. 152–154; Nicholas Bethell, *The Great Betrayal: The Untold Story of Kim Philby's Greatest Coup* (Hodder and Stoughton, London, 1984), pp. 37–42.

61. Lucas and Morris, p. 102.

62. *Foreign Relations of the United States, 1949*, vol. 1, *National Security Affairs and Foreign Economic Policy* (Government Printing Office, Washington, D.C., 1977), pp. 285–287. The NSC 45/1 report published in the FRUS volume

approves the development of adequate airfields in the United Kingdom and Cairo-Suez area, required for emergency war plans. "Airfield Construction in the United Kingdom and the Cairo-Suez Area." The latter was the subject of a memo from Secretary Forrestal to Souers at the NSC.

63. Kim Philby, *My Silent War* (Ballantine Books, New York, 1983), p. 151.

CHAPTER TEN

1. Ludwell Lee Montague, *General Walter Bedell Smith as Director of Central Intelligence* (Pennsylvania State University Press, University Park, 1992), p. 202. Memorandum from Allen W. Dulles to Mathias F. Correa and William H. Jackson, New York, January 21, 1949, National Archives, Central Intelligence Agency Records, Job 80-MO1009A, Box 1, Folder 12, no classification marking. Smith quickly began to search for a single installation after he assumed command in October 1950.

2. A number of malicious press reports on the CIG (even by the *New York Times*) had become so serious a problem that on June 26, 1947, CIG director Hillenkoetter raised the subject at a meeting of the National Intelligence Authority. The reports were undoubtedly based on falsifications circulated by those opposed to the CIG, including the FBI and the service intelligence agencies. Secretary Forrestal suggested Hillenkoetter contact the leading newspaper publishers, which Hillenkoetter had already done. Minutes of the Tenth meeting of the National Intelligence Authority, Central Intelligence Agency Historical Files, HS/HC-245, Job 84-00473R, Box 3, Top Secret.

3. Phillip Knightley, *The Second Oldest Profession* (W. W. Norton, New York, 1987), pp. 242–247. Knightley repeats these errors in *The Master Spy* (Alfred A. Knopf, New York, 1989), p. 153.

4. Arthur B. Darling, *The Central Intelligence Agency* (Pennsylvania State University Press, University Park, 1990), pp. 42–74. Darling was the CIA's first official historian. His history covered the 1946–1950 period and was particularly critical of the service chiefs and the State Department in frustrating Vandenberg's and Hillenkoetter's ability to manage the CIG and the CIA as an effective national intelligence agency. Written in 1951 and not declassified until 1989 (and then incompletely), it is a confusing and monotonous epic of acronyms and cross-references.

5. Montague, pp. 35–38, 76–77. Montague's history was written in the late 1960s but wasn't declassified until 1990. Heavy deletions were made, including all references to the CIA's liaison with foreign intelligence agencies, MI6 among them. Montague served with both the CIG and the CIA. His analysis is more readable, lively, and penetrating than Darling's. Although it concentrates on Smith's reign, it analyzes the CIA prior to the general's arrival in October 1950, when the agency was virtually "moribund" as a functioning organization. Montague, p. x.

6. Memorandum from the Executive Secretary of the Intelligence Survey Group (Blum) to Allen W. Dulles, Mathias F. Correa, and William H. Jackson, Washington, April 12, 1948, National Archives, Central Intelligence Agency Records, Job 86-B00269R, Box 5, Secret.

7. Smith's views on Dulles and Wisner are in Montague, pp. 91–92, 95–96. White's comment on the two is in Tom Bower, *A Perfect English Spy: Sir Dick White and the Secret War, 1935–1990* (St. Martin's Press, New York, 1995), p. 207. It was evidently made in an interview.

8. Montague, p. 47.

9. The CIA deficiencies in scientific intelligence collection are contained in the Memorandum from the Assistant Director for Scientific Intelligence (Machle) to the Director of Central Intelligence (Hillenkoetter), Washington, September 29, 1949, National Archives, Central Intelligence Agency Records, Job 84-T00286R, Box 5, Folder 1, Top Secret. Subject: Inability of OSO to Accomplish Its Mission.

10. Montague, pp. 28, 80–81, 186–187.

11. Stephen Penrose's two-thousand-word January 2 memorandum went far beyond Galloway and the OSO in criticizing every aspect of the CIA's operational performance. Letter from the Secretary of Defense's Special Assistant (McNeil) to Mathias F. Correa, Washington, February 2, 1948, National Archives, Central Intelligence Agency Records, Job 86-B00269R, Box 5, Personal and Secret.

12. Memorandum from the Assistant Director for Policy Coordination, Central Intelligence Agency (Wisner) to the Counselor of the Department of State (Bohlen), Washington, April 15, 1949, National Archives, RG 59, Records of the Department of State, Records of the Executive Secretariat, NSC Files, Lot 63 D 351, NSC 50, Box 4207, Secret, Eyes Only.

13. Montague, pp. 80, 101, 188.

14. Memorandum of Conversation, April 16, 1948, National Archives, RG 59, Records of the Department of State, Records of the Assistant Secretary for Administration, Subject Files 1044–1048, Lot 53 D 28, Special Assistant for Research and Intelligence, Box 19, Secret.

15. Russell Jack Smith, *The Unknown CIA: My Three Decades with the Agency* (Pergamon-Brasseys, Washington, D.C., 1989), p. 42. Lovett's disparagement of CIA intelligence collection and Admiral Hillenkoetter is in the National Archives, RG 59, Records of the Department of State, Records of the Executive Secretariat, NSC Files, Lot 66 D 148, Box 1555.

16. "Copy of an Undated Report of Meredith Gardner," Records of National Security Agency Public Release, Copies of Records Relating to Project Venona 1941–1947, National Archives, RG 457, Box 4, Job NN3–457–98–001, Top Secret.

17. Memorandum from Director of Central Intelligence Hillenkoetter to the Chief of Naval Operations (Denfeld), Washington, June 18, 1948, National

Archives, Central Intelligence Agency Historical Files, HS/CSG-605, Job 83–0036, Box 4, Folder 10, Top Secret. Subject: Project for High-level Balloon Research and Development.

18. Nicholas Bethell, *The Great Betrayal: The Untold Story of Kim Philby's Greatest Coup* (Hodder and Stoughton, London, 1984), p. 149.

19. Kim Philby, *My Silent War* (Ballantine Books, New York, 1983), p. 156. Many British readers took Philby at his word and Angleton's reputation grew. The error duplicated in Philby's incorrectly identifying the CIA's OSO acronym is insignificant except to indicate how widely and uncritically accepted was Philby's factual detail in *My Silent War*. See Patrick Seale and Maureen McConville, *Philby: The Long Road to Moscow* (Simon and Schuster, New York, 1973), p. 201; Knightley, *The Master Spy*, p. 155; and Bethell, p. 98. Andrew Boyle makes a more significant error when he identifies Angleton as the "effective head of [CIA] counter-intelligence." Boyle, *The Fourth Man* (Dial Press, New York, 1979), p. 345.

20. Bower, p. 383.

21. Yuri Modin, *My Five Cambridge Friends* (Farrar, Straus, Giroux, New York, 1994), p. 262. Philby told Knightley in Moscow that Angleton "wanted to use me for his own deception plans." Knightley, *The Master Spy*, p. 140.

22. Oleg Penkovsky was a senior GRU officer in Moscow in 1961–1962 who provided MI6 and the CIA with secrets on Soviet weapons and missile technology. He was arrested in late 1962 in Moscow and shot.

23. Tom Mangold, *Cold Warrior: James Jesus Angleton* (Simon and Schuster, New York, 1991), pp. 65, 168.

24. W. Scott Lucas and C. J. Morris, "A Very British Crusade," in Richard Aldrich, ed., *British Intelligence Strategy and the Cold War, 1945–1951* (Routledge, New York, 1992), pp. 101–102; Bethell, pp. 36–38.

25. Lucas and Morris, pp. 102–103; Bethell, pp. 38–39; Beatrice Heuser, "Covert Action in UK and US Concepts of Containment," in Aldrich, *British Intelligence Strategy and the Cold War, 1945–1951*, p. 70.

26. Dmitri Volkogonov, *Stalin: Triumph and Tragedy* (Grove Weidenfeld, New York, 1988), p. 537.

27. Milovan Djilas, *Conversations with Stalin* (Harcourt, Brace and World, New York, 1962), pp. 107–115, 171–186. Djilas is the most authentic source in identifying the reason for Soviet-Yugoslav differences.

28. Memorandum from the Chief of the Special Procedures Group (Cassady) to Director of Central Intelligence Hillenkoetter, Washington, June 30, 1948, National Archives, Central Intelligence Agency Historical Files, HS/CSG-615, Job 83–00036, Box 4, Folder 10, Top Secret. Subject: Covert Propaganda to Exploit Tito-Cominform Dispute.

29. Evan Thomas, *The Very Best Men: The Early Years of the CIA* (Simon and Schuster, New York, 1995), p. 20.

30. Letter from Acting Secretary of State Lovett to Secretary of Defense Forrestal, Washington, October 1, 1948, National Archives, RG 59, Records of the Department of State, Decimal File 1945–1949, 101.61/10–146, Top Secret.

31. Townsend Hoopes and Douglas Brinkley, *Driven Patriot: The Life and Times of James Forrestal* (Random House, New York, 1992), pp. 312–314; Peter Grose, *Operation Rollback* (Houghton Mifflin, Boston, 2000), pp. 46–47.

32. Bethell, pp. 39–40, 132–134.

33. Ibid., p. 118.

34. Memorandum from Secretary of Defense Johnson to Director of Central Intelligence Hillenkoetter, Washington, October 6, 1949, National Archives, Central Intelligence Agency Historical Files, HS/CSG-2051, Job 83–00739R, Box 2, Folder 12, Top Secret. Subject: Support of Covert Operations of CIA.

35. The SSU cable to Munich is in Grose, p. 130. General Magruder's opposition to the Albanian operation is in Thomas Powers, *The Man Who Kept the Secrets: Richard Helms and the CIA* (Alfred A. Knopf, New York, 1979), p. 44.

36. Philby falsely implied the CIA had a hand in Bandera's later assassination in Munich. Philby, pp. 157, 163–165. A KGB assassin confessed to the killing years later.

37. Thomas, p. 31.

38. Heuser, p. 70.

39. Djilas, pp. 181–182.

40. Bethell, pp. 58–63, 105–106.

41. Ibid., pp. 79–97.

42. Joan Didion, "The Lion King," *New York Review of Books*, vol. 44, no. 20 (December 18, 1997), p. 14.

43. George Schultz, *Turmoil and Triumph: My Years as Secretary of State* (Charles Scribner Sons, New York, 1993), pp. 323, 336. The East German and Russian presence in Grenada was reported to Secretary Schultz by State's Political-Military Bureau (PM), which maintains liaison with the Pentagon, including the Defense Intelligence Agency. The DIA's field reports by defense attachés based on their sources, contacts, or agents (human intelligence, or Humint) are often the most unreliable of all intelligence reports when not dealing with order of battle matters and more often than not are completely worthless. CIA intelligence information cables from the field warn that they are purely information reports, not "finally evaluated intelligence," and always assess their sources (in the source attribution they also disguise intelligence gathered by technical means, the most reliable of all). The East German and Soviet presence vanished like a will o' the wisp after the military incursion.

44. Bethell, pp. 4–5. Bethell insists "there can be no doubt" that Philby told his KGB control in London of the Albanian operation and of "the short term plans" for an incursion on the Albanian coast the first week of October. None of the KGB files available in Moscow support that conclusion.

45. Powers, p. 47.

46. Christopher Andrew and Vasili Mitrokhin, *The Mitrokhin Archive* (Penguin Books, London, 1999), pp. 120, 205–207.

CHAPTER ELEVEN

1. Adam Ulam, *Stalin: The Man and His Era* (Beacon Press, Boston, 1973), p. 654.

2. Dmitri Volkogonov, *Stalin: Triumph and Tragedy* (Grove Weidenfeld, New York, 1988), p. 537.

3. Stephen L. Rearden, *History of the Secretary of Defense: The Formative Years* (Office of the Secretary of Defense, Washington, D.C., 1984), pp. 337, 346, 364–369.

4. Volkogonov, pp. 653–654.

5. Viacheslav Molotov, *Molotov Remembers: Inside Kremlin Politics* (Ivan Dee, Chicago, 1993), pp. 59, 63. Molotov's concern about provoking a U.S. response is also mentioned by Milovan Djilas, *Conversations with Stalin* (Harcourt, Brace and World, New York, 1962), p. 131.

6. Vladimir M. Zubok, "Stalin," in John Lewis Gaddis, ed., *Cold War Statesmen Confront the Bomb: Nuclear Diplomacy since 1945* (Oxford University Press, London, 1999), p. 58. Zubok draws on two Russian works by Yu V. Votinsev and Grigory Kissunko published in Moscow in 1993 and 1996.

7. Edward Spiers, "The British Nuclear Deterrent," in *Retreat from Power* (Macmillan, London, 1981), p. 155.

8. Julian Lewis, *Changing Direction: British Military Planning* (Sherwood, London, 1988), pp. 295, 319–320, 332; Peter Malone, *The British Nuclear Deterrent* (St. Martin's Press, New York, 1984), p. 6.

9. The ban on any OPC operations involving U.S. war plans is explicitly set forth in NSC-10/2, "The National Security Council Directive on Office of Special Projects," Washington, June 18, 1948, National Archives, RG 273, Records of the National Security Council, Top Secret.

10. Richard J. Aldrich, *The Hidden Hand* (Overlook Press, Woodstock, 2002), pp. 371–374. Aldrich cites a Ministry of Defense document of July 1, 1946: "Future Developments in Weapons and Methods of War."

11. Records of the Ministry of Defense, DFE 28/181, London Controlling Section, Public Record Office. The report on Drew's visit is too obscure to draw any conclusions. It did conclude that the U.S. Orange team seemed to be "losing touch with reality." It had operated for some time.

12. Gregg Herkin, *The Winning Weapon: The Atomic Bomb in the Cold War, 1945–1950* (Random House, New York, 1982), p. 317.

13. Anthony Cave Brown, *C: Winston Churchill's Spymaster* (New York, Macmillan, 1988), p. 745.

14. Anthony Cave Brown, *Treason in the Blood: H. St. John Philby, Kim Philby, and the Spy Case of the Century* (Houghton Mifflin, Boston, 1994), p. 402.

15. William Corson, *The Armies of Ignorance* (Dial Press, New York, 1977), pp. 326–328.

16. F. W. Winterbotham, *The Ultra Secret* (Dell Publishing, New York, 1974), p. 232.

17. Kenneth Strong, *Intelligence at the Top: The Recollections of a British Intelligence Officer* (Doubleday, New York, 1969), p. 243.

18. Ludwell Montague, *General Walter Bedell Smith as Director of Central Intelligence* (Pennsylvania State University Press, University Park, 1992), pp. 186–189, 246.

19. General Sibert left his papers to Cave Brown, who deposited them with the Georgetown University library in Washington. Several years ago, in an attempt to resolve the various inconsistencies in Cave Brown's book, I visited the library and asked to see the Sibert papers. After a phone call to Cave Brown, the librarian refused access.

20. Steven T. Ross, *American War Plans, 1945–1950* (Frank Cass, London, 1988), pp. 96–111; Kenneth W. Condit, *History of the Joint Chiefs of Staff*, vol. 2, *The Joint Chiefs of Staff and National Policy, 1947–1949* (Office of Joint History, Office of the Chairman of the Joint Chiefs of Staff, Washington, D.C., 1996), p. 160.

21. David Leigh, *The Wilson Plot* (Pantheon, New York, 1988), p. 73; Cave Brown, *Treason in the Blood*, pp. 399–403; Tom Bower, *A Perfect English Spy: Sir Dick White and the Secret War, 1935–1990* (St. Martin's Press, New York, 1995), pp. 298–299, 306. Bower claims White told Wilson of Philby's confession in Beirut. According to Bower, Philby told MI6's Elliott he had been recruited by his ex-wife Litzi, had recruited Burgess and Maclean, and broke contact with the KGB in 1949.

22. Montague, pp. 58, 59, 64.

23. John Newhouse, *War and Peace in the Nuclear Age* (Alfred A. Knopf, New York, 1989), pp. 58–60.

24. Bower, p. 208.

25. Cipher from Air Ministry in London to B.F.A.S. Washington, Message for Nowell from Medhurst, MSX 808, National Archives, RG 341, Air Force Plans Project Decimal File 1942–1954, SG 581 (TS), Box 743.

26. Cave Brown, *Treason in the Blood*, p. 423.

27. Robert Lamphere and Tom Shachtman, *The FBI-KGB War* (Random House, New York, 1986), pp. 85, 191.

28. Kim Philby, *My Silent War* (Ballantine Books, New York, 1983), p. 185.

29. Phillip Knightley, *The Master Spy* (Alfred A. Knopf, New York, 1989), p. 157.

30. Richard J. Aldrich, ed., *Espionage, Security, and Intelligence in Britain, 1945–1970* (Manchester University Press, Manchester, 1998), p. 39. Aldrich was citing a document in the National Archives.

31. Genrikh Borovik, *The Philby Files* (Little, Brown, Boston, 1994), p. 269.

32. Those figures were given in the House of Commons by Prime Minister Attlee on July 24, 1950, in response to a question by a Laborite member, S. O. Davies, who asked for the strength of "foreign armed forces on our soil." Davies opposed British participation in the Korean War, which he blamed the United States for initiating. *Kessing's Contemporary Archives* (Kessing's Publications, London, July 1950), p. 10873.

33. David T. Fauta, " 'The Long Pull' Army: NSC-68, the Korean War, and the Creation of the Cold War U.S. Army," *Journal of Military History,* 61, 1 (January 1997), pp. 93–120.

34. Kenneth Strong, *Men of Intelligence: A Study of the Roles and Decisions of Chiefs of Intelligence from World War I to the Present Day* (St. Martin's Press, New York, 1972). On p. 114 of Strong's book is a remarkable photograph taken at a March 1966 meeting in Washington of the U.S. Intelligence Board. Ranking officials of every U.S. intelligence agency were present—the CIA, the NSA, the DIA, the AEC, the FBI, the State Department, and the army, navy, and USAF. Strong was the only non-American present, evidence enough of the confidence and trust he continued to enjoy.

35. Ibid., p. 115.

36. Aldrich, *Espionage, Security, and Intelligence in Britain 1945–1970,* p. 194. The Tedder quotation is taken from Russia Committee minutes included by Aldrich and found in Foreign Office files at the Public Record Office.

CHAPTER TWELVE

1. Peter Wright, *Spy Catcher* (Viking, New York, 1987), p. 185; Nigel West and Oleg Tsarev, *The Crown Jewels* (Yale University Press, New Haven, 1999), p. 182.

2. William Empson, *The Collected Poems* (Harcourt, Brace, New York, 1949), p. 86.

APPENDIX A

1. NSA Venona Historical Monograph no. 6 explains that eleven and possibly all twelve Maclean cables date from 1944, six from New York to Moscow and six from Washington. In fact the New York cables date from 1944 and the Washington cables from 1945.

2. VIKTOR was Russian Lieutenant General Pavel Mikhailovich Fitin. From 1940 until 1946 he was the head of the KGB First Chief Directorate (Foreign Intelligence). Christopher Andrew and Oleg Gordievsky, *KGB: The Inside Story of Its Foreign Operations from Lenin to Gorbachev* (HarperCollins, New York, 1990), p. 649.

3. Meredith Gardner, "Development of the 'G'–HOMER [GOMER] Case" (October

11, 1951), p. 2. Records of National Security Agency Public Release, Copies of Records Relating to Project Venona 1941–1947, National Archives, RG 457, Box 4.

4. Government Code and Cipher School and Government Communications Headquarters, Venona Project Records, Material from "H" (Donald Maclean), HW 15/32, Public Record Office.

APPENDIX B

1. Yuri Modin, *My Five Cambridge Friends* (Farrar, Straus, Giroux, New York, 1994).

2. Anthony Cave Brown, *Treason in the Blood: H. St. John Philby, Kim Philby, and the Spy Case of the Century* (Houghton Mifflin, Boston, 1994), p. 430.

Index

127, 129–131, 135–139, 150, 155–
156, 166, 187, 194, 203, 213, 218–
220, 223, 231; Maclean counterespionage deception, 5, 103–106,
108–115, 117, 128–130, 135, 146–
147, 155–157, 223, 230–231; suspicion of Philby, 66–67, 129–
130, 135–136, 149; World War II
service, 64–65
White Paper, September *1955*, 6–7,
13, 15, 46, 84, 86, 117, 119, 147,
229–230
Wilson, Harold, 193, 213
Wilson, General Henry Maitland,
234
Wisner, Frank, 172, 187, 189–190,

194, 197–198; Bedell Smith's
views of, 187
Wright, Colonel Edwin K., 186–191,
212
Wright, Peter, 145–146, 155, 240–
241

Yalta Conference, 73–74, 82–83,
117, 161; Declaration on Liberated Europe, 74, 78, 80; Declaration on Poland, 73–76, 78–79, 82
Yugoslavia, 82, 169, 182, 195–196,
199–200

Zog, King, 200–201
Zukok, Vladimir, 165